RECENT ADVANCES IN BRAIN-COMPUTER INTERFACE SYSTEMS

Edited by **Reza Fazel-Rezai**

Recent Advances in Brain-Computer Interface Systems
Edited by Reza Fazel-Rezai

Published by InTech

Janeza Trdine 9, 51000 Rijeka, Croatia

Publishing Process Manager Iva Lipovic

Technical Editor Teodora Smiljanic

Cover Designer InTech Design Team

Additional hard copies can be obtained from orders@intechopen.com

Recent Advances in Brain-Computer Interface Systems, Edited by Reza Fazel-Rezai
p. cm.
ISBN 978-953-307-175-6

For EU product safety concerns:
IN TECH d.o.o., Prolaz Marije Krucifikse Kozulić 3, 51000 Rijeka, Croatia,
info@intechopen.com or visit our website at intechopen.com.

Meet the editor

Dr. Reza Fazel-Rezai received his BSc. and M.Sc. in Electrical Engineering and Biomedical Engineering in 1990 and 1993, respectively. He received his Ph.D. in Electrical Engineering from the University of Manitoba in Winnipeg, Canada in 1999. From 2000 to 2002 he worked in industry as a senior research scientist and research team manager. Then he joined academia at Sharif University of Technology and later the University of Manitoba as Assistant Professor in 2002 and 2004, respectively. Currently he is Assistant Professor and the Director of Biomedical Signal Processing Laboratory at the Department of Electrical Engineering, University of North Dakota, USA. His research interests include biomedical signal and image processing, brain computer interface, EEG signal processing, seizure detection and prediction, neurofeedback, and human performance evaluation based on EEG signals.

Contents

Preface

Communication and the ability to interact with the environment are basic human needs. Millions of people worldwide suffer from such severe physical disabilities that they cannot even meet these basic needs. Even though they may have no motor mobility, however, the sensory and cognitive functions of the physically disabled are usually intact. This makes them good candidates for Brain Computer Interface (BCI) technology, which provides a direct electronic interface and can convey messages and commands directly from the human brain to a computer. BCI technology involves monitoring conscious brain electrical activity via electroencephalogram (EEG) signals and detecting characteristics of EEG patterns via digital signal processing algorithms that the user generates to communicate. It has the potential to enable the physically disabled to perform many activities, thus improving their quality of life and productivity, allowing them more independence and reducing social costs. The challenge with BCI, however, is to extract the relevant patterns from the EEG signals produced by the brain each second.

A BCI system has an input, output and a signal processing algorithm that maps the inputs to the output. The following four major strategies are considered for the input of a BCI system: 1) the P300 wave of event related potentials (ERP), 2) steady state visual evoked potential (SSVEP), 3) slow cortical potentials and 4) motor imaginary.

Recently, there has been a great progress in the development of novel paradigms for EEG signal recording, advanced methods for processing them, new applications for BCI systems and complete software and hardware packages used for BCI applications. In this book a few recent advances in these areas are discussed. In the first chapter hardware and software components along with several applications of BCI systems are discussed. In chapters 2 and 3 several signal processing methods for classifying EEG signals are presented. In chapter 4 a new paradigm for P300 BCI is compared with traditional P300 BCI paradigms. Chapters 5 and 6 show how a visual evoked potential (VEP)-based BCI works. In chapters 7 and 8 a visuo-motor-based and natural motor control-based BCI systems are discussed, respectively. New applications of BCI systems for control and biometry are discussed in chapter 9. Finally, the recent competition in BCI held in 2010 along with a short summary of the submitted projects are presented in Chapter 10.

As the editor, I would like to thank all the authors of different chapters. Without your contributions, it would not be possible to have a quality book, help in growth of BCI systems and utilize them in real-world applications.

Dr. Reza Fazel-Rezai
University of North Dakota
Grand Forks, ND,
USA

Reza@UND.edu

1

Hardware/Software Components and Applications of BCIs

Christoph Guger, Günter Edlinger and Gunther Krausz
g.tec medical engineering GmbH/ Guger Technologies OG
Austria

1. Introduction

Human-Computer interfaces can use different signals from the body in order to control external devices. Beside muscle activity (EMG-Electromyogram), eye movements (EOG-Electrooculogram) and respiration also brain activity (EEG-Electroencephalogram) can be used as input signal. EEG-based brain-computer interface (BCI) systems are realized either with (i) slow cortical potentials, (ii) the P300 response, (iii) steady-state visual evoked potentials (SSVEP) or (iv) motor imagery.

Potential shift of the scalp EEG over 0.5 - 10 s are called slow cortical potentials (SCPs). Reduced cortical activation goes ahead with positive SCPs, while negative SCPs are associated with movement and other functions involving cortical activation (Birbaumer, 2000). People are able to learn how to control these potentials, hence it is possible to use them for BCIs as Birbaumer and his colleagues did (Birbaumer, 2000, Elbert, 1980). The main disadvantage of this method is the extensive training time to learn how to control the SCPs. Users need to train in several 1-2 h sessions/week over weeks or months.

The P300 wave was first discovered by Sutton (Sutton, 1965). It elicits when an unlikely event occurs randomly between events with high probability. In the EEG signal the P300 appears as a positive wave about 300 ms after stimulus onset. Its main usage in BCIs is for spelling devices, but one can also use it for control tasks (for example games (Finkea, 2009) or navigation (e.g. to move a computer-mouse (Citi, 2008)). When using P300 as a spelling device, a matrix of characters is shown to the subject. Now the rows and columns (or in some paradigms the single characters) of the matrix are flashing in random order, while the person concentrates only on the character he/she wants to spell. For better concentration, it is recommended to count how many times the character flashes. Every time the desired character flashes, a P300 wave occurs. As the detection of one single event would be imprecise, more than one trial (flashing of each character) has to be carried out to achieve a proper accuracy.

Krusienski et al. (Krusienski, 2006) evaluated different classification techniques for the P300 speller, wherein the stepwise linear discriminant analysis (SWLDA) and the Fisher's linear discriminant analysis provided the best overall performance and implementation characteristics. A recent study (Guger 2009), performed on 100 subjects, revealed an average accuracy level of 91.1%, with a spelling time of 28.8 s for one single character. Each character was selected out of a matrix of 36 characters.

Steady state visual evoked potentials (SSVEP)-based BCIs use several stationary flashing sources (e.g. flickering LEDs, or phase-reversing checkerboards), each of them flashing with another constant frequency. When a person gazes at one of these sources, the specific frequency component will increase in the measured EEG, over the occipital lobe. Hence, when using different light sources, each of them representing a predefined command, the person gives this command by gazing onto the source. The classification is either done by FFT-based spectrum comparison, preferably including also the harmonics (Müller-Putz, 2005), or via the canonical correlation analysis (CCA) (Lin, 2006). A third possibility is via the minimum energy approach which was published by O. Friman et.al. in 2007 (Friman, 2007) and requires no training.

Typical SSVEP applications are made for navigation, for example Middendorf et al. (Middendorf, 2000) used SSVEPs to control the roll position of a flight simulator. The number of classes varies between two and eight, although Gao et al. (Gao, 2003) established an experiment with even 48 targets. Bakardijan et al. (Bakardijan, 2010) investigated SSVEP responses for frequencies between 5 and 84 Hz to find the strongest response between 5.6 Hz and 15.3 Hz peaking at 12 Hz. With their frequency-optimized-eight-command BCI they achieved a mean success rate of 98 % and an information transfer rate (ITR) of 50 bits/min. Bin et al. (Bin, 2009) reports of a six-target BCI with an average accuracy of 95.3% and an information transfer rate of 58 ± 9.6 bits/min.

Although most SSVEP-based BCIs work with gaze shifting towards a source, recent studies (Allison, 2009, Zhang, 2010) proofed that only selective attention onto a pattern alone is sufficient for control. The latter paper achieved an overall classification accuracy of 72.6 +/- 16.1% after 3 training days. Therefore also severely disabled people, who are not able to move their eyes, can control an SSVEP-based BCI.

When subjects perform or only imagine motor tasks, an event related desynchronization (ERD) (Pfurtscheller & Neuper, 1997) and an event related synchronization (ERS) is detectable by changes of EEG rhythms on electrodes close to the respective sensorimotor areas. The ERD is indicated by a decrease of power in the upper alpha band and lower beta band, starting 2 seconds before movement onset on the contra lateral hemisphere and becomes bilaterally symmetrical immediately before execution of movement (Pfurtscheller, 1999). An ERS appears either after termination of the movement, or simultaneously to the ERD, but in other areas of the cortex. The decrease/increase is always measured in comparison to the power in a reference interval, for example a few seconds before the movement occurs. For classification there are several approaches used. The simplest one is by calculating the bandpower in a specific frequency band and consecutive discrimination via a Fisher linear discriminant analysis. Other classification strategies are support vector machines (SVM) (Solis-Escalante, 2008), principal component analysis (PCA) (Vallabhaneni, 2004), or common spatial patterns (CSP) (Guger, 2003)

2. Components and signals

For BCI experiments the subject or the patient is connected via electrodes or sensors to a biosignal amplifier and a data acquisition unit (DAQ board) containing the analog-to-digital conversion (as shown in Figure 1). Then the data are passed to the real-time system to perform the feature extraction and classification. Important is that the real-time system works fast enough to present feedback to the subject via a stimulation unit. The feedback represents the BCI output and allows the subject to learn the BCI control faster. For system update and data collection a central control unit managing several systems is of advantage.

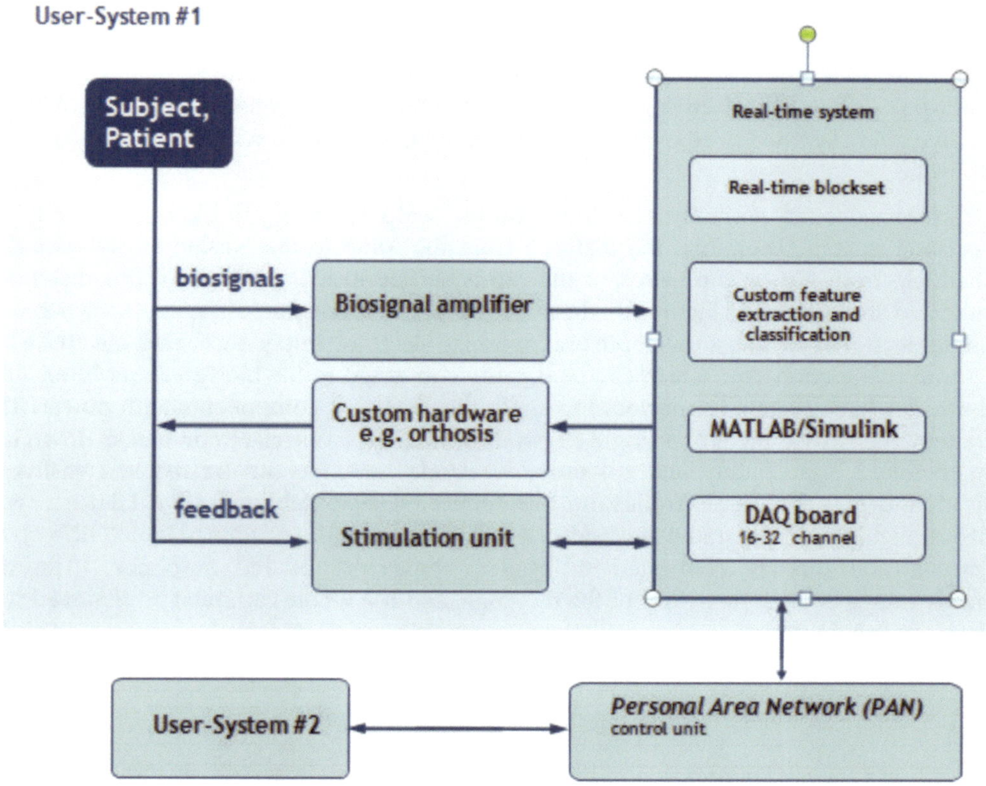

Fig. 1. BCI components to run real-time experiments

2.1 Electrodes

For EEG measurements normally single disk electrodes made of gold or Ag/AgCl are used (see Figure 2). Gold electrodes are maintenance free and have a good frequency response for EEG, EMG or ECG measurements. For DC derivations with EEG frequencies below 0.1 Hz Ag/AgCl electrodes perform better than gold electrodes. Passive electrodes consist only of the disk material and are connected with the electrode cable and a 1.5 mm medical connector to the biosignal amplifier. Active electrodes have a pre-amplifier with gain 1-10 inside the electrode which makes the electrode less sensitive to environmental noise such as power line interference and cable movements. Because of this fact, active electrodes also work if the electrode-skin impedance is higher than for passive electrodes (should be below 10 kOhm). Active electrodes have system connectors to supply the electronic components with power. Fig.A, Fig.B and Fig.C show EEG electrodes that can be fitted into EEG caps, Fig.D shows an ECG/EMG electrode which is placed close to the muscle/heart. Electrodes of type A and D can also be used for EOG recordings.

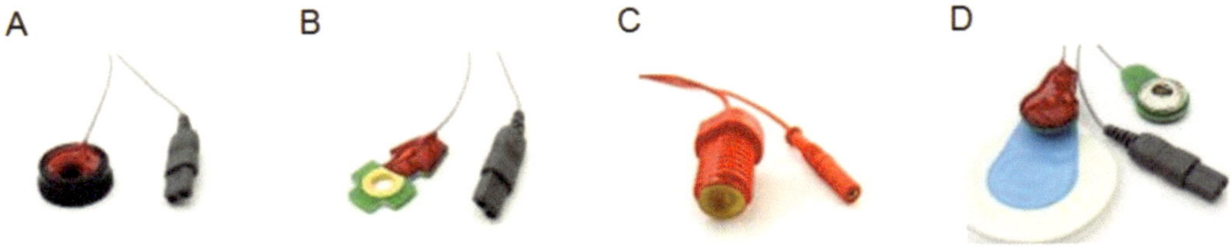

Fig. 2. Electrodes for EEG, ECG, EOG,... measurements. A: Active single electrode with multi-pole connector; B: active gold electrode with multi-pole connector; C: screw-able passive gold electrode to adjust location; D: active ECG electrode with disposable Ag/AgCl electrode

EEG electrodes are normally distributed on the scalp according to the international 10-20 electrode system. Therefore, the distance from the Inion to the Nasion is first measured. Then, electrode Cz on the vertex of the cap is shifted exactly to 50 % of this distance, as indicated in Figure 3A. Figure 3B shows a cap with 64 positions. The cap uses screwable single electrodes to adjust the depth and optimize electrode impedance. Each electrode has a 1.5 mm safety connector which can be directly connected to the biosignal amplifier. Active electrodes have system connectors to supply the electronic components with power. There are two main advantages of a single electrode system: (i) if one electrode breaks down it can be removed immediately and (ii) every electrode montage can be realized easily. The disadvantage is that all electrodes must be connected separately each time. Hence, caps are also available with integrated electrodes. All the electrodes are combined in one ribbon cable that can be directly connected to system connectors of the amplifiers. The main disadvantage is the inflexibility of the montage, and the whole cap must be removed if one electrode breaks down.

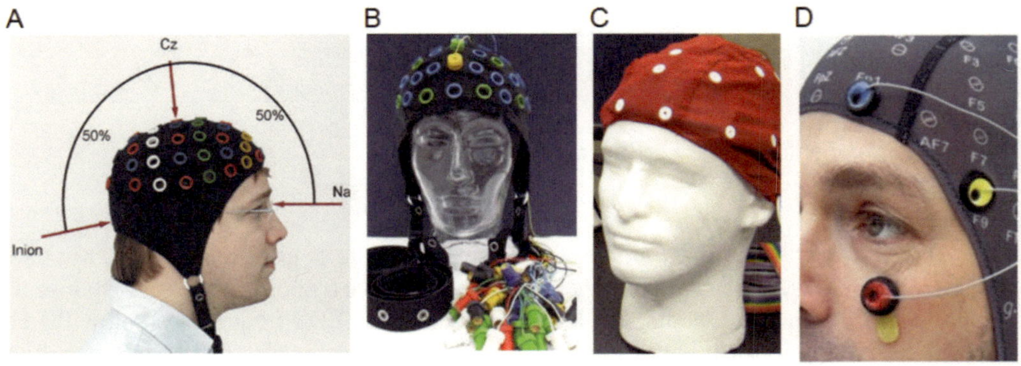

Fig. 3. Electrode caps. A: Electrode positioning according to the 10/20 electrode system. B: Electrode cap with screwable single passive or active electrodes. C: Electrode cap with build-in electrodes with a specific montage. D: Electrode cap with active electrodes

Active electrodes avoid or reduce artifacts and signal noise resulting from high impedance between the electrode(s) and the skin (e.g. 50/60 Hz coupling, artifacts caused by electrode or cable movements, distorted signals or background noise). Figure 4 shows a comparison of active and passive electrodes. Active electrodes were mounted on positions F1 (channel 1), C1 (channel 2), O1 (channel 3) with g.GAMMAgel (no abrasion) and passive electrodes were mounted on positions F2 (channel 4), C2 (channel 5) and O2 (channel 6) with abrasive gel. Active and passive electrodes are located next to each other to allow a better comparison. The ground electrode was located on position FPz. The active electrodes were referenced against the right ear. The passive electrodes are referenced against the left ear. Five conditions were compared: (i) eye movements, (ii) biting, (iii) cable artefacts, (iv) active head movements by the person himself and (v) passive head movements done by a second person.

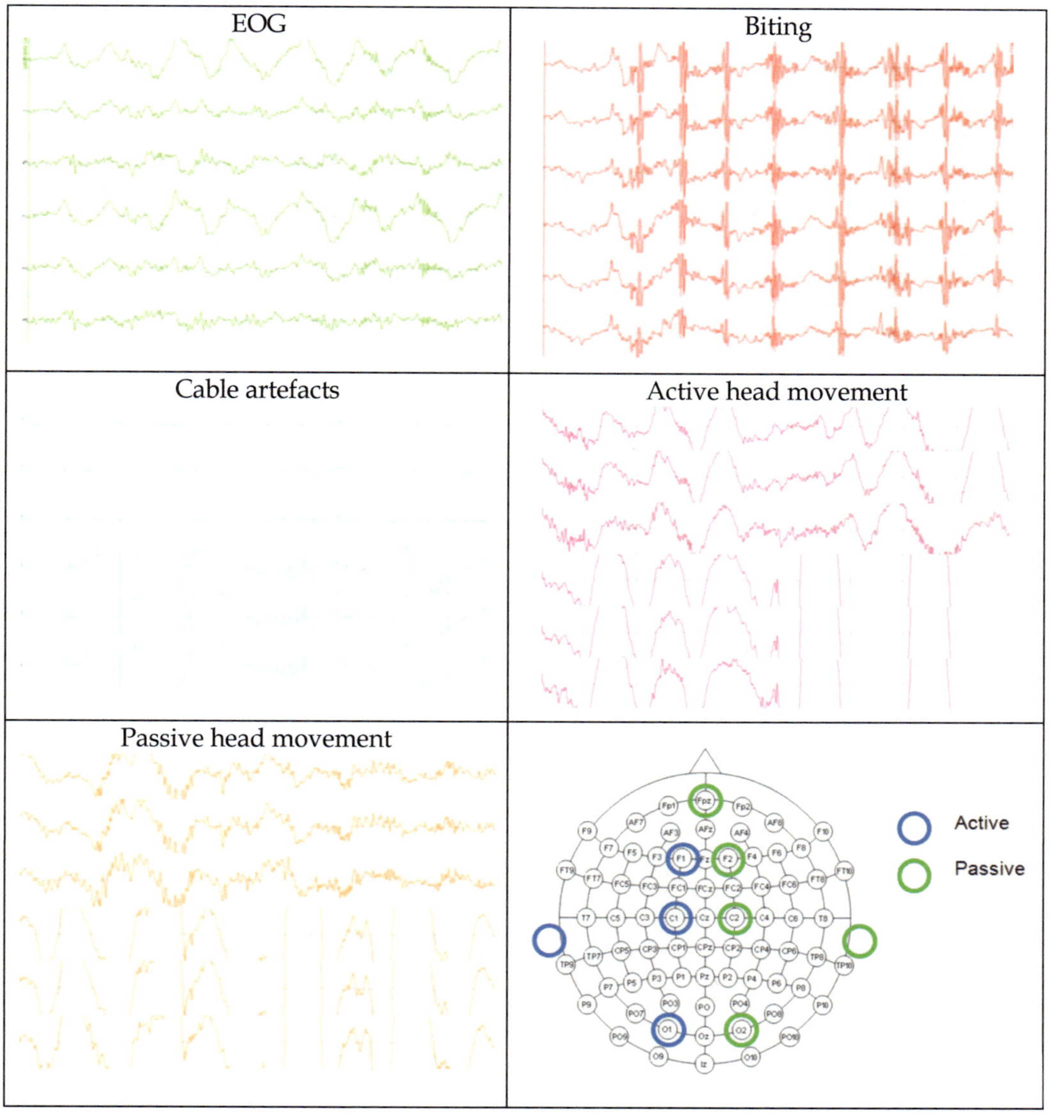

Fig. 4. Comparison of active and passive electrodes. The first three channels in each plot are recorded with active electrodes, the last three channels with passive electrodes

EYE MOVEMENTS -The channels closer to the eyes (1 and 4) show higher EOG artefacts than central and occipital channels. Both passive and active electrodes show a similar EOG contamination which is also clear because both pick up the same source signal.

BITING - Biting produces an EMG contamination almost equally on all channels and there is no difference between active and passive electrodes because both pick up the same source signal.

CABLE ARTEFACTS - Cable artefacts are produced by touching or shaking the cables. The active electrodes are almost unaffected while the passive electrodes show large movement artefacts.

ACTIVE HEAD MOVEMENTS - Active head movements produce fewer artefacts with active electrodes compared to passive ones. Artefacts for both electrodes can occur because of skin-electrode movements. Passive electrodes are mostly affected by the cable movements initiated by the head movements.

PASSIVE HEAD MOVEMENTS - Passive head movements have lower accelerations than active head movements and therefore the artefacts are smaller and mostly visible with passive electrodes.

2.2 Biosignal amplifier

One of the key components of a physiological recording and analysis system is the biosignal amplifier. Figure 5 illustrates g.USBamp and a block diagram of the amplifier.

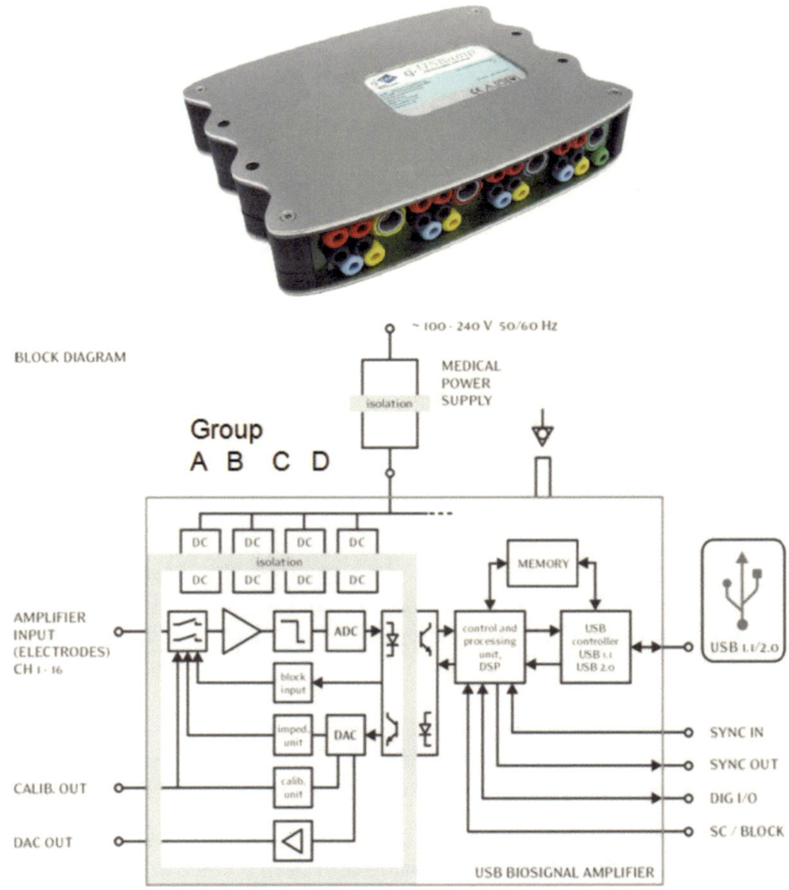

Fig. 5. Biosignal amplifier and block diagram

This device has 16 input channels, which are connected over software controllable switches to the internal amplifier stages and anti-aliasing filters before the signals are digitized with sixteen 24 Bit ADCs. The device is also equipped with digital to analog converters (DAC) enabling the generation of different signals like sinusoidal waves, which can be sent to the inputs of the amplifiers for system testing and calibration. Additionally, the impedance of each electrode can be checked by applying a small current to the individual electrodes and measuring the voltage drops. All these components are part of the so-called applied part of the device, as a subject or patient is in contact to this part of the device via the electrodes. All following parts of the device are separated via optical links from the subject/patient.
The digitized signals are passed to a digital signal processor (DSP) for further processing. The DSP performs an over-sampling of the biosignal data, band pass filtering, Notch filtering to suppress the power line interference and calculates bipolar derivations. These processing stages eliminate unwanted noise from the signal, which helps to ensure accurate and reliable classification. Then the pre-processed data are sent to a controller which transmits the data via USB 2.0 to the PC. One important feature of the amplifier is the over-sampling capability. Each ADC is sampling the data at 2.4 MHz. Then the samples are averaged to the desired sampling frequency of e.g. 128 Hz. Here a total of 19.200 samples are averaged, which improves the signal to noise ratio by the square root of 19.200 = 138,6 times.
For EEG or ECoG (Electrocorticogram) recordings with many channels, multiple devices can be synchronized. One common synchronization signal is utilized for all ADCs, yielding a perfect non delayed acquisition of all connected amplifiers. This is especially important for evoked potential recordings or recordings with many EEG channels. If only one ADC with a specific conversion time is used for many channels, then a time lag between the first channel and the last channel could be the result (e.g. 100 channels * 10 μs = 1 ms). Important is also that biosignal acquisition systems provide trigger inputs and outputs to log external events in synchrony to the data or to send trigger information to other external devices such as a visual flash lamp. Digital outputs can also be used to control external devices such as a prosthetic hand or a wheelchair. An advantage here is to scan the digital inputs together with the biosignals to avoid time-shifts between events and physiological data. A medical power supply that works with 230 or 110 V is required for physiological recording systems that are used mainly in the lab. For mobile applications like the controlling a wheelchair, amplifiers which run on battery power are also useful.
For invasive recordings, only devices with an applied part of type CF are allowed. For EEG measurements, both BF and CF type devices can be used. The difference here is the maximum allowed leakage current. Leakage current refers to electric current that is lost from the hardware, and could be dangerous for people or equipment. For both systems, the character F indicates that the applied part is isolated from the other parts of the amplifier. This isolation is typically done based on opto-couplers or isolation amplifiers. For a BF device, the ground leakage current and the patient leakage current must be ≤100 μA according to the medical device requirements, such as IEC 60601 or EN 60601. These refer to widely recognized standards that specify details of how much leakage current is allowed, among other details. For a CF device, the rules are more stringent. The ground leakage current can also be ≤100μA, but the patient leakage current must be ≤10 μA only.
The next important feature is the number of electrodes used. For slow wave approaches or oscillations in the alpha and beta range and P300 systems, a total of 1-8 EEG channels are sufficient (Birbaumer, 2000, Krusienski, 2006, Guger, 2003). BCIs that use spatial filtering,

such as common spatial pattern (CSP), require more channels (16-128) (Ramoser, 2000). For ECoG recordings, 64-128 channel montages are typically used (Leuthard, 2004). Therefore, stack-able systems might be advantageous because they can extend the functionality with future applications. A stack-able e.g. 64-channel system can also be split into four 16-channels systems if required for some experiments.
The signal type (EEG, ECoG, evoked potentials - EP, EMG, EOG) also influences the necessary sampling frequency and bandwidth of the amplifier. For EEG signals, sampling frequencies of 256 Hz with a bandwidth of 0.5 – 100 Hz are typically used (Guger, 2001). For ECoG recordings, sampling frequencies of 512 or 1200 Hz are applied with a bandwidth of 0.5 - 500 Hz (Leuthardt, 2004). A special case are slow waves, where a lower cut - off frequency of 0.01 Hz is needed (Birbaumer, 2000). For P300 based systems, a bandwidth of 0.1 - 30 Hz is typically used (Sellers, 2006). Notch filters are used to suppress the 50 Hz or 60 Hz power line interference. A notch filter is typically a narrow band-stop filter having a very high order. Digital filtering has the advantage that every filter type (Butterworth, Bessel, etc), filter order, and cut-off frequency can be realized. Analog filters inside the amplifier are predefined and can therefore not be changed. The high input range of g.USBamp of ±250 mV combined with a 24-bit converter (resolution of 29 nV) allows measuring all types of biosignals (EMG, ECG, EOG, EPs, EEG, ECoG) without changing the amplification factor of the device.

2.3 Real-time processing environment

Physiological recording systems are constructed under different operating systems (OS) and programming environments. Windows is currently the most widely distributed platform, but there are also implementations under Windows Mobile, Linux and Mac OS. C++, LabVIEW (National Instruments Corp., Austin, TX, USA) and MATLAB (The MathWorks Inc., Natick, USA) are mostly used as programming languages. C++ implementations have the advantages that no underlying software package is needed when the software should be distributed, and allow a very flexible system design. Therefore, a C++ Application Program Interface (API) was developed that allows the integration of the amplifiers with all features into programs running under Windows or Windows Mobile. The main disadvantage is the longer development time. The BCI2000 software package was developed with the C API (Schalk, 2004).
Under the MATLAB environment, several specialized toolboxes such as signal processing, statistics, wavelets, and neural networks are available, which are highly useful components for a BCI system. Signal processing algorithms are needed for feature extraction, classification methods are needed to separate biosignal patterns into distinct classes, and statistical functions are needed e.g. for performing group studies. Therefore, a MATLAB API was also developed, which is seamlessly integrated into the Data Acquisition Toolbox. This allows direct control of the amplification unit from the MATLAB command window to capture the biosignal data in real-time and to write user specific m-files for the data processing. Furthermore, standard MATLAB toolboxes can be used for processing, as well as self-written programs. The MATLAB processing engine is based upon highly optimized matrix operations, allowing very high processing speed. Such a processing speed is very difficult to realize with self-written C code.
Beside the MATLAB and C API it is also useful to have a rapid prototyping environment that allows to create different BCI experiments rapidly. Such an environment was designed under

Simulink and allows the real-time processing of EEG data. The following BCI experiments were realized with this "Highspeed On-line Processing for Simulink" software package.

2.3.1 Motor imagery

To train a user to control a BCI with motor imagery a training paradigm is necessary that is synchronized with the EEG data acquisition and real-time analysis. Therefore the subject is seated in front of the computer screen where the paradigm is shown. The user has the task to wait until an arrow pointing either to the right or left side of the screen occurs (using bipolar EEG derivation around C3 and C4). The direction of the arrow instructs the subject to imagine a right or left hand movement for 3 seconds. Then, after some delay, the next arrow appears. The direction of the arrows is randomly chosen, and about 40-200 trials are typically used for further processing. The EEG data, together with the time points of the appearance of the arrows on the screen, are loaded for off-line analysis to calculate a subject-specific weight vector (WV) which is used for the feedback experiment.
A Simulink model for the real-time analysis of the EEG patterns is shown in Figure 5. Here 'g.USBamp' represents the device driver reading data from the biosignal amplifier into Simulink. Then the data is converted to 'double' precision format and connected to a 'Scope' for raw data visualization and to a 'To File' block to store the data in MATLAB format. Each EEG channel is further connected to 2 'Bandpower' blocks to calculate the power in the alpha and beta frequency range (both ranges were identified with the ERD/ERS and spectral analysis). The outputs of the band-power calculation are connected to the 'BCI System', i.e. the real-time LDA implementation which multiplies the features with the weight vector WV. The 'Paradigm' block is responsible for the presentation of the experimental paradigm in this case the control of the arrows on the screen and the feedback.

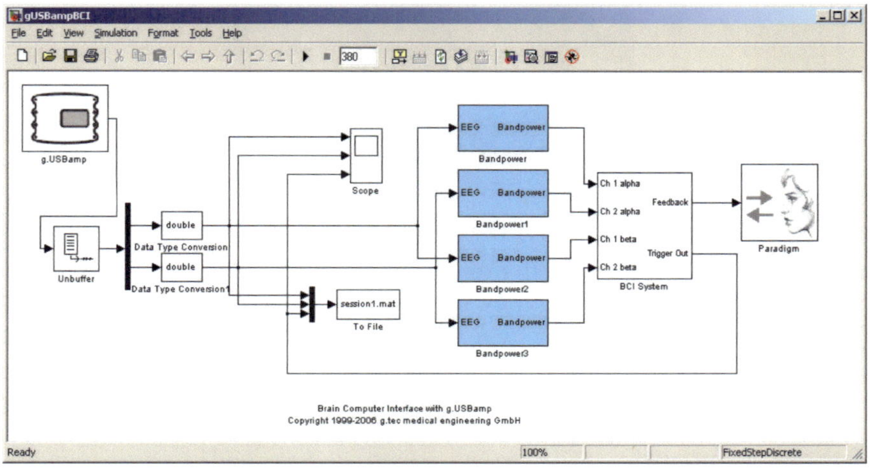

Fig. 5. Simulink model for the real-time feature extraction, classification and paradigm presentation

2.3.2. P300

A P300 spelling device can be based on a 6 x 6 matrix of different characters displayed on a computer screen. The row/column speller flashes a whole row or a whole column of characters at once in a random order as shown in Figure 6. The single character speller flashes only one single character at an instant in time. This yields of course to different communication rates; with a 6 x 6 matrix, the row/column approach increases speed by a factor of 6. The underlying phenomenon of a P300 speller is the P300 component of the EEG, which is seen if an attended and relatively uncommon event occurs. The subject must concentrate on a specific letter he/she wants to write (Sellers, 2006, Guger, 2009). When the character flashes on, the P300 is induced and the maximum in the EEG amplitude is reached typically 300 ms after the flash onset. Several repetitions are needed to perform EEG data averaging to increase the signal to noise ratio and accuracy of the system. The P300 signal response is more pronounced in the single character speller than in the row/column speller and therefore easier to detect (Guger, 2009).

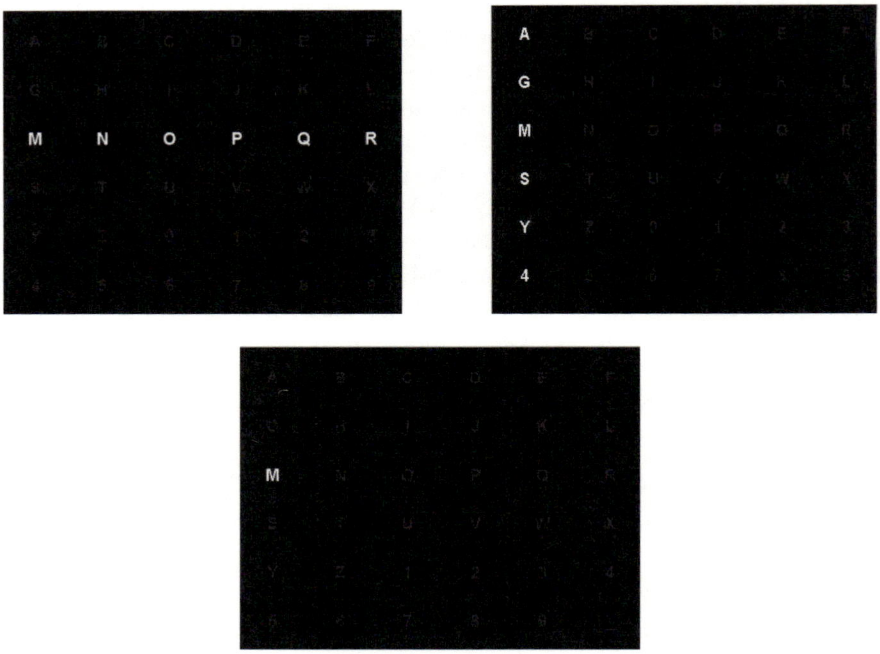

Fig. 6. Left, mid panels: row/column speller. Right panel: single character speller

For training, EEG data are acquired from the subject while the subject focuses on the appearance of specific letters in the copy spelling mode (positions Fz, Cz, Pz, Oz, P3, P4, PO7, PO8). In this mode, an arbitrary word like LUCAS is presented on the monitor. First, the subject counts whenever the L flashes. Each row, column, or character flashes for e.g.100ms per flash. Then the subject counts the U until it flashes 15 times, and so on. These data, together with the timing information of each flashing event, are then loaded for off-line analysis. Then, the EEG data elicited by each flashing event are extracted within a specific interval length and divided into sub-segments. The EEG data of each segment are averaged and sent to a step-wise linear discriminant analysis (LDA). The LDA is trained to separate the target characters, i.e. the characters the subject was concentrating on (15 flashes x 5 characters), from all other events (15 x 36 – 15 x 5). This yields again a subject specific weight vector WV for the real-time experiments. It is very interesting for this approach that the LDA is trained only on 5 characters representing 5 classes and not on all 36 classes. This

is in contrast to the motor imagery approach where each class must also be used as a training class. The P300 approach allows minimizing the time necessary for EEG recording for the setup of the LDA. However, the accuracy of the spelling system increases also with the number of training characters.
After the setup of the WV the real-time experiments can be conducted with the Simulink model shown in Figure 7.

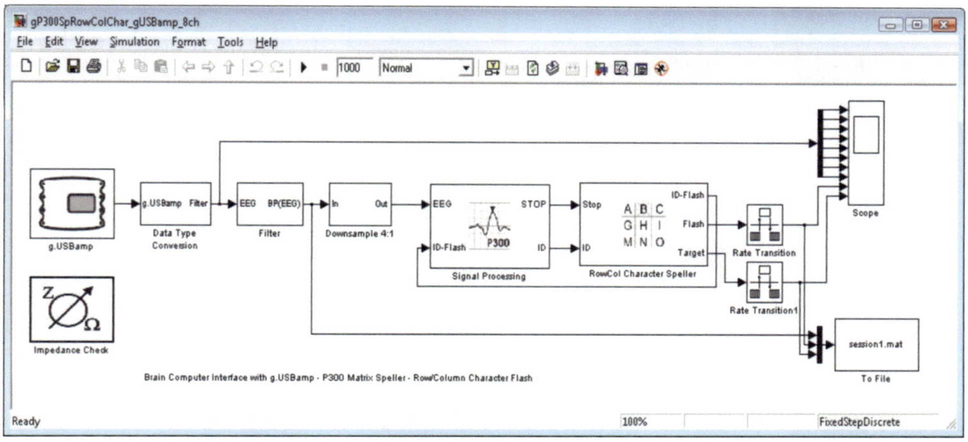

Fig. 7. Real-time Simulink model for P300 experiment

The device driver 'g.USBamp' reads again the EEG data from the amplifier and converts the data to double precision. Then the data are band pass filtered ('Filter') to remove drifts and artifacts and down sampled to 64 Hz ('Downsample 4:1'). The 'RowCol Character Speller' block generates the flashing sequence and the trigger signals for each flashing event and sends the 'ID' to the 'Signal Processing' block. The 'Signal Processing' block creates a buffer for each character. After all the characters flashed, the EEG data is used as input for the LDA and the system decides which letter was most likely investigated by the subject. Then this character is displayed on the computer screen. Nowadays, the P300 concept allows very reliable results with high information transfer rates (Thulasidas, 2006, Krusienski, 2006, Guger, 2009).

2.3.3 SSVEP

The SSVEP stimulation is realized with a 12x12cm box (see Figure 8) equipped with four LED-groups containing three LEDs each. Additionally four arrow LEDs were added to indicate at which LED the user should look during the training. The LEDs are controlled by a microcontroller connected to the computer via USB. The accuracy of the produced frequencies has to be very accurate to make the feature extraction more reliable (frequency error is < 0.025 Hz).
The EEG-data is derived with eight gold electrodes placed mostly over visual cortex on positions POz, PO3, PO4, PO7, PO8, O1, O2 and Oz of the international 10-20 system. The reference electrode is placed at the right earlobe and a ground electrode at position FPz.
The EEG data is analyzed with several feature extraction and classification methods resulting in a classification output for each method. Each classifier has a discrete output in the form of a number (1, 2, 3 and 4) that corresponds to a certain LED. Finally in the last processing stage, the change rate/majority weight analysis step adds a 0 to this set of outputs. The device driver of the robot transforms these five numbers semantically to

driving commands (0-stop, 1-forward, 2-right, 3-backward, 4-left) and sends them to the robot, which moves and gives the feedback to the user.

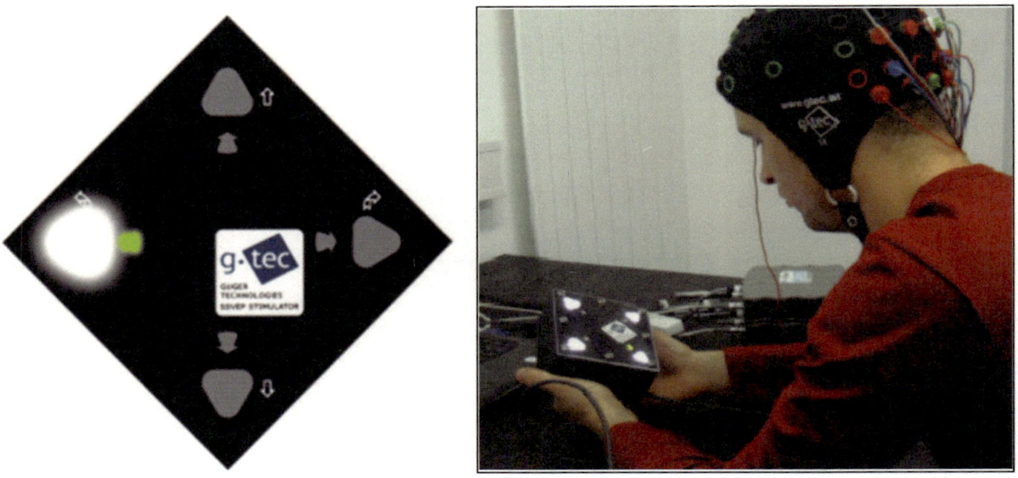

Fig. 8. SSVEP stimulation box and EEG recording

The four LEDs are flickering with different frequencies (10, 11, 12 and 13 Hz). These frequencies have been chosen in preceding off-line tests and showed good performance for the test subjects and are also known from literature to give good accuracy (Friman, 2007). During training the subject has to look at each of the LEDs for several seconds which are controlled by the paradigm. Beside the EEG data also the instruction at which LED the user should look at is logged to harddisk.

All the components of the BCI system are shown in Figure 9. EEG data are recorded with a sampling rate of 256 Hz with the g.USBamp block. Then in the Preprocessing block Laplacian derivations are performed. Each Laplacian derivation is composed of one center signal X_C and an arbitrary number $n > 1$ of side signals $X_{S,1}, i = 1, \dots, n$ which are arranged symmetrically around the center signal. These signals are then combined to a new signal $Y_j = n \cdot X_c - (X_{S,1} + \dots + X_{S,n})$ where j is the index of the derivation.

Two different methods are used to calculate features of the EEG data. One is the minimum energy approach (ME) (Friman, 2007) which requires no training. This algorithm is fed with raw EEG-data channels since it selects the best combination of channels by itself. First of all the EEG-data gets "cleaned" of potential SSVEP-signals. After that operation the signals contain just the unwanted noise. Now a weight vector is generated, which has the property of combining the channels in a way, that the outcome has minimal energy. Now SSVEP detection is done utilizing a test statistic which calculates the ratio between the signal with an estimated SSVEP-response and the signal where no visual stimulus is present. This is done for all stimulation frequencies and all EEG-channels. The output of this classifier is the index of the frequency with the highest signal/noise ratio.

As second method a Fast Fourier Transformation (FFT) and linear discriminant analysis (LDA) using the Laplacian derivations is used. First of all the incoming data gets transformed to the frequency spectrum with a 1024-point FFT. A feature vector is extracted by taking the values of the stimulation frequencies and their 1st and 2nd harmonics. With

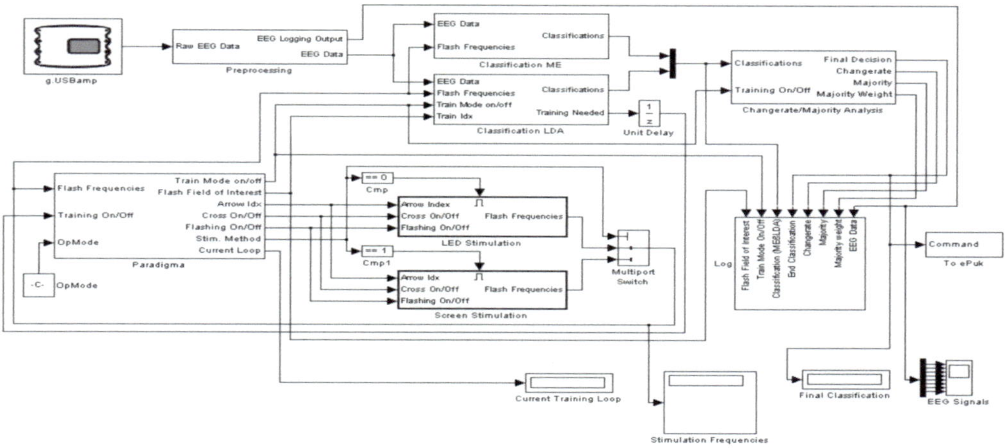

Fig. 9. SSVEP Simulink model. g.USBamp, Preprocessing, Classification ME (Minimum Energy)/LDA and Changerate/Majority Analysis blocks perform the real-time analysis of the EEG data. The block Paradigm controls the training sequence of the LED Stimulation. Beside LEDs also the computer screen can be used as stimulation unit. Furthermore EEG data is visualized and stored

these feature vectors a weight/bias vector must be generated for each user in a training procedure. When the training was completed successfully the LDA classifier can then be used to classify new feature vectors to one of the stimulation frequency indices. In the model used for the experiments described in this paper four ME classification units and four FFT+LDA classification units were used with different EEG channels as inputs.

The last step is a procedure called change rate/majority weight analysis. By having multiple classification units configured with slightly different input data there will be in general random classification results on noise input. This effect is used on one side to produce a zero decision when the outputs of the classifiers are changing heavily and are very different. On the other side a low change rate and a high majority weight (the number of classifications of the different algorithms which are pointing in the same direction) can be used to strengthen the robustness of the decision. Calculation is made on the last second. Default thresholds of 0.25 for change rate and 0.75 (1 - all outputs are pointing into the same direction) for majority weight were used.

The first step of the procedure is to look at the change rate. If it is above the threshold the procedure returns a final classification result of 0 which corresponds to a stop command. Otherwise, if it is below the threshold the next step is to look at the majority weight. If this is above the threshold the majority is taken as final result, otherwise the final output is again 0. The final classification is then sent to external device such as a robot.

3. Accuracies achieved with different BCI principles

Results are presented of 81 subjects who tested a P300 based system, of 99 subjects who tested a motor imagery based BCI system and of 3 subjects who tested a SSVEP based system.

The subjects participating in the P300 study had to spell a 5 character word with only 5 minutes of training. EEG data were acquired to train the system while the subject looked at a 36 character matrix to spell the word WATER. During the real-time phase of the experiment, the subject spelled the word LUCAS.

For the P300 system 72.8 % were able to spell with 100 % accuracy and less than 3 % did not spell any character correctly as shown in Table 1 (Guger, 2009). Interesting is also that the Row-Column Speller reached a higher mean accuracy compared to the single character speller which produces higher P300 responses. This can be explained by the longer selection time per character for the SC speller.

Classification Accuracy [%]	**Row-Column Speller: Percentage of sessions (N=81)**	**Single Character Speller: Percentage of Sessions (N=38)**
100	72.8	55.3
80-100	88.9	76.3
60-79	6.2	10.6
40-59	3.7	7.9
20-39	0.0	2.6
0-19	1.2	2.6
Average Accuracy of all subjects	91.0	82.0
Mean of subjects who participated in RC and SC (N=19)	85.3	77.9

Table 1. Classification accuracy for P300 experiments

The subjects participating in the motor imagery study had to move 40 times a cursor to the right or left side of the computer monitor. Training and classifier calculation were performed with 40 imaginations of left and right hand movement initiated by an arrow pointing to the left and right side.

For motor imagery 6.2 % achieved an accuracy above 90 % and 6.7 % performed with almost random classification accuracy between 50-59 % as shown in Table 2 (Guger, 2003).

Classification accuracy [%]	**Percentage of subjects (N=99)**
90-100	6.2
80-89	13.0
70-79	32.1
60-69	42.0
50-59	6.7
	100

Table 2. Classification accuracy for motor imagery

The subject using the SSVEP based system had to control a robot to a desired location by making 12 choices. The difference to the motor imagery and P300 experiments is that with SSVEP a continuous control signal was realized. For motor imagery and P300 at a specific time point the classification was performed, while for SSVEP the classification was done continuously every 250 ms. As shown in Table 3 subject 1 had an overall error rate of 9.5%. The error rate consisted of no decisions and wrong classes. A fraction of 28.3% of the error rate were wrong classifications. An error of 9.5% seems to be high, but it includes also the breaks between the stimulations. In total 1088 classifications were made during one run and consisted of the following periods: 20 sec pause at the beginning + 3 times 15 seconds LED stimulation + 7 seconds pause after each stimulation. This was repeated 4 times for each LED and gives in total 1088 classification time points. Out of the 1088 decisions only 28 wrong classifications were made during the whole experiment including the breaks. No decisions were only made for 71.7 % of the 9.5 % errors.

Subject	Error [%]	No decision [%]	Wrong class [%]
S1	9.5	71.7	28.3
S2	23.5	92.7	7.3
S3	18.9	75.0	25.0
Mean	17.3	79.8	20.2

Table 3. Classification accuracy for SSVEP

Table 4 compares the 3 BCI principles. As mentioned before, motor imagery and the P300 speller performed the classification at one specific time point and had 6.2 and 72.8 % of the users with more than 90 % accuracy. In contrast the SSVEP BCI classified every 250 ms continuously. If the SSVEP BCI makes the decision only at a certain time point all subjects reached more than 90 % accuracy. It must be noted that for the P300 system the random classification accuracy is 1/36, for the motor imagery system it is 1/2 and for SSVEP it is 1/5. The training time and the montage time of the electrodes was almost equal for P300, motor imagery and SSVEP.

	Motor imagery	P300 speller	SSVEP
Population with 90-100% accuracy	6.2%	72.8%	100%
Training time [min]	6 min	5 min	5 min
Number of electrodes	5	9	9
Random classification accuracy [%]	50 %	1/36	1/5
Decision time for one character	60 s	45 s with 15 flashes	0.25 s

Table 4. Comparison of motor imagery, P300 speller and SSVEP

This study shows that high spelling accuracy can be achieved with the P300 BCI system using approximately five minutes of training data for a large number of non-disabled subjects. The large differences in accuracy between the motor imagery and P300/SSVEP suggest that with limited amount of training data the P300 based BCI is superior to the motor imagery BCI. Overall, these results are very encouraging and a similar study should be conducted with subjects who have ALS to determine if their accuracy levels are similar.

Summarizing it can be said that a P300 based system is suitable for spelling applications, but also e.g. for Smart Home control with several controllable devices. The motor imagery and SSVEP based systems are suitable if a continuous control signal is needed.

4. Applications

4.1 Twitter

One growing application area of BCIs is the control of social environments that allow the user to participate like a healthy person in daily live activities. Therefore 2 frequently used social networks - Twitter and Second Life - were interfaced to the BCI.

Twitter (Twitter Inc.) is a social network that enables the user to send and read messages. The messages are limited to 140 characters and are displayed in the authors profile page. Messages can be sent via the Twitter website or via smart phones or SMS (Short Message Service). Twitter provides also an application programming interface to send and receive SMS. Figure 10 shows an UML diagram of the actions required to use the service Twitter. The standard P300 spelling matrix with 6 x 6 characters was redesigned to cover all the necessary actions for Twitter. Therefore the first two lines contain now the commands to operate the service and the remaining characters are used for spelling itself. The matrix contains now 6 x 9 = 54 characters instead of 36.

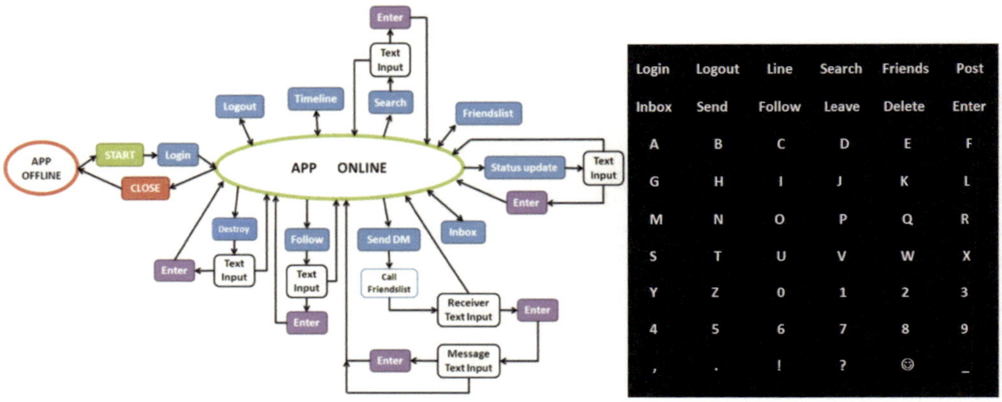

Fig. 9. UML diagram of service Twitter

To interface the BCI system with Twitter the API functions according to Table 5 were used.

BCI command	Description	Twitter API function
Login	Performs authentification	Login account verify credentials
Logout	Logout from Twitter	Logout
Line	Get the 20 newest messages of the user and of friends	Status home timeline
Search	Search for other twitter users	Search
Friends	Get list of friends	Status friendslist
Post	Update user status	Status update
Inbox	Get 20 newest messages from inbox	Direct messages
Send	Send twitter message	Direct direct messages
Follow	Add a friend	Friendships/create
Leave	Cancel a friendship	Friendships/destroy

Table 5. API function for service Twitter

Initially the subject was trained with 10 training characters to calculate a weight vector for testing the Twitter-BCI. Then another user was asking questions via Twitter and the BCI User had to answer one questions on each day. Therefore in total the BCI User had to use the interface on 9 different days and selected between 6 and 36 characters each day. Interesting is to compare the beginning with the end of the study. The first session lasted 11:09 min and the user spelled 13 characters, but made 3 mistakes. The user had the instruction to correct any mistake and this yielded to an average of 51 seconds selection time per character. In comparison in the last session the user spelled 27 characters in 6:38 min with only 1 mistake and an average selection time of 15 seconds per minute. Also the number of flashes per character was reduced from 8 to only 3 flashes to increase the speed.

Tweets	Charac.	Duration [mm:ss]	Errors	Flashes	Time per character [s]
Friend: Which kind of Brain-Computer Interface do you use?					
BCI: P300 GTEC BCI	13	00:11:09	3	8	51
Friend: Are you using the g.GAMMAsys?					
BCI: Exactly!	7	00:06:18	1	8	54
Friend: Active or passive electrodes? For explanation: the active system avoids or reduces artefacts and signal noise.					
BCI: Active electrodes	17	00:06:10	0	5	22
Friend: The mounting of the active system is very comfortable. You do not need to prepare the skin first, do you?					
BCI: you are absolutely right	24	00:08:55	1	5	22
Friend: How many electrodes are needed to run the BCI?					
BCI: For P300 we usually use 8 electrodes	36	00:14:21	2	5	24
Friend: What amplifier are you using for the Brain-Computer Interface?					
BCI: g.MOBIlab+	10	00:04:42	1	5	28
Friend: How long does it take to code the software for the BCI for **TWITTER?**					
BCI: 3 Weeks	7	00:03:13	1	4	28
Friend: How many characters are you able to write within a minute?					
BCI: 3 TO 4	6	00:03:15	0	5	33
Friend: Did you get faster in writing during this period?					
BCI: Yes, from 2 to 4 characters	27	00:06:38	1	3	15

Table 6. Questions and text input with the BCI system, errors and speed

4.2 Second Life (SL)

Second Life is a free 3D online virtual world developed by the American company Linden Lab. It was launched on June 23, 2003. In September 2008 Linden Lab announced that there were 15 million registered accounts whereas on average 60 000 users are online at the same time. The free client Software "Second Life Viewer" and an account are necessary to participate.

One of the main activities in Second Life is socializing with other so-called residents whereas every resident represents a person of the real world (see Figure 10). Furthermore it is possible to hold business meetings, to take photographs and make movies, to attend courses,...Communication takes place via text chat, voice chat and gestures.

For ALS or locked-in patients Second Life allows them to participate like any other user.

Fig. 10. Screenshot of Second Life

The P300 BCI system was interfaced with a Second Life (SL) controller implemented as a C++ S-function. Important is to run the BCI system and SL on separate computers to have enough performance.

To control Second Life three masks were developed: i) the main mask as shown in Figure 11 which has 31 characters, (ii) the mask for chatting (55 characters) and a mask (iii) for searching (40 characters).

Each of our symbols on the P300 mask represents actually a specific key, key combination or sequence of keys of a keyboard and therefore a specific function in Second Life. If now a certain symbol is selected, Second Life is notified to execute this individual action with keyboard events.

An important component of the Second Life matrix is the stand-by character on top right position as BCI systems are designed for disabled persons who cannot switch-on or switch-off the system on their own. If the user selects the character twice in a row the BCI system is switched off until the character is selected again twice. This makes it quite unlikely that a decision is made without attending to the BCI system.

Fig. 11. BCI mask to walk forward/backward, turn left/right, slide left/right, climb, teleport home, show map, turn around, activate/deactivate running mode, start/stop flying, decline, activate/deactivate mouselook view, enter search mask, take snapshot, start chat, quit and stand-by

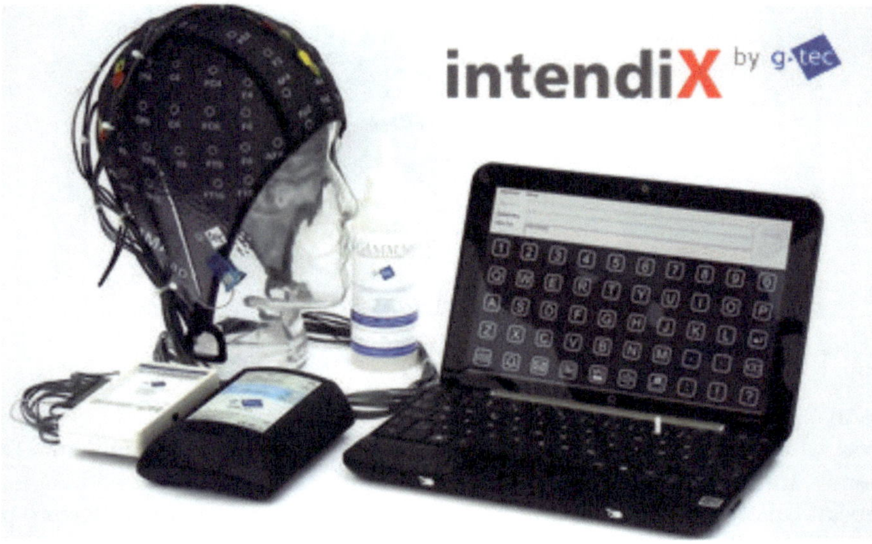

Fig. 12. IntendiX running on the laptop and active electrodes

4.3 intendiX

intendiX® is designed to be installed and operated by caregivers or the patient's family at home. The system consists of active EEG electrodes to avoid abrasion of the skin, a portable

biosignal amplifier and a laptop or netbook running the software under Windows (see Figure 12). The electrodes are integrated into the cap to allow a fast and easy montage of the intendiX equipment.
The intendiX software allows viewing the raw EEG to inspect data quality, but indicates automatically to the unexperienced user if the data quality on a specific channel is bad. If the system is started up for the first time, a user training has to be performed. Therefore usually 5-10 training characters are entered and the user has to copy the characters. The EEG data is used to calculate the user specific weight vector which is stored for later usage. Then the software switches automatically into the spelling mode and the user can spell freely. The input screen is shown in Figure 13.
The user can perform different actions: (i) copy the spelled text into an Editor, (ii) copy the text into an email, (iii) send the text via text-to-speech facilities to the loud speakers, (vi) print the text or (v) send the text via UDP to another computer. For all these services a specific icon exists.
The number of flashes for each classification can be selected by the user or the user can also use a statistical approach that detects automatically the required number of flashes and if the user is working with the BCI system. The later one has the advantage that no characters are selected if the user is not looking at the matrix or does not want to use the speller.

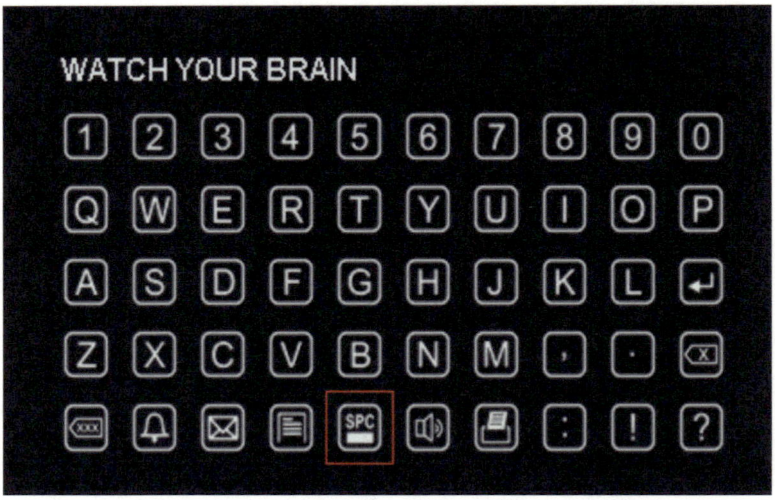

Fig. 13. User interface with 50 characters and computer keyboard like layout

4.4 SM4All – smart home control with BCI

Beside virtual worlds BCI systems can also be used to control real environments. Therefore smart homes are developed that allow independent living for handicapped people. Within an European Union project called SM4All (www.sm4all-project.eu) a middleware platform is developed that allows to control multiple domotic devices with a BCI system.
The SM4All system consists of three layers as shown in Figure 12:

1. The Pervasive Layer gives access to the hardware infrastructure. Different devices and sensors can communicate with the layer (lights, washing machine, doors, temperature sensors, ...) and the embedded software on top of them make services available to the composition layer.

2. The Composition Layer consists of all the components needed to automatically satisfy user needs. It contains the user profile and context manager that prepares the home and user interface according to certain states of the house. Services are described in the repository.
3. The User Layer provides the interface for controlling the house either with a web-interface on a computer or with the BCI system.

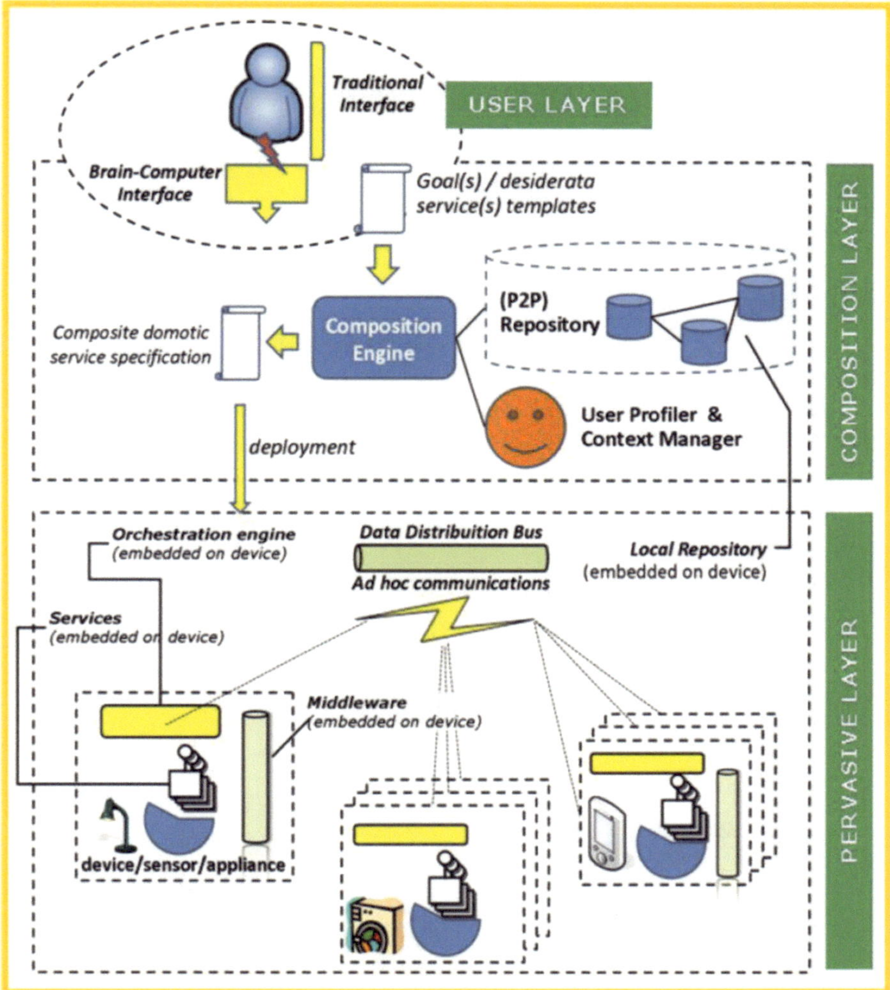

Fig. 12. The SM4ALL architecture

Between the Composition Layer and the User Interface is the abstract adaptive interface (AAI) that extracts all currently available actions for certain services for the user interface as shown in Figure 13. All available services are shown in the user interface and are ordered according to the priority of the service. The user can now simply click with the mouse on the web-interface or can use the P300 BCI system to initiate an action. Both transmit the command via SOAP messages to the SM4All system and therefore from any computer with internet connection the house can be controlled.

Fig. 13. BCI interface and web interface

A light is for example 1 service with 2 actions because it can be switched on and off. Therefore the control icon allows either to switch on or off the light. Figure 14 shows the service TV. The TV can be in several different states and the arrows between represent the actions that must be selectable with the web-interface or BCI system.

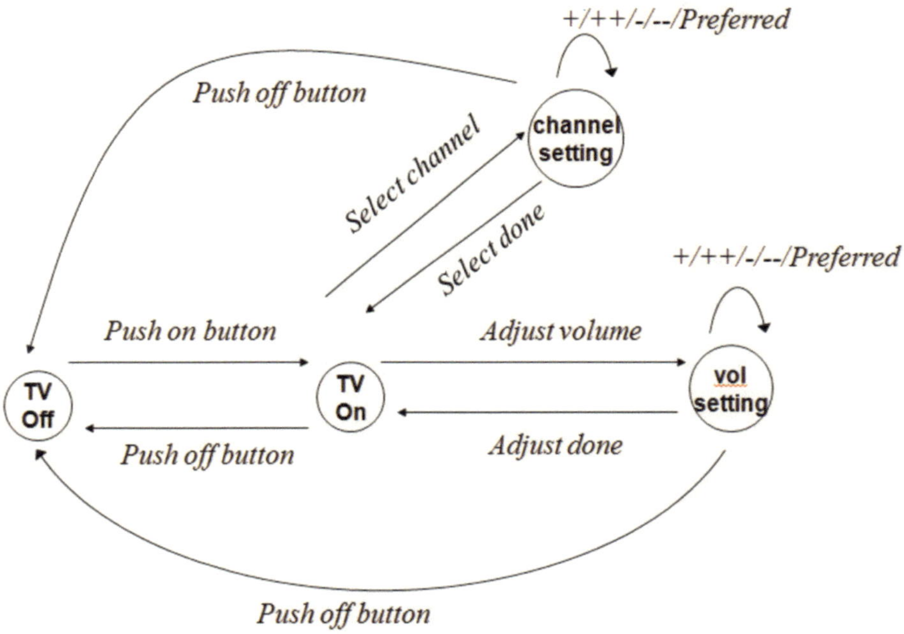

Fig. 14. Description of service TV with several actions

In future the SM4all system will be able to control many different domotic devices from different manufacturers and this makes it simple for handicapped people to have access to them and to life independent.

5. Acknowledgements

This work was funded by EC projects Presenccia, SM4all, BrainAble, Decoder, Better.

6. References

Allison, B. Z., McFarland, J., D., Schalk, G., Zheng, S. D., M., J. M., et al. (2008). Towards an independent brain-computer interface using steady state visual evoked potentials. Clin Neurophysiol , 399-408.

Bakardjian, H., Tanaka, T., & Cichocki, A. (2010). Optimization of SSVEP brain responses with application to eight-command Brain–Computer Interface. Neurosci. Lett. , 34-8.

Bin, G., Gao, X., Yan, Z., Hong, B., & Gao, S. (2009). An online multi-channel SSVEP-based brain–computer interface using a canonical correlation analysis method. Journal of Neural Engineering , 6pp.

Birbaumer, N., Kubler, A., Ghanayim, N., Hinterberger, T., Perelmouter, J., Kaiser, J., Iversen, I., Kotchoubey, B., Neumann, N., Flor, H. (2000). The thought translation device (TTD) for completely paralyzed patients. IEEE Trans.Rehabil.Eng, 8(2): p. 190-193.

Citi, L., Poli, R., Cinel, C., & Sepulveda, F. (2008). P300-based BCI mouse with genetically-optimized analogue control. IEEE Transactions on Neural Systems and Rehabilitation Engineering , 51-61.

Elbert T, Rockstroh B, Lutzenberger W, Birbaumer N. Biofeedback of slow cortical potentials. Electroenceph clin Neurophysiol 1980;48:293–301.

Finkea, A., Lenhardt, A., & Ritter, H. (2009). The MindGame: a P300-based brain-computer interface game. Neural Networks , 1329-1333.

Friman, O., Volosyak, I., Graser, A.: Multiple channel detection of Steady-State Visual Evoked Potentials for brain-Computer interfaces. IEEE Transactions on Biomedical Engineering, 54, 742--750, (2007).

Gao, X., Xu, D., Cheng, M., & S., G. (2003). A BCI-Based Environmental Controller for the Motion-Disabled. IEEE Trans. Neural Sys. and Rehab. Eng. , 137-140.

Guger, C., Ramoser, H., and Pfurtscheller, G. (2000). Real-time EEG analysis with subject-specific spatial patterns for a Brain Computer Interface (BCI). IEEE Trans Neural Syst Rehabil Eng., 8: p. 447-456.

Guger, C., Schlögl, A., Neuper, C., Walterspacher, D., Strein, T., and Pfurtscheller, G. (2001) Rapid prototyping of an EEG-based brain-computer interface (BCI). IEEE Trans. Rehab. Engng., vol. 9 (1): p. 49-58.

Guger, C., Edlinger, G., Harkam, W., Niedermayer, O., and Pfurtscheller, G. (2003). How many people are able to operate an EEG-based brain computer interface? IEEE Trans. Rehab. Engng., vol. 11: p. 145-147.

Guger, C., Daban, S., Sellers, E., Holzner, C., Krausz, G., Carabalona, R., et al. (2009). How many people are able to control a P300-based brain-computer interface (BCI)? Neuroscience Letters , 94-98.

Krusienski, D.J., Sellers, E.W., Cabestaing, F., Bayoudh, S., McFarland, D.J., Vaughan, T.M., and Wolpaw, J.R. (2006). A comparison of classification techniques for the P300 Speller. J.Neural Eng, 3(4): p. 299-305.

Leuthardt, E.C., Schalk, G., Wolpaw, J.R., Ojemann, J.G., and Moran, D.W. (2004). A brain-computer interface using electrocorticographic signals in humans. J. Neural Eng., 1: p. 63-71.

Lin Z., Zhang C., Wu W., & X., G. (2006). Frequency recognition based on canonical correlation analysis for SSVEP-based BCIs. IEEE Trans Biomed Eng. , 2610-2614.

Middendorf, M., McMillan, G., Calhoun, G., & Jones, K. S. (2000). Brain-computer interfaces based on the steady-state visual-evoked response. IEEE Transactions on Rehabilitation Engineering , 211-214.

Muller-Putz, G.R., Scherer, R., Brauneis, C., and Pfurtscheller, G. (2005). Steady-state visual evoked potential (SSVEP)-based communication: impact of harmonic frequency components. J.Neural Eng, 2(4): p. 123-130.

Pfurtscheller, G., Neuper, C., Flotzinger, D., and Pregenzer, M. (1997). EEG-based discrimination between imagination of right and left hand movement. Electroenceph. clin. Neurophysiol., 103: p. 642-651.

Pfurtscheller, G., Neuper, C., Guger, C., Obermaier, B., Pregenzer, M., Ramoser, H., and Schlögl, A. (2000). Current trends in Graz brain-computer interface (BCI) research. IEEE Trans. Rehab. Engng., vol. 8: p. 216-219.

Schalk G, McFarland DJ, Hinterberger T, Birbaumer N, Wolpaw JR. BCI2000: a general-purpose brain-computer interface (BCI) system. IEEE Trans Biomed Eng. 2004 Jun;51(6):1034-43.

Sellers, E.W., Krusienski, D.J., McFarland, D.J., Vaughan, T.M., and Wolpaw, J.R. (2006). A P300 event-related potential brain-computer interface (BCI): the effects of matrix size and inter stimulus interval on performance. Biol.Psychol., 73(3): p. 242-252.

Sellers, E.W., and Donchin, E. (2006). A P300-based brain-computer interface: initial tests by ALS patients. Clin.Neurophysiol., 117(3): p. 538-548.

Sutton, S., Braren, M., Zubin, J., & John, E. R. (1965). Evoked-Potential Correlates of Stimulus Uncertainty. Science , 1187-1188.

Thulasidas, M., Cuntai, G., and Jiankang, W. (2006). Robust classification of EEG signal for brain-computer interface. IEEE Trans Neural Syst Rehabil Eng., 14(1): p. 24-29.

Vallabhaneni, A., "Motor imagery task classification for brain computer interface applications using spatiotemporal principle component analysis". Neurol Res. 2004 Apr ;26 (3):282-7 15142321 Cit:5

Waldhauser, M. (2006). Offline and online processing of evoked potentials. Master thesis, FH Linz.

Wolpaw J. R., Birbaumer N., McFarlanda D.J., Pfurtscheller G., Vaughan T. M. (2002). Brain-computer interfaces for communication and control", Clinical Neurophysiology, Volume 113, Issue 6, Pages 767-791.

Zhang, D., Maye, A., Gao, X., B., H., Engel, A. K., & Gao, S. (2010). An independent brain-computer interface using covert non-spatial visual selective attention. J Neural Eng., 16010. Epub 2010 Jan 19.

2

Applied Advanced Classifiers for Brain Computer Interface

José Luis Martínez, Antonio Barrientos
Politechnic University of Madrid
Spain

1. Introduction

Since that Dr. Hans Berger discovered the electrical nature of the brain, it has been considered the possibility to communicate persons with external devices only through the use of the brain waves (Vidal, 1973).
Brain Computer Interface technology is aimed at communicating with persons using external computerised devices via the electroencephalographic signal as the primary command source (Wolpaw, J.R.; et al., 2000), (Birbaumer, N; et al., 2000). In the first international meeting for BCI technology it was established that BCI *"must not depend on the brain's normal output pathways of peripheral nerves and muscles"* (Wolpaw, J. R.; et al., 2002). The primary uses of this technology are to benefit persons with blocking diseases, such as: Amiotrophic Lateral Sclerosis (ALS), brainstem stroke, or cerebral palsy; or persons whom have suffered some kind of traumatic accident like for example paraplegic (E. Donchin and K. M. Spencer and R. Wijesinghe, 2000).
Actually different types of classifications can be established for BCI technology, from the physiologic point of view BCI devices can be classified in exogenous and endogenous. The exogenous devices provide some kind of stimuli to the user and they analyse the user's responds to them, examples of this class are devices based on visual evoked potential or P300 (E. Donchin and K. M. Spencer and R. Wijesinghe, 2000). On the contrary, the endogenous devices do not depend on the user's respond to external stimuli, they base their operation in detecting and recognising brain-wave patterns controlled autonomously by the user, examples of this class are devices based on the desynchronisation and synchronisation of μ and β rhythms (Wolpaw, J. R.; et al., 2002), (Pfurtscheller et al., 2000a), (Pineda, J.A. et al., 2003).
But in any case, independently of the classification criteria, an algorithm that detects, acquires, filters, learns and classifies the electroencephalographic signal is required in order to control an external device using thoughts, associating some mental patterns to device commands, as it is shown in the block diagram of Figure 1, (Kostov, A., 2000), (Pfurtscheller et al., 2000b).
The first block is in charge of acquiring and amplifying the brain signal, allocating the electrodes on specific places on the scalp in case of using superficial electrodes, or inside the brain in case of using intracortical ones; in the second block the signal is sampled, quantified and codified at periodic intervals of time in order to digitalize it, to simplify the following phases the digitalised signal may be filtered, for example to reduce the noise level obtaining a better SNR signal or identifying and processing artifacts. After this, in oder to obtain a set

of parameters that represent the temporal window of the acquired brain signal the process of feature extraction is performed, because the main changes in brain activity are associated to changes in the power amplitude of band frequencies, spectrograms based on FFT are used to obtain initial feature vectors of six components (Obermaier et al., 2001) (Proakis & Manolakis, 1997).

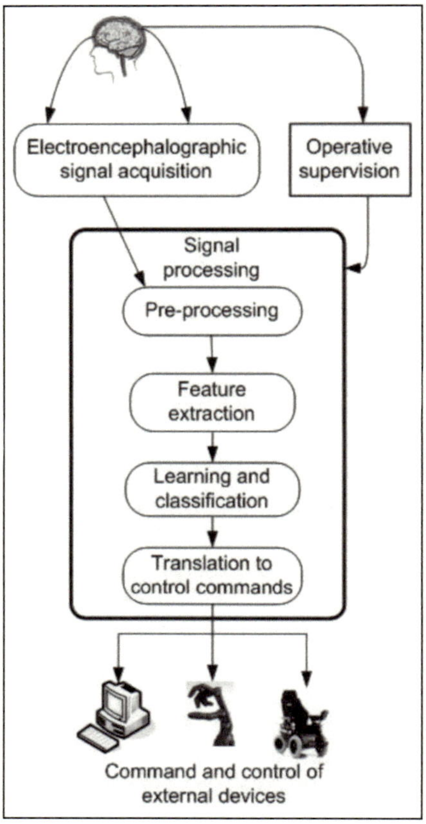

Fig. 1. Block diagram of a BCI device.

In the next block the features are processed in order to detect a specific event in the case of exogenous devices, or for identifying, learning, and recognising signal cerebral patterns, that are going to be used as inputs for the following block that translates them to control commands of the external device.

Finally, but not less important, is the Operative Supervision block which sets the operative mode of the BCI device under the user's supervision, this is if the device is operating in on-line / off-line mode, or if it is modifying its internal parameters during the learning phase in order to adjust to the user's cerebral activity.

In the experiments considered for this paper only two electroencephalographic channels "C3 and C4" have been considered to capture the endogenous electroencephalographic signal from the subject. In order to facilitate the use of this technology it is important to make it easy to use, the "cosmosis" or how the user's looks like wearing the BCI device is also important, this is the reason that the number of electrodes employed in these devices is a global key feature, as the fewer of electrodes used, the higher the comfort (Wolpaw, 2007).

This chapter deals with the application of these concepts for developing BCI devices, focusing in the classification of the user's cerebral activity.
The contents of this chapter are distributed in the following sections:

- The first section contemplates this introduction.
- The second section briefly describes the signal processing phase and the selection of the features that describe the user's cerebral activity.
- In the third section is analysed the discrimination capability between the feature vector populations sampled when the user develop three different cognitive tasks.
- Afterwards, in the fourth section, it is assessed the best component combination of the feature vector in order to reduce the feature space dimensionality improving the discrimination capability.
- The fiveth section describes different types of advanced classifiers based on: Neural Networks, Hidden Markov Models, and Support Vector Machines .
- The experiments, carried on with signal sampled from real users, are described in the sixth section. The different experimental paradigms, results, and analysis, are explained in it.
- Finally the seventh section is devoted to conclusions.

2. Signal processing and feature selection

The tests described below were carried out on five male healthy subjects, one of them has been trained before, but the other four were novice in the use of the system.
In order to facilitate the mental concentration on the proposed activities, the experiments were carried on in a room with low level of noise and under controlled environmental conditions, all electronic equipments external to the experiment around the subject were switched off to avoid electromagnetic artifacts. The subjects were sat-down in front of the acquisition system monitor, at 50 cm from the screen, their hands were in a visible position, the supervisor of the experiment controlled the correct development of it.
Two different types of experimental procedures had been considered for the acquisition of the user's cerebral signal. In the first one, the user concentrates on the proposed cognitive tasks meanwhile the system registers the cerebral activity but without communicating any feedback about the signal classification.
In the second type of experiments the user receives the classification feedback from a simple classifier based on artificial neural networks. These neural networks have been trained with registers associated to each cognitive task obtained from the previous kind of experiments.
Because in the first type of experiments there is not any kind of feedback they are named Off-line experimental procedures, in contrast to the second class called On-line experimental procedures.
The flow of activities for each experimental procedure are described in the following subsections.

2.1 Flow of the activities for the Off-line experimental procedure

The experimental process is shown on Figure 2.

- *Test of system devices.* It checks the correct level of battery, and state of the electrodes.
- *System assembly.* Device connections: superficial electrodes (Au-Cu), battery, bio-amplifier (g.BSamp by g.tec), acquisition signal card (PCI-MIO-16/E-4 by National Instrument), computer.

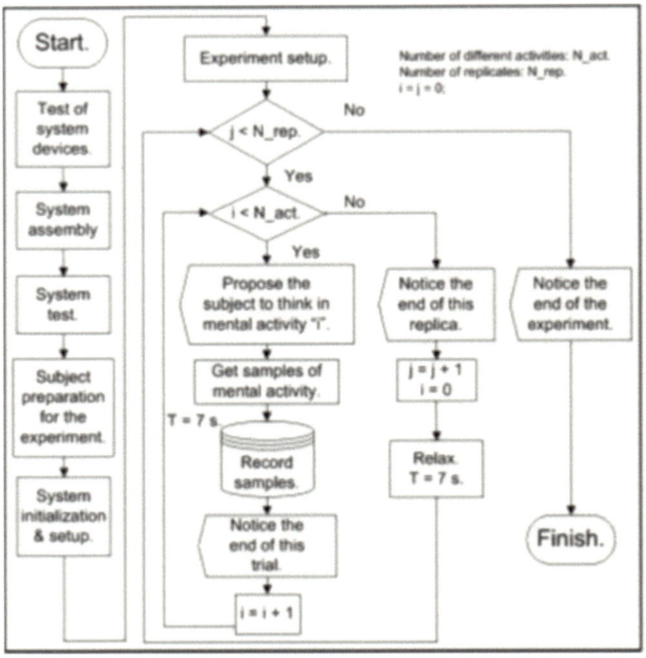

Fig. 2. Diagram of the experiment realization.

- *System test.* Verifies the correct operation of the whole system. To minimise noise from the electrical network the Notch filter (50Hz) of the bio-amplifier is switched on.
- *Subject preparation for the experiment.* Application of electrodes on subject's head. Impedance $\leq$ 4KOhms.
- *System initialisation and setup.* Verification of data register. It is monitored the signal evolution, in the spectrogram should appear a very low component of 50 Hz.
- *Experiment setup.* The supervisor of the experiment sets-up the number of replications, $N_{rep} = 10$, and the quantity of different mental activities. The duration of each trial is $t = 7s$, the acquisition frequency is $f_s = 384Hz$. The system suggests to the subject to think about the proposed mental activity. A short relax is allowed at the end of each trial.

2.2 Flow of the activities for the On-line experimental procedure

In these tests, a cursor in the centre of the screen and a square goal are shown to the subject, the square goal appears half the trials on the left of the screen and the other half on the right. The subject shall try to move the cursor towards the goal thinking in the cognitive tasks proposed in the Off-line experiments. The experimental On-line process is shown on Figure 3.

- *Experiment set-up.* This phase determines the cognitive tasks used to move the cursor to the left and to the right, the number of trials and the time for each trial.
- *Display initialisation.* It initialises the display, for even trials the goal is on the right, for odds on the left.
- *Data acquisition.* In this phase 128 samples per electroencephalographic channel are acquired at $fs = 384Hz$.

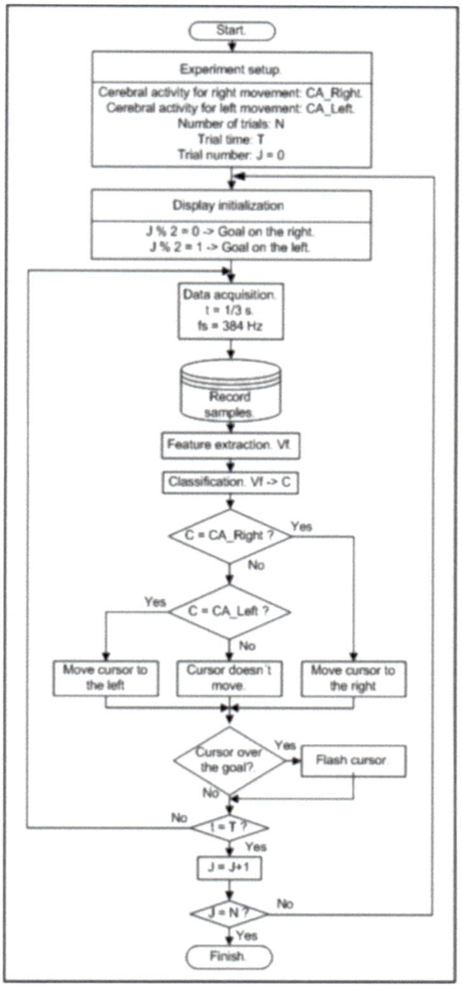

Fig. 3. Diagram of the On-line experiment realization.

- *Record samples.* The previous samples are recorded for a posterior analysis.
- *Feature extraction.* A vector of features is extracted from the acquired samples.
- *Classification.* The vector of features is classified as belonging to one of the previous mental tasks, and the associated movement is performed; if the vector can't be classified in any of the cerebral activities, the cursor doesn't move. If the trial time is exceeded a new trial is carried out until the *N* trials had been performed.

2.3 Position of electrodes

Electrodes were placed in the central zone of the skull, next to C3 and C4 (Penny, W. D.; et al., 2000), two pair of electrodes were placed in front of and behind of Rolandic sulcus, this zone is one with the highest discriminant power, it takes signal from motor and sensory areas of the brain (Birbaumer, N; et al., 2000), (Neuper, C.; et al., 2001).
Reference electrode was placed on the right mastoid, two more electrode were placed near to the corner of the eyes to register blinking.

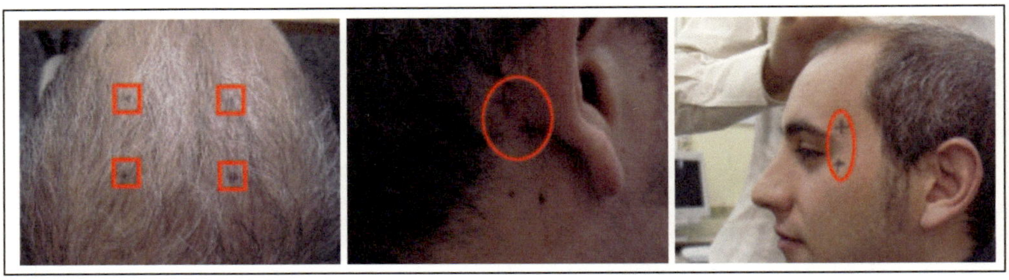

Fig. 4. Electrode placement.

2.4 Description of cognitive tasks

The supervisor of the experiment suggests the subject to figure out the following mental activities:

Activity A. Mathematical task. Recursive subtraction of a prime number, i.e. 7, from a big quantity, i.e. 3.000.000.

Activity B. Movement task. The subject imagines moving their limbs or hands, but without the materialisation of it.

Activity C. Relax. The subject is relaxed.

These tasks will be the cerebral patterns to differentiate among them (Neuper, C.; et al., 2001).

2.5 Computational process

This section describes the procedure applied to recorded signal just before its classification.

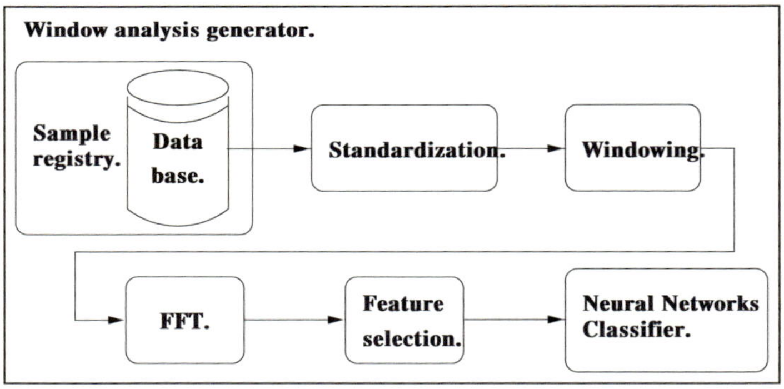

Fig. 5. Computational process flow.

2.5.1 Window analysis generator

In this block the registered signal is chopped in packages of samples, similar to the bundles of samples obtained from an acquisition card in an on-line BCI application. The number of samples in each package is a compromise between the goodness of the classification and the amount of time taken by this classification. An algorithm with very good classification and low number of mistakes will take a very big package, so the time between classifications will be also very big, it will do the algorithm useless for a real on-line BCI system, neither a very fast algorithm with small packages of samples but with a high number of mistakes will be useful.

In this work we have considered packages of 128 samples, the sample frequency is $F_s = 384Hz$, so it is possible to obtain a classification latency of $t = 1/3s$.

The duration of each activity is 7s, so there will be 21 classifications obtained from each register, no overlap between windows have been considered.

2.5.2 Standardisation

To compare the signal of different sessions is necessary to standardise the samples, avoiding for example that variations in the impedance of the electrodes changes the classification result. The standardisation of each analysis window consists in the subtraction of the average value and the division by the standard deviation, eqs. 1 to 3.

$$\mu = \frac{\sum_{i=1}^{N} x_i}{N} \tag{1}$$

$$\sigma^2 = \frac{\sum_{i=1}^{N} (x-\mu)^2}{N} \tag{2}$$

$$x' = \frac{x-\mu}{\sigma} \tag{3}$$

2.5.3 Windowing

The frequency leakage effect occurs when signals with low frequency components are chopped or processed with temporal windows with sharp edges, in this case in the spectrogram appears high frequency components as it is shown in Figure 6, (Harris, 1978).

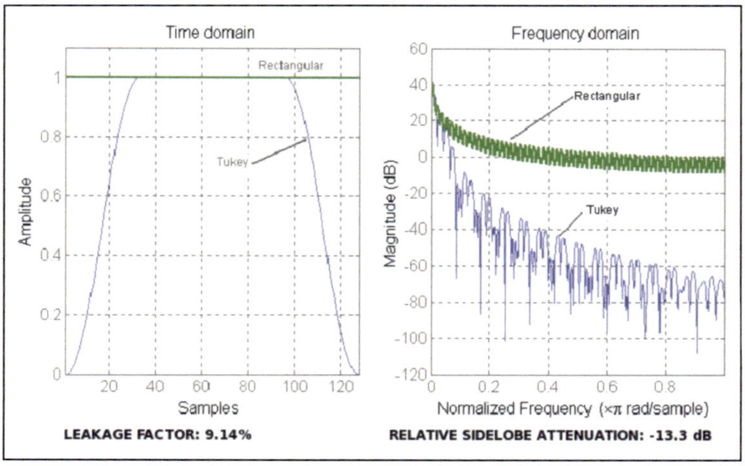

Fig. 6. Example of leakage effect.

In order to minimise this effect, seven different types of preprocessing windows have been applied to the standardised signal. The following types of windows have been considered:

- Rectangular window. $h(n) = 1$.
- Triangular or Bartlett's window. $h(n) = 1 - \frac{2|n - \frac{M-1}{2}|}{M-1}$.
- Blackman's window. $h(n) = 0.42 - 0.5cos(\frac{2\pi n}{M-1}) + 0.08cos(\frac{4\pi n}{M-1})$.
- Hamming's window. $h(n) = \frac{1}{2}(1 - cos(\frac{2\pi n}{M-1}))$.
- Hanning's window. $h(n) = 0.54 - 0.46cos(\frac{2\pi n}{M-1})$.

- Kaiser's window. $h(n) = \frac{I_o\left[\alpha\sqrt{(\frac{M-1}{2})^2-(n-\frac{M-1}{2})^2}\right]}{I_o[\alpha(\frac{M-1}{2})]}.$
- Tukey's window. $h(n) = \frac{1}{2}\left[1+cos(\frac{n-(1+\alpha)(M-1)/2}{(1-\alpha)(M-1)/2}\pi)\right]$
  $\frac{\alpha(M-1)}{2} \leq |n-\frac{M-1}{2}| \leq \frac{M-1}{2}.$
- Time domain sequence: $h(n), 0 \leq n \leq M-1.$[1]

With the use of a window which gets good separability between mental patterns, the classifier will be easier, faster and the results more reliable.

2.5.4 FFT

The cerebral activity becomes apparent mainly through the frequency components of the electroencephalographic signal. Different kind of mental activities have different frequency components, (Harris, 1978),(Neuper, C.; et al., 2001),(Penny, W. D.; et al., 2000). For this reason it is necessary to transform the sampled time domain signal to frequency domain, so a Fast Fourier Transform is applied to each block of 2^7 sampled data.

$$X(k) = \sum_{n=0}^{N-1} x(n)W_N^{k_n} \qquad 0 \leq k \leq N-1 \tag{4}$$

$$W_N = e^{-\frac{2\pi j}{N}} \tag{5}$$

Having in mind that the sample frequency is 384Hz, the frequency resolution is:

$$\Delta f = \frac{384Hz}{128} = 3Hz. \tag{6}$$

In this application the useful information is in the amplitude of the frequency components, so the phases are discarded, we focus our attention on the spectrograms of each of the analysis windows. Considering the properties of the Fourier Transform and that the signal in the time domain only have real components, in the Nyquist frequency is produced the reflection effect, so the signal information is in the first halve of the components, (Harris, 1978).

2.5.5 Feature selection

A vector of six features is extracted from each signal analysis window. This vector, table 1, is made up as the mean of the amplitudes of the frequency bands. Because the frequency of normal human brain is under 40-50Hz, only frequencies between 6 and 38Hz have been considered.

3. Statistical analysis procedure

In order to assess if it is possible to discriminate between the samples acquired when the user was performing the proposed cognitive tasks, the statistical technique of bilateral contrast test is applied to each population pair of features obtained from each cognitive activity. Each component of the vector is considered to determine its significance and separability power. Bilateral contrast makes use of population variance, if the equality of both population variances is rejected it is necessary to apply a correction factor in the degrees of freedom. These

[1] M = length of the filtering window

FFT index.	Frequency.	Denomination.
1 - 2	0 - 5	Not considered
3	6 - 8	θ.
4	9 - 11	α_1.
5	12 - 14	$\alpha 2$.
6 - 7	15 - 20	β_1.
8 - 10	21 - 29	β_2.
11 - 13	30 - 38	β_3.
14 - 64	39 - 192	Not considered

Table 1. Feature vector.

contrasts were applied to samples of both electroencephalographic channels preprocessed with each type of filtering window.

- *Bilateral contrast to the variance ratio.* The equality of variances is obtained with $R = 1$.
  n_1 : sample size of the first population.
  n_2 : sample size of the second population.
  σ_1 : variance of the first population.
  σ_2 : variance of the second population.
  $\hat{S_1}$: variance estimation of the first population.
  $\hat{S_2}$: variance estimation of the second population.
  $F =$ Fisher distribution.
  $T =$ Student distribution.

  Null hypothesis H_o vs. alternative hypothesis H_1.

$$H_o : \frac{\sigma_1}{\sigma_2} = R \quad vs. \quad H_1 : \frac{\sigma_1}{\sigma_2} \neq R \tag{7}$$

Considering that:

$$\frac{(n_1 - 1)\hat{S_1}}{\sigma_1} \rightsquigarrow \chi^2_{n_1 - 1} \qquad \frac{(n_2 - 1)\hat{S_2}}{\sigma_2} \rightsquigarrow \chi^2_{n_1 - 1} \tag{8}$$

$$\frac{\frac{1}{n_1-1}\frac{(n_1-1)\hat{S_1}}{\sigma_1}}{\frac{1}{n_2-1}\frac{(n_2-1)\hat{S_2}}{\sigma_2}} = \frac{\sigma_2}{\sigma_1}\frac{\hat{S_1}}{\hat{S_2}} \rightsquigarrow F_{n_1-1,n_2-1} \tag{9}$$

Therefore under the fulfillment of the null hypothesis:

$$F_{Exp} = \frac{1}{R}\frac{\hat{S_1}}{\hat{S_2}} \rightsquigarrow F_{n_1-1,n_2-1} \tag{10}$$

The acceptance zone of H_o is:

$$a_{teo} = F_{(n_1-1,n_2-1,1-\frac{\alpha}{2})} \tag{11}$$

$$b_{teo} = F_{(n_1-1,n_2-1,1-\frac{\alpha}{2})} \tag{12}$$

$$a_{teo} \leq F_{Exp} \leq b_{teo} \tag{13}$$

- *Bilateral contrast of two independent normal and homocedastic populations.* Null hypothesis H_o vs. alternative hypothesis H_1.

$$H_o : \mu_1 - \mu_2 = \Delta \quad vs. \quad H_1 : \mu_1 - \mu_2 \neq \Delta \tag{14}$$

The variances of the both population are equal but unknown.

$$T_{Exp} = \frac{(\bar{X_1} - \bar{X_2}) - (\mu_1 - \mu_2)}{\sqrt{\hat{S}(\frac{1}{n_1} + \frac{1}{n_2})}} \tag{15}$$

In which $\hat{S}$ is the pseudo-variance of $\hat{S_1}$ and $\hat{S_2}$

$$\hat{S} = \frac{(n_1 - 1) * \hat{S_1} + (n_2 - 1) * \hat{S_2}}{n_1 + n_2 - 2} \tag{16}$$

The zone of H_o acceptance is: $$T_{Teo} = t_{(n_1+n_2-2,1-\frac{\alpha}{2})} \tag{17}$$

If $|T_{Exp}| \leq T_{Teo}$ then H_o is accepted, on the contrary H_1 is accepted and H_o is rejected.

- *Bilateral contrast of two independent normal and heterocedastic populations.* The null hypothesis H_o and alternative hypothesis are similar to the previous ones, the statistical measure is:

$$T_{Exp} = \frac{(\bar{X_1} - \bar{X_2}) - (\mu_1 - \mu_2)}{\sqrt{\frac{\hat{S_1}}{n_1} + \frac{\hat{S_2}}{n_2}}} \leadsto t_f \tag{18}$$

In which f is the number of degrees of freedom calculated with the Welch's formula:

$$f = \frac{(\frac{\hat{S_1}}{n_1} + \frac{\hat{S_2}}{n_2})^2}{\frac{1}{n_1+1}(\frac{\hat{S_1}}{n_1})^2 + \frac{1}{n_2+1}(\frac{\hat{S_2}}{n_2})^2} - 2 \tag{19}$$

In this case the zone of H_o acceptance is:

$$T_{Teo} = t_{(f,1-\frac{\alpha}{2})} \tag{20}$$

If $|T_{Exp}| \leq T_{Teo}$ then H_o is accepted, on the contrary it is assumed that the populations are different.

The results of these analyses are graphically shown in the subsection 6.2.1.

4. Reduction of the feature space dimensionality

Linear Discriminant Analysis is a preprocessing technique used in machine learning, its objective is to find the best combination of features that separate two or more types of objects or events. The result can be used as linear classifier or as a technique to reduce the feature space dimension before the classification process.
Under the consideration that it is possible to discriminate between electroencephalographic samples acquired when the user was performing the suggested cognitive tasks, the next phase is to find the best combination of features that separates in an optimal way the registers of these mental tasks.
In machine learning a preprocessing technique called Linear Discriminant Analysis finds automatically this combination of features. The result can be used as linear classifier or as a technique to reduce the feature space dimension before the classification process.

4.1 Linear discriminant analysis

Supposed C classes of observations, Linear Discriminant Analysis is a preprocess technique that finds the transformation matrix W which separates in an optimal way two or more classes. LDA considers maximising the following objective:

$$J(W) = \frac{W^T S_B W}{W^T S_W W} \tag{21}$$

where S_B is the between classes scatter matrix, and S_w is the within classes scatter matrix, the definitions of the both matrices are:

$$S_B = \sum_c N_c(\mu_c - \bar{x})(\mu_c - \bar{x})^T \tag{22}$$

$$S_W = \sum_c \sum_{i \in c} (x_i - \mu_c)(x_i - \mu_c)^T \tag{23}$$

$$\mu_c = \frac{1}{N_c} \sum_{i \in c} x_i \tag{24}$$

$$\bar{x} = \frac{1}{N} \sum_i x_i = \frac{1}{N} \sum_c N_c \mu_c \tag{25}$$

and N_c is the number of samples in class c.
Because J is invariant to rescaling of the vectors $W \to \alpha W$, hence it is possible to choose W such that the denominator is $W^T S_W W = 1$. So the problem of maximising J can be transformed to the following constrained optimisation problem,

$$min_W \quad -\frac{1}{2} W^T S_B W \tag{26}$$

$$s.t. \quad W^T S_W W = 1 \tag{27}$$

corresponding to the Lagrangian,

$$L_P = -\frac{1}{2} W^T S_B W + \frac{1}{2} \lambda (W^T S_W W - 1) \tag{28}$$

With solution (the halves are added for convenience):

$$S_B W = \lambda S_W W \Rightarrow S_W^{-1} S_B W = \lambda W \tag{29}$$

This is a generalised eigen-problem, and using the fact that S_B is symmetric positive definite and can hence be written as $S_B^{\frac{1}{2}} S_B^{\frac{1}{2}}$, where $S_B^{\frac{1}{2}}$ is constructed from its eigenvalue decomposition as $S_B = U \Lambda U^T \to S_B^{\frac{1}{2}} = U \Lambda^{\frac{1}{2}} U^T$. Defining $V = S_B^{\frac{1}{2}} W$ it is get

$$S_B^{\frac{1}{2}} S_W^{-1} S_B^{\frac{1}{2}} V = \lambda V \tag{30}$$

this is a regular eigenvalue problem for a symmetric positive definite matrix, with solutions λ_k as eigen-values and V_k as eigen-vectors, which leads to solution:

$$W = S_B^{-\frac{1}{2}} V \tag{31}$$

Plugging the solution back into the objective $J(W)$, it is found that the desired solution which maximise the objective is the one with largest eigenvalues.

4.2 Operational procedure

1. Samples from each mental tasks are obtained.
   X_a Mathematical Activity.
   X_b Movement imagination.
   X_c Relax.
2. Statistical definition of all populations:

$$\bar{\mu_a} = E[x_a] \quad S_a = E[(x_a - \bar{\mu_a})(x_a - \bar{\mu_a})^T] \tag{32}$$
$$\bar{\mu_b} = E[x_b] \quad S_b = E[(x_b - \bar{\mu_b})(x_b - \bar{\mu_b})^T] \tag{33}$$
$$\bar{\mu_c} = E[x_c] \quad S_c = E[(x_a - \bar{\mu_c})(x_c - \bar{\mu_c})^T] \tag{34}$$

3. Calculation of the scattering matrices (eq.22 & 3).
4. Application of LDA optimising criterion (eq.30).
5. Calculation of the transformation matrix, W (eq.31), formed by the eigen-vectors, V_k, which eigen-values are bigger than $1 * 10^{-4}$ ordered form high to low magnitudes.
6. Once the transformation matrices have been obtained, the data sets are transformed using LDA transform. The decision region in the transformed space is a hyperplane of lower dimension than the feature space.

$$X_a \Rightarrow \quad X'_a = W^T * X_a \tag{35}$$
$$X_b \Rightarrow \quad X'_b = W^T * X_b \tag{36}$$
$$X_c \Rightarrow \quad X'_c = W^T * X_c \tag{37}$$

7. For classification problems once the LDA transformations are completed, Euclidean or Mahalanobis distances to the centre of each class could be used to classify new vectors. The smallest value among the c distances classifies the new vector as belonging to class c.

In order to evaluate the feedback effect over the discrimination capability the Off-line and On-line experimental procedures described respectively on subsections 2.1 and 2.2 were carried out on five healthy male subjects obtaining the results shown in subsection 6.2.2

5. Classifier description

This section briefly presents the different types of classifiers used in the experimental procedures.

5.1 Neural networks classifiers for BCI devices

Once that the discrimination capability of the electroencephalographic signals has been assessed and analysed the possibility for the reduction of the original feature space without affecting the discrimination capability, the next step is the application of different families of supervised classifiers to the electroencephalographic signal and analysing the results.
One of these family of classifiers is based on different types of artificial neural networks. This section describes the architecture of three types of classifiers based on: Radial Basis Functions (RBF), Probabilistic Neural Networks (PNN), and Multi-Layer Perceptrons (MLP) (Bishop, 1995), (Ripley, 1996).
For each type of neural network two architectures of classifiers were implemented (refer to Figure 7).
Each classifier applies the following procedure to the vector of features extracted previously:

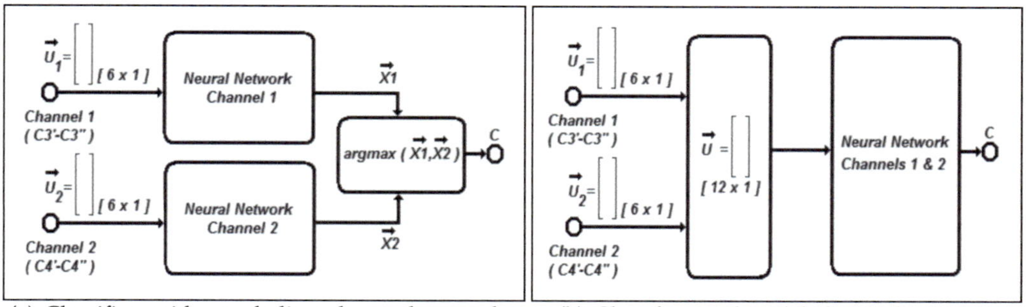

(a) Classifiers with two dedicated neural networks. (b) Classifiers with a global neural network.

Fig. 7. Architecture of classifiers.

1. Determination of the learning (50%), test (25%) and validation (25%) data sets.
2. Calculation of the normalisation matrix for the learning data set.
3. Application of Principal Component Analysis to the learning data set in order to reduce the dimensionality of the data input space.
4. Learning of the input data set by the neural network.
5. Application of the neural network to the test data set. If the error test is less than the goal error ($1e^{-5}$), then the learning process is stopped. Otherwise, the network is trained again.
6. Estimation of the network performance error.
7. Application of the neural net to the whole data set and result registration.
8. Calculation of the confusion matrices for each experiment.

5.1.1 Multi-Layer Perceptron Classifier

The setup parameters used in this classifier are:

Parameter	Value
Learning algorithm	Levenberg-Marquardt (Backpropagation)
Number of output neurons	3
Goal error	$1e^{-5}$
Epochs	400
Max. fail	5
Mem. reduc.	1
Min. grad.	$1e^{-10}$
μ	$1e^{-3}$
μ_{dec}	0.1
μ_{inc}	10
μ_{max}	$1e^{-5}$

Table 2. Parameters for MLP Classifiers.

5.1.2 Radial Basis Function Classifier

The setup parameters used in this classifier are:

- Number of hidden neurons: The learning algorithm used by this type of neural networks determines the number of neurons that are in the hidden layer through an iterative process (Horward Demuth, 2006). That is, it starts with a reduced number of hidden neurons, which are increased as long as the goal error is not achieved or a maximum number of neurons is reached.
- Spread constant : 0.25 (Determine the zone of influence of each neuron).

$$a = e^{-(||w-p||b)^2} \tag{38}$$

  In which:
  - a: Output of the neuron.
  - w: Weight vector.
  - p: Input vector.
  - b: Spread constant.
- Number of output neurons : 3. One for each cognitive activity.

5.1.3 Probabilistic Neural Network Classifier

The setup parameters used in this classifier are:

- Number of hidden neurons: The learning algorithm used as many hidden neurons as pairs of input vector - target vectors were in the learning data set.
- Spread constant : 0.25 (Determines the zone of influence of each neuron, same expression as eq.38).
- Number of output neurons : 3. One for each cognitive activity.

5.2 Adaptive bi-stage classifier based on RBF-HMM

In this section it is described an adaptive bi-stage classifier. The first stage is based on Radial Basis Function neural networks, which provides sequences of pre-assignations to the second stage, that it is based on three different Hidden Markov Models, each one trained with pre-assignation sequences from the cognitive activities between classifying. The segment of EEG signal is assigned to the HMM with the highest probability of generating the pre-assignation sequence.
The algorithm is tested with real samples of electroencephalografic signal, from five healthy volunteers using the cross-validation method. The results allow to conclude that it is possible to implement this algorithm in an on-line BCI device. The results also shown the huge dependency of the percentage of the correct classification from the user and the setup parameters of the classifier.

5.2.1 Introduction.

In Figure 8 is shown the block diagram of the algorithm for the proposed classifier.
In it can be appreciated how the classification of the considered segment of the EEG signal is obtained after the evaluation of the probability generation of the pre-assignation sequence provided by three Hidden Markov Models.

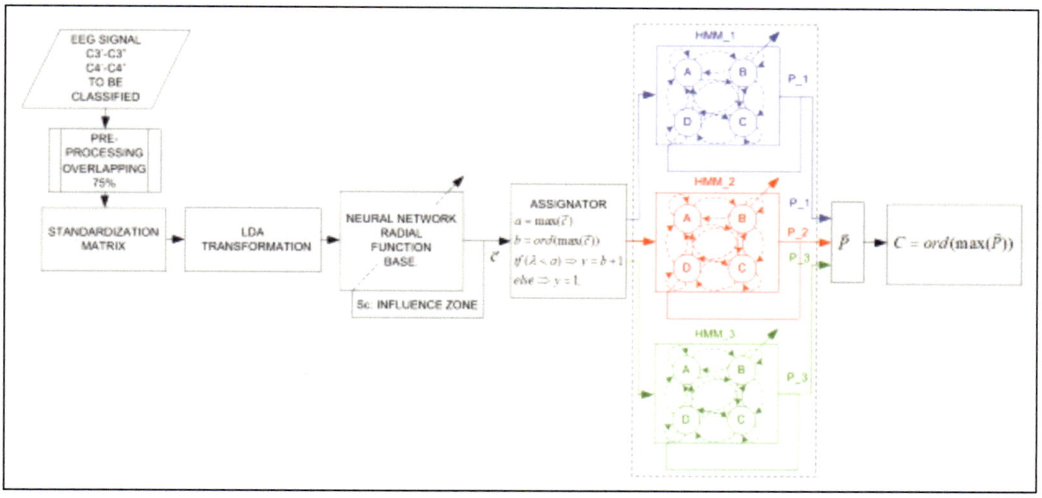

Fig. 8. Block diagram of the classifier.

There are as many Hidden Markov Models as cognitive activities to be considered for the classification, each model is trained with pre-assignation sequences of data of the cognitive activity associated to it.
The pre-assignation sequence of data are provided by a neural network, which inputs are the vectors of features obtained after the preprocessing of the segment of EEG signal, as it is described in the following subsections.

5.2.2 Training of the neural network

The considered neural network is the type of Radial Function Basis. This type of neural network is characterised by the learning of the position of the samples in the training set and by the interpolation capability between them (Bishop, 1995).
In Figure 9 is represented the architecture of this type of neural network.

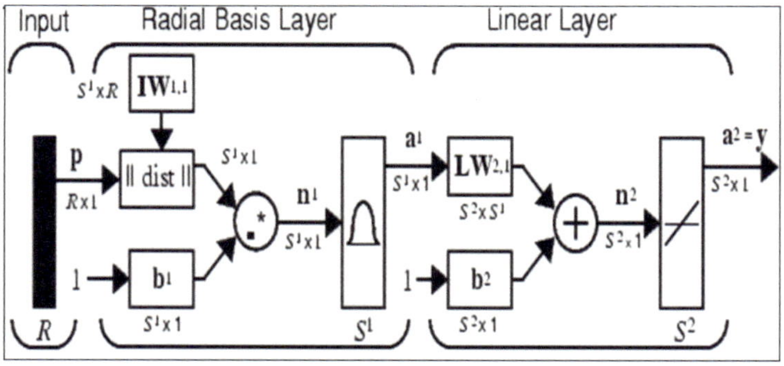

Fig. 9. Architecture of the RBF neural network.

From previous studies it has been concluded that this type of neural network behaves better than other types of neural networks, as for example Multi-Layer Perceptrons or Probabilistic Neural Networks (Martinez, J.L.; Barrientos, A., 2008).
The activation function is:

$$radbas(x) = e^{-x^2}; \quad x = (\vec{w} - \vec{p}) * S_c \tag{39}$$

In where $\vec{w}$ and S_c are respectively the weights and influence zone constant of each neuron, and $\vec{p}$ is the position of the considered sample.
During the learning phase the neurons of the hidden layer learn the position of the samples of the learning set, $\vec{w}$; during the test phase when a new sample $\vec{p}$ is presented, it is computed the distance between the sample and the learned positions, the nearest neurons to the sample will proportionate higher activation values than the rest of the neurons.
For the learning process are considered vectors of features from the EEG signal, acquired when the user was performing one of the different cognitive activities considered for the classification. The learning set is composed by the 75% of all the sample set, and the other 25% is considered for validation. After the determination of the learning and validation sets, the input vectors to the neural network are normalised, and with LDA technique is reduced their dimensionality projecting the original input vectors in the direction of the highest discrimination capability (Martinez, J.L.; Barrientos, A., 2007).
In order to minimise the over-learning effect, the RBF learning process allows a dynamic growth of the number of neurons in the hidden layer. In the output layer are considered as many linear neurons as cognitive activities between discriminate. Finally in the assignation block on Figures 8, it is weighted the output vector of the neural network and it assigns the input vector to the activity with highest output value provided it is higher than a threshold λ, on the contrary if the value is lower than λ, the input vector is labelled as unclassified.
On operation, once the neuronal network has been trained, when a new vector is presented, the cognitive activity with samples nearer to it will provide a higher activation level, and the corresponding output will have a higher value than the others cognitive activities.

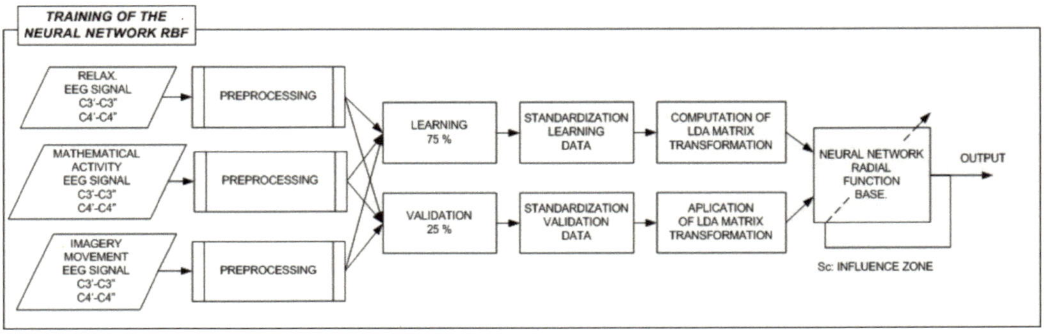

Fig. 10. Training of the RBF neural network.

5.2.3 Description of Hidden Markov Models

A Hidden Markov Model is a double stochastic statistical model, it consists of a Markov process with unknown and non-observable parameters, and a observed model which parameters depend stochastically from the hidden states. A stochastic process is called a Markovian process if the future does not depend from the past, only from the known present; considering the stochastic variable $q(t-1)$ the transition probability in the instant t is defined as $P(q_t = \sigma_t | q_{t-1} = \sigma_{t-1})$. A Markov chain is formally defined with the pair (Q, A), where $Q = \{1, 2, ..., N\}$ are the possible estates of the chain and $A = [a_{ij}]$ is the transition matrix of the model, with the constrains:

$$0 \leq a_{ij} \leq 1; \qquad 1 \leq i,j \leq N \tag{40}$$

$$\sum_{j=1}^{N} a_{ij} = 1; \qquad 1 \leq i \leq N \tag{41}$$

The transition and emission probabilities depends from the actual estate and no from the former estates.

$$\begin{aligned} P(q_t = j | q_{t-1} = i, q_{t-2} = k, ...) &= \\ = P(q_t = j | q_{t-1} = i) &= a_{ij}(t) \end{aligned} \tag{42}$$

Formally a discrete HMM of first grade is defined by the 5-tuple: $\lambda = \{Z, Q, A, B, \pi\}$, in where:

- $Z = \{V_1, V_2, ..., V_M\}$ is the alphabet or discrete set of M symbols.
- $Q = \{1, 2, ..., N\}$ is the set of N finite estates.
- $A = [a_{ij}]$ is the transition matrix of the model.
- $B = (b_j(Q_t))_{NxM}$ is the matrix of emission symbols, also known as observation matrix.
- $\pi = (\pi_1, \pi_2, ..., \pi_N)$ is the prior probability vector of the initial estate.

The parameters of a HMM are $\lambda = \{A, B, \pi\}$. There are three types of canonic problems associated to HMM (Rabiner, 1989)(Rabiner & Juang, 1986):

1. Given the parameters of the model, obtain the probability of a particular output sequence. This problem is solved through a forward-backwards algorithm.
2. Given the parameters of the model, find the most probable sequence of hidden estates, that could generate the given output sequence. This problem is solved through the use of Viterbi algorithm.
3. Given an output sequence, find the parameters of the HMM. This problem is solved through the use of Baum-Welch algorithm.

The HMM have been applied specially in speech recognition an generally in the recognition of temporal sequences, hand written, gestures, and bioinformatics (Rabiner & Juang, 1986).

5.2.4 Training of the Hidden Markov Models

The HMM's are trained with sequences of pre-assignations coming from the EEG samples, as it is shown in the Figure 11.

For each cognitive activity a particular HMM, with the following characteristics, is trained:

- Number of hidden estates: 4.
- Number of different observable objects: 4

In the training phase, chains of nine pre-assignations were used. In a previous experiment with synthetic samples, it was concluded that for the proposed architecture of Hidden Markov Models the highest percentage of correct classifications were obtained with chains of nine elements.

After the training or solution of the third canonic problem, the probability matrices of state transitions and observation matrices are determined. The Viterbi algorithm is used in order to determine the probability that a model generates the proposed sequence.

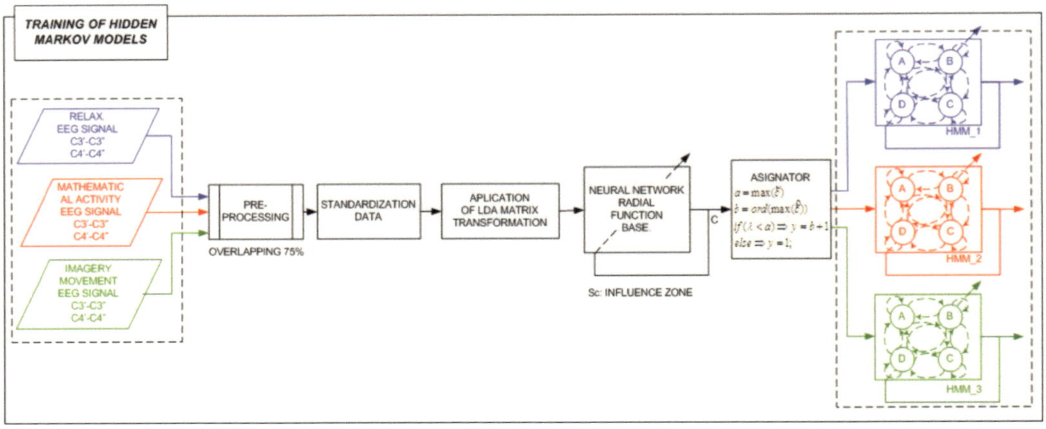

Fig. 11. Training of the HMM.

5.3 Classifier based on Support Vector Machines

Under the denomination of Support Vector Machines are known a set of supervised learning methods that belong to the generalised linear classifiers with applicability into classification and regression problems.

It structure is based on a net of static kernels operating over feature vectors which have been transformed to a space with higher dimension than the original feature space, see Figure 12.

The main property of the SVMs is its good generalisation capability founded on the determination of a hiperplane with maximum separation distance between the transformed vector of each class. This separation distance is the one between to hiperplanes parallel to the optimum separation hiperplane containing at least one transformed vector called support vector. It is assumed that as bigger is this distance, bigger is the generalisation capability.

The operations performed by a SVM classifier are:

- Transformation of the sample data or input feature vectors to a higher dimension space through the application of the kernel function ϕ. The objective is to formulate the classification problem using the kernel function.
- Obtaining of the optimum hiperplane which maximises the distance between the considered classes. If the input vectors are lineally separable, the optimum hiperplane besides the maximisation of the separability, minimises the penalty function that considers the incorrect classifications.

6. Description of experimental procedures and results

6.1 Esperimental procedures

6.1.1 LDA procedure

The Figure 13 represents the activity diagram associated to the experimental procedure used with the Linear Discriminant Analysis technique.

The experimental procedure is performed with the feature vectors obtained after processing the samples of electroencephalogram activity with each type of preprocessing window.

In order to assess the discriminant power of each type of preprocessing window a bilateral contrast test is performed with the transformed populations of feature vectors.

The results are graphically represented in subsection 6.2.2.

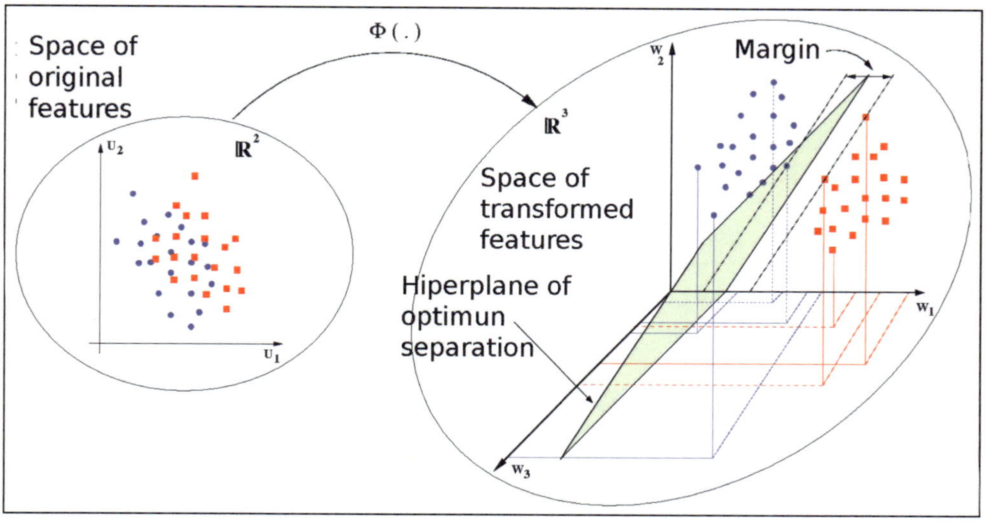

Fig. 12. Operacional description of Support Vector Machines.

6.1.2 Procedure for classifiers based on Artificial Neural Networks

The Figure 14 represents the activity diagram associated to the experimental procedure used with the Artificial Neural Networks classifiers.

- The first stage loads the registers sampled when the user performed the different mental tasks and associates them to each proposed cognitive activity. After this the data sets are normalised and reduced their dimension through LDA.
- In the second stage the learning data sets are defined; 50% of the samples are used for the learning data set, 25% for the validation data set, and the other 25% for the testing data set.
- In the third stage the classifiers are created, trained, validated and tested using respectively the previous data sets.
- In the fourth and last stage the confusion matrices are obtained and saved.

The results are graphically represented in subsection 6.2.3.

6.1.3 Procedure for RBF-HMM bi-stage classifier

The Figure 15 represents the activity diagram for the experimental procedure used with the RBF-HMM classifier. It is composed by four different blocks:

- The first block generates the different data sets for learning and testing, considering the three different cognitive tasks. The cross validation procedure is used for the results, ten different repetitions of cross validation are considered, in each repetition a different data set session is reserved for the validation, employing the rest data sets for learning and testing.
- In the second block the pre-classifier based on RBF is trained.
- In the third block three different Hidden Markov Models are trained, one for each cognitive activity, considering pre-assignation sequences of nine elements.
- Finally in the fourth block the validation procedure is performed and the results saved.

The results are graphically represented in subsection 6.2.4.

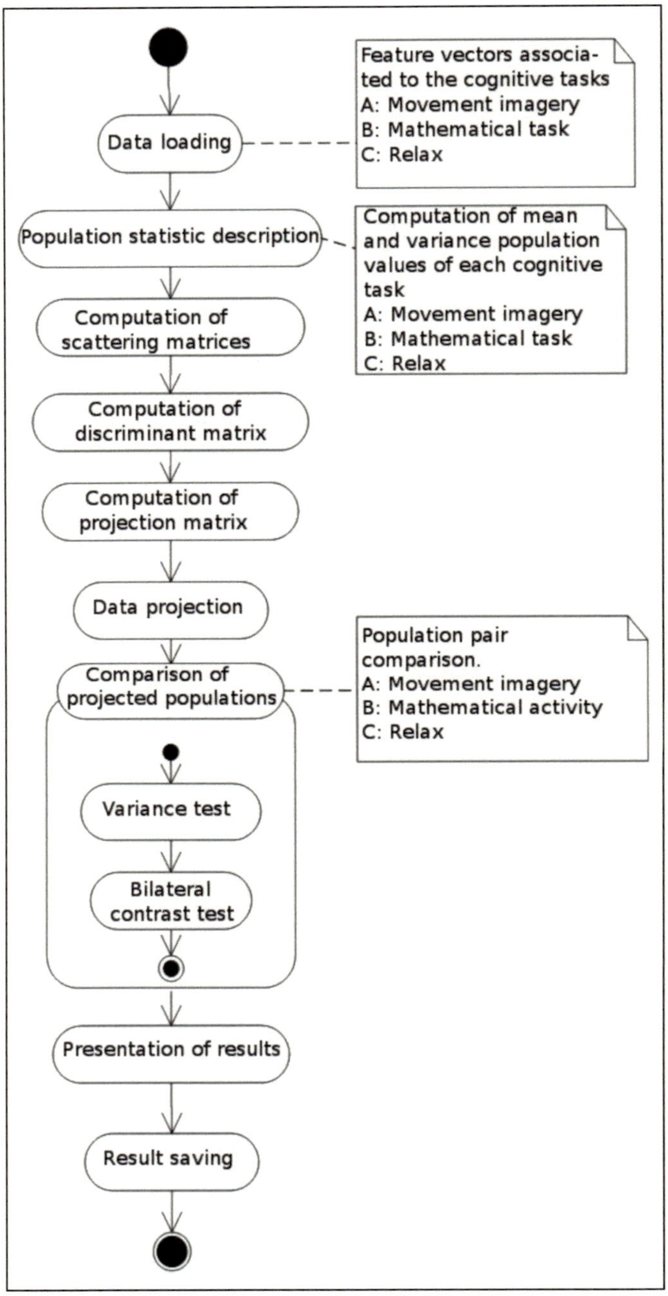

Fig. 13. Experimental procedure for LDA.

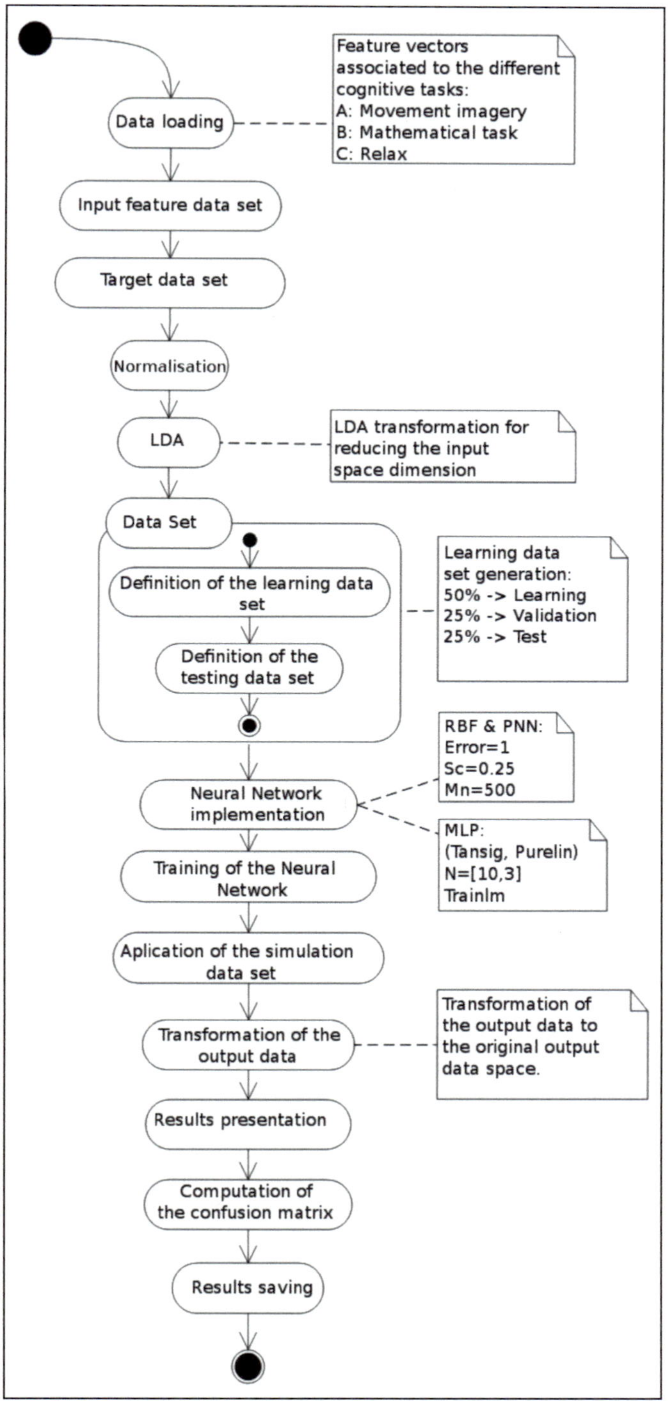

Fig. 14. Experimental procedure for ANN classifiers.

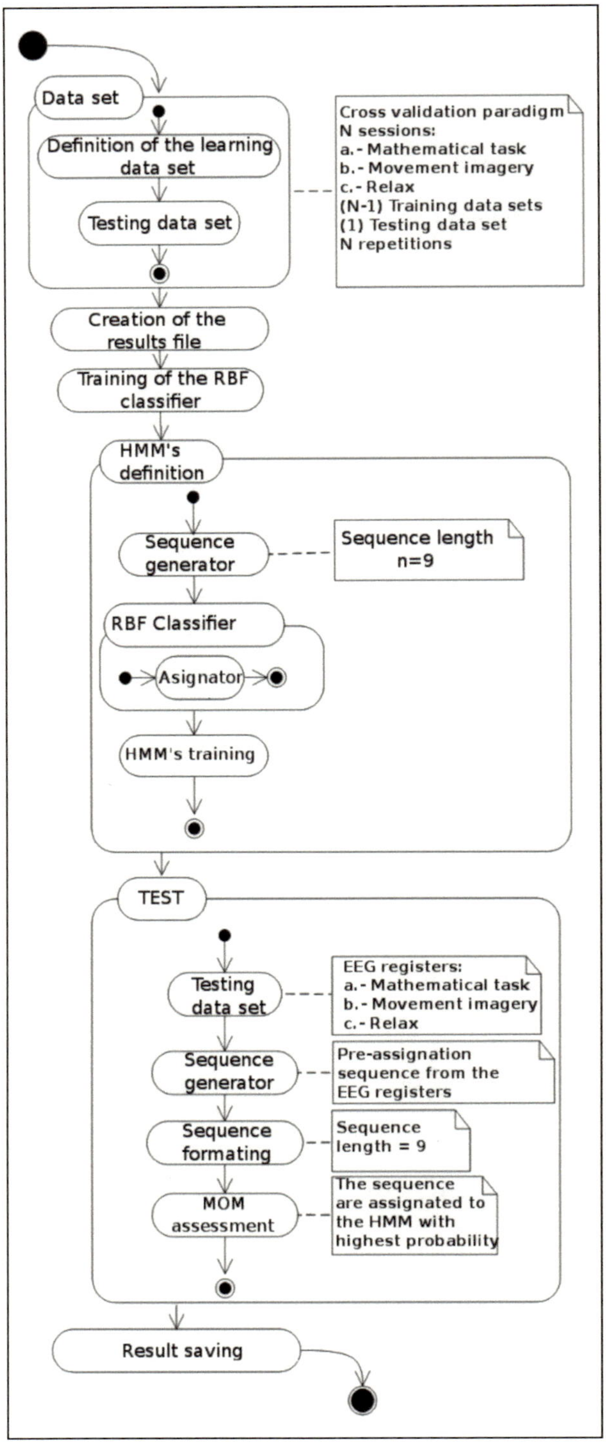

Fig. 15. Experimental procedure for RBF-HMM classifier.

6.1.4 SVM procedure

The Figure 16 represents the experimental procedure used with the SVM classifiers. In the first stage the data sets of each cognitive activity are loaded. In the second stage the SVM classifiers are created with the different kernel parameters, the training and testing data sets are defined, and the classifiers are trained considering three subclassifiers under the one against one classification paradigm.
Finally in the last stage a classification test is performed and the results saved. The results are graphically represented in subsection 6.2.5.

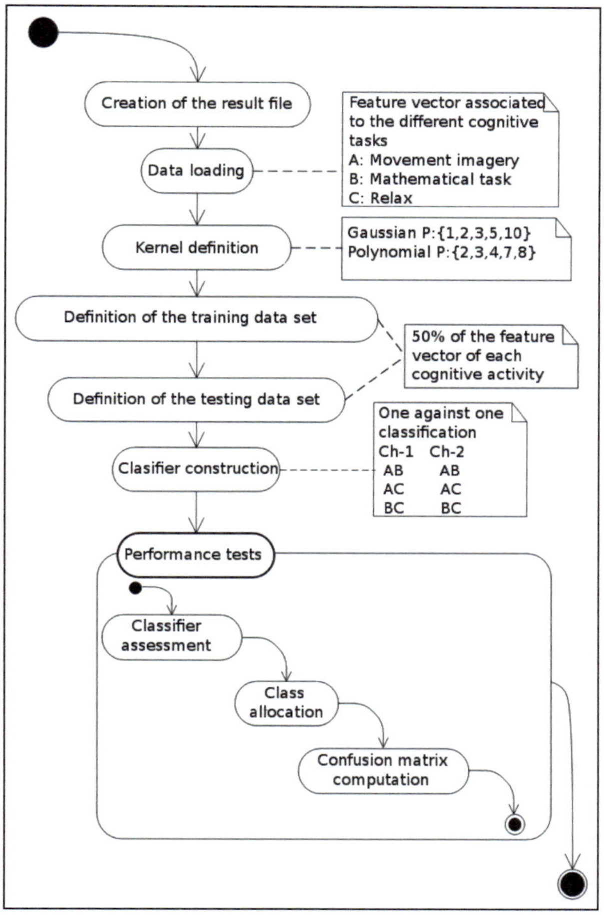

Fig. 16. Experimental procedure for SVM classifiers.

6.2 Results

6.2.1 Results of the statistical analysis procedure

The following figures summarise the results of the former tests.
The contrasts between mental activities are shown on the horizontal axis. The Figure 17 shows the results of the contrast tests between the cognitive tasks for channel one: $C3' - C3''$, meanwhile the Figure 18 shows the results for channel two: $C4' - C4''$.

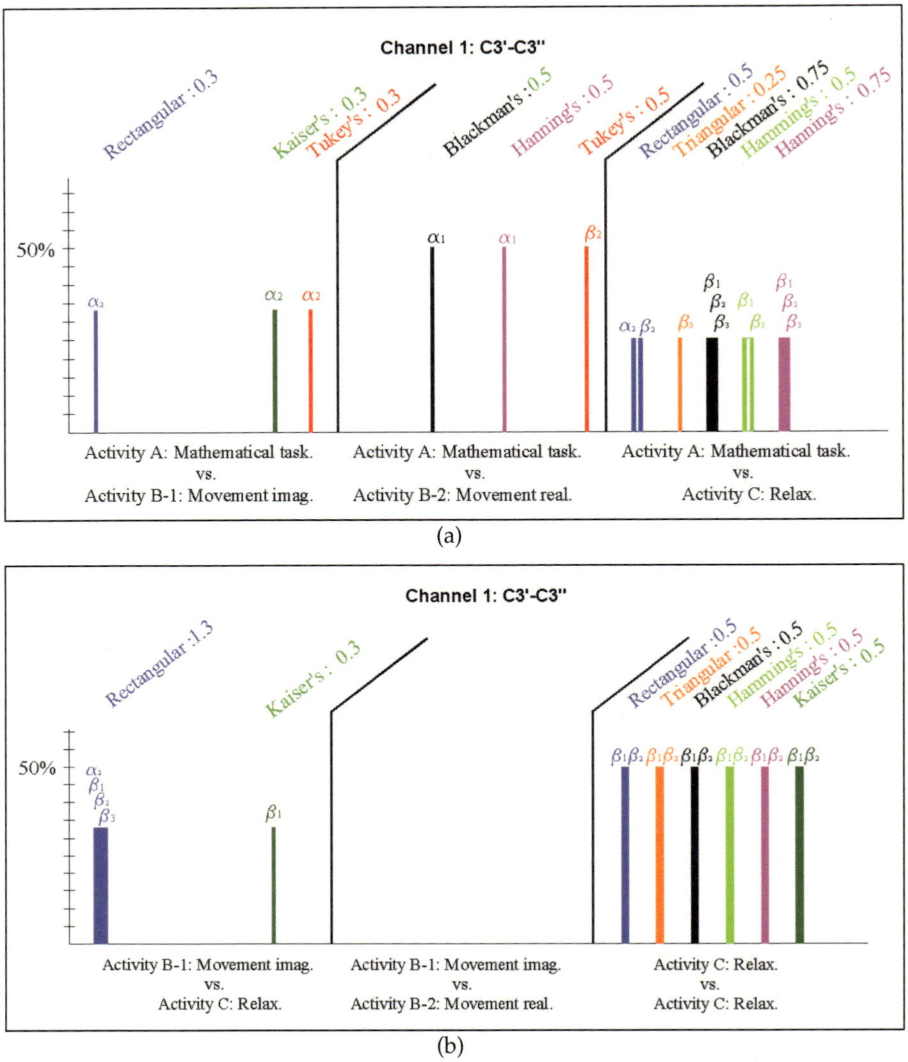

Fig. 17. Results channel 1.

All the seven types of windows have been applied to each comparison.[2] In the top of each figure appears both the type of window and a number. This number indicates the average of significant features obtained with this window, it is the total of the features that shown statistical evidence of difference, $p < 0.05$, divided by the number of times the experiment has been replicated.
Finally in the bars are the significant features for each kind of window[3], in the vertical axis is the percentage of times that this feature has been significant.
Making a comparison between **mathematical activity** and **movement imagination** the result is, that among all windows, the Tukey's and Kaiser's windows are the ones with more

[2] See sections 2.5.3 and 3.
[3] See section 2.5.5.

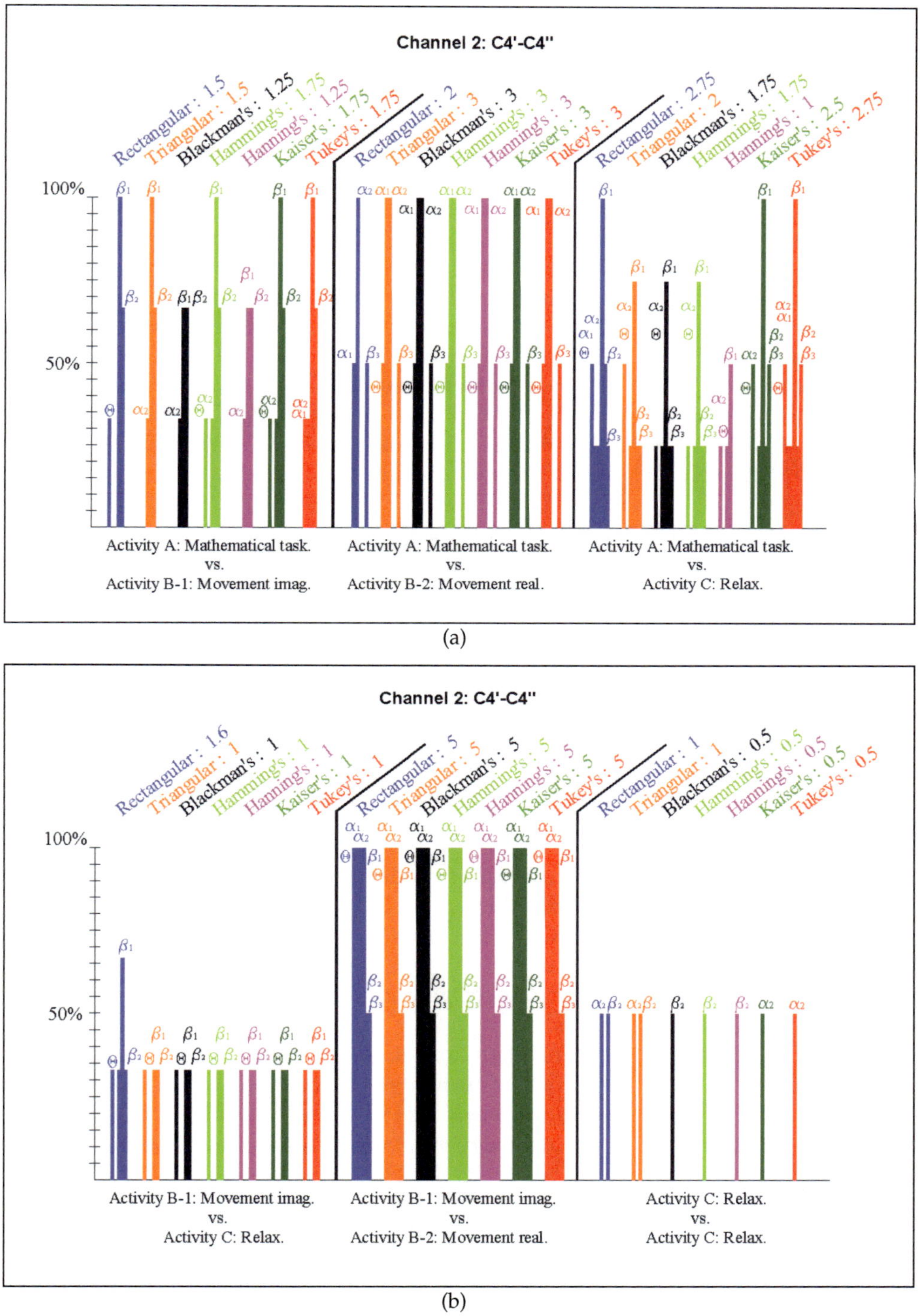

Fig. 18. Results channel 1.

significant features. Among features, the most significant are β_1 and β_2 for all kind of windows.
In the comparison between **mathematical activity** and **movement realization** the result is that the most significant windows are Hanning's, Tukey's and Blackman's, and the most significant features are α_1 and α_2.
Taking **mathematical activity** versus **relax**, the result is that the rectangular and Tukey's windows are the most significant. The component of the feature vector with more discriminating power is β_1 followed by β_2 and β_3.
Comparing **movement imagination** and **relax**,the obtained result is that the rectangular window is the most significant. The features with more significant power are θ β_1 y β_2.
Movement imagination versus **movement realization** are the two mental activities with more discriminating power. The most important features are $\theta, \alpha_1, \alpha_2$, and β_1. All types of windows obtain a very good result.
Making the comparison between **relax** activities appears significant difference between populations in the features α_2 and β_2 of the channel 2, and β_1 β_2 of channel 1. It is a case of false positive identification due to the noise in the signal, for this reason the window with better behaviour is the Tukey's one, it only detect a false positive in α_2.

6.2.2 Results of reduction of the feature space dimensionality

The LDA technique produces only two eigen-values bigger than $1 * 10^{-4}$ for all the experiments, this originates that only two eigen-vectors are considered in the transformation matrix, W, hence the population of the six dimension feature vectors are projected in a 2D space: X_1, X_2. Matrices in eqs. 43 and 44 show typical experimental values for λ and W.

$$\lambda = \begin{pmatrix} 0.109 & 0 \\ 0 & 0.020 \end{pmatrix} \tag{43}$$

$$W = \begin{pmatrix} \theta & \alpha_1 & \alpha_2 & \beta_1 & \beta_2 & \beta_3 \\ -0.06 & 0.22 & 0.05 & -0.05 & 0.06 & -0.9 \\ -0.37 & 0.01 & -0.002 & -0.56 & 0.73 & 0.16 \end{pmatrix}^T \tag{44}$$

In figures 19 and 20 are presented the results of the bilateral contrast test for the transformed coordinate X_1 and X_2 respectively, considering the Off-line and On-line experiments. The figures show for each channel (C3'-C3" and C4'-C4"), and for each type of preprocessing window, the results p of the associated probability of the bilateral contrast tests between the mental tasks. In order to represent the dispersion of the results the mode value and bars from 15th to 85th percentile have been used.
The comparisons between the discrimination capabilities of On-line and Off-line experiments are shown in the figures 19 and 20. From the bilateral contrast test carried out with a significant level of $\alpha = 2.5\%$, $\alpha = 1 - p$, represented in Figure 19 for X_1, it is obtained that in almost all cases the null hypothesis H_o, which maintains the equality in the populations of the features associated to the mental tasks, shall be rejected for both types of experiments; it is observed that p values obtained in the comparison of mathematical task versus motor imagery, p values are lower for the On-line case in both channels and with all types of preprocessing windows than the ones p values obtained for the Off-line case; the dispersion of the results is similar in both experiments. It is also shown that for X_1, channel C4'-C4" performs better than C3'-C3". The best results are obtained for X_1 with Tukey's and Kaiser's windows. The same analysis for X_2, Figure 20, shows that the difference rarely appears for Off-line experiments, and in any case for in the On-line cases, $p < 0.975$. The same analysis for X_2, figures 10 to 15, shows that

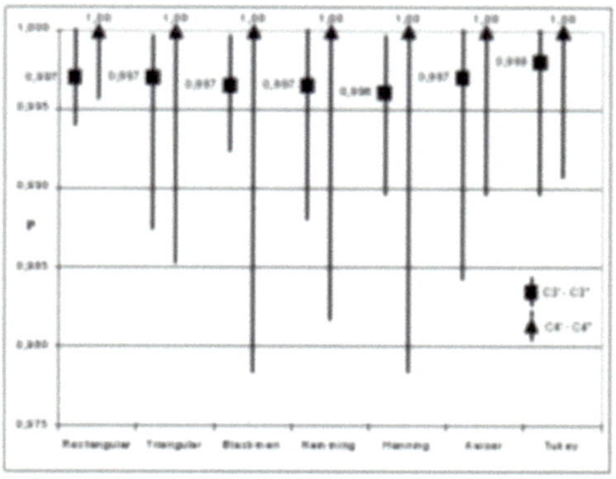

(a) Off-line. Math task vs. Motor imagery. X1.

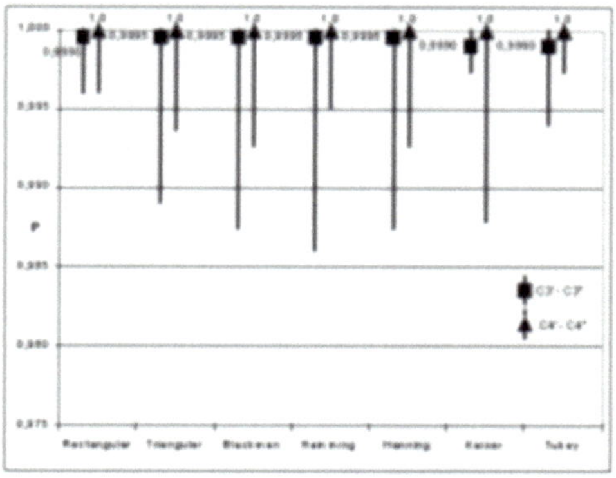

(b) Off-line. Motor imagery vs. Relax. X1.

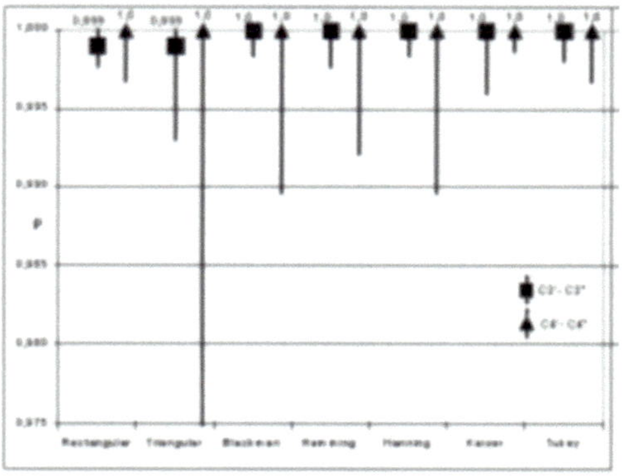

(c) Off-line. Motor imagery vs. Relax. X1.

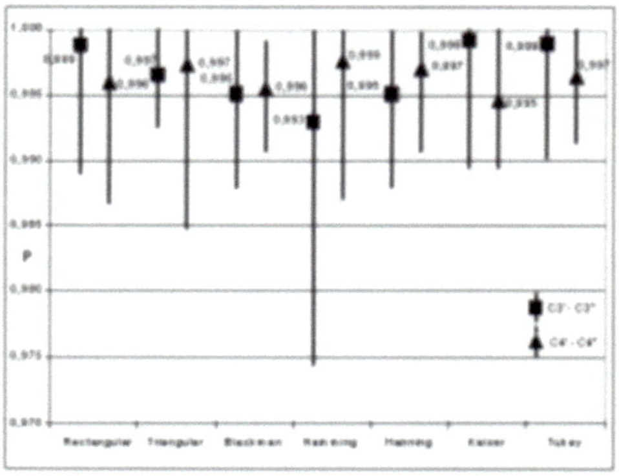

(d) On-line. Math task vs. Motor imagery. X1.

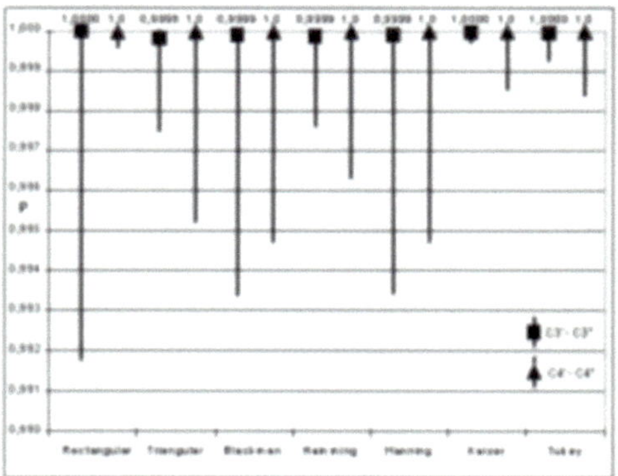

(e) On-line. Math task vs. Relax. X1.

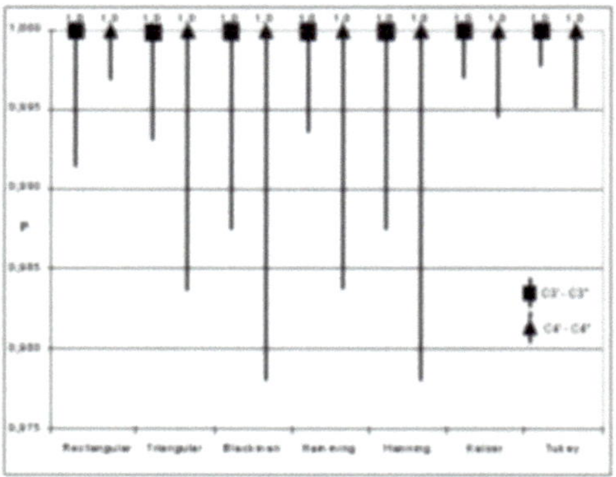

(f) On-line. Math task vs. Relax. X1.

Fig. 19. Off-line. Math task vs. Motor imagery. Coordinate X1.

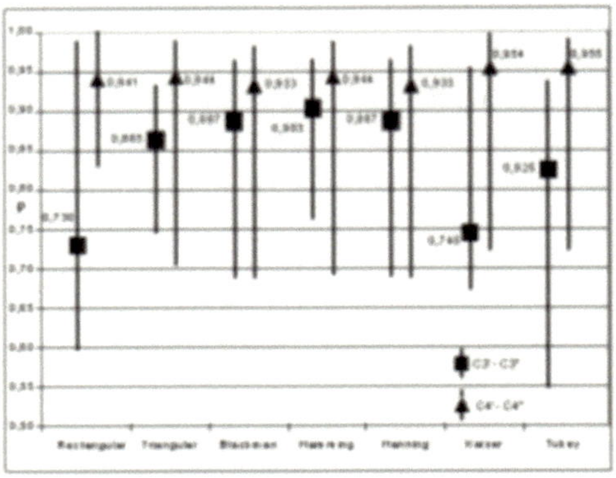

(a) Off-line. Math task vs. Motor imagery. X2.

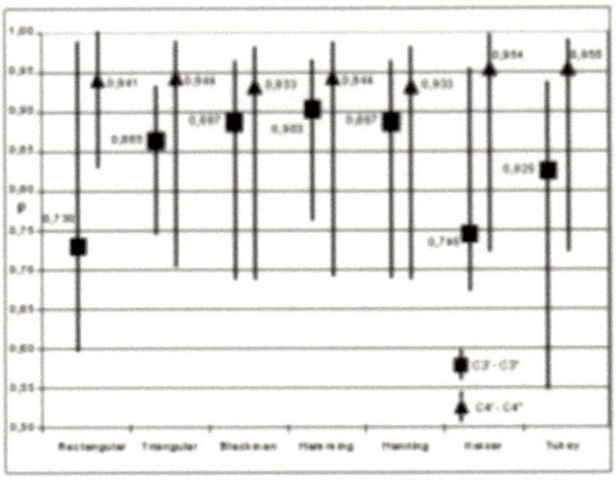

(b) Off-line. Math task vs. Relax. X2.

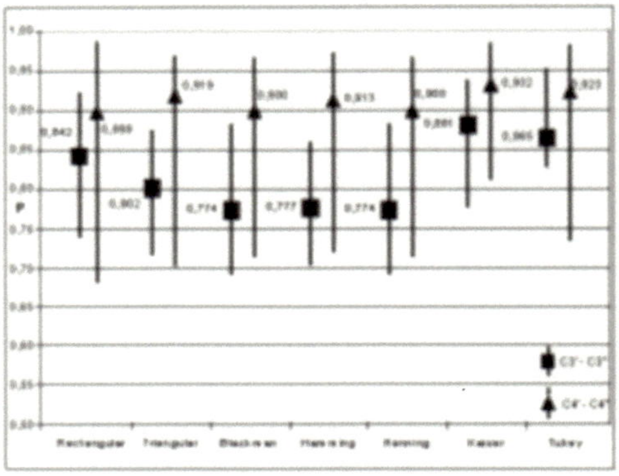

(c) Off-line. Motor imagery vs. Relax. X2

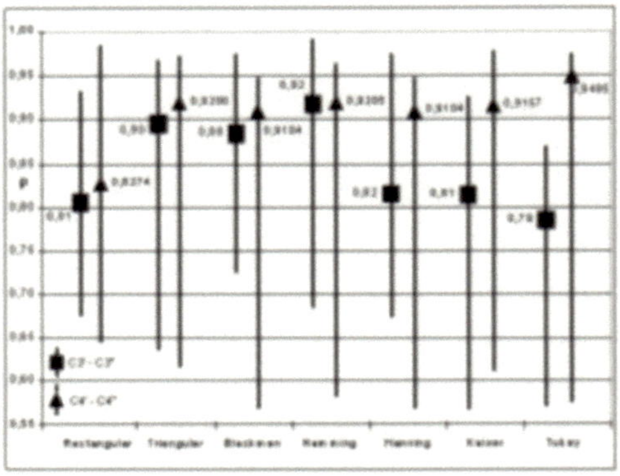

(d) On-line. Math task vs. Motor imagery. X2.

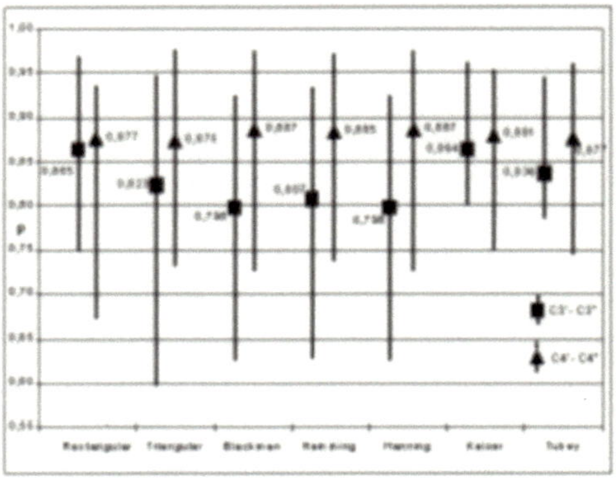

(e) On-line. Math task vs. Relax. X2.

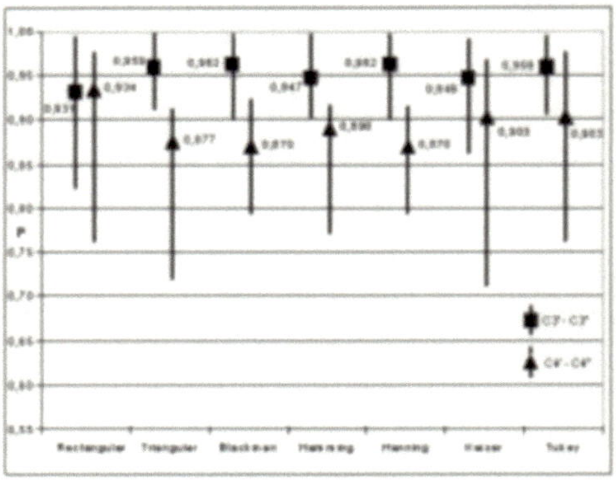

(f) On-line. Motor imagery vs. Relax. X2.

Fig. 20. Off-line. Math task vs. Motor imagery. Coordinate X2.

the difference rarely appears for Off-line experiments, and in any case for in the On-line cases, $p < 0.975$.
On average, for both types of experiments, all preprocessing windows show statistical difference between mental tasks; the best results, with higher quantities for the mode values and lower dispersion, are obtained for X_1 with Tukey's and Kaiser's preprocessing windows. From the numerical results is observed that as higher the eigen-value magnitude, case of X_1, the higher the value of one component of the eigen-vector, normally in β frequency band, by the contrary, as lower the eigen-value more the contribution of the rest of eigen-vector components.
The highest contrast power is obtained in the comparison of *Motor imagery* vs. *Relax*, it is followed by *Mathematical task* vs. *Relax*, and the lowest is for *Mathematical task* vs. *Motor imagery*.

6.2.3 Results of Neural Networks Classifiers for BCI devices

The figures 21 to 23 summarize on vertical axis the percentage of correct classifications that were obtained from the confusion matrices and applied to each one of the three classifiers. It should be noted that the scale was broken in order to convey the scattered results. On the horizontal axis are displayed the different types of preprocessing windows that were considered.
For each preprocessing window, there appears a bar with the results of each classifier: maximum, minimum and median percentage values.
For each volunteer, the first two figures show the correct classifications obtained from each dedicated neural network: C3 $\Rightarrow$ Channel 1, and C4 $\Rightarrow$ Channel 2. The third figure shows the correct classifications obtained when the classifier was based on only one neural net. It gathers the feature vectors of both electroencephalographic channels at the same time.
The following considerations can be extracted from an analysis of the results:

- The data obtained from the experiments suggests that classifiers that were based on Probabilistic Neural Networks or Radial Basis Functions perform better than classifiers that were based on MLP (i.e., approximately 84% versus 33% of correct classifications). This indicates that the interpolation capability of the RBF outweighs the extrapolation capability of the MLP. A similar percentage of approximately 88% of correct classifications was obtained by N.Nicolau using classifiers based on Support Vector Machines with Gaussian kernels (Georgiou; & M.Polycarpou, 2008). A.Ferreira reported similar results in the best case of experiments for a robotic wheelchair using SVM as classifier (Andre Ferreira, Teodiano Freire, Mario Sarcinelli, Jose Luis Martin Sanchez, et al., 2009).
- Result stability. For all tests, the procedure was replicated three times, wherein both PNN and RBF classifiers produced the same confusion matrices. Thus, instead of the MLP classifiers, different matrices were produced for each replica. This indicates that with the proposed training data sets, the MLP classifiers are unable to differentiate between the different tasks. (In the learning phase the RBF nets allocate the center of each radial basis function, meanwhile the MLP nets get the weights associated to the inputs of each neuron, if there is not a clear difference in the training sets of the input data populations, the MLP classifiers are unable to stablish the difference between them (Bishop, 1995), (Ripley, 1996)). It also explains the rate of correct classifications obtained with PNN, RBF and MLP neural networks.
- A comparison of PNN and RBF classifiers shows that, in some cases, the PNN produced better classification rates but also a higher variability. It should be noticed that although

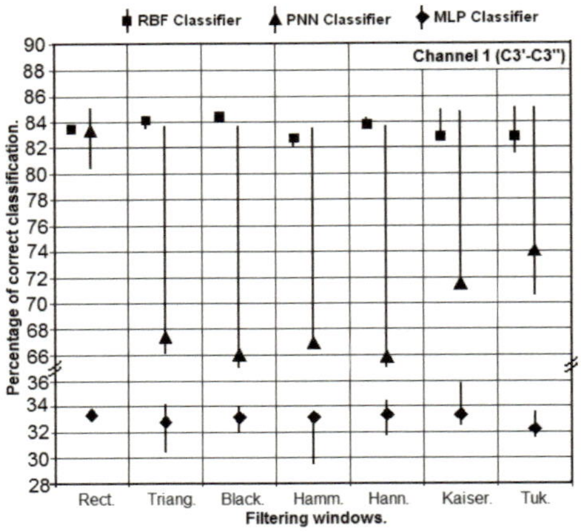

(a) Volunteer A. Correct classification C 1.

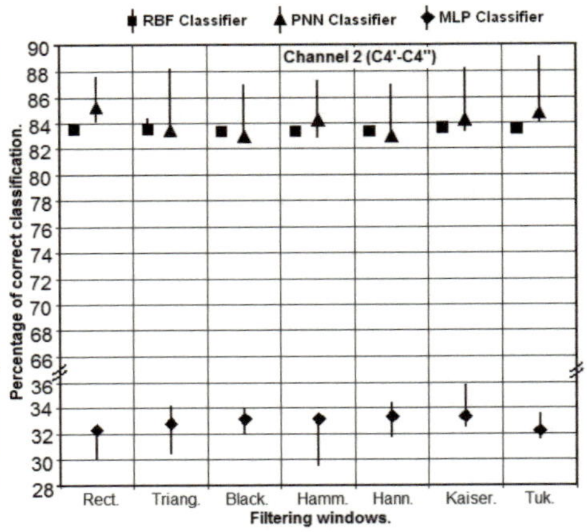

(b) Volunteer A. Correct classification C 2.

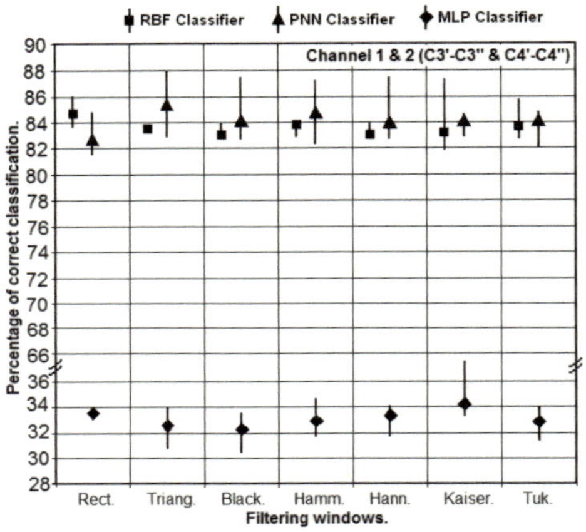

(c) Volunteer A. Correct classification C 1 & 2.

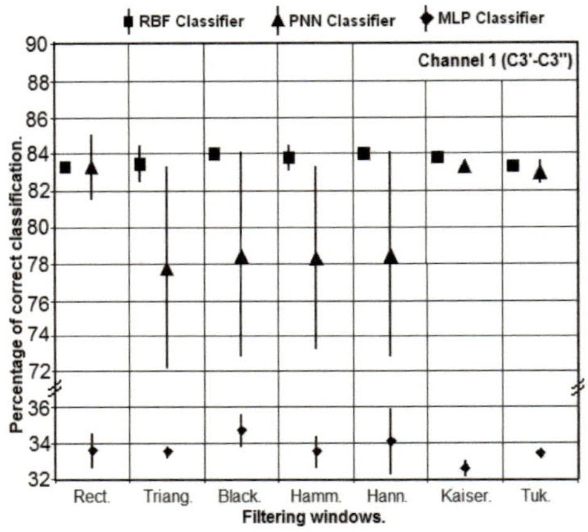

(d) Volunteer B. Correct classification C 1.

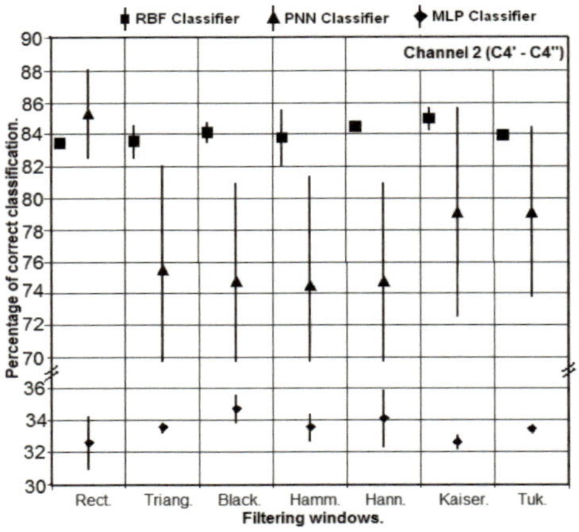

(e) Volunteer B. Correct classification C 2.

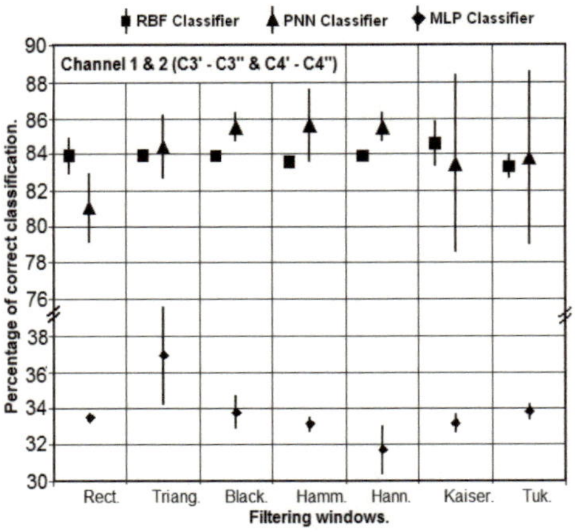

(f) Volunteer B. Correct classification C 1 & 2.

Fig. 21

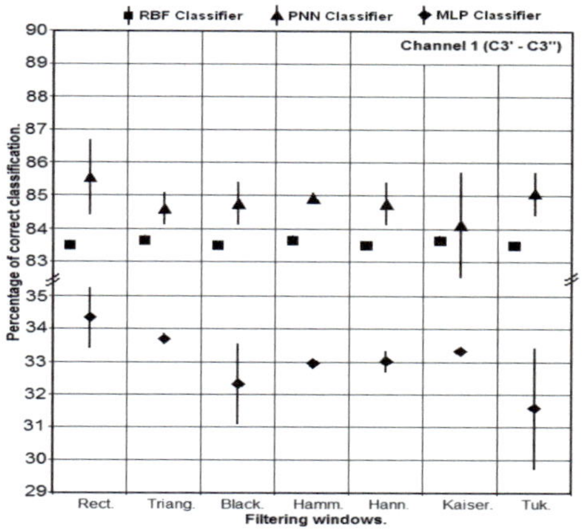

(a) Volunteer C. Correct classification C 1.

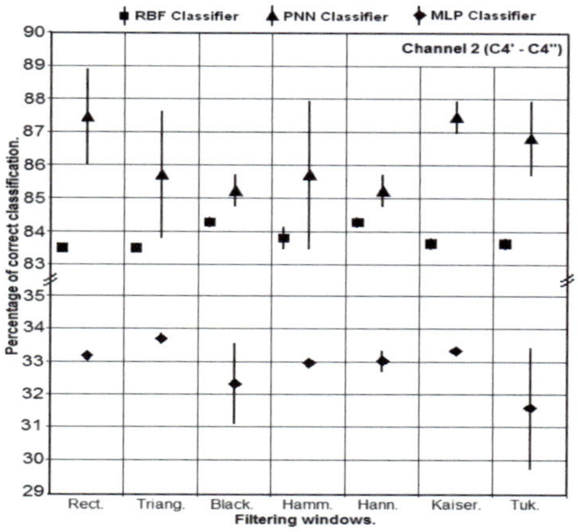

(b) Volunteer C. Correct classification C 2.

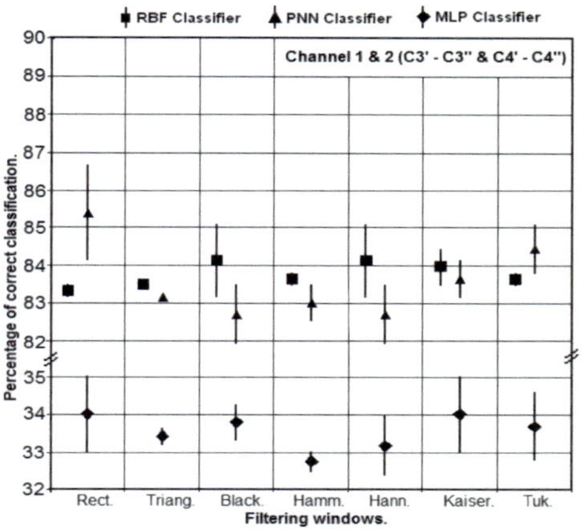

(c) Volunteer C. Correct classification C 1&2.

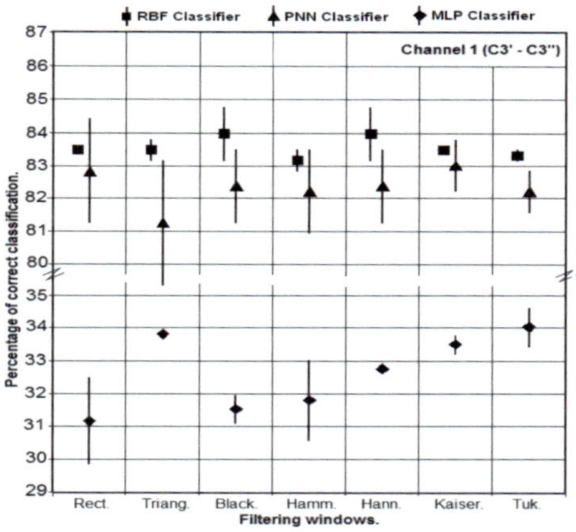

(d) Volunteer D. Correct classification C 1.

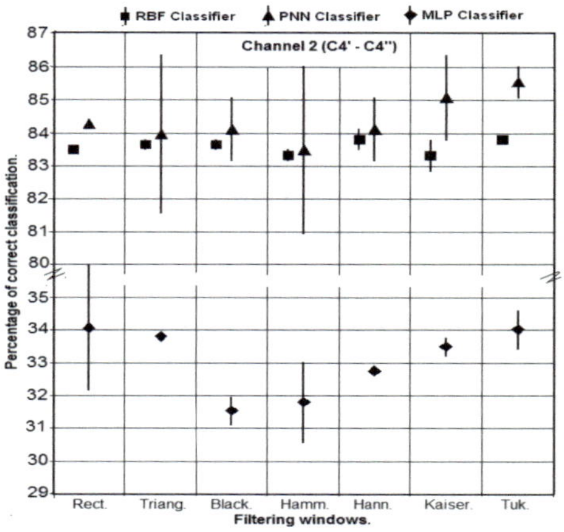

(e) Volunteer D. Correct classification C 2.

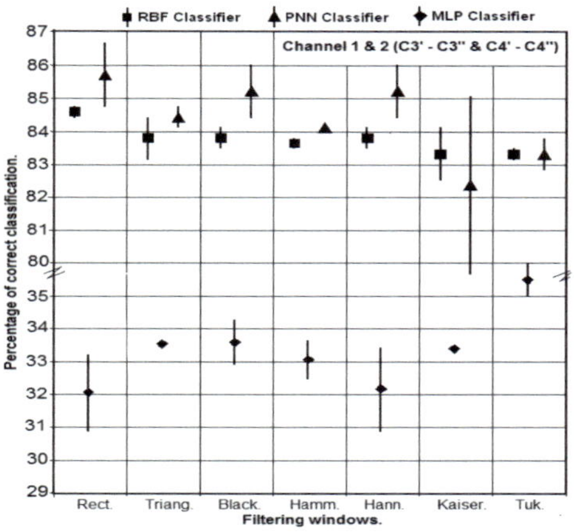

(f) Volunteer D. Correct classification C 1&2.

Fig. 22

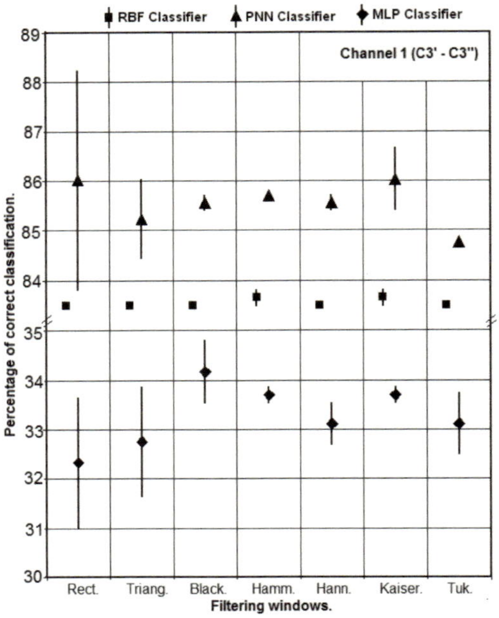

(a) Volunteer E. Correct classification C 1.

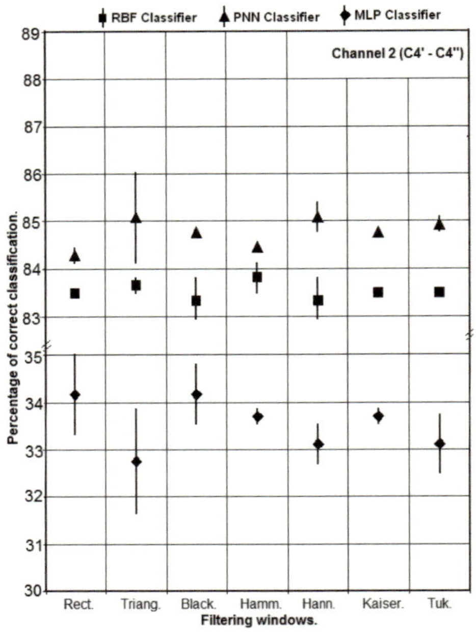

(b) Volunteer E. Correct classification C 2.

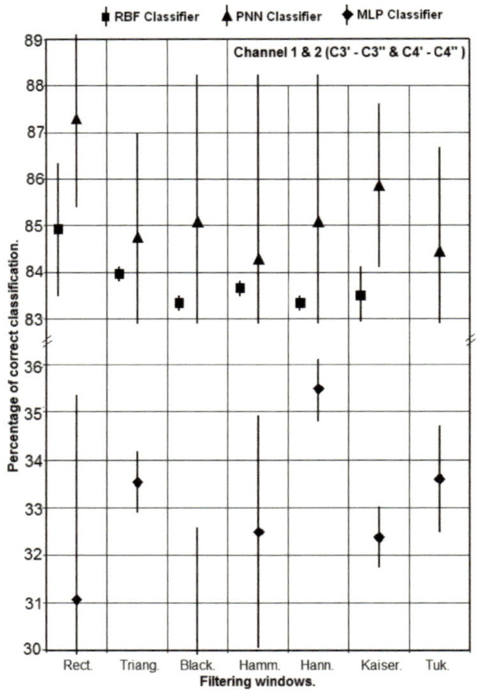

(c) Volunteer E. Correct classification C 1 & 2.

Fig. 23

RBF's and PNN's are both based on radial basis functions, in the case of PNN's exist as much functions as samples in the training set, whereas in the case of RBF's this quantity is determined through an iterative process and it is usually lower (Horward Demuth, 2006). This may cause the overlearning of the training data set and a lower generalization capability for PNN's which explains its higher variability (Bishop, 1995).

- Classifiers based on only one neural network, and that simultaneously consider features obtained from both electroencephalographic channels, do not always perform better than classifiers based on two neural networks, one for each channel.
- A consideration of different types of preprocessing windows demonstrates that the results with lowest variability values are achieved with Kaiser's, Tukey's, and rectangular windows. This corroborates the conclusions of previous studies concerning the influence of preprocessing windows in mental tasks discrimination capability (Martinez, J.L.; Barrientos, A., 2006),(Martinez, J.L.; Barrientos, A., 2007). On average, however, similar classification rates are obtained for all. This indicates that although the type of preprocessing window is important, the behaviour of the classifier is even more relevant.

6.2.4 Results of adaptative bi-stage classifier based on RBF-HMM

In order to test the behavior of the proposed algorithm, determine the influence of the threshold assignation parameter (λ), and the influence zone of the neuron (S_c), the EEG samples of the session tests from the volunteers were used as follows.

6.2.4.1 Evaluation of the learning capability.

With a subset of 75% of the all EEG samples, the algorithm was trained with different λ and S_c values[4]:

$\lambda =$	0.55	0.65	0.8

$S_c =$	0.5	0.95

After the learning, the same samples were processed with the trained algorithm, and a comparison between the results obtained with the algorithm and the ones employed for the learning was done, in all cases a 100% of correct classification has been obtained.

6.2.4.2 Evaluation of the generalization capability.

After the good results obtained from the learning phase, a cross-validation methodology is used to estimate the generalization capability. From the whole ten sessions, nine are used for learning and one is used for validation, the process is repeated ten times changing each time the session used for validation.
In the following tables are shown the results obtained for each volunteer, considering the λ and S_c parameters.
For each combination, the process is replicated three times. In the upper row it is shown the number of correct classifications. In the lower row it is shown the percentage of improvement against a naive classifier.
From the results of the proposed classification algorithm, it is observed that:

- The learning capability is better that the one achieved only with the RBF neural network (Martinez, J.L.; Barrientos, A., 2008).

[4] These values have been fixed after a seek in wide with the samples of the first volunteer.

$S_c = 0.5$ $\lambda = 0.65$			$S_c = 0.95$ $\lambda = 0.55$			$S_c = 0.5$ $\lambda = 0.55$			$S_c = 0.95$ $\lambda = 0.80$		
94	103	103	94	81	87	93	92	87	86	97	81
+4	+14	+14	+4	-10	-3	+3	+2	-3	-4	+8	-10

Table 3. Volunteer: Al01.

$S_c = 0.5$ $\lambda = 0.65$			$S_c = 0.95$ $\lambda = 0.55$			$S_c = 0.5$ $\lambda = 0.55$			$S_c = 0.95$ $\lambda = 0.80$		
103	97	92	118	109	118	97	87	86	117	106	110
+14	+8	+2	+31	+21	+31	+8	-3	-4	+30	+18	+22

Table 4. Volunteer: Ro01.

$S_c = 0.5$ $\lambda = 0.65$			$S_c = 0.95$ $\lambda = 0.55$			$S_c = 0.5$ $\lambda = 0.55$			$S_c = 0.95$ $\lambda = 0.80$		
106	97	110	87	90	107	99	106	107	98	108	99
+18	+8	+22	-3	0	+19	+10	+18	+19	+9	+20	+10

Table 5. Volunteer: Ja01.

$S_c = 0.5$ $\lambda = 0.65$			$S_c = 0.95$ $\lambda = 0.55$			$S_c = 0.5$ $\lambda = 0.55$			$S_c = 0.95$ $\lambda = 0.80$		
109	102	104	83	92	92	106	91	110	86	87	92
+21	+13	+15	-8	+2	+2	+18	+1	+22	-4	-3	+2

Table 6. Volunteer: Da01.

$S_c = 0.5$ $\lambda = 0.65$			$S_c = 0.95$ $\lambda = 0.55$			$S_c = 0.5$ $\lambda = 0.55$			$S_c = 0.95$ $\lambda = 0.80$		
106	97	110	87	90	107	99	106	107	91	76	99
+18	+8	+22	-3	0	+19	+10	+18	+19	+1	-15	+10

Table 7. Volunteer: Ra01.

$S_c = 0.5$ $\lambda = 0.65$			$S_c = 0.95$ $\lambda = 0.55$			$S_c = 0.5$ $\lambda = 0.55$			$S_c = 0.95$ $\lambda = 0.80$		
102	102	98	102	107	114	103	105	96	116	99	98
+13	+13	+9	+13	+19	+26	+14	+16	+6	+29	+10	+9

Table 8. Volunteer: Ra02.

- From the analysis of the results of the replicas it has been detected that the variability in the percentage of correct classifications is caused by the HMM's, both in the learning and validation phases. The sequences of pre-assignations provided by the neural network were stable, but the generation probabilities of the HMM's changed in each replica. In the learning phase the HMM's probabilities allowed a perfect classification, but they were not maintained in the cross validation phase; for this stage a lower percentage of correct classification was obtained, as it is summarized in the tables 3 to 8. But until in this case, almost in all replicas, the cross-validation test results were better than the ones hoped from a naive classifier.
- The values of correct classifications depend highly from the user. There has not been identified a pair of λ and S_c values which proportionate the highest percentage of correct classification for all users. The discrepancy in the results between RA1 and RA2 is explained by the user's learning process, session RA1 is previous to RA2.

6.2.5 Results of SVM

This section presents graphically the results obtained from the application to eleven experimental sessions, following the off-line procedure in 6.1.4, the SVM classifier described in the subsection 5.3.
In order to determine the SVM classifier with biggest generalisation capability or the classifier with highest percentage of correct classifications and lower number of support vectors the following values for the kernel parameters in procedure 6.1.4 have been considered.

Kernel type.	Kernel parameter value.
Gaussian	$1, 2, 3, 5$ y 10.
Polynomial	$2, 3, 4, 7$ y 8.

Table 9. Kernel function family and Kernel parameters.

In figures 24 to 27 the following figures are shown for each cerebral channel and type of SVM kernel, the percentage of correct classifications and support vectors obtained for each classifier taking in consideration each type of the processing windows.
The percentages are shown in box diagrams with the notch in the mean value and its uncertainty represented by the size of the box, the segments in both extremes of each box represent the variability[5]. If there are outlander samples they are represented by small empty circles at the extreme of each segments.
From the inspection of the results of classifiers based on Gaussian kernels it is observed that:

- When the zone of influence of the kernel function increases the percentage of correct classifications is reduced independently of the electroencephalographic channel and processing window type. It goes from 100% of correct classifications for $n = 1$ to $90\% - 80\%$ with Tukey's, Kaiser's and rectangular window types[6] with gaussian kernels with $n = 10$.
- When the parameter of the gaussian kernel increases, the percentage of support vector reduces, it goes from 100% of learning data set with $n = 1$, to $85\% - 74\%$ for $n = 10$. The lower values are achieved for rectangular, Tukey's and Kaisser's type of window.

Performing the same analysis with the results of classifiers based on polynomial kernels it is observed that:

- When the order of the polynomial kernel increases the number of support vector is reduced, getting 100% of correct classifications with kernels of order four or higher with Tukey's, Kaiser's and rectangular processing window types.
- With kernel of order four or higher the percentage of support vector is established between 45% and 50% of the learning data set depending on the processing window type, the lowest percentage are obtained with Tukey's, Kaiser's and rectangular's window types, the lowest variability is obtained with the last one.
- Comparing both electroencephalographic channels it is observed that the behaviour of the right one, C2, it is better than the left one, C1.

The classifiers based on Gaussian kernels trend to over-learn the training data set, when the kernel parameter is small all training samples become support vectors, meanwhile the

[5] The length of each segment is 1.5 times the standard deviation.
[6] For the rest of window types the percentage of correct classification is lower.

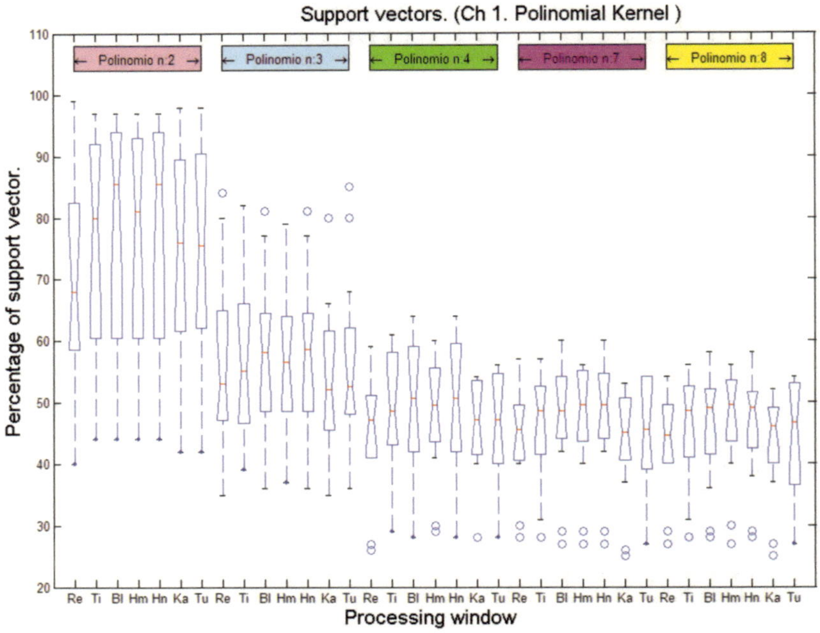

(a) Polinomial Kernel.

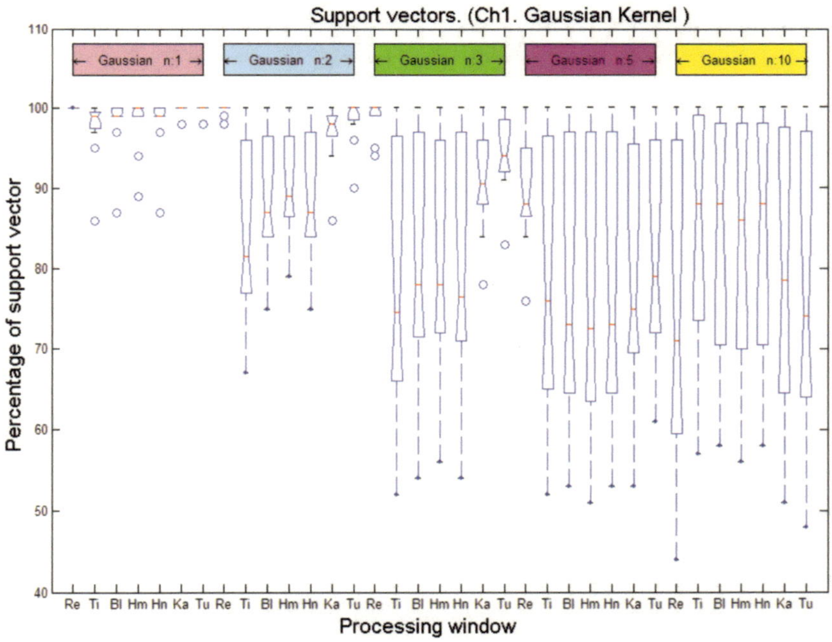

(b) Gaussian Kernel.

Fig. 24. Percentage of support vector. Channel 1.

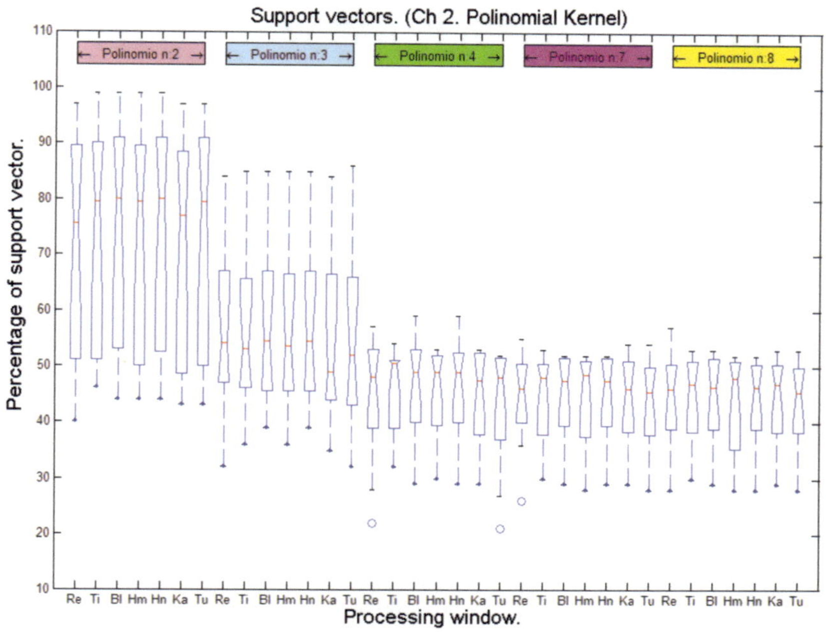

(a) Polinomial Kernel.

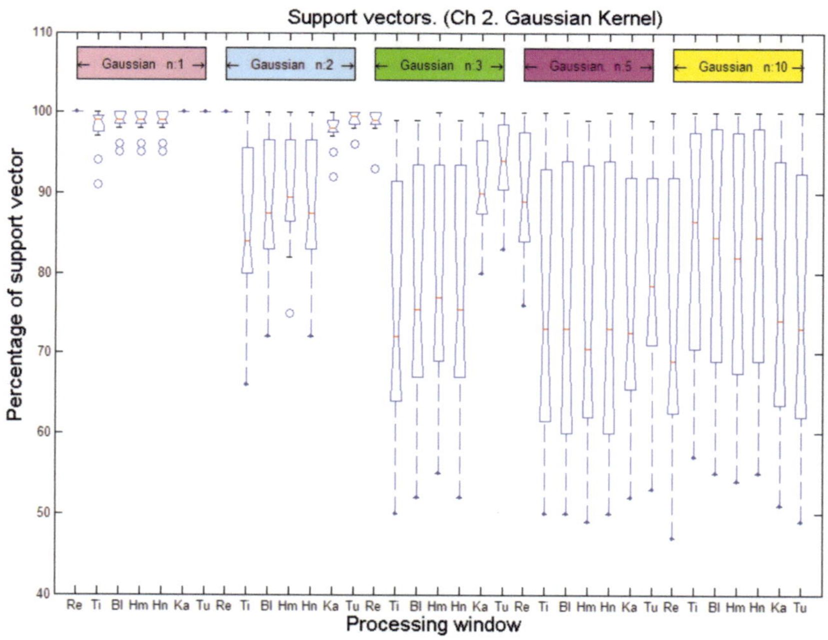

(b) Gaussian Kernel.

Fig. 25. Percentage of support vector. Channel 2.

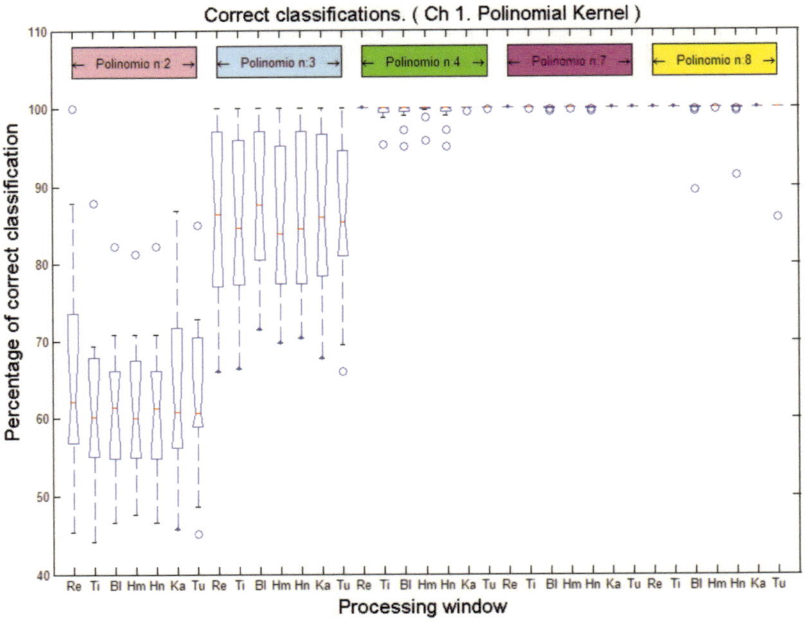

(a) Polinomial Kernel.

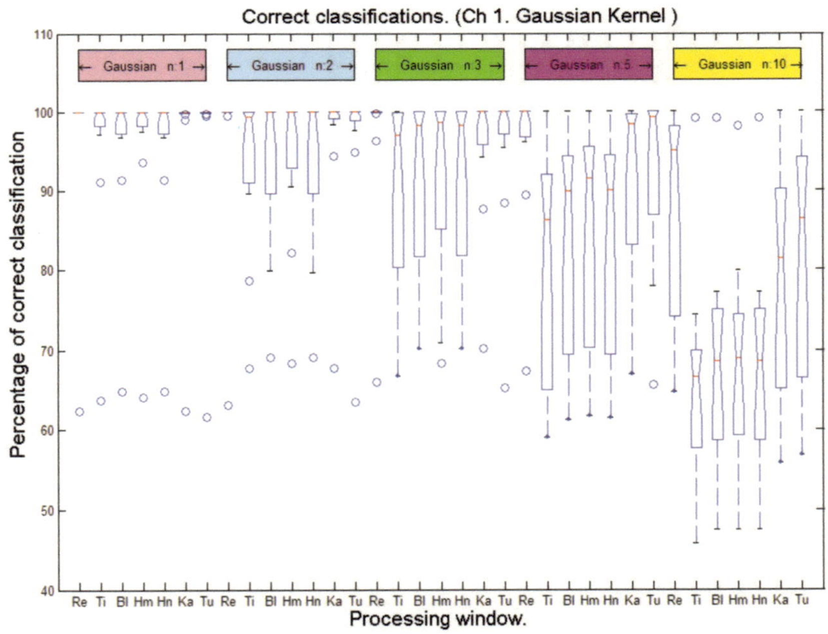

(b) Gaussian Kernel.

Fig. 26. Percentage of correct classifications. Channel 1.

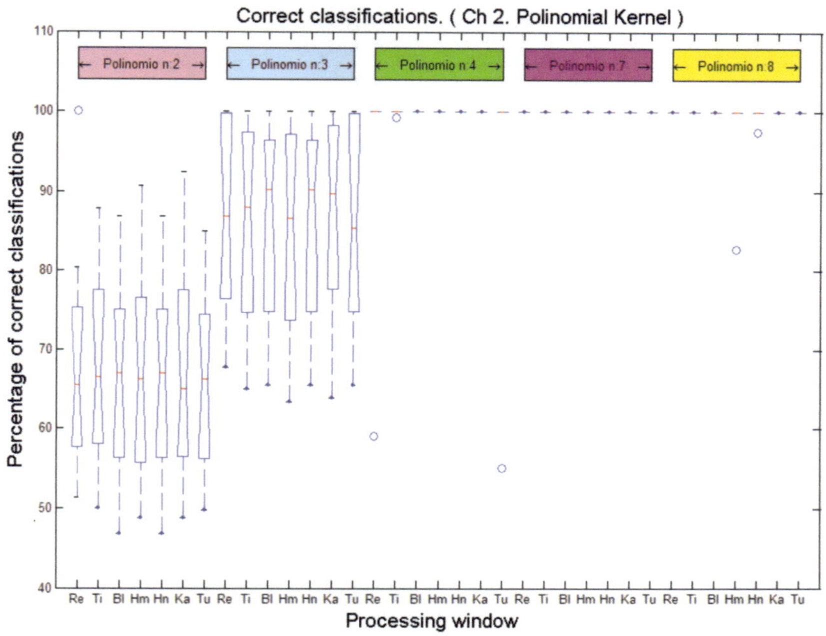

(a) Polinomial Kernel.

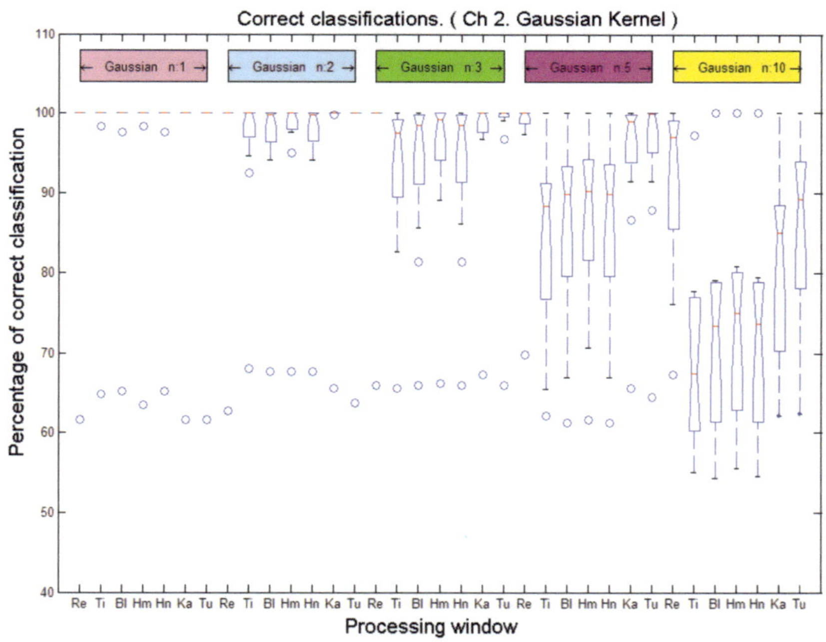

(b) Gaussian Kernel.

Fig. 27. Percentage of correct classifications. Channel 2.

parameter increases the number of support vectors decreases, but in the same way the percentage of correct classifications is reduced.
As it can be seen in the firsts points of the former analysis, the best results are obtained with the Tukey's, Kaiser's and rectangular processing windows.
The classifiers based on polynomial kernels do not over-learns the training data set, because as it is shown in the third and fourth items of the former analysis, when the polynomial order of the kernel increases the number of support vector reduces, but on the contrary the percentage of correct classification gets bigger, nevertheless for polynomial kernels with order higher than five there is not an improvement in their behaviour.
The classifiers based on polynomial kernels exhibit better behaviour than the classifiers based on Gaussian kernels, with polynomial kernels of order four and higher practically a percentage of 100% of correct classification is achieved with 45% – 50% of support vectors, meanwhile the classifiers with gaussian kernels need 74% – 85%, this means that the generalization capability of polynomial kernels is bigger than the Gaussian ones.
The better results of channel two is in line with the exposition in 6.2.2.

7. Conclusions

A classifier which discriminates between mathematical activity and movement imagination should consider the Tukey's window as filtering window, and the features α_1, β_1 and β_2.
It is important to note that the Tukey's window minimises false positive, so it is more reliable than the others types of window.
In these test the channel two (C4) is more significant than channel one(C3), it is probably due to the subject dexterity, more tests should be realized with left-handed and right-handed subjects to determine the influence of it.
It has been statistically proven that through the use of LDA technique it is possible to reduce the dimensionality of the original input feature space, meanwhile the discrimination capability between the proposed mental tasks is maintained, allowing the control of external devices through the association of these tasks to device commands.
From the experiment results carried out by five volunteers under the Off-line an On-line experimental procedures, it is possible to conclude that the user's feedback influence provokes a lower discrimination capability, but enough to be used in an On-line BCI device,(Pineda, J.A. et al., 2003).
It is also shown that Tukey's and rectangular preprocessing windows improve the discrimination capability between the considered mental tasks.
The LDA technique allows to weight the power amplitude of frequency bands, and at the same time, allows to reduce the feature input space maintaining the particularities of the considered cerebral activities. On the other hand, eigen-vector analysis shows that the discrimination power is manifested over β band, mainly β_2 and β_3, they are the vector components with highest contributions in the transformation matrices.
From the result analysis of classifiers based on neural networks are obtained the following conclusions:

1. It is feasible to discriminate between mental tasks using the user's electroencephalographic signal from only the two proposed channels: $C3' - C3''$ and $C4' - C4''$ (J. del R. Millan, 2003).
2. In the case of vectors of features that are based on the power of the signal frequency bands, the election of classifiers based on RBF's shows better classification rates than those that are based on MLP. A similar conclusion is obtained by Garrett in (Peterson, 2003).

3. Classifiers that are based on an architecture with multiple neural networks (one for each electroencephalographic channel, followed by a block that weighs the classification results given by the networks) are in a better position to produce higher correct classification rates than those classifiers that are based on only one neural network.
4. The use of Kaiser's or Tukey's preprocessing window allows for an increase in the mental tasks discrimination capability and improves the behaviour of the classifier.

On the other hand, from the analysis of the results of the adaptative bi-stage classifier it is possible to conclude that the information inside the pre-assignation sequences improves the classification capability, therefore the Hidden Markov Model technique is useful for the extraction and use of this information in an On-line BCI device.
The scattering of the maximum values, of the correct classifications obtained from the cross-validation tests, shows that the combination of λ and S_c parameters are highly dependent on the user, for this reason a BCI device based in this kind of algorithm should have a setup stage, that allows to initialise correctly these parameters.
The algorithm behaves better than a naive algorithm, but it is not as good as it should be taking into account the good results obtained during the learning phase. The size of the learning data set is critical in the results obtained during the validation phase. With a bigger learning data set the validation results will improve, because of the minimisation of the overlearning.
Finally from the analysis and discussion of the results of the tests carried out using classifiers based on MSV, the following conclusions are obtained:

- It is better to choose polynomial kernels instead of Gaussian ones.
- The architecture of the classifier should employ polynomial kernels of order 4 or 5 (it is preferable to choose 5 in order to maximise the generalisation capability of the classifier, but not higher because it does not mean an improvement in the classifier behaviour); and using a processing window of the Tukey's, Kaiser's and rectangular types.

8. References

Andre Ferreira, Teodiano Freire, Mario Sarcinelli, Jose Luis Martin Sanchez, et al. (2009). Evaluation of psd components and aar parameters as input features for a svm classifier applie to a robotic wheelchair, *Proceedings of the BIODEVICES International Conference on Biomedical Electronics and Devices.* 1(1): 7–12.

Birbaumer, N; et al. (2000). The thought translation device (TTD) for completely paralyzed patients, *IEEE TRANS. ON REH. ENG.* 8(2): 190–193.

Bishop, C. M. (1995). *Neural Networks for Pattern Recognition*, Oxford University Press, Great Britain.

E. Donchin and K. M. Spencer and R. Wijesinghe (2000). The mental prosthesis: assessing the speed of a P300-based brain-computer interface, *IEEE Transactions on Rehabilitation Engineering* 8(2): 174–179.

Georgiou;, N. N. J. & M.Polycarpou (2008). Autoregressive features for thought to speech converter, *Proceedings of the BIODEVICES International Conference on Biomedical Electronics and Devices.* 1(1): 11–16.

Harris, F. J. (1978). On the Use of Windows for Harmonic Analysis with the Discrete Fourier Transform.

Horward Demuth, e. a. (2006). *Neural Network Toolbox. User's Guide*, 5 edn, The MathWorks.

J. del R. Millan (2003). Adaptative brain interfaces., *Communications of the ACM.* (46): 74–80.

Kostov, A. (2000). Parallel man-machine training in development of EEG-based cursor control., *IEEE TRANS. ON REH. ENG.* 8(2): 203–205.

Martinez, J.L.; Barrientos, A. (2006). The windowing Effect in Cerebral Pattern Classification. An Application to BCI Technology., *IASTED Biomedical Engineering BioMED 2006* pp. 1186–1191.

Martinez, J.L.; Barrientos, A. (2007). Linear Discriminant Analysis on Brain Computer Interface., *2007 IEEE. International Symposium on Intelligent Signal Processing. Conference Proceedings Book.* pp. 859–864.

Martinez, J.L.; Barrientos, A. (2008). BRAIN COMPUTER INTERFACE. Comparison of Neural Networks Classifiers., *Proceedings of the BIODEVICES International Conference on Biomedical Electronics and Devices.* 1(1): 3–10.

Neuper, C.; et al. (2001). Motor Imagery and Direct Brain-Computer Communication., *Proceedings of the IEEE* 89(7): 1123–1134.

Obermaier, B., Neuper, C., Guger, C. & Pfurtscheller, G. (2001). Information transfer rate in a five-classes brain-computer interface, *IEEE Transactions on Neural Systems and Rehabilitation Engineering* 9(3): 283–288.

Penny, W. D.; et al. (2000). EEG-based communication: A pattern recognition approach, *IEEE TRANS. ON REH. ENG.* 8(2): 214–215.

Peterson, D. G. D. A. (2003). Comparison of linear, nonlinear, and feature selection methods for eeg signal classification., *Neural Systems and Rehabilitation Engineering.* (11): 141–144.

Pfurtscheller et al. (2000a). Brain oscillations control hand orthosis in a tetraplegic., *Neuroscience Letters* 1(292): 211–214.

Pfurtscheller et al. (2000b). Current trends in Graz brain-computer interface (BCI) research., *IEEE TRANS. ON REH. ENG.* 8(2): 216–219.

Pineda, J.A. et al. (2003). Learning to Control Brain Rhythms: Making a Brain-Computer Interface Possible., *IEEE TRANS. ON REH. ENG.* 11(2): 181–184.

Proakis, J. G. & Manolakis, D. G. (1997). *Tratamiento digital de señales : [principios, algoritmos y aplicaciones]*, Prentice-Hall, Madrid.

Rabiner, L. R. (1989). A Tutorial on Hidden Markov Models and Selected Applications in Speech Recognition.

Rabiner, L. R. & Juang, B. H. (1986). An Introduction to Hidden Markov Models.

Ripley, B. D. (1996). *Pattern Recognition and Neural Networks*, Cambridge University Press, United Kingdom.

Vidal, J. J. (1973). Toward direct brain-computer communication, *Annu. Rev. Biophys. Bioeng.* 2: 157–180.

Wolpaw, J. R. (2007). Brain-Computer Interfaces as New Brain Output Pathways, *The Journal of Physiology* .

Wolpaw, J. R.; et al. (2002). Brain-Computer interface for communication and control., *Clinical Neurophysiology* 113: 767–791.

Wolpaw, J.R.; et al. (2000). Brain-Computer Interface Technology: A Review of the First International Meeting., *IEEE TRANS. ON REH. ENG.* 8(2): 164–171.

3

Feature Extraction by Mutual Information Based on Minimal-Redundancy-Maximal-Relevance Criterion and Its Application to Classifying EEG Signal for Brain-Computer Interfaces

Abbas Erfanian, Farid Oveisi and Ali Shadvar
Iran University of Science and Technology
Iran

1. Introduction

Dimensionality reduction of the raw input variable space is an essential preprocessing step in the classification process. In general, it is desirable to keep the dimensionality of the input features as small as possible to reduce the computational cost of training a classifier as well as its complexity (Torkkola, 2003; Murillo & Rodriguez, 2007). Moreover, using large number of features, when the number of data is low, can cause degradation of the classification performance (Chow & Huang, 2005). Reduction of the number of input features can be done by selecting useful features and discarding others (i.e., feature selection) (Battiti, 1994; Kwak & Choi, 2002; Peng et al., 2005; Estèvez et al., 2009; Sindhwani et al., 2004) or extracting new features containing maximal information about the class label from the original ones (i.e., feature extraction) (Torkkola, 2003; Hild II et al., 2006; Kwak, 2007; Murillo & Rodriguez, 2007).

In this paper, we focus on feature selection methods. A variety of linear feature extraction methods have been proposed. One well-known feature extraction methods may be principal component analysis (PCA) (Li et al., 2006). The purpose of PCA is to find an orthogonal set of projection vectors or principal components for feature extraction from given training data through maximizing the variance of the projected data with aim of optimal representing the data in terms of minimal reconstruction error. However, in its feature extraction for classification tasks, PCA does not sufficiently use class information associated with patterns and its maximization to the variance of the projected patterns might not necessarily be in favor of discrimination among classes, thus naturally it likely loses some useful discriminating information for classification.

Linear discrimination analysis (LDA) is another popular linear dimensionally reduction algorithm for supervised feature extraction (Duda et al., 2001). LDA computes a linear transformation by maximizing the ratio of between-class distance to within-class distance, thereby achieving maximal discrimination. In LDA, a transformation matrix from an n-dimensional feature space to a d-dimensional space is determined such that the Fisher criterion of between-class scatter over within-class scatter is maximized. LDA algorithm assumes the sample vectors of each class are generated from underlying multivariate

Normal distributions of common covariance matrix but different means (i.e., homoscedastic data). Over the years, several extensions to the basic formulation of LDA have been proposed (Yu & Yang, 2001; Loog & Duin, 2004). Recently, a method based on Discriminant Analysis (DA) was proposed, known as Subclass Discriminant Analysis (SDA), for describing a large number of data distributions (Zhu & Martinez, 2006). In this approach, the underlying distribution of each class was approximated by a mixture of Gaussians. Then a generalized eigenvalue decomposition was used to find the discriminant vectors that best (linearly) classify the data,

Independent component analysis (ICA) has been also used for feature extraction. ICA is a signal processing technique in which observed random data are linearly transformed into components that are statistically independent from each other (Hyvarinen, Karhunen & Oja, 2001). However, like PCA, the method is completely unsupervised with regard to the class information of the data. A key question is which independent components (ICs) carry more information about the class label. Kwak & Choi (2003) proposed a method for standard ICA to select a number of ICs (i.e., features) that carry information about the class label and a number of ICs that do not. It was shown that the proposed algorithm reduces the dimension of feature space while improving classification performance. We have already used ICA-based feature extraction for classifying the EEG patterns associated with the resting state and the imagined hand movements (Erfanian & Erfani, 2004) and demonstrated the improvement of the performance.

One of the most effective approaches for optimal feature extraction is based on mutual information (MI). MI measures the mutual dependence of two or more variables. In this context, the feature extraction process is creating a feature set from the data which jointly have largest dependency on the target class and minimal redundancy among themselves. In computing the mutual information, one needs to know the multivariate probability density function which is almost impossible to estimate.

To overcome this problem, in (Torkkola, 2003; Hild II, Erdogmnus, Torkkola & Principe, 2006), a method was proposed, known as MRMI, for learning linear discriminative feature transform using an approximation of the mutual information between transformed features and class labels as a criterion. The approximation is inspired by the quadratic Renyi entropy which provides a non-parametric estimate of the mutual information. No simplifying assumptions, such as Gaussian, need to be made about the densities of the classes. However, there is no general guarantee that maximizing the approximation of mutual information using Renyi's definition is equivalent to maximizing mutual information defined by Shannon. Moreover, MRMI algorithm is subject to the curse of dimensionality (Hild II, Erdogmnus, Torkkola & Principe, 2006). To overcome the difficulties of MI estimation for feature extraction, Parzen window modeling was also employed to estimate the probability density function (Kwak, 2007). However, Parzen model may suffer from the "curse of dimensionality," which refers to the overfitting of the training data when their dimension is high (Murillo & Rodriguez, 2007). Due to this difficulty, some recent works on information-theoretic learning have proposed the use of alternative measures for MI (Murillo & Rodriguez, 2007) by means of an entropy estimation method that has succeeded in independent component analysis (ICA). The features are extracted one by one with maximal dependency to the target class. Although, the mutual information between the features and the classes is maximized, but the proposed scheme does not produce minimal information redundancy between the extracted features.

All the above mentioned methods are based on the idea that a linear projection on the data is applied that maximizes the mutual information between the transformed features and the class labels. Finding the linear mapping was performed using standard gradient descent-ascent procedure which suffers from becoming stuck in local minima.
The purpose of this paper is to introduce an efficient method to extract feature with maximal dependency to the target class and minimal redundancy among themselves using only one-dimensional MI estimates. The proposed method has been applied to the problem of the classification of electroencephalogram (EEG) signals for EEG-based brain-computer interface (BCI). Moreover, the results of proposed method was compared to the results obtained using PCA, ICA, MRMI, and SDA. The results confirm that the classification accuracy obtained by Minimax-MIFX is higher than that achieved by existing feature extraction methods and by full feature set.

2. Methods

2.1 Definition of mutual information

Mutual information is a non-parametric measure of relevance between two variables. Shannon's information theory provides a suitable formalism for quantifying this concepts. Assume a random variable $\boldsymbol{X}$ representing continuous-valued random feature vector, and a discrete-valued random variable $\boldsymbol{C}$ representing the class labels. In accordance with Shannon's information theory, the uncertainty of the class label C can be measured by entropy $H(C)$ as

$$H(C) = -\sum_{c \in C} p(c) \log p(c) \tag{1}$$

where $p(c)$ represents the probability of the discrete random variable $\mathbf{C}$. The uncertainty about C given a feature vector $\boldsymbol{X}$ is measured by the conditional entropy as

$$H(C|X) = -\int_x p(\mathbf{x}) \left(\sum_{c \in C} p(c|\mathbf{x}) \log p(c|\mathbf{x}) \right) d\mathbf{x} \tag{2}$$

where $p(c|\mathbf{x})$ is the conditional probability for the variable $\boldsymbol{C}$ given $\boldsymbol{X}$.

In general, the conditional entropy is less than or equal to the initial entropy. It is equal if and only if one has independence between two variables $\boldsymbol{C}$ and $\boldsymbol{X}$. The amount by which the class uncertainty is decreased is, by definition, the mutual information, $I(X;C) = H(C) - H(C|X)$, and after applying the identities $p(c,\mathbf{x}) = p(c|\mathbf{x})p(\mathbf{x})$ and $p(c) = \int_x p(c,\mathbf{x})d\mathbf{x}$ can be expressed as

$$I(X;C) = \sum_{c \in C} \int_x p(c,\mathbf{x}) \log \frac{p(c,\mathbf{x})}{p(c)p(\mathbf{x})} d\mathbf{x} \tag{3}$$

If the mutual information between two random variables is large, it means two variables are closely related. Indeed, MI is zero if and only if the two random variables are strictly independent.

2.2 Minimax mutual information approach to feature extraction

The optimal feature extraction requires creating a new feature set from the original features which jointly have largest dependency on the target class (i.e., maximal dependency). Let us denote by $\mathbf{x}$ the original feature set as the sample of continuous-valued random vector, and by discrete-valued random variable C the class labels. The problem is to find a linear mapping $\mathbf{W}$ such that the transformed features

$$\mathbf{y} = \mathbf{W}^T\mathbf{x} \tag{4}$$

maximizes the mutual information between the transformed features Y and the class labels C, $I(Y,C)$. That is, we seek

$$\mathbf{W}_{opt} = \arg \max_{\mathrm{W}} I(Y;C) \tag{5}$$

$$I(\boldsymbol{Y},C) = \sum_{c \in C} \int \ldots \int p(y_1 \ldots y_m) \log \frac{p(y_1 \cdots y_m, c)}{p(y_1 \cdots y_m)p(c)} dy_1 \cdots dy_m \tag{6}$$

However, it is not always easy to get an accurate estimation for high-dimensional mutual information. It requires the knowledge on the underlying probability density functions (pdfs) of the data and the integration on these pdfs. Moreover, due to the enormous computational requirements of the method, the practical applicability of the above solution to complex classification problems requiring a large number of features is limited.

To overcome the abovementioned practical obstacle, we propose a heuristic method for feature extraction which is based on minimal-redundancy-maximal-relevance (minimax) framework. The max-relevance and min-redundancy criterion has been already used for feature selection (Battiti, 1994; Kwak & Choi, 2002; Peng et al., 2005). It was proved theoretically that minimax criteria is equivalent to maximal dependency (6) if one feature is added at one time (Peng et al., 2005). This criterion is given by

$$J = \left\{ I(x_i;c) - \beta \sum_{x_s \in S} I(x_i;x_s) \right\} \tag{7}$$

According to this criteria, at each time, a new feature x_i is selected with maximal dependency to the target class (i.e., $\max_{x_i} I(x_i;c)$) and minimal dependency among the new feature and already selected features (i.e., $\min_{x_i} \sum_{x_s \in S} I(x_i;x_s)$). The parameter β is the redundancy parameter which is used in considering the redundancy among input features and regulates the relative importance of the MI between the new extracted feature and the already extracted features with respect to the MI with the output class.

In this paper, we modify these criteria for purpose of feature extraction, namely minimax feature extraction, as follows:

$$J = \left\{ I(y_i;c) - \beta \sum_{y_s \in S} I(y_i;y_s) \right\}; \quad y_i = \mathbf{w}_i^T\mathbf{x} \tag{8}$$

where y_i and y_s are the new and already extracted features, respectively. The parameter β was assigned the value $1/m$, where m is the number of already extracted features. The proposed feature extraction method is an iterative process which begins with an empty feature set and additional features are created and included one by one such that the criteria (8) maximized. Formally, the problem can be stated as

$$\mathbf{w}_{opt} = \arg \max_{\mathrm{w}} \left\{ I(y_i;c) - \beta \sum_{y_s \in S} I(y_i;y_s) \right\}; \quad y_i = \mathbf{w}_i^T \mathbf{x} \tag{9}$$

We use a genetic algorithm (GA) (Goldberg, 1989) for mutual information optimization and learning the linear mapping $\mathbf{w}$. Unlike many classical optimization techniques, GA does not rely on computing local first- or second-order derivatives to guide the search process; GA is a more general and flexible method that is capable of searching wide solution spaces and avoiding local minima (i.e., it provides more possibilities of finding an optimal or near-optimal solution). To implement the GA, we use Genetic Algorithm and Direct Search Toolbox for use in Matlab (The Mathworks, R2007b). The algorithm starts by generating an initial population of random candidate solutions. Each individual (chromosomes) in the population is then awarded a score based on its performance. The value of the fitness function (i.e., the function to be optimize) for an individual is its score. The individuals with the best scores are chosen to be parents, which are cut and spliced together to make children. The genetic algorithm creates three types of children for the next generation: Elite children, Crossover children, and Mutation children. Elite children are the individuals in the current generation with the best fitness values. These individuals automatically survive to the next generation. Crossover children are created by combining the genes of two chromosomes of a pair of parents in the current population. Mutation, on the other hand, arbitrarily alters one or more genes of a selected chromosome, by a random change with a probability equal to the mutation rate. These children are scored, with the best performers likely to be parents in the next generation. After some number of generations, it is hoped that the system converges with a near-optimal solution.

In this application, the genetic algorithm is run for 70 generations with population size of 20, crossover probability 0.8, and uniform mutation probability of 0.01. The number of individuals that automatically survive to the next generation (i.e., elite individuals) is selected to be 2. The scattered function is used to create the crossover children by creating a random binary vector and selects the genes where the vector is a 1 from the first parent, and the genes where the vector is a 0 from the second parent.

One is to implement MI-based feature extraction scheme, estimation of MI always poses a great difficulties as it requires the knowledge on the underlying probability density functions (pdfs) of the data and the integration on these pdfs. One of the most popular ways to estimate mutual information for low-dimensional data space is to use histograms as a pdf estimator. Histogram estimators can deliver satisfactory results under low-dimensional data spaces. Trappenberg et al. (2006) have compared a number of MI estimation algorithms including standard histogram method, adaptive partitioning histogram method (Darbellay & Vajda, 1999), and MI estimation based on the Gram-Charlier polynomial expansion (Trappenberg et al., 2006). They have demonstrated that the adaptive partitioning histogram method showed superior performance in their examples. In this work, we used a two-dimensional mutual information estimation using adaptive partitioning histogram method.

The minimax MI-based feature extraction can be summarized by the following procedure:

1. Initialization:
   - Set $\mathbf{x}$ to the initial feature set;
   - Set $\mathbf{s}$ to the empty set;
2. Feature extraction (repeat until desired number of features are extracted).
   - Set $J = \left\{ I(\mathbf{w}_i^T\mathbf{x},c) - \beta \sum_{y_s \in S} I(\mathbf{w}_i^T\mathbf{x};y_s) \right\}$ as the fitness function;
   - Initialize the GA;
     - Specify type, size, and initial values of population;
     - Specify the selection function (i.e., how the GA chooses parents for the next generation);
     - Specify the reproduction operators (i.e., how the genetic algorithm creates the next generation)
   - Find the weighting vector that maximize the fitness function and denote it as $\mathbf{w}_{opt}$;
   - Extract the feature, $y = \mathbf{w}_{opt}^T\mathbf{x}$;
   - Put y into $\mathbf{s}$;
3. Output the set $\mathbf{s}$ containing the extracted features.

3. Experimental setup and data set

3.1 Our experiments

The EEG data of five healthy right-handed volunteer subjects were recorded at a sampling rate of 256 from positions Cz, T5, Pz, F3, F4, Fz, and C3 by Ag/AgCl scalp electrodes placed according to the International 10-20 system. The eye blinks were recorded by placing an electrode on the forehead above the left brow line. The signals were referenced to the right earlobe. Data were recorded for 5 s during each trial experiment and low-pass filtered with a cutoff 45 Hz. Depending on the cue visual stimuli which was appeared on the monitor of computer at 2 s, the subject imagines either right-hand grasping or right-hand opening. If the visual stimuli was not appeared, the subject did not perform a specific task. In the present study, the tasks to be discriminated were the imagination of hand grasping and the idle state. The imaginative hand movement can be hand closing or hand opening. There were 200 trails acquired from each subject during each experiment day.

One of the major problems in developing an online EEG-based BCI is the ocular artifact suppression. In this work, eye blink artifacts are suppressed automatically by using a neural adaptive noise canceller (NANC) proposed in (Erfanian & Mahmoudi, 2005). The structure of adaptive noise canceller is shown in Fig. 1. The primary signal is the measured EEG data from one of the EEG channels. The reference signal is the data recorded from the forehead electrode. Here the adaptive filter is implemented by means of a multi layer perceptron neural network.

3.2 BCI competition III-data set IIIb

To validate the proposed MI-based feature extraction and classification methods for brain-computer Interfaces, the algorithms were also applied to the data set IIIb of "BCI Competition III (Blankertz et al., 2006).". This data set contained 2-class EEG data from 3

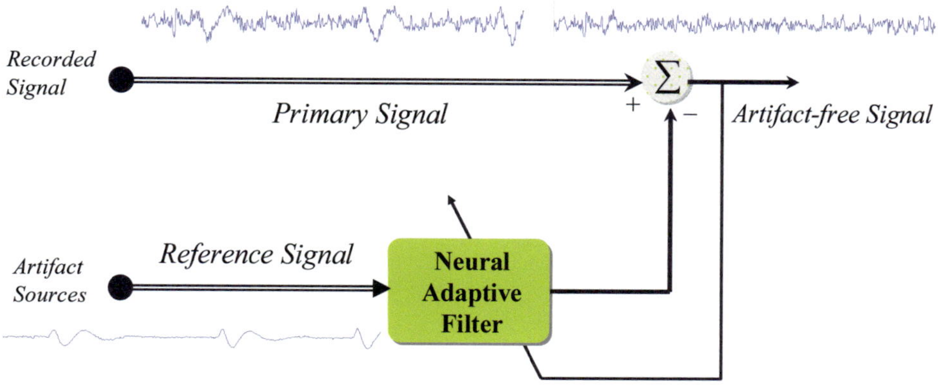

Fig. 1. The structure of the neural adaptive noise canceller used for online ocular artifact suppression.

Subjects. Each data set contained recordings from consecutive sessions during a BCI experiment.Thee experiment consists of 3 sessions for each subject. Each session consisted of 9 runs and each run consisted of 40 feedback trials. For each subject the total number of trials is 1080. The recordings were made with a bipolar EEG amplifier from g.tec (Guger Technologies OEG Austria) . The EEG was sampled with 125 Hz, it was filtered between 0.5 and 30 Hz with Notchfilter on. The experiment was based on the basket paradigm (Vidaurre et al., 2006). In each trial, the subject saw a black screen for a fixed length pause (3 s). Then, two different colored baskets (green and red) appeared at the bottom of the screen. At this moment, also a little green ball appeared at the top of the screen. After 1 s more, the ball began to fall downward with constant speed. The horizontal position of the ball was directly controlled by the output of the classifier. The subject's task was to control the green ball by the imagination of left- or right-hand movements, and try to keep it as long as possible in the side where the green basket appeared. The duration of each trial was 7 s,

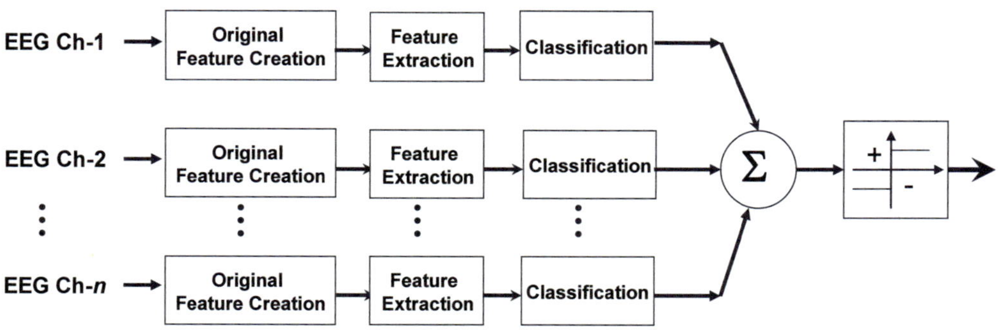

Fig. 2. The block diagram of a multiple classifier for EEG classification.

3.3 Multiple classifier

A multiple classifier is employed for classification of extracted feature vectors. The *Multiple Classifier is* used if different sensors are available to give information on one object. Each of the classifiers works independently on its own domain. The single classifiers are built and trained for their specific task. The final decision is made on the results of the individual classifiers. In this work, for each EEG channel, separate classifier is trained and the final decision is implemented by a simple logical majority vote function. The desired output of each classifier are -1 or +1. The output of classifiers is added and the *signum function* is used for computing the actual response of the classifier. The block diagram of classification process is shown in Fig. 1. The diagonal linear discrimination analysis (DLDA) (Krzanowski, 2000) is here considered as the classifier. The classifier is trained to distinguish between rest state and imaginative hand movement.

4. Results

4.1 Our experiments

Original features are formed from 1-s interval of EEG data of each channel, in the time period 2.3-3.3 s, during each trial of experiment. The window starting 0.3 s after cue presentation is used for classification. The number of local extrema within interval, zero crossing, 5 AR parameters, variance, the mean absolute value (MAV), and 1-Hz frequency components between 1 and 35 Hz constitute the full set of features with size 44. In this application, the genetic algorithm was run for 70 generations with population size of 20, crossover probability 0.8, and mutation probability of 0.01. For each channel, one classifier is designed. The classifier is trained to distinguish between rest state and imaginative hand movement. The imaginative hand movement can be hand closing or hand opening. From 200 data sets, 100 sets are randomly selected for training, while the rest is kept aside for validation purposes. Training and validating procedure is repeated 10 times and the results are averaged.

Fig. 3 shows the classification accuracy for subject ST during different experiment days for different sizes of feature set obtained by minimax-MIFX, PCA, MRMI, and ICA methods. During the first day, the best classification accuracy as high as 75.0% was obtained using minimax-MIFX with 5 features. During the second day, the best results obtained are 72.9% with 10 features using ICA, 72.3% using MRMI and 71.1% using Minimax-MIFX with 5 features, and 71.9% using full feature set. During the third experiment day, the best classification accuracy obtained is 83.4% by using Minimax-MIFX with 5 features, while the rate is 74.0% with full feature set. Fig. 2 (d) shows the average classification accuracies over three experiment days for the subject ST. It is observed that the Minimax-MIFX method provides a better performance compared to the other feature extraction methods. On average, the best rate for the subject ST is 76.5% which is obtained by Minimax-MIFX method with 5 extracted features. The average classification performance of SDA for the subject ST is 73.96% which is poorer than that obtained by the Minimax-MIFX. The performance for full feature set is 72.43%. It is observed that the best performance of MRMI method takes place when the number of extracted to be small. It should be noted that the MRMI method is subject to the curse of dimensionality as the number of extracted feature increases (Hild II et al., 2006). Due to this fact and low computation speed of MRMI, this method are performed for extraction of 5 and 10 features.

Fig. 4 shows the average of classification accuracies over three days for all other subjects. The best classification accuracy is obtained by the Minimax-MIFX in all subject and is 78.4% with 5 features in AE, 80.0% with 10 features in ME, 78.37% with 20 features in BM, and 78.3% with 10 features in MM. Fig. 3(e) shows the average of classification accuracy over all subjects. The classification performance obtained using ICA method is almost the same as that obtained using PCA. The best performance of MRMI method is achieved when five extracted features are used for classification. However, the performance of MRMI degrades as the number of extracted features increases. The results indicate that classification accuracy obtained by the Minimax-MIFX method is generally better than that obtained by other methods. The best classification accuracy as high as 78.0% is obtained by minimax-MIFX method only with 5 extracted features. The average performance of SDA is 77.85% which is identical to that obtained using minimax-MIFX.

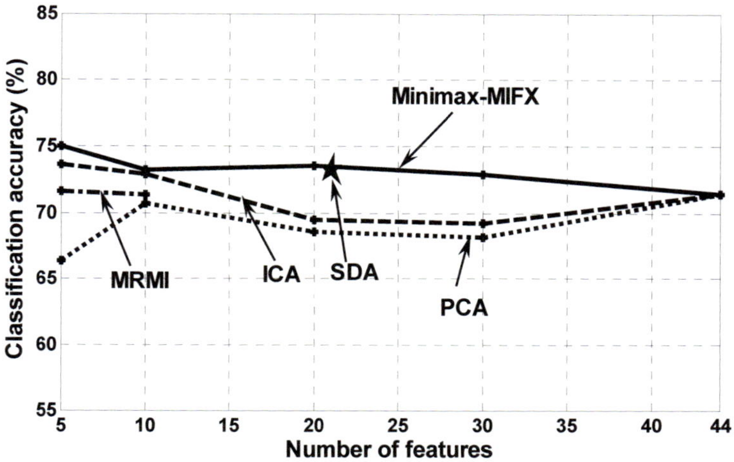

(a)

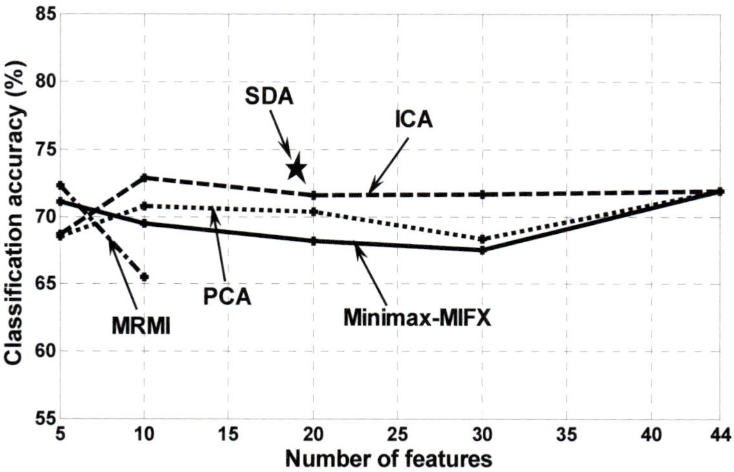

(b)

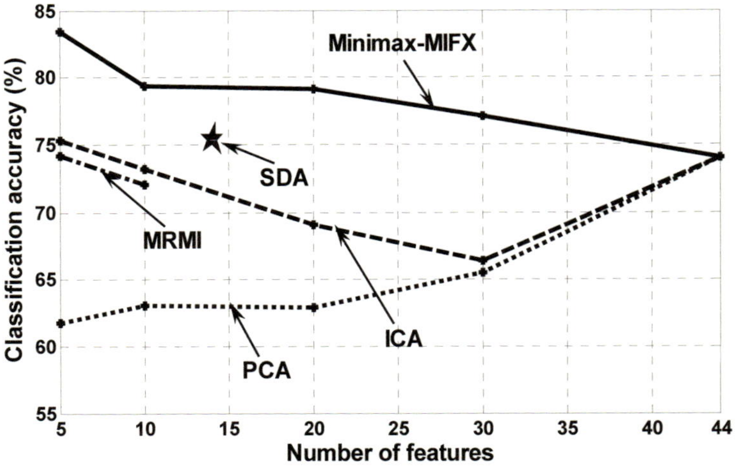

(c)

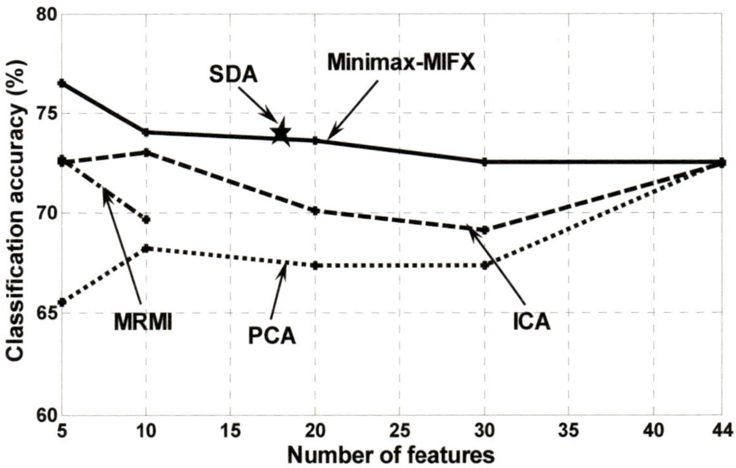

(d)

Fig. 3. Classification accuracy for subject ST with different sizes of feature set obtained by different feature extraction methods: (a-c) Different experiment days. (d) Average classification accuracy over different days.

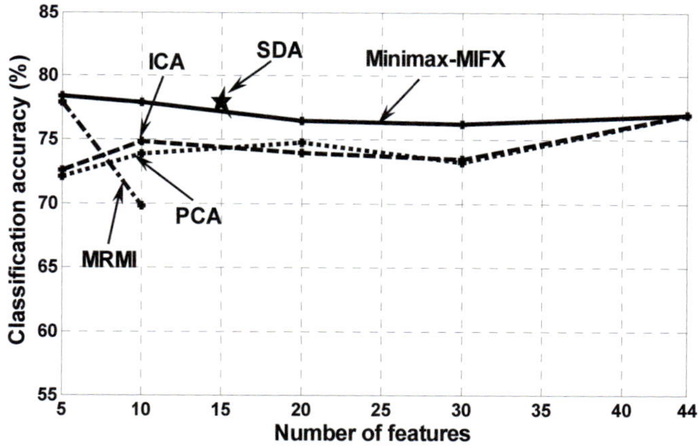
ICA
SDA
Minimax-MIFX
PCA
MRMI
Classification accuracy (%)
Number of features

(a)

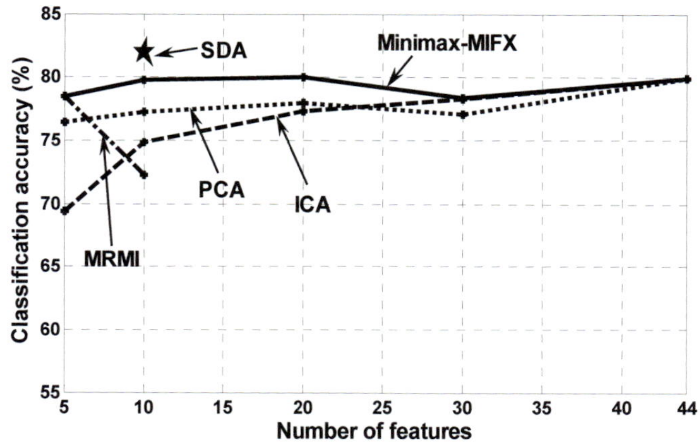
SDA
Minimax-MIFX
PCA
ICA
MRMI
Classification accuracy (%)
Number of features

(b)

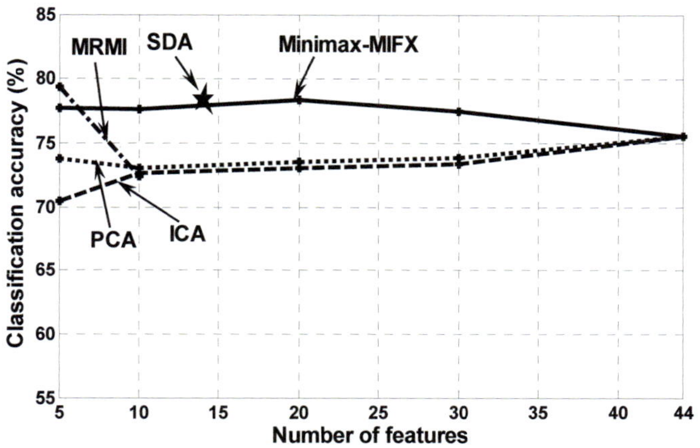
MRMI
SDA
Minimax-MIFX
PCA
ICA
Classification accuracy (%)
Number of features

(c)

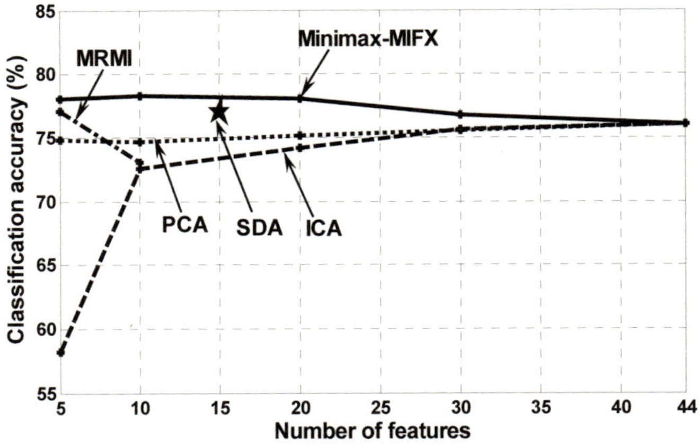

(d)

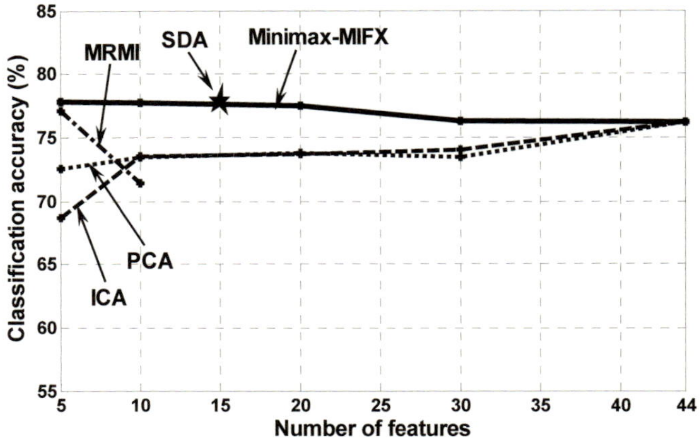

(e)

Fig. 4. The average of classification accuracy over the three days for the subjects AE (a), ME (b), BM (c), and MM (d). Average classification accuracy over all days and all subjects (e).

4.2 BCI Competition III-Data Set IIIb

For classification, the features are extracted from 3-s epoch of EEG data recorded from channels C3 and C4 in the interval 4-7 s. A classifier is trained to differentiate between EEG patterns associated with left- and right-hand movement imagery. The entire feature set are formed from each data window, separately and consist of 23 features including the number of local extrema within interval, zero crossing, energy of 8 wavelet packet nodes of a three level decomposition, 5 AR parameters, variance, the mean absolute value (MAV), the first three eigenvalues of correlation matrix, and the relative power in three common frequency bands of EEG spectral density—theta (4–8 Hz), alpha (9–14 Hz), and beta (15–30 Hz). From 1080 feature sets, 540 sets are assigned for training of each classifier, while the rest is kept aside for validation purposes.

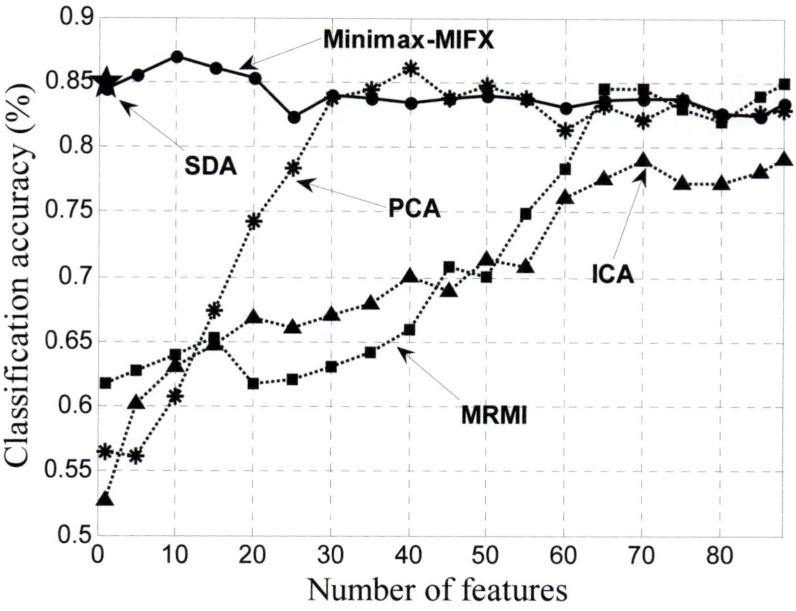

(a)

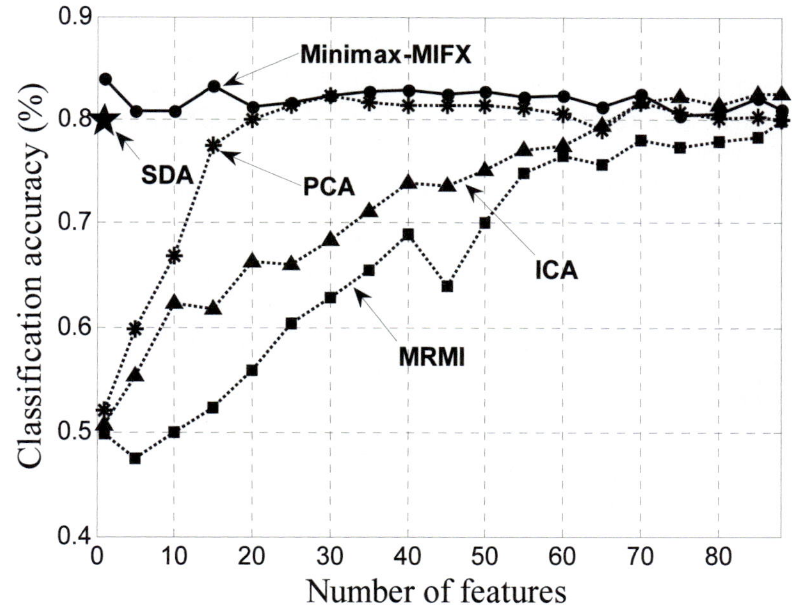

(b)

Fig. 5. Classification accuracy obtained by using different feature extraction methods for BCI Competition III-Data Set IIIb for two subjects S4 (a) and X11 (b).

Fig. 5 shows the classification accuracies obtained by different feature extraction methods for different number of extracted features. In subject S4, the best classification accuracies obtained are 87.0% using minimax-MIFX with 10 extracted features, 86.1% using PCA with 36 features, 79.1% using ICA with 68 features, 85.1% using MRMI with 70 extracted features, and 77.2% using full feature set. In subject X11, it is observed that the best classification accuracy was achieved by using the proposed feature extraction method which is 84.1% with only one extracted feature. The accuracy rate with full feature set in subject X11 is 82.9%.
The results show that that minimax-MIFX provides a robust performance against changes in the number of features extracted, while the performance of other feature extraction methods is sensitive with respect to the number of features.

5. Conclusion

In this paper, we have proposed a novel approach for feature extraction which is based on mutual information. The goal of mutual information-based feature extraction (MIFX) is to create new features from transforming the original features such that the dependency between the transferred features and the target class is maximized. However, the estimation of MI poses great difficulties as it requires the estimating the multivariate probability density functions (pdfs) of the data space and the integration on these pdfs. The proposed MIFX method iteratively creates a new feature with maximal dependency to the target class and minimal redundancy among the new feature and previously extracted features. Our minimax-MIFX scheme avoids the difficult multivariate density estimation in maximizing dependency and minimizing redundancy. Only two-dimensional (2-D) MIs are directly estimated, whereas the higher dimensional MIs are analyzed using the 2-D MI estimates. The effectiveness of the proposed method was evaluated by using the classification of EEG signals during hand movement imagination and the results compared to the performance of some existing feature extraction methods including PCA, ICA, SDA, and MRMI. Moreover, the MIFX algorithms were also applied to the data set IIIb of BCI Competition III. The results demonstrate that the classification accuracy can be improved by using the proposed feature extraction scheme compared to the existing feature extraction methods.

6. References

Battiti, R. (1994). Using mutual information for selecting features in supervised neural net learning. *IEEE Transaction Neural Networks*, Vol. 5, No. 4, (July 1994) pp. (537-550), ISSN 1045-9227.

Blankertz B. & Muller, K. (2004). The BCI competition 2003: progress and perspectives in detection and discrimination of EEG single trials, *IEEE Transaction Biomedical Engineering*, Vol. 51, No. 6, (June 2004) pp. (1044-1051), ISSN 0018-9294.

Blankertz, B.; Müller, K. R.; Krusienski, D.; Schalk, G.; Wolpaw, J. R.; Schlögl, A.; Pfurtscheller, G.; Millán, J. R.; Schröder, M. & Birbaumer, N. (2006). The BCI competition III: validating alternative approaches to actual BCI problems. *IEEE Transaction on Neural Systems and Rehabilitation Engineering*, Vol. 14, No. 2, (June 2006) pp. (153-159), ISSN 1534-4320.

Chow, T. & Huang, D. (2005). Estimating optimal feature subsets using efficient estimation of high-dimensional mutual information. *IEEE Transaction Neural Network*, Vol. 16, No. 1, (January 2005) pp. (213-224), ISSN 1045-9227.

Darbellay, G. & Vajda, I. (1999). Estimation of the information by an adaptive partitioning of the observation space. *IEEE Transaction Information Theory*, Vol. 45, No. 4, (May 1999) pp. (1315-1321), ISSN 0018-9448.

Duda, R.O.; Hart, P.E. & Stork, D. (2001). *Pattern Classification*. Wiley, second edition ISBN 0-471-05669-3.

Erfanian, A. & Erfani, A. (2004). ICA-based classification scheme for EEG-based brain-computer interface: the role of mental practice and concentration skills. *26th Annual International Conference of the IEEE/EMBS*, pp. 235 - 238, ISBN 0-7803-8439-3, USA, September 2004, San Francisco.

Erfanian, A. & Mahmoudi, B. (2005). Real-time ocular artifacts suppression using recurrent neural network for EEG-based brain computer interface, *Medical & Biological Engineering & Computation*, Vol. 43, No. 2, (March 2005) pp. (296-305), ISSN 0140-0118.

Estèvez, P. A.; Tesmer, M.; Perez, C. A. & Zurada, J. M. (2009). Normalized mutual information feature selection. *IEEE Transaction Neural Networks*, Vol. 20, No. 2, (February 2009) pp. (189 - 201), ISSN 1045-9227.

Goldberg, D. E. (1989). Genetic algorithms in search, *Optimization and Machine Learning*. Addison-wesley, ISBN 0201157675, Boston, MA, USA.

Hild II, K. E.; Erdogmnus, D.; Torkkola, K. & Principe, J. C. (2006). Feature extraction using information-theoretic learning. *IEEE Transaction Pattern Analysis and Machine Intelligence*, Vol. 28, No. 9, (September 2006) pp. (1385-1393), ISSN 0162-8828.

Hyvarinen, A.; Karhunen, J. & Oja, E. (2001). *Independent Component Analysis*, John Wiley & Sons, ISBN 9780471405405.

Krzanowski, WJ. (2000). Principles of multivariate analysis: *a user's perspective*, Oxford University Press, Oxford, ISBN 9780198507086.

Kwak, N. (2007). Feature extraction based on direct calculation of mutual information. *International Journal of Pattern Recognition and Artificial Intelligence*, Vol. 21, No. 7, (november 2007) pp. (1213-1231), ISSN 0218-0014.

Kwak, N. & Choi, C. H. (2002). Input feature selection for classification problems. *IEEE Transaction Neural Networks*, Vol. 13, No. 1, (January 2002) pp. (143–159), ISSN 1045-9227.

Kwak, N. & Choi, C. H. (2003). Feature extraction based on ICA for binary classification problems. *IEEE Transaction Knowledge and Data Engineering*, Vol. 15, No. 6, (November/December 2003) pp. (1374-1388), ISSN 1041-4347.

Lemm, S.; Schäfer, C. & Curio, G. (2004). BCI competition 2003—data set III: probabilistic modeling of sensorimotor μ rhythms for classification of imaginary hand movements. *IEEE Transaction Biomedical Engineering*, Vol. 51, No. 6, (June 2004) pp. (1077–1080), ISSN 0018-9294.

Li, H.; Jiang, T. & Zhang, K. (2006). Efficient and robust feature extraction by maximum margin criterion. *IEEE Transaction Neural Networks*, Vol. 17, No. 1, (January 2006) pp. (157–165), ISSN 1045-9227.

Loog, M. & Duin, R. P. W. (2004). Linear dimensionality reduction via a heteroscedastic extension of LDA: the Chernoff criterion. *IEEE Transaction Pattern Analysis and Machine Intelligence*, Vol. 26, No. 6, (June 2004) pp. (732-739), ISSN 0162-8828.

Murillo, J. & Rodriguez, A. (2007). Maximization of mutual information for supervised linear feature extraction. *IEEE Transaction Neural Network*, Vol. 18, No. 5, (September 2007) pp. (1433-1441), ISSN 1045-9227.

Peng, H.; Long, F. & Ding, C. (2005). Feature selection based on mutual information: criteria of max-dependency, max-relevance, and min-redundancy. *IEEE Transaction Pattern Analysis and Machine Intelligence*, Vol. 27, No. 8, (august 2005) pp. (1226-1238), ISSN 0162-8828.

Sindhwani, V.; Rakshit, S.; Deodhar, D.; Erdogmus, D.; Principe, J. & Niyogi, P. (2004). Feature selection in MLPs and SVMs based on maximum output information. *IEEE Transaction Neural Networks*, Vol. 15, No. 4, (July 2004.) pp. (937–948), ISSN 1045-9227.

Torkkola, K. (2003). Feature extraction by non-parametric mutual information maximization. *Journal of Machine Learning Research*, Vol. 3, No. 7-8, (March 2003) pp. (1415–1438), ISSN 1533-7928.

Trappenberg, T.; Ouyang J. & Back A. (2006). Input variable selection: mutual information and linear mixing measures. *IEEE Transaction Knowledge and Data Engineering*, Vol. 18, No. 1, (january 2006) pp. (37-46), ISSN 1041-4347.

Vidaurre, C.; Schlöogl, A.; Cabeza, R.; Scherer, R. & Pfurtscheller, G. (2006). A fully on-line adaptive BCI. *IEEE Transaction Biomedical Engineering*, Vol. 53, No. 6, (June 2006) pp. (1214-1219), ISSN 0018-9294.

Yu, H. & Yang, J. (2001). A direct LDA algorithm for high-dimensional data—with applications to face recognition. *Pattern Recognition*, Vol. 34, No. 11, (October 2001) pp. (2067-2070), ISSN 0031-3203.

Zhu, M. & Martinez, A. M. (2006). Subclass discriminant analysis. *IEEE Transaction Pattern Analysis and Machine Intelligence*, Vol. 28, No. 8, (august 2006) pp. (1274-1286), ISSN 0162-8828.

4

P300-based Brain-Computer Interface Paradigm Design

Reza Fazel-Rezai and Waqas Ahmad
University of North Dakota
USA

1. Introduction

In this chapter, we will explore the P300 wave of visual evoked potentials (VEP), which has become the most popular form of event-related potentials (ERP) in past few decades, its applications and future advancements in the field of P300-based brain computer interface (BCI). The focus of the chapter will be on different design issues considered so far and important challenges to be considered for designing a new P300-based BCI paradigm. In addition, different applications of P300-based BCI systems will be discussed briefly.

Applications of electroencephalography (EEG) or the 'brain signals' are emerging rapidly and new ways have been innovated for communication and fast transfer of data between the brain and these applications. Over the last two decades, BCI has made significant progress and substantial research is going on to communicate with the human brain (Wolpaw et al., 2002). One of the few breakthroughs of BCI is a P300-based BCI speller (Farwell & Donchin, 1988). There have been many research studies based on the original design introduced by Farwell and Donchin (Donchin et al., 2000; Serby et al., 2005; Sellers et al., 2006; Fazel-Rezai, 2007; Ramanna & Fazel-Rezai, 2007) with the significant improvement in the accuracy and speed. The Farwell-Donchin paradigm (Farwell & Donchin, 1988) is a well known and most widely used paradigm for the visually evoked potential based BCI speller, in which, characters and numbers are represented in a grid of six-by-six matrix.

Although different variations in the visual paradigm have been analyzed (Salvaris & Sepulveda, 2009), they are mostly based on the matrix representation of characters. The P300-based speller is especially useful for people with amyotrophic lateral sclerosis (ALS), brainstem stroke, brain or spinal cord injury, cerebral palsy, muscular dystrophies, multiple sclerosis and other diseases which impair them to communicate in a normal way.

Several shortcomings of existing P300-based BCIs have been identified (Fazel-Rezai, 2007 & Fazel-Rezai & Abhari, 2009), and many research groups have tried to overcome those shortcomings. However, more progress should be made in resolving many of the challenges issues to move BCI into the realm of practicality and to take it outside research laboratories into practical applications.

The chapter will be organized as follows. In the first few sections, we will introduce the basics on the VEP and P300. In the subsequent sections, more detailed applications of BCI speller program involving the design and development issues affecting the accuracy and speed along with classic Farwell-Donchin paradigm will be discussed. Furthermore, we will share our experience of implementing innovative ideas on changing the Farwell-Donchin paradigm, leading to a new direction in terms of BCI speller paradigm. The chapter concludes with future trends in this area.

2. Event-Related Potentials (ERPs)

ERPs are electrocortical potentials generated in the brain during the presentation of stimulus. The stimulus could be generated by a sensor or a psychological event. It generates a time delay wave in EEG that can be detected by after processing EEG signals. These methods can be a simple averaging technique, in which, EEGs are averaged over total time (time from presenting the stimulus to time when EEG settles down) or advanced approaches such as linear discreminant analysis or support vector machine algorithms. There are different types of ERPs based on the source of stimulus presentation such as visual, auditory and tactile. This chapter discusses the P300 which is a form of visually evoked potential (VEP) and focuses on the P300 wave in ERP.

2.1 P300 wave

The P300 wave also known as P3 is the most important and studied component of ERPs, which can be recorded/measured after the stimulus presentation in an EEG. The P300 is observed in an EEG as a significant positive peak 300 ms to 500 ms after an infrequent stimulus is presented to a subject. The actual origin of the P300 is still unclear. It is suggested to be related to the end of the cognitive processing, to memory updating after information evaluation or to information transfer to consciousness (Bernat et al., 2001; Gonsalvez & Polich, 2002). Typical peak latency of this positive wave occurs around 300 ms for most users; therefore, it is called as P300 wave. In the typical P300-based experiments three different types of paradigms are being used; 1) single-stimulus, 2) oddball, and 3) three-stimulus paradigm.

The single-stimulus paradigm includes one type of stimuli called target. In a typical oddball paradigm, the subject is normally presented with target and standard (or irrelevant) stimuli. The three-stimulus paradigm consists of target, standard and distractor. Distractors are also referred as probes or novels. Novel stimuli in a three-stimulus paradigm are presented infrequently and produce a P300 component that is large over the frontal/central area and is different from the typical parietal maximum P300 discrimination (Comerchero & Polich, 1999). This 'novelty' P300 is called the P3a which is totally different from the P300 in response to the target stimulus (P3b). Furthermore, P3a's peak is bifurcated with shorter latency compare to P3b. It also habituates relatively faster discrimination (Comerchero & Polich, 1999). The P3a is a subcomponent of P300, which is significant in EEG produced in the frontal/central part of the scalp (Courchesne et al., 1984; Knight, 1984; Yamaguchi & Knight, 1991) also sometimes referred as novelty P300. Its generation does not depend on stimulus novelty but is solely based on the target discrimination (Comerchero & Polich, 1999) and habituation (Soltana, M., & Knight, R, 2000). The P3b is referred to as the maximum potential P300 from the target stimulus (Courchesne et al., 1975; Squires et al., 1975). It has been used for cognitive purposes in the field of psychology. The P3b has been successfully applied for task experiments related activities are as a measurement of workload.

3. P300 detection

P300 detection is usually done by averaging method, in which several trials are averaged (Farwell & Donchin, 1988) due to the fact that brain signal is a combination various brain activities and artifacts such as noise is also accumulated during the recording process. During averaging, the P300 is extracted based on attended stimulus. Different approaches have been used for the feature extraction and classification of P300 based systems. In this section, we will briefly describe the necessary steps for P300 detection.

3.1 Preprocessing

Prepocessing of EEG signals is an important step before extracting any feature. It is done after data acquisition. Preprocessing usually enhances the signal and improve signal to noise ratio (SNR). A typical step in preprocessing is bandpass filtering. Bandpass filters are designed to remove DC bias and high frequency noises. In preprocessing, channel selection with respect to data decimation is determined in a way to enhance the classification performance. Segments of data are collected and moving average filter is applied for best performance (Krusienski et al., 2006).

3.2 Classification

Different classification methods have been used in P300 based BCI systems. Some of them includes linear discriminant analysis (LDA), support vector machines (SVM), stepwise linear discriminant analysis (SWLDA), Fisher's linear discriminant (FLD), Baysian linear discriminant analysis (BLDA), Pearson's correlation method, linear support vector machine (LSVM) and Gausian support vector machine (GSVM). A brief description for each of these methods is given in the following sections.

a. *Linear Discriminant Analysis (LDA)*

Linear discriminant analysis (LDA) is very popular pattern classification technique and out performs SVM classifiers for the P300 detection (Mirghasemi et al., 2006). Two modified versions of LDA are used for P300 classification: Fisher linear discriminant analysis (FLDA) and stepwise linear discriminant analysis (SWLDA).

b. *Fisher linear Discriminant Analysis (FLDA)*

Fisher discriminant analysis is a robust and easy to calculate method for determining the maximum distance between two classes. In the case of binary decision making process, both the FLDA and least-square regression are equivalent. The FLDA is more favorable classification technique against noise as compare to SVM (Blankertz et.al., 2002; Krusienski, 2006).

c. *Stepwise Linear Discriminant Analysis (SWLDA)*

Stepwise linear discriminant analysis is an extension of FLDA, in which only those features are selected for the discrimination analysis which are suitable for classification purposes, thus reduces the number of features required for classification. Farwell and Donchin used stepwise linear discrimination analysis for 6 X 6 row/column paradigm (Farwell & Donchin, 1988), which later used to assess the speed of P300-based BCI by Donchin (Donchin, Spencer & Wijesinghe, 2000) with the help of discrete wavelet transform (DWT). The data used for classification in the ERP is the combined averages for rows and columns instead of individual averages for rows and columns (Donchin et. al., 2000). This may have resulted an improvement in the accuracy and the communication rate for the BCI system.

d. *Baysian Linear Discriminant Analysis (BLDA)*

Baysian linear discriminant analysis (BLDA) is an extension of FLDA. Unlike FLDA, Baysain analysis performs estimation techniques to compute the discriminant vector for classification purposes (Huang & Zhou, 2008). Target values are set through regression analysis in a Baysian frame work and training can be performed in a more quick way as compare to that of FLDA.

e. *Support Vector Machine (SVM)*

Support vector machines (SVM) is a machine learning technique which is very useful for the binary classification purpose. SVMs are used with Kernal functions which define transformation function. (Müller et al., 2001; Krusienski et al., 2006; Vapnik, 1995; Blankertz et.al., 2002). The SVM are suitable for practical purposes, where high transfer rates are required along with least amount of data. (Kaper et al., 2004; Thulasidas et.al., 2006)

f. *Gaussian Support Vector Machine (GSVM)*

Gaussian support vector machines (GSVM) is a nonlinear method used for classification of the EEG data for BCI speller program (Krusienski, 2006). The GSVM are used with Kernal functions which define nonlinear transformation and may cause difficulty for computations of data for large support vectors. (Krusienski, 2006; Vapnik, 1995; Müller et.al., 2001; Blankertz et.al., 2002).

g. *Maximum Likelihood (ML)*

ML classifiers are used for feature detection using a priori knowledge (Haykin, 1983; Serby et al., 2005). They provide a wide range of decision classes with the use of threshold values set for these classes. Serby used ML method for comparison with other techniques for BCI speller programs (Serby et al., 2005).

h. *Independent Component Analysis (ICA)*

Independent component analysis is a blind source separation technique used for recovering source signals from background noise or mixture of other signals using reconstruction. Different filtering techniques are used for preprocessing the source signal before being sent to ICA. Similar to ML, in ICA threshold value calculations are based on features in the source signals. Threshold values depend on number of trials and decision making is very fast as compared to the other methods (Serby et al., 2005). ICA's can be very effective as both temporal and spatial information is provided as the a priori knowledge (Xu et al., 2004).

4. Applications of P300

P300 has several of applications developed over the past few decades. Extensive progress in the research in this field result numerous applications from P300-based speller (virtual keyboard) to smart home applications and from lie detector to sending emails over the internet browsers. We will describe these applications in detail in the following sections.

4.1 Lie detectors

Information processing in the human brain generates an activity in the brain signal and can be recorded in the form of EEG. These EEGs can further be processed to find the deceptions. Farwell and Donchin investigated that activity through experiment and find out the different brain wave activities for two groups of subjects (Farwell & Donchin, 1991). The brain activity for the subjects who committed mock crime was different than that of those who did not take part in mock crime (Farwell & Donchin, 1991). Cacioppo devised a method for the lie detection using EEG assuming that the brain would process the stimuli differently if the brain wave association for two stimuli is different (Cacioppo et al., 1994). In 1993, Farwell introduced a technique based on brain electrical activities to spot a liar (Farwell 1995). His invention was based on the fact that P300 is elicited when the subject is confronted with particular stimulus that he/she has prior knowledge of. Certain stimuli, such as a crime scene or specific gun's picture, produce P300 if they look familiar to the subject (Farwell & Smith, 2001). This stimulus could be a word, phrase, or picture (Farwell & Smith, 2001). He defined three different types of stimuli in his method: Irrelevant, Target and Probe. The subject is given a list of specific stimuli called 'Target' and instructed to perform a task which is pressing a particular button in response. 'Irrelevant' stimuli are not relevant while 'Probes' are related to the situation under investigation. Probes elicit P300 if the subject is knowledgeable. On the other hand, they have the same effect as the irrelevant for a subject who is not knowledgeable about the situation (Farwell, 1995). Even though Farwell has claimed his technique is 100% accurate (Farwell & Smith, 2001) it has never been subject to independent review.

4.2 Smart homes

Smart homes are P300 based BCI systems that can be used for controlling the various applications in a home. Guger used a P300 based BCI system for smart home with high accuracy and reliability (Guger et al., 2009). They tested the system on a virtual reality based smart home. The results showed that different trivial control commands like switching TV channels, opening and closing doors and windows, turning light on and off, using phone, play music, operate a camera, walk around the house or move to a specific location in a smart home were performed successfully (Guger et al., 2009).

4.3 P300-based internet browsing

Like many other applications of P300, internet browsing through P300 potentials is a practical approach to provide more degree of freedom to the ALS patients. The user selection of various internet links and suffering through pages was performed (Muglerab et al., 2008) which later even extended to the use of virtual keyboard and mouse (Sirvent et al., 2010) for the P300 based internet browsing.

4.4 BCI spellers

BCI spellers can be used as a communication tool by people with neuromuscular disorders (Wolpaw et al., 1991). It is especially useful for people with amyotrophic lateral sclerosis (ALS), brainstem stroke, brain or spinal cord injury, cerebral palsy, muscular dystrophies, multiple sclerosis and other diseases which impair patients to communicate in a normal way. Recently, there has been progress in improving P300 speller accuracy and speed. Various P300 stimuli presentation paradigms have been proposed. They are described in more details in the following sections.

5. P300 speller paradigms

A typical P300 speller consists of data collection, signal processing and classification (Wolpaw et al., 2000). In the data collection, a paradigm should be presented to subject to evoke the P300. P300-based BCI speller proved to be very useful in detecting the characters and symbols with high accuracy. However, there is a trade-off between increasing the communication rate and lowering the errors. Despite all the research progress made in the field of P300-based BCI speller program, there are several challenging issues that should be addressed to move the P300 BCI into practical applications. In this section, we discuss those problems and challenging issues in more detail.

a. *Crowding Effect*

Crowding effect occurs when target object is surrounded by the similar objects. It makes it difficult for the user to identify the target (Bouma 1970; Feng et al., 2007; Toet & Levi 1992; Van den Berg et al., 2007). Crowding effect may be caused by the inaccurate spatial distribution of the characters around the visual periphery of the spelling paradigm and leads to the error during spelling process (Strasburger, 2005). The matrix based design of RC paradigms is prone to this effect and it is hard to pay attention to many characters in the visual periphery. Increasing the size of characters in the visual paradigm would cause the cramming of the characters further leading to increase the crowding effect. One way to decrease the crowding effect is to scale up the size of the character while reducing the number of characters in the matrix paradigm which would provide less degree of freedom to the user due to decrease vocabulary size (Treder & Blankertz, 2010). The crowding effect can be observed in both row/column and checkerboard paradigms to be explained later.

b. *Adjacency Problem*

Adjacency errors occur most frequently in locations which are closer to the target items (Fazel-Rezai, 2007). These errors occur as the non-target items near to target flashes and attract user attention producing P300 which is averaged out with the target items. Adjacency problems can either be reduced by making sure the there is no flash in the non target items adjacent to item or by increasing the gap between the matrix elements as well as reducing the number of character/regions being intensified.

c. *Repetition Blindness*

Repetition blindness is a phenomenon which occurs due to the repetition of the two target items with non target items, causing errors during the detection process (Kanwisher, 1987). Repetition blindness may be due to lack of visual cues in the visual presentation of the paradigms. Visual paradigms with crowding effect may cause errors due to repetition blindness; however repetition blindness is less evident in recent paradigms due to their better visual presentation of stimulus (Townsend et al., 2010).

d. *Fatigue*

Fatigue is one of the causes for error in the BCI-speller programs. After several trials the subjects feels it difficult to keep concentrating due to tiredness. Fatigue can be reduced by innovation in the design of visual paradigms and make it easy for the users. Another way of avoiding fatigue could be reducing the spelling time i.e., by increasing the communication rate for typing.

e. *User Acceptability*

User acceptability is one of the important considerations for a speller program. Different speller paradigms have been proposed to provide more degree of freedom to user during spelling process. Factors such as crowding effect, adjacency problems and repetition blindness are related to the user acceptability.

In the following sections, several paradigms for the P300 generation are discussed.

5.1 Row / Column (RC) paradigm

Farwell and Donchin proposed the first BCI row-column speller in which a user is presented a with six-by-six matrix of alphanumeric characters (Farwell and Donchin, 1988) as shown in Figure 1. These characters are intensified in rows and columns in a random order. The intersection of the target row and column creates the P300 in EEG signals and, therefore, detection of the target character. Due to very low amplitude of the P300 in EEG, the classification of the P300 requires numbers of flashes to achieve high accuracy. It is the most widely discussed and used for P300 BCI. The probability of target being flashed is 0.17 (1/6), which is capable of producing robust a P300 (Polich, 1986; Polich, 1987; Duncan-Johnson & Donchin, 1982).

Fig. 1. Row/column paradigm (Farwell and Donchin, 1988)

The drawback with such system was that the more time required isolating the targets as more flashes are required. However fewer character set would eliminate this problem but limits the vocabulary size. Guger studied the RC paradigm for both P300 and motor imagery-based BCI system and discovered that only 89% of 81 RC subjects spell with accuracy 80-100%, while using motor imagery with 99 subjects, only 19% of subjects were able to achieve 80-100% accuracy (Guger et al., 2009).

5.2 Variations of Row / Column (RC) paradigms

The Farwell and Donchin paradigm has been quite popular among the research groups and have been tested with various configurations. Salvaris investigated modifications in the background color, font size, font style and increasing or decreasing the display area to analyze the classification difference between simple modifications to the visual protocol for the speller (Salvaris & Sepulveda, 2009). They found that although no visual protocol was the best for all subjects, the best performances were obtained with the white background visual protocol and the worst performance was obtained with the small symbol size protocol. Allison further investigated the relationship between the matrix size and EEG measures, detection accuracy and user preferences (Allison & Pineda, 2003). Their results indicated that the larger matrices evoked larger P300 amplitude and the matrix size did not significantly affect the performance or preferences. To further explore that relationship, Sellers manipulated the size of the character matrix and the duration of inter stimulus interval (ISI) between intensifications and concluded that the online accuracy was highest for the 3x3 matrix with 175-ms ISI condition, while the bit rate was highest for the 6x6 matrix 175-ms with ISI condition (Sellers et al., 2006). Guger studied the use of a row-column along with a single character paradigm of the BCI speller over the normal subjects to see the subsequent improvement in the overall accuracy of the system (Guger et al., 2009). Although the row-column paradigm provides more accuracy and bit rate as compared to the single character, Allison and Pineda suggested the multiple flash approaches may be more efficient and faster basis for a P300 BCI system (Allison & Pineda, 2003). Fazel-Rezai investigated adjacency problem in the matrix based P300- speller and suggested redesigning the matrix-based paradigm to remove the human error (Fazel-Rezai, 2007). Townsend et al. presented a checkerboard paradigm which is superior to the row-column paradigm in performance and user acceptability (Townsend et al., 2010). Checkerboard paradigm also eliminated the double flash problem as wells as adjacency problems. However, due to its visual design and increase in the matrix size to 8x9, the row column paradigm is hampered by the crowding effect (Treder & Blankertz, 2010) as the matrix may contains symbols which are hard to pay attention. Hence, it leads to less degree of freedom for the user. Other studies including tactile P300 BCI (Brouwer & Van Erp, 2010), and auditory P300 BCI (Nijboer et al., 2008) stimuli presentation approaches have also been used as an alternative to the present visual approaches.

5.3 Single Character (SC) paradigm

In a single character (SC) paradigm, a character flashes in a random order individually. Guger compared both SC and RC paradigm (Guger et al., 2009) and results suggests that only 55.3% (N=38) were able to spell with 100% accuracy in SC paradigm as compared to the 72.3% (N=81) of the subjects were able to spell with 100% accuracy in the RC paradigm.

Fig. 2. Single character paradigm (Guger et.al., 2009)

5.4 Checkerboard (CRB) Paradigm

The checkerboard paradigm (CBP) is originally based on the idea of using RCP in a checkerboard style. This eliminates the errors like adjacency problems and double flash. However it could be prone to the crowding effect as that of found in single character (SC) (Townsend et al., 2010).

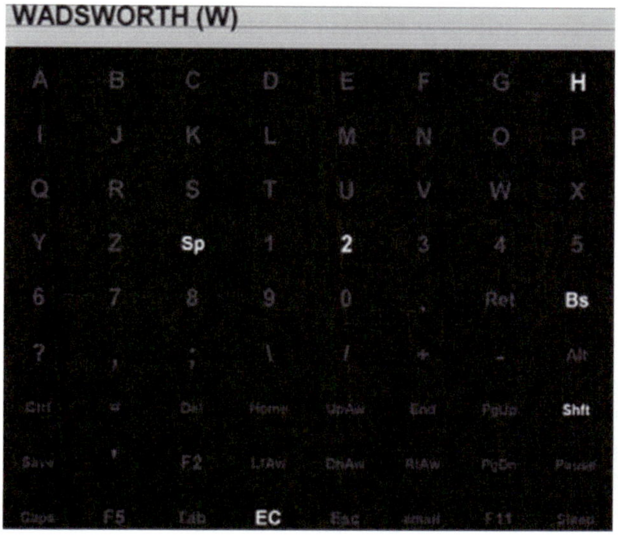

Fig. 3. Checkerboard paradigm of 8 x 9 matrix (Townsend et.al., 2010)

5.5 Region-based paradigm

In the region based (RB) paradigm (Fazel-Rezai & Abhari, 2009), seven sets of characters arranged into seven different regions in level 1 as shown in Figure 4. These regions are intensified to the user in random order. After successful selection of a region, characters in the selected region are again subdivided into seven regions consisting of single characters in level 2. The single characters are again intensified in a random order to find the particular character. The 7-region paradigm not only provides more input character set, but also reduces the crowding effect and adjacency problem. In this section, we discuss two

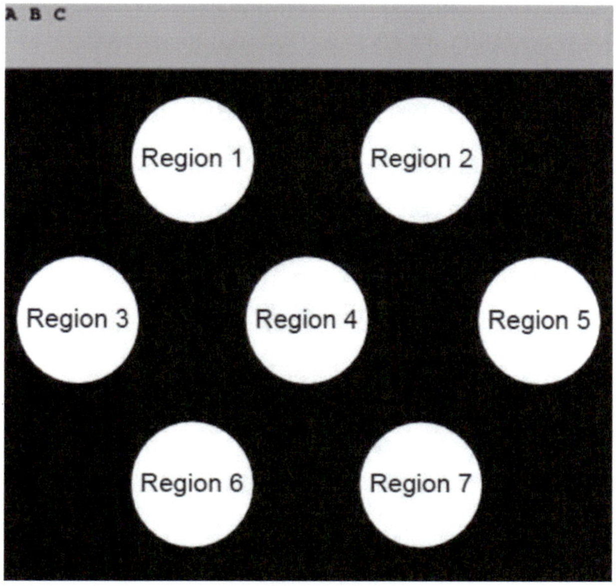

Fig. 4. Location of seven regions in the RB paradigm

variations of RB paradigm (RB1 and RB2). In RB1 paradigm, characters are placed in seven regions in alphabetical orders. However, in RB2, the frequency of characters usage (Zim, 1948; Lewand, 2000) was considered in distributing them into regions. Characters with close probability of usage were placed in one region. The list of characters used in seven regions in RB1 and RB2 paradigms in level 1 is shown in Table 1. In level 2, each region consists of only one character from the selected region in level 1.

	RB1 Paradigm	*RB2 Paradigm*
Region 1	A B C D E F G	E T A O N R I
Region 2	H I J K L M N	S H D L F C M
Region 3	O P Q R S T U	U G Y P W B V
Region 4	V W X Y Z 1 2	K X J Q Z 1 2
Region 5	3 4 5 6 7 8 9	3 4 5 6 7 8 9
Region 6	0 / * - + . ?	0 / * - + . ?
Region 7	" ! @ # $ % &	" ! @ # $ % &

Table 1. List of characters in each region in level 1 of RB1 and RB2 paradigms.

6. A Comparison among SC, RC and RB Paradigms

In this section, we present results obtained by the BRAIN (Biomedical research And INnovation) team in the Biomedical Signal Processing Laboratory, the University of North Dakota.

6.1 Experiments

The experiments were approved by the Internal Review Board (IRB-201006-372) at University of North Dakota. Six subjects (all males, between 20 to 25 years old) participated in the experiment. Each participant completed four experimental paradigms in a random order and three trails were taken for each session. All the subjects were asked to spell two words (WATER and LUCAS). Products of g.tec (Guger Technologies, Austria) including g.GAMMAbox and g.USBamp for recording and g.BSanalysis for classification were used. Six flashes with flash time 100 ms and blank time of 60 ms were considered. EEG signals were recorded from eight channels at FZ, CZ, PZ, OZ, P3, P4, PO7, and PO8 locations. An electrode at the FPZ location was considered as a ground channel and one electrode on the right earlobe was considered as a reference channel. Data was sampled with a frequency of 256 Hz and filtered by a 0.1 Hz highpass, a 30 Hz lowpass filter. Linear discriminant analysis (LDA) was used for classification purpose.

6.2 Results

The results for two target characters 'WATER' and 'LUCAS' to find the corresponding accuracy for each phrase for six subjects. We then find the combined averaged accuracy for both phrases against each user and plotted as Fig. 4. A summary of individual accuracies can be seen in Table 2.

The graph in Figure 5 shows the combined average accuracy for the two words for each user as shown in the last row of Table 2. It can be seen from the graph that the average accuracy for RB1 and RB2 is greater than that of RC and SC.

Subjects	Paradigms RC		SC		RB1		RB2	
	WATER	LUCAS	WATER	LUCAS	WATER	LUCAS	WATER	LUCAS
Subject 1	93.3	100	73.3	66.7	100	86.7	96.7	96.7
Subject 2	93.3	73.3	53.3	46.7	93.3	76.7	96.7	80
Subject 3	100	100	93.3	100	100	100	100	100
Subject 4	93.3	60	93.3	66.7	100	100	96.7	93.3
Subject 5	60	53.3	60	46.7	83.3	83.3	96.7	86.7
Subject 6	93.3	100	86.7	86.7	93.3	96.7	96.7	100
Average	88.9	81.1	76.7	68.9	95.0	90.6	97.3	92.8
	85		72.8		92.8		95.1	

Table 2. Accuracy (in percentage) of spelling two words (WATER and LUCAS) for four paradigms.

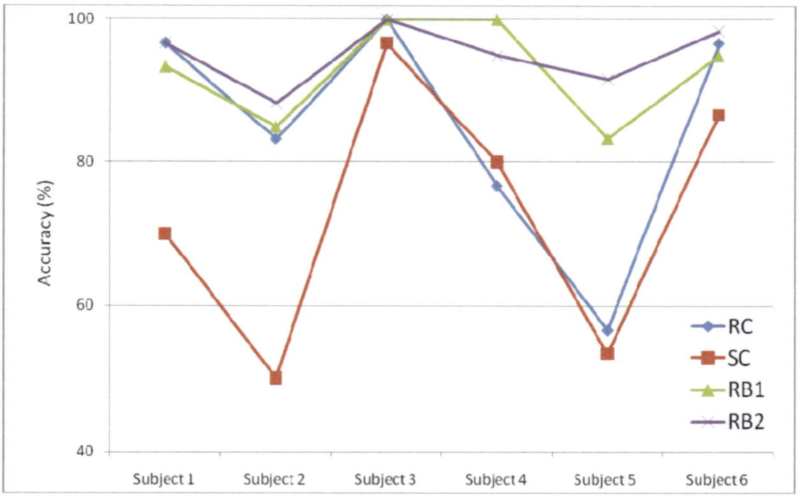

Fig. 5. Average accuracy for two phrases for six subject in four paradigms

The overall improvement in accuracy for the RB paradigms is much better for this set of subjects with minimal training and no prior experience with RB paradigm. Furthermore, fewer numbers of errors were reported as compared to RC and SC paradigms. However, RC paradigm reported less number of errors as compared to that of SC paradigm. We also determine the user acceptability for all four paradigms and a questionnaire was filled out by the subjects at the end of experiment. Users rated on a scale from 1 to 10, where 1 is lowest and 10 is highest, for parameters such as level of fatigue and difficulty to use the paradigm. The level of fatigue was highest for SC paradigm and found lowest for RB1. However, RB2 showed more fatigue among the users as compared to that of RC. One might attribute this due to most frequently use characters were placed in RB1. However, there is a substantial improvement in user acceptability in terms of difficulty to use parameter as asked in the questionnaire. Subjects found RB1 most easy to use while RB2 was rated as second highest. Both RC and RB1 have marginal difference, but SC rated as most difficult to use as shown in Fig. 6.

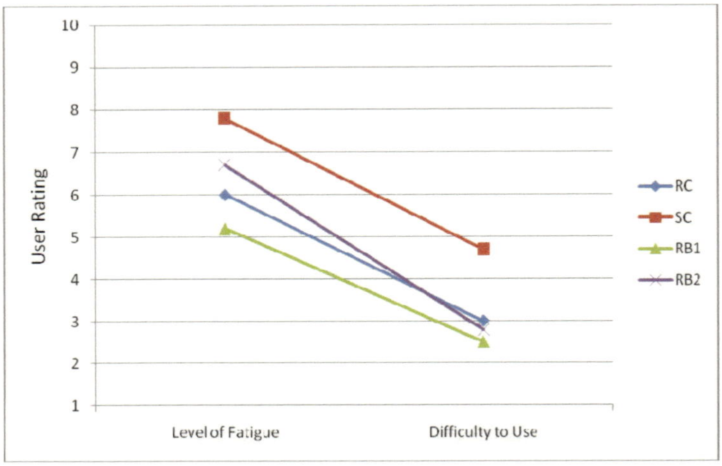

Fig. 6. Average of two parameters rated from 1-10 by six users for all four paradigms.

6.3 Region accuracy

We further extended our experiments to find out which one of regions had lesser probability of errors. This will help us to place the most frequently characters in the regions with the least probability of error. This will further reduce the probability of error as less frequently used characters can be fit into the high error region as compared to most frequently characters. For that purpose, another experiment was performed to determine and analyze the accuracy rate for each region. We have used the same experiment method and material as described in Section 6.1. A single set of seven characters i.e., ABCDEFG was considered for all the seven regions, so that each user has same set in each region. This helps us to compare the error for each region.

Twenty random trials were performed for each individual user. The results are shown in Fig. 7. It shows the total errors occurred for each individual region. It can be seen from that graph that maximum number of errors occurs for region 4 which is located in the center in RB paradigm.

Fig. 7. Total number of errors for each region for 5 subjects

7. Future trends in research

P300-based BCI can be very helpful to the people with neuromuscular disorder. BRAIN team at the Biomedical Signal Processing Laboratory, the University of North Dakota is working further to improve the overall accuracy and user acceptability of the BCI speller program. It is planned to further improve the results by incorporating more subject data. Further research on RB paradigms is going on to make it more robust and easy to use for the subjects.

8. Acknowledgment

We would like to thank Scott Gavett and Eric Schneider for their help in developing the test programs. Financial support from ND EPSCoR through National Science Foundation Grant #EPS-0814442 is gratefully acknowledged.

9. References

Allison, B. Z. & Pineda, J. A. (2003). ERPs evoked by different matrix sizes: implications for a brain computer interface (BCI) system. *IEEE Trans Neural Syst Rehabil,* Vol. 11, pp. 110-3.

Allison, B. Z. & Pineda, J. A. (2006). Effects of SOA and flash pattern manipulations on ERPs, performance, and preference: Implications for a BCI system. *International Journal of Psychophysiology* Vol. *59, No. 2,* pp. 127-140.

Bernat, E.; Shevrin, H. & Snodgrass, M. (2001). Subliminal visual oddball stimuli evoke a P300 component. *Clinical Neurophysiology*, Vol. 112, pp. 159-171.

Blankertz, B.; Curio, G. & Müller, K.R. (2002). Classifying single trial EEG: Towards brain computer interfacing, In T. G. Dietterich, S. Becker, and Z. Ghahramani, editors, *Advances in neural information processing systems 14*, Cambridge, MA, 2002, MIT Press.

Bostanov, V. (2004). BCI competition 2003-data sets Ib and IIb: feature extraction from event-related brain potentials with the continuous wavelet transform and the t-value scalogram, *IEEE Trans. Biomed. Eng.* Vol. 51 pp. 1057-61

Bouma, H. (1970). Interaction effects in parafoveal letter recognition. *Nature* Vol. 226, pp. 177-178.

Brouwer, A. M.; Van Erp, J. B. F. & Brouwer, A. M. (2010). A tactile P300 brain-computer interface. *Frontiers in Neuroscience* Vol. 4, No. 19, pp. 1-12

Cacioppo, J.T.; Petty, R. E.; Losch, M. E. & Crites, S. L. (1994). Psychophysiological approaches to attitudes: Detecting affective dispositions when people won't say, can't say, or don't even know. In S. Shavitt & T. C. Brock (Eds.), *Persuasion: Psychological Insights and Perspectives*, pp 43-69. Boston: Allyn & Bacon.

Comerchero, M. D. & Polich, J. (1999). P3a and P3b from typical auditory and visual stimuli, *Clinical Neurophysiology* Vol. 110, pp. 24-30.

Courchesne, E.; Hillyard, S.A. & Galambos, R. (1975). Stimulus novelty, task relevance and the visual evoked potential in man *Electroenceph. clin. Neurophysiol.*, Vol. 39, pp. 131-143.

Courchesne, E.; Kilman, B. A.; Galambos, R. & Lincoln, A. (1984). Autism processing of novel auditory information assessed by event-related brain potentials. *Electroenceph. clin. Neurophysiol.*, Vol. 59, pp. 238–248.

Donchin, E. & Smith, D. B. (1970). The contingent negative variation and the late positive wave of the average evoked potential. *Electroenceph clin Neurophysiol;* Vol. 29, pp. 201–203.

Donchin, E.; Spencer, K. M. & Wijesinghe, R. (2000). The mental prosthesis: assessing the speed of a P300-based brain-computer interface *IEEE Trans. Rehabil. Eng.* Vol. 8, pp. 174–9

Farwell, L. A. & Donchin, E. (1988). Talking off the top of your head: toward a mental prothesis utilizing event-related brain potentials. *Electroenceph clin Neurophysiol* Vol. 70 pp. 510–523.

Farwell, L. A. & Donchin, E. (1991). The truth will out : Interogative ploygraphy ("lie detection") with event-related brain potentials. *Psycholophysiology*, Vol. 28, pp. 531-47.

Farwell, L. A., (1995). Method and apparatus for truth detection, *Patent number: 5406956;* Filing date: Feb 11, 1993; Issue date: Apr 18.

Farwell, L. A. & Smith, S. S, (2001). Using brain MERMER testing to detect concealed knowledge despite efforts to conceal, *Journal of Forensic Sciences* Vol. 46, No. 1, pp. 1-9.

Fazel-Rezai, R. (2007). Human error in p300 speller paradigm for brain-computer interface. *The 29th Annual International Conference of the IEEE Engineering in Medicine and Biology Society*, Lyon, France.

Fazel-Rezai, R. & Abhari, K. A region-based P300 speller for brain-computer interface. *Canadian Journal of Electrical and Computer Engineering*, Vol. 34, No. 3, pp. 81-85.

Fazel-Rezai, R. (2009). P300-based speller brain-computer interface, in Recent Advances in Biomedical Engineering, Naik, G. R. Editor, IN-TECH: Austria, pp. 137-148.

Feng, C.; Jiang, Y. & He, S. (2007). Horizontal and vertical asymmetry in visual spatial crowding effects. *Journal of Vision* Vol. 7, No. 2, pp. 1-10.

Gonsalvez, C. J. & Polich, J. (2002). P300 amplitude is determined by target-to-target interval. *Psychophysiology*, Vol. 39, pp. 388–396.

Guger, C.; Daban, S.; Sellers, E.; Holzner, C.; Krausz, G.; Carabalona, R.; Gramatica, F; & Edlinger, G. (2009). How many people are able to control a P300-based brain-computer interface (BCI). *Neurosci. Lett.* Vol. 462, No. 1, pp. 94-98.

Guger, C.; Holzner, C.; Grönegress, C.; Edlinger, G. & Slater, M. (2009). Brain–computer interface for virtual reality control. *Proceedings of ESANN* 2009, pp. 443–448.

Huang, A. & Zhou, W. (2008). BLDA approach for classifying P300 potential, *7th Asian-Pacific Conference on Medical and Biological Engineering,* Springer, pp. 341.

Kanwisher, N.G. (1987). Repetition blindness: type recognition without token individuation. *Cognition,* Vol. 27, pp. 117–143.

Kanwisher, N.G. (1991). Repetition blindness and illusory conjunctions: errors in binding visual types with visual tokens. *J. Exp. Psychol. Hum. Percept. Perform.* Vol. 17, pp. 404–421.

Kaper, M., Meinicke, P., Grossekathoefer, U., Lingner, T. & Ritter H. (2004). BCI competition 2003—Data set IIb: Support vector machines for the P300 speller paradigm, in *IEEE Trans. Biomed. Eng.*, Vol. 51, pp. 1073–1076.

Knight, R.T. (1984). Decreased response to novel stimuli after prefrontal lesions in man. *Electroenceph. clin. Neurophysiol.,* Vol. 59, pp. 9–20.

Krusienski, D.; Sellers, E.; Cabesing, F.; Bayoudh, S.; McFarland, D.; Vaughan, T. & Wolpaw, J. (2006). A comparaison of classification techniques for the P300 speller. *Journal of Neural Engineering,* Vol. 6, pp. 229-305.

Lewand, R. (2000). *Cryptological mathematics,* The Mathematical Association of America. ISBN 978-0883857199.

Mirghasemi, H.; Fazel-Rezai, R. & Shamsollahi, M. B. (2006). Analysis of P300 classifiers in brain computer interface speller, in *Proc. Annu. Int. IEEE EMBS Conf.* 2006, pp. 6205-6208.

Müller, K.-R.; Mika, S.; Rätsch, G.; Tsuda, K. & Schölkopf, B. (2001). An introduction to kernel-based learning algorithms, *IEEE Transactions on Neural Networks,* Vol. 12, No. 2, pp. 181–201.

Mugler, E.; Bensch, M.; Halder, S.; Rosenstiel, W.; Bogdan, M.; Birbaumer, N.; & K¨ubler, A., (2008). Control of an Internet browser using the P300 event-related potential. *Int. J. Bioelectromagn.,* Vol. 10, No. 1, pp. 56–63.

Nijboer, F.; Furdea, A.; Gunst, I.; Mellinger, J.; McFarland, D. J.; Birbaumer, N. & Kübler A. (2008). An auditory brain-computer interface (BCI). *J. Neurosci. Methods* Vol. 167, No. 1, pp. 43-50.

Ramanna, S. & Fazel-Rezai, R. (2007). A robust P300 detection based on rough sets. *Transactions on Rough Sets,* Vol. 5 pp. 207-223

Salvaris, M. & Sepulveda, F. (2009). Visual modifications on the P300 speller BCI paradigm. *Journal of Neural Engineering* Vol. 6 pp. 046011.

Sellers, E. W.; Krusienski, D. J.; McFarland, D. J.; Vaughan, T. M. & Wolpaw, J. R. (2006). A P300 event-related potential brain-computer interface (BCI): The effects of matrix size and inter stimulus interval on performance. *Biol. Psychol.* Vol. 73, No. 3, pp. 242-252.

Serby, H.; Yom-Tov, E. & Inbar, G. F. (2005). An improved P300-based brain-computer interface. *IEEE Trans. Neur. Syst. Rehabil. Eng,.* Vol. 13, pp. 89–98.

Sirvent, J.; Azorín, J.; Iáñez, E.; Úbeda, A. & Fernández, E. (2010). P300-Based Brain-Computer Interface for Internet Browsing. *Trends in Practical Applications of Agents and Multiagent Systems,* pp. 615-622.

Soltana, M. & Knight, R. (2000). Neural origins of the P300. *Critical Reviews in Neurobiology,* Vol. 14, No. 3, pp. 199-224.

Squires, N.K.; Squires, K.C. & Hillyard, S.A. (1975). Two varieties of longlatency positive waves evoked by unpredictable auditory stimuli in man. *Electroenceph. clin. Neurophysiol.,* Vol. 38, pp. 387–401.

Strasburger, H. (2005). Unfocussed spatial attention underlies the crowding effect in indirect form vision. *Journal of Vision,* Vol. 5, No. 11, pp. 1024-37.

Sutton, S.; Braren, M.; Zubin, J. & John, E. R. (1965). Evoked correlates of stimulus uncertainty. *Science,* Vol. 150, pp. 1187–1188.

Toet, A. & Levi, D. M. (1992). The two-dimensional shape of spatial interaction zones in the parafovea. *Vision Res.,* Vol. 32, No. 7, pp. 1349-1357.

Townsend, G.; LaPallo, B.; Boulay, C.; Krusienski, D.; Frye, G.; Hauser, C.; Schwartz, N.; Vaughan, T.; Wolpaw, J. & Sellers, E. (2010). A novel P300-based brain–computer interface stimulus presentation paradigm: Moving beyond rows and columns. *Clinical Neurophysiology* Vol. 121(7), pp. 1109-1120.

Thulasidas, M.; Guan, C.; & Wu, J. (2006). Robust classification of EEG signal for brain computer interface. *IEEE Transactions on Neural Systems and Rehabilitation Engineering* Vol. 14, No. 1, pp. 24–29

Treder, M. & Blankertz, B. (2010). (C)overt attention and visual speller design in an ERP-based brain-computer interface. *Behavioral and Brain Functions* Vol. 6, pp. 28 doi:10.1186/1744-9081-6-28

Vapnik, V. (1995). *The nature of statistical learning theory*. Springer Verlag, New York.

Walter, W. G.; Cooper, R.; Aldridge, V. J.; McCallum, W.C. & Winter, A. L. (1964). Contingent negative variation: an electric sign of sensorimotor association and expectancy in the human brain. *Nature*, Vol. 203, pp. 380–384.

Wolpaw, J. R.; Birbaumer, N.; Heetderks, W. J.; McFarland, D. J.; Peckham, P. H.; Schalk, G.; Donchin, E.; Quatrano, L. A.; Robinson, C. J.; & Vaughan, T. M. (2000). Brain-computer interface technology: A review of the first international meeting IEEE *Transactions on Rehabilitation Engineering*, Vol. 8, No. 2, pp. 164-173.

Xu, N.; Gao, X.; Hong, B.; Miao, X.; Gao, S. & Yang, F. (2004). BCI competition 2003 Data Set IIb: Enhancing P300 wave detection using ICA-based subspace projections for BCI applications. *IEEE Trans. Biomed. Eng.* Vol. 51, No. 6, pp.1067- 1072.

Yamaguchi, S. & Knight, R.T. (1991). P300 generation by novel somatosensory stimuli. *Electroenceph. clin. Neurophysiol.*, Vol. 78, pp. 50–55.

Zim, H. (1948). *Codes and secret writing*. New York: Morrow.

5

Brain Computer Interface Based on the Flash Onset and Offset Visual Evoked Potentials

Po-Lei Lee[1,2], Yu-Te Wu[2], Kuo-Kai Shyu[1] and Jen-Chuen Hsieh[2]
[1]*Department of Electrical Engineering, National Central University,*
[2]*Institute of Brain Science, National Yang-Ming University,*
Taiwan

1. Introduction

Severe motor disabilities can limit one's ability in communication, especially for patients suffering from amyotrophic lateral sclerosis (ALS), severe cerebral palsy, head trauma, multiple sclerosis, and muscular dystrophies who are incapable of conveying their intentions (locked-in syndrome) to the external environment. For the last several decades, a considerable amount of research effort has been devoted towards the development of novel communication techniques which are independent of peripheral nerves and muscles. One promising method is the use of neural activities, for example, electroencephalography (EEG) or intracortical neural activities, arising from the human brain, as control or communication signals. Such techniques are referred to as 'brain computer interfaces' (BCIs) (Wolpaw et al., 2000).

Several EEG-based BCI systems have been developed with elaborately designed paradigms to induce endogenous or exogenous neuroelectric signals which were detected and translated into control signals for communication purposes. Endogenous BCI communicates with environments independent of sensatory responses or muscles which enable users to control external environments directly. For examples, Pfurtscheller et al. (2000) measured sensorimotor mu rhythms during subject's imagery movements and achieved a high recognition rate of 90%; Blankertz et al. (2007) constructed Berlin Brain-Computer Interface (BBCI) with high ITR (>35 bits/min) based on detections of the modulations of sensorimotor rhythms due to motor imagery; Birbaumer et al. (1999) developed a Thought Translation Device (TTD) to measure slow cortical potentials (SCPs) for a binary selection task; Mason & Birch (2000) designed an asynchronous detector to control a binary switch by using the detected motor-related potentials (MRPs) filtered within 1-4 Hz. However, the ITRs of endogenous BCIs are relatively low (between 5 and 25 bits/min) because the performance of translation algorithm in extracting reliable features can be easily degraded by the undesired characteristics of neuroelectric signals, such as artifacts, task-unrelated EEG, and large variability in latencies. Besides, the subjects participated in the endogenous BCIs usually require extensive training for generating specific patterns. The exogenous BCIs, on the contrary, require parts of user's sensation ability involved in a stimulating environment to induce sensatory neurophysiological activities, such as P300-based (Donchin et al., 2000; Meinicke et al., 2003), VEP (visual evoked potential)-based (Lee et al., 2005; Lee et al., 2006; Sutter, 1992), SSVEP (steady-state visual evoked potential)-based (Cheng et al., 2002; Cheng et al., 2006; Kelly et al.,2005; Middendorf et al., 2000; Trejo et al. 2006) and SSSEP (steady-state somatosensory evoked potential)-based systems (Muller-Putz et al., 2006). Neurophysiological activities induced from sensation inputs are self-regulated by the users with specific patterns which can be easily distinguished to achieve high ITRs (>25 bits/min). Especially, the ITRs of P300-based and VEP-based BCIs can be as high as 50.5 bits/min (Meinicke et al., 2003) and 43 bits/min (Wang et al, 2006), respectively, with the aid of support vector machine and bipolar channel design.

BCI systems with high information transfer rates (ITRs) require fast-responding bio-signals and a reliable translation algorithm to convert such signals into control commands. Visual stimulation using flashes of light is a popular and easy means to elicit flash visual evoked potentials (FVEPs) with short latencies short enough to be useful in a BCI. Specifically, FVEP manifests four major peaks: N1, P1, N2, and P2, with latencies less than 200 ms after flash onset or offset (Spehlmann, 1985). In the present study, an exogenous BCI system was developed for users who have sensitive visual acuity (e.g., users are capable of distinguishing two objects in space with 3° visual angle apart). The proposed BCI was constructed based on the central flash FVEPs, which were induced from abrupt light onsets and offsets, to generate control signals with high ITR. When the subjects pay their attention on the target and according to the neural connections and interactions of the route from the retina to the primary visual cortex, visual stimuli at central visual fields can generate the so-called 'cortical magnification' which makes the central FVEPs more prominent than any FVEPs evoked from peripheral visual fields (Odom et al., 2004; Sutter, 1992). In order to remove the contamination of peripheral FVEPs from central FVEPs, we designed flickering sequences with mutually independent flash onsets (or offsets) generated by random ON and OFF durations. Since FVEP in human visual cortex is time-locked and phase-locked to the timing of flash onset (or offset) (Spehlmann, 1985), EEG data segmented based on the flash onset (or offset) timing of one chosen flickering sequence will contain time-locked FVEPs of the chosen flickering sequence mixed with non-time-locked FVEPs induced from other flickering sequences. By applying a simple averaging process, the intentionally manipulated time-locked and non-time-locked properties conduce the time-locked FVEPs to being enhanced concurrently with the suppression of non-time-locked FVEPs. After comparing the averaged onset and offset responses and referring to the characteristic of "cortical magnification", the stimulus producing the onset and offset FVEPs with the largest peak-to-valley features was identified as the gazed target. The flickering sequences with mutually independent flash onsets (or offsets) will be termed as "mutually independent flickering sequences" in the followings for convenience purpose.

Some other VEP-based BCI systems have been proposed in recent years. Two of them were gaze-dependent systems, one was based on the fast multifocal visual evoked potential (FMFVEP) (Sutter, 1992) and the other on the steady-state visual evoked potential (SSVEP) (Cheng et al., 2002). The flickering stimuli of FMFVEP-based system were generated by a pseudo-random binary sequence with a fixed time lag between any two adjacent channels. Each entire pseudo-random sequence was convoluted with a standard VEP response to create a so-called "expected response". By finding the maximum correlation between the measured EEG signals and the expected response of each flickering stimulus, the gazed stimulus was recognized. Instead of using a binary sequence with fixed flickering frequency, each stimulus in the SSVEP-based system was designed to have its own flickering frequency. The gazed target was identified by finding the stimulus which contributes maximum power of SSVEP at Fourier spectrum. However, there are limitations in these two gaze-dependent systems. The FMFVEP-based method presumed identical response of VEP across all trials and used it as template in correlation computation (Sutter, 1992). Such a stringent assumption was irreconcilable with the truth (Jung et al., 2001; Tang et al., 2002) and the resultant correlation may not be optimal in detecting the gazed target. In the SSVEP-based method, the flickering frequencies were confined to be lower than 14 Hz due to the frame rate of PC monitor, and flickering frequencies around alpha band should also be excluded to avoid the interference of spontaneous alpha rhythm (Salmelin and Hari, 1994). These two constraints may reduce the available flickering channels and communication bandwidth.

Another type of VEP-based BCI system requests users to pay attention to flickering stimuli for regulating the SSVEP responses (Kelly et al., 2005; Trejo et al., 2006). The operation of such attention-regulated SSVEP systems is independent of eye movements, which is suitable for users who have well-preserved visual acuity but are incapable of moving their eyes. Nevertheless, the attention-regulated SSVEP systems are usually designed with few flickering channels (FCs) since too many FCs may distract user's attention and result in poor performance. Besides, attention maintenance in operating the system relies on user's experience and it usually requires users to take a training procedure (e.g., 3 minutes) before they can achieve accuracies higher than 80% (Trejo et al., 2006). Another problem is the evaluation of system performance. Owing to the inter-individual variations on attention maintenance and time lag for successful attention modulation, Trejo et al. (2006) reported that the lag for each attention modulated SSVEP was in a range of 1~5 seconds which limited the bandwidth of ITR.

The current system, originated from our previous BCI work in which only the flash-onset induced VEP was employed (Lee et al., 2005; Lee et al., 2006), was designed by taking the additional distinguishable feature from offset FVEP into account, not only to improve the detection accuracy of gazed stimuli but also achieve better ITR.

2. Materials and methods

2.1 Visual stimuli and task

The visual stimuli were presented on a 17-inch ViewSonic LCD monitor (model VG724; reaction time < 3 ms; 60 frames/s) with a distance of 40~50 centimeters away from the viewer. The full screen was partitioned into several flickering channels. Each flickering channel (FC) was designed to be a rectangle (subtended angle = 3°) overlaid with a small cross-hair and driven by a flickering sequence consisting of alternative ON and OFF (illumination-extinction) states. The small cross hairs were used to draw subjects' attention so that subjects could fixate their gaze at the centers of the FCs. The luminance of ON and OFF state in each FC were 168.7 candelas (cd/m2) and 8.1 cd/m2, respectively, measured by a luminance meter (LS-110; Konica Minolta Photo Imaging Inc., USA) resulting in Michelson contrast of 90.3 %. Duration of each ON or OFF state was a concatenation of two segments, one with a fixed length of 116.7 ms (7 frames) and the other with a variable length which was uniformly distributed between 0 ms and 233.3 ms (0~14 frames). In other words, the duration of each ON or OFF state was between 116.7 and 350 ms and its mean is 233.3 ms. Of note is that the fixed duration was designed to prevent the major visual response of current onset or offset FVEP overlapped with the incoming offset or onset FVEP, and the random duration was used to generate temporal independence of flash onsets (or offsets) among different flickering sequences (see Discussion section).

To demonstrate the stability and applicability of the proposed FVEP system, one control study and one application study were designed and tested. In the control study, 25 FCs, namely from FC-1 to FC-25, were presented in an arrangement of 5×5 grid (see Fig. 1A). Subjects were asked to gaze binocularly at the center of each FC for one-minute recording. In the application study, 12 flickering channels were displayed as a pseudo telephone keypad consisting of ten digits '0-9', one Backspace 'B' and one Enter 'E' (see Fig. 1B). The Backspace 'B' was reserved for the future use of correcting error input and was not used in the study. Subjects were asked to stare at the target stimuli one by one until the most prominent central onset and offset FVEPs could be detected for the identification of gazed stimulus. A representative digit or a letter was sent out right after recognition of gazed-stimulus. All subjects were instructed to complete a string: 0287513694E.

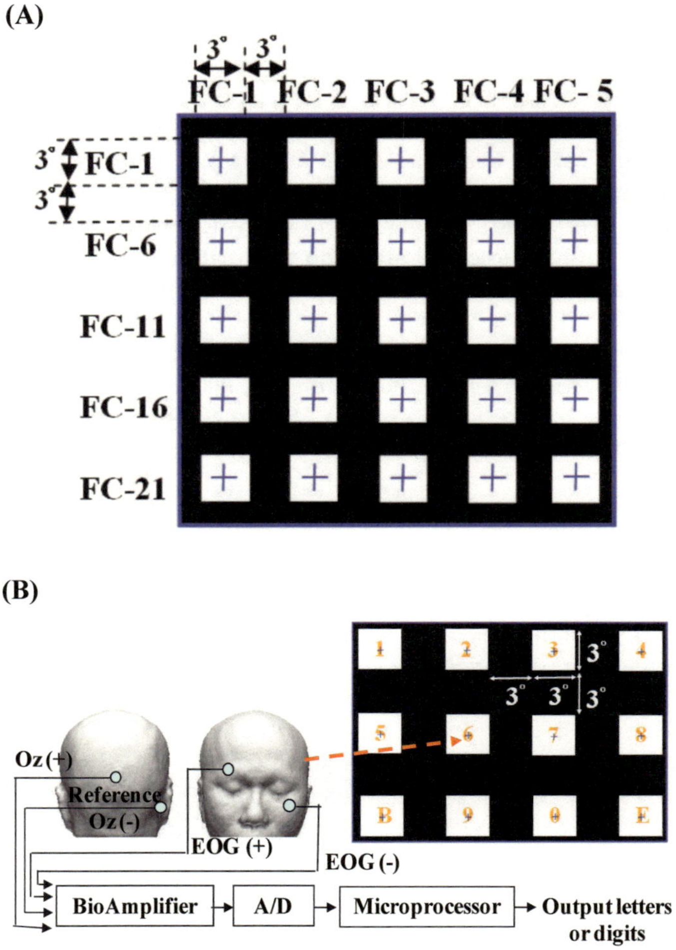

Fig. 1. The visual stimuli used in inducing onset and offset FVEPs. (A) 25 flickering channels, labeled by FC-1, ..., FC-25, were presented in a 5×5 grid in the control study. (B) 12 flickering channels were designed as a pseudo telephone keypad consisting of 10 digits '0-9', one Backspace 'B' and one Enter 'E' in the application study. One EEG channel at the Oz position and the other reference electrode at the right mastoid were utilized.

2.2 Subjects and EEG recordings

Five healthy volunteers (three males and two females), ages from 25 to 32 years, were recruited to participate in our studies. Each subject had corrected Snellen visual acuity of 6/6 or better, with no history of clinical visual disease. All subjects gave informed consent, and the study was approved by the Ethics Committee of Institutional Review Board, Taipei Veterans General Hospital, Taiwan. Two of the five subjects (Subject I and II both were male) had one-hour experience in this visual stimulation task while the other three were naïve subjects. VEPs were recorded with a whole-head 40-channel EEG system (bandpass, 0.05-50 Hz; digitized at 250 Hz; Nu Amplifier; Neuroscan Inc., USA), while subjects sat on a comfortable armchair in a dimly illuminated room. Two out of the 40 EEG channels were respectively used as bipolar horizontal and vertical electro-oculograms (EOG); one was placed below and above the left eye and the other at the bilateral outer canthi. The signals recorded from two additional electrodes placed on left and right mastoids were averaged and used as the reference to all EEG channels. The inter-electrode impedances were kept below 5 KΩ during recording. It should be noted that the use of whole-head EEG recording in the control study is only for demonstration purpose. In the application study, only one EEG channel was placed at the Oz position (Fisch & Spehlmann, 1999) and another one reference electrode at the right mastoid (see Fig. 1B), rather than using the whole-head EEG. An additional bipolar electroculargraphy (EOG) channel was placed on the upper site of right eye and the lower site of the left eye to monitor eye movements. The threshold level for rejecting artifact-contaminated epochs was set at 100 μV in both control and application studies. The EEG recordings were bandpass filtered, within 0.1-50 Hz, to remove 60 Hz and low-frequency drifts, followed by digitization (NI-PCI 6071E, National Instruments). All the aforementioned computations and signal processing procedures presented in the following sections were implemented by the LabVIEW software (National Instruments, USA) to achieve on-line analysis.

2.3 Peak-to-valley amplitudes Amp_{onset} and Amp_{offset} in the onset and offset FVEPs

In our study, the flickering stimuli are driven by flickering sequences with ON and OFF alternative states. The FVEPs, induced by flash onsets and offsets, referring to onset FVEP and offset FVEP, respectively, were measured and used as features for detecting gazed stimuli. Both the onset and offset FVEPs have two major negative and two positive peaks within 200 ms after flash onset and offset (Spehlmann, 1985), which were termed as $N1_{onset}$, $P1_{onset}$, $N2_{onset}$, and $P2_{onset}$ in onset FVEP (see Fig. 2A and 2C) and $N1_{offset}$, $P1_{offset}$, $N2_{offset}$, and $P2_{offset}$ in offset FVEP (see Fig. 2B and 2D), respectively. Topographies in subject I (see Fig. 2E and 2F) and subject III (see Fig. 2G and 2H) also demonstrated that the $P2_{onset}$ and $P1_{offset}$ were induced from occipital areas. In normal subjects, the $N2_{onset}$ and $P2_{onset}$ peaks were usually the most robust (Spehlmann, 1985; Odom et al., 2004). The amplitude difference between $N2_{onset}$ and $P2_{onset}$ peaks, denoted by Amp_{onset}, and that between $N1_{offset}$ and $P1_{offset}$ peaks, denoted by Amp_{offset}, were calculated and their sum, Amp_{onset}+Amp_{offset}, was used for detecting gazed stimulus. Examples of the onset and offset FVEPs from two subjects were shown in Fig. 2. The latencies of $N2_{onset}$, $P2_{onset}$, $N1_{offset}$, and $P1_{offset}$ peaks were represented by $t_{\_onset\_n2}$, $t_{\_onset\_p2}$, $t_{\_offset\_n1}$, and $t_{\_offset\_p1}$, respectively (see Fig. 2C and 2D). Because the presence of the latencies of $N2_{onset}$, $P2_{onset}$, $N1_{offset}$, and $P1_{offset}$ peaks could vary from trial to trial during experiments, the four peaks were searched in a time window by extending ±15 ms (Lee et al., 2006) around the timing of the peaks (illustrated by shaded windows in Fig. 2C and 2D) obtained from the control study.

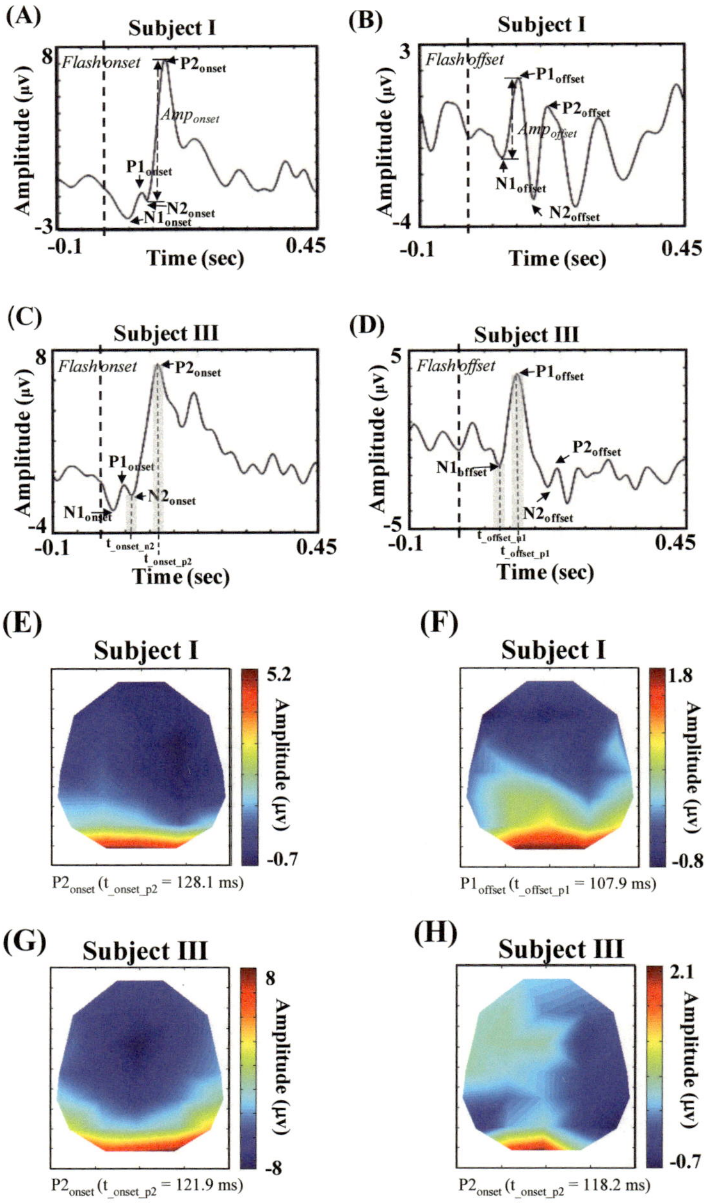

Fig. 2. Examples of the measured onset and offset FVEPs. Both the onset and offset FVEPs have two major negative and two positive peaks within 200 ms after flash onset and offset, termed as $N1_{onset}$, $P1_{onset}$, $N2_{onset}$, and $P2_{onset}$ in onset FVEP and $N1_{offset}$, $P1_{offset}$, $N2_{offset}$, and $P2_{offset}$ in offset FVEP, respectively, which are all marked by arrows. (A) the onset FVEP in subject I. (B) the offset FVEP in subject I. (C) the onset FVEP in subject III. (D) the offset FVEP of subject III. The shaded areas are the time windows used for searching $N2_{onset}$, and $P2_{onset}$, $N1_{offset}$, and $P1_{offset}$. (E) the topography of $P2_{onset}$ in subject I. (F) the topography of $P1_{offset}$ in subject I. (G) the topography of $P2_{onset}$ in subject III. (H) the topography of $P1_{offset}$ in subject III.

2.4 Determination of gazed target by detecting the largest $Amp_{onset}+Amp_{offset}$ among the averaged responses of all flickering channels

The EEG recordings at Oz were inevitably contaminated by peripheral onset and offset FVEPs induced from non-target visual stimuli. Since FVEPs are time-locked and phase-locked to the visual stimulus (Sutter, 1992), onset and offset FVEPs induced from the central visual field are synchronized to the flash onsets and offsets of the gazed flickering stimulus, respectively. Peripheral visual responses that are asynchronous to the flash onsets and offsets of central visual stimulus can be suppressed using a simple averaging process. By comparing the averaged onset and offset responses, the stimulus producing the onset and offset FVEPs with the largest peak-to-valley features was identified as the gazed target.

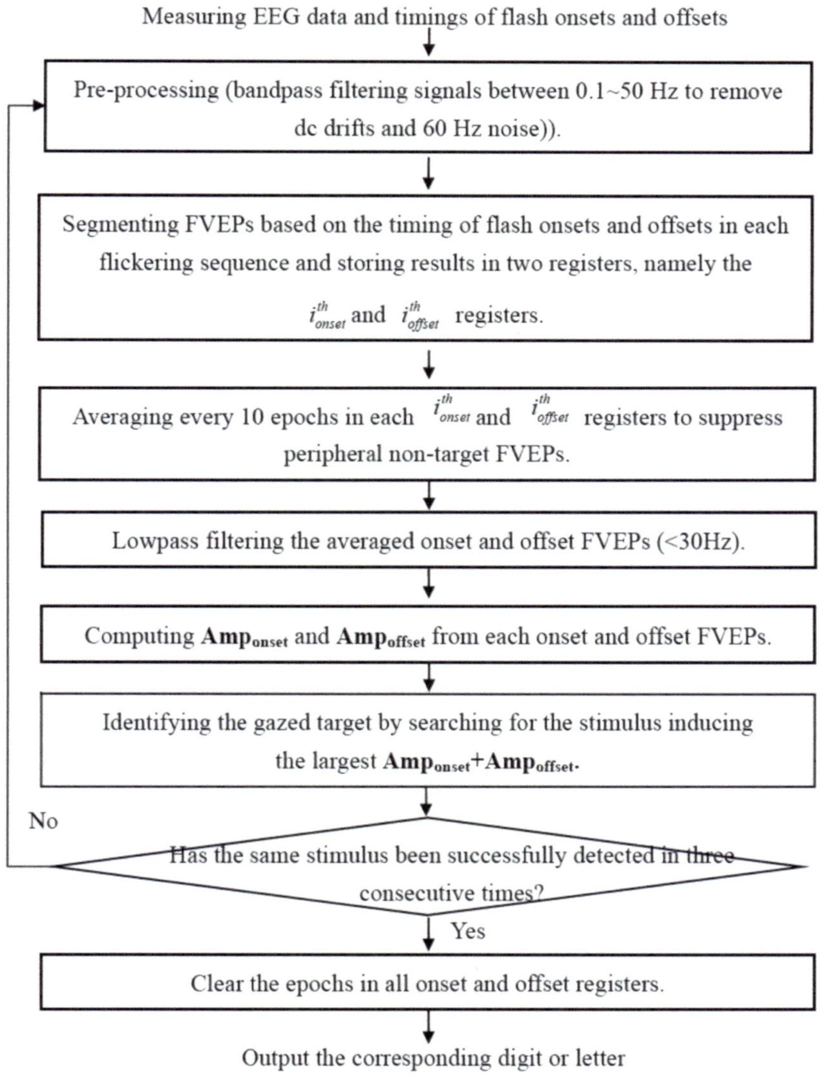

Fig. 3. The overall signal processing flow chart of the FVEP-based BCI system.

To suppress such interferences from non-target stimuli via averaging, the ON and OFF durations were designed to be random and all the flickering pattern sequences were generated in a manner that they were mutually independent. The Oz-EEG signals were segmented into epochs based on the flash onset or offset in the ith flickering sequences, i.e., from -0.1 to 0.45s, and stored in two computer registers, namely the i^{th}_{onset} and i^{th}_{offset} registers, respectively. To detect the gazed target, first, every N epochs (N=10 in our implementation) in both i^{th}_{onset} and i^{th}_{offset} registers were averaged followed by lowpass (<30Hz) filtering (zero-phase, 6th-order, IIR Butterworth filter) to produce noise-suppressed onset and offset FVEPs. Second, the Amp_{onset} and Amp_{offset} induced from all flickering channels were computed. Third, the stimulus producing the largest Amp_{onset}+Amp_{offset} was recognized as the gazed target. Finally, the screen letter or digit representing the identified stimulus was sent out with a concurrent auditory bio-feedback presented to the subject, along with resetting the i^{th}_{onset} and i^{th}_{offset} registers. In our current design, a gazed stimulus was detected in every one second and was confirmed as the target after three consecutively successful detections, i.e., a letter or digit was sent out in every three seconds. The overall processing flowchart is summarized in Fig. 3.

3. Results

The primary advantage of current design of mutually independent flickering sequences is to enhance the visual responses arising from target stimuli while suppressing the interference from surrounding non-target flickering channels via averaging. Figure 4 illustrates the detection of largest Amp_{onset} and Amp_{offset} when one of subjects (subject I) was focusing binocularly on the stimulus FC-13 located at the center of the 5×5 grid in the control study. The first panel shows the flickering sequences of stimulus FC-13 and the induced EEG signals at Oz, where the vertical solid and dashed lines indicates the flash onsets and offsets of flickering sequence FC-13, respectively. The Oz signals were segmented based on the flash onsets and offsets in the flickering sequence of stimulus FC-13 and the averaged results of every 10 consecutive segmented epochs were displayed in the panel labeled by FC-13 Onset and FC-13 Offset. Temporal waveforms in the remaining panels labeled by FC-j Onset and FC-j Offset, j = 1 and 25, were generated in the same manner based on the flash onsets and offsets of flickering stimulus FC-j. Figure 5 provides another overall view of the averaged onset and offset FVEPs in which the location of each subplot corresponds to the location of associated stimulus. Since the central onset (or offset) FVEPs were time-locked and phase-locked to the flash onsets (or offsets) of the target flickering sequence but the peripheral FVEP epochs were asychronized to such flash onsets (or offsets), the averaged onset and offset FVEPs induced from stimulus FC-13 exhibited the largest Amp_{onset} and Amp_{offset} after averaging and have been successfully segregated from the surrounding flickering sequences. Figure 6 shows that the 10-trial averaged onset and offset FVEPs provoked from stimulus FC-13 can only be recognized at O1, O2 and Oz channels in the occipital area, validating the use of single Oz channel in the application study.

To further assess the detection accuracy of using the onset and offset FVEPs, each subject was instructed to gaze binocularly at the center of each flickering channel for one-minute recording in the control study. The detection of gazed FC was performed one by one continuously until all of the twenty-five FCs were processed. Different numbers of epochs were averaged to compute the values of Amp_{onset}+Amp_{offset} for the subsequent estimation of

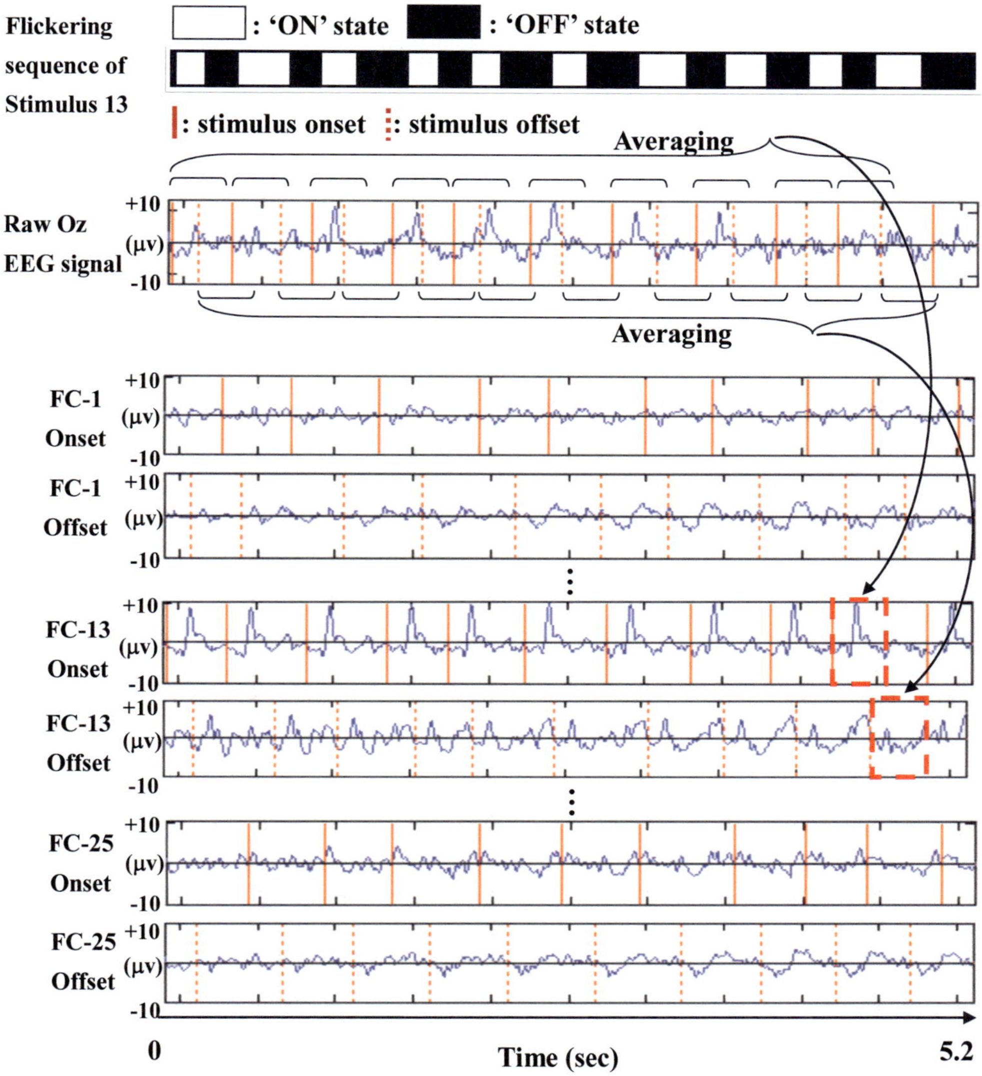

Fig. 4. Extraction of central onset and offset FVEPs when a subject stares at stimulus FC-13 in the control study. The first panel shows the flickering stimulus sequence, namely FC-13, where vertical solid and dashed marks denote the flash onsets and offsets, respectively. The Oz-EEG signals are segmented based on the flash onsets and offsets in stimulus FC-13 followed by averaging every 10 consecutive segmented epochs and results are displayed in the panel labeled by FC-13 Onset and FC-13 Offset. Temporal waveforms in the remaining panels labeled by FC-j Onset and FC-j Offset, j=1 and 25, show the results generated in the same manner based on the flash onsets and offsets of flickering stimulus FC-j. The averaged onset and offset FVEPs induced from stimulus FC-13 exhibited the largest Amp_{onset} and Amp_{offset} so that FC-13 was identified as the target stimulus.

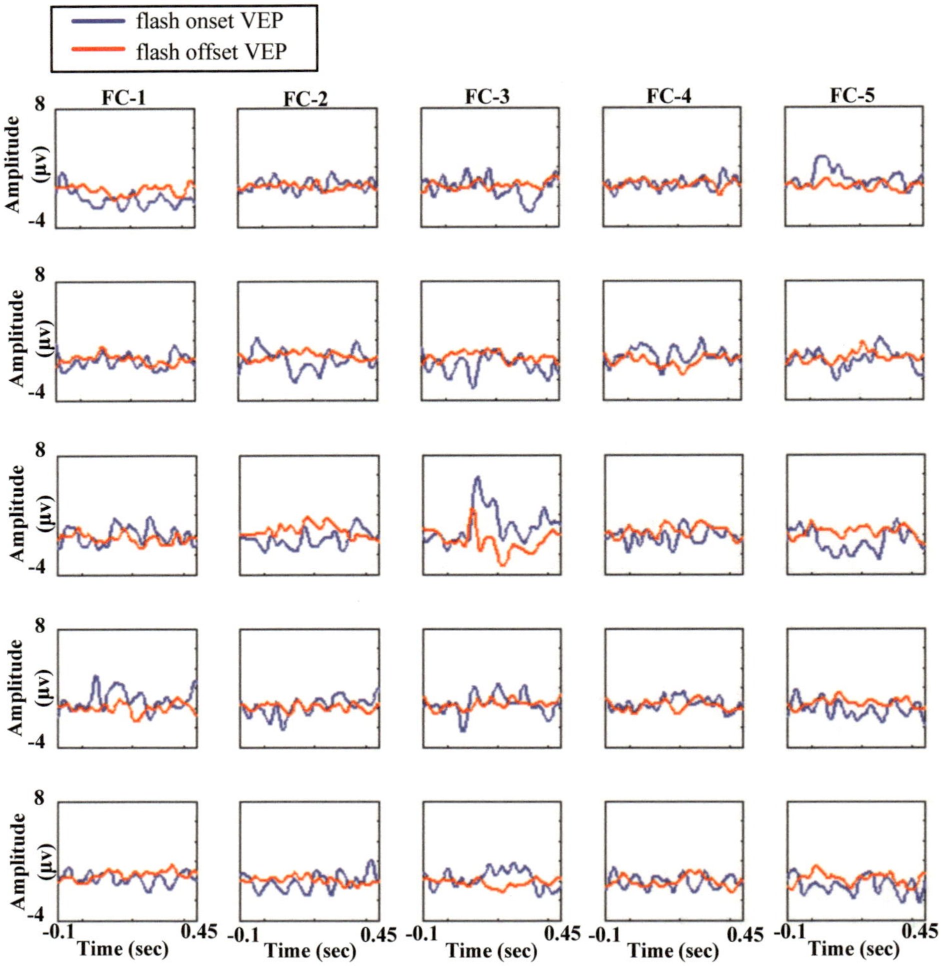

Fig. 5. Overall view of averaged central onset and offset FVEPs when a subject stares at stimulus FC-13 in the control study. Averaged onset (blue curve) and offset (red curve) FVEPS obtained from the procedure described in Fig. 3 are displayed in the subplots of a 5x5 array. Position of each subplot corresponds to the position of the stimulus used in the control study. The onset and offset FVEPs in the panel FC-13 shows the most prominent onset and offset FVEPs.

detection accuracy of gazed target, which was defined as the number of correct detections ($N_{correct}$) divided by the total detection number (N_{total}), i.e., $N_{correct}/N_{total}$. Figure 7 depicts the mean detection accuracies over the five participants with 1, 5, 10, 15, 20, 25, 30, and 35 epochs being averaged using $Amp_{onset}+Amp_{offset}$ (dashed curve) and Amp_{onset} (solid curve), respectively. The mean accuracies of using $Amp_{onset}+Amp_{offset}$ were 31.8%, 73.8%, 97.4%, 99.5%, 100%, 100%, 100%, and 100%, respectively, in comparison with that of using Amp_{onset} which were 27.8%, 67.0%, 91.2%, 95.0 %, 95.8%, 99.0%, 99.4%, and 99.8%, respectively, and that of using Amp_{offset} which were 27.7%, 45.3%, 57.5%, 78.3%, 92.0%, 98.1%, 99.2%, and 99.5% (dotted curve), respectively. The resulting accuracies from each individual were further presented in Table 1A and 1B, respectively, where the accuracies of using

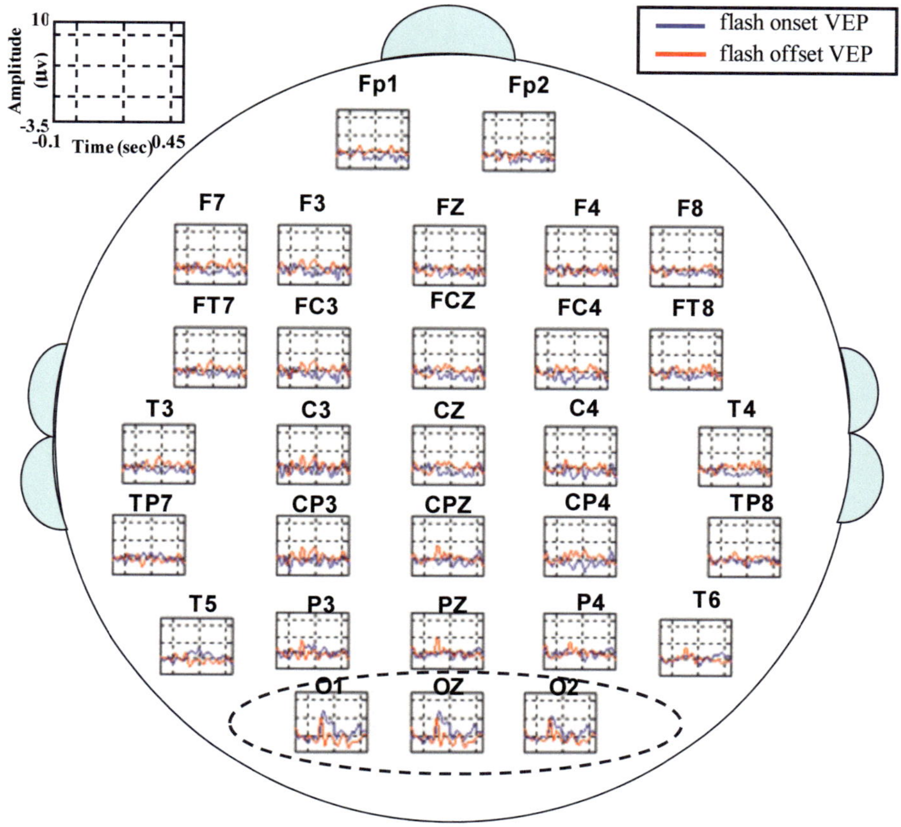

Fig. 6. Whole-head channel plot of ten-trial averaged FVEPs. The 10-trial averaged onset and offset FVEPs resulted from stimulus FC-13 can only be identified at O1, O2 and Oz channels in the occipital area, validating the use of single Oz channel in the application study.

$Amp_{onset}+Amp_{offset}$ with 10-epoch averages were significantly higher in comparison with that of using Amp_{onset} with 10-epoch averages (paired *t*-test, $p<0.05$), and reached 100% when 20 or more epochs were averaged. To compromise the computational efficiency and accuracy in the current BCI system, 10-epoch averages were adopted since accuracy higher than 95% has been achieved.

Averages and standard deviations of the latencies and amplitudes of the $N2_{onset}$, $P2_{onset}$, $N1_{offset}$, and $P1_{offset}$ peaks induced from the twenty-five flickering channels for each subject in the control study were computed on the basis of 100 epochs (Table 2A and Table 2B). Results elucidated small variations (less than 5 ms) in the latencies of four featured peaks (Table 2A) as well as relative significance between Amp_{onset} and Amp_{offset}, where the mean value of Amp_{offset} (3.41µv) over five subjects was about half (45.6%) of the mean value of Amp_{onset} (7.47µv), suggesting the reliability of onset and offset FVEPs in the proposed FVEP-based BCI system. In addition, the short latencies (the longest one occurred at $P2_{onset}$ peaks with 130 ms) endorse the feasibility of high communication rate.

In the application study, each subject was requested to produce a string '0287513694E'. The letter 'B' was not used in this experiment since it was used for the purpose of correcting erroneous spelling. By detecting the largest values of $Amp_{onset}+Amp_{offset}$ among the

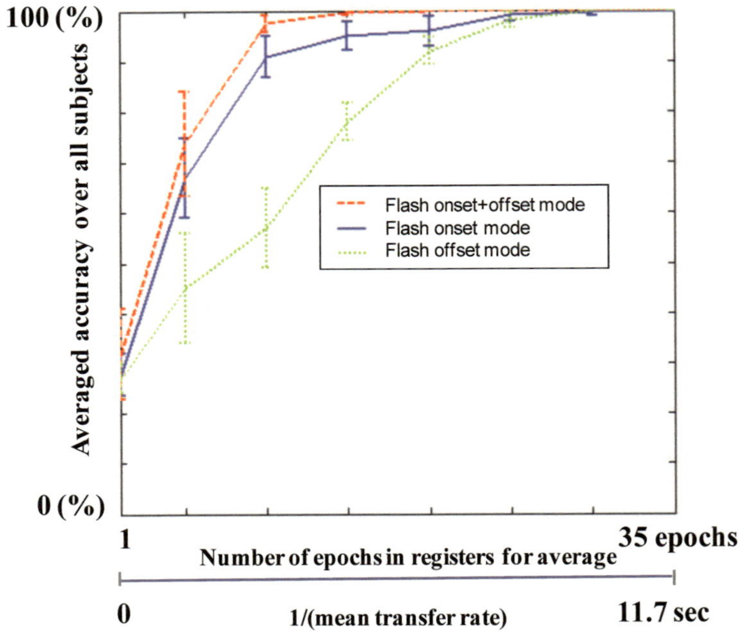

Fig. 7. Comparison of $Amp_{onset}+Amp_{offset}$, Amp_{onset}, and Amp_{offset} detected accuracies. Five subjects with 1, 5, 10, 15, 20, 25, 30, and 35 averaged epochs are used for comparison. The mean accuracies of using $Amp_{onset}+Amp_{offset}$ are 31.8%, 73.4%, 97.4%, 99.5%, 100%, 100%, 100%, and 100%, respectively, compared to that of using Amp_{onset} which are 27.8%, 67.0%, 91.2%, 95.0%, 95.8%, 99%, 99.4%, and 99.8%, respectively.

averaged responses of all flickering channels, the gazed FC was determined in every second by a personal computer (CPU 3.0 GHz/ 1GB RAM). Whenever each gazed digit or letter was confirmed for three consecutive times by the system, the subject was prompted by voice feedback to proceed with the next digit/letter. All five participants completed the string with minor errors, which were marked underlined. In addition to the accurate rate, $N_{correct}/N_{total}$, the command transfer interval (CTI) and information transfer rate per minute (ITR) were also computed. The command transfer interval, CTI, was defined as total experimental time (T_{total}) divided by the number of total output digits and letters, i.e., T_{total}/N_{total}. The information transfer rate per minute (ITR) was computed by

$$\frac{Bits}{command} = \log_2 N + P\log_2 P + (1-P)\log_2[(1-P)/(N-1)] \quad (1)$$

$$ITR = \frac{Bits}{command} \cdot \frac{60}{CTI} \quad (2)$$

where N is the total number of stimuli and P is the accuracy (Kelly et al., 2005). The mean accuracy of using $Amp_{onset}+Amp_{offset}$ was 92.18 %, and the mean CTI and ITR were 5.52 sec/command and 33.65 bits/min, respectively.

All subjects who took part in this study have successfully completed a string (see Table 3A and 3B) with few errors either using the Amp_{onset}+Amp_{offset} or Amp_{onset}. Nevertheless, the familiarity of experiment and attention of subjects may affect the detection rates. In this study, two of the five subjects had one-hour training before this task while the other three were naïve subjects. We observed that the experienced subjects have better concentration on the target stimulus than the naïve subjects who were distracted occasionally by surrounding non-target stimuli. For example, subject IV has incautiously shifted his gaze on the wrong stimulus '7' after selected '3' (see Table 3). The experienced group (i.e., subject I and II) has performed superiorly with faster ITR (45.73 bits/min) and higher accuracy (100%) than the naïve group from which the ITR and accuracy were 25.06 bit/min and 86.07%, respectively.

(A) Results of using Amp_{onset}+Amp_{offset}.

	Number of epochs for averaging							
Subject	1	5	10	15	20	25	30	35
I	30%	88%	98%	100%	100%	100%	100%	100%
II	23%	66%	97%	99%	100%	100%	100%	100%
III	31%	79%	98%	100%	100%	100%	100%	100%
IV	28%	62%	95%	99%	100%	100%	100%	100%
V	47%	74%	99%	100%	100%	100%	100%	100%
Average	31.8%	73.8%	97.4%	99.5%	100%	100%	100%	100%

(B) Results of using Amp_{onset}.

	Number of epochs for averaging							
Subject	1	5	10	15	20	25	30	35
I	33%	76%	91%	97%	98%	99%	100%	100%
II	24%	63%	85%	90%	91%	97%	98%	99%
III	32%	74%	94%	96%	97%	100%	100%	100%
IV	25%	65%	93%	96%	97%	100%	100%	100%
V	25%	57%	93%	95%	96%	99%	99%	100%
Average	27.8%	67.0%	91.2%	95.0%	95.8%	99.0%	99.4%	99.8%

Table 1. Comparison of the results using Amp_{onset}+Amp_{offset} and Amp_{onset}.

(A) Latencies of onset and offset FVEP features.

Subject	Onset FVEP		Offset FVEP	
	$N2_{onset}$	$P2_{onset}$	$N1_{offset}$	$P1_{offset}$
I	95.5±3.45	127.8±2.38	75.2±3.83	108.3±3.21
II	82.3±3.29	125.2±3.21	72.2±4.19	109.3±4.22
III	74.1±2.13	121.3±2.55	81.8±3.81	118.7±2.25
IV	78.2±3.71	118.9±2.53	78.6±3.14	112.1±4.91
V	92.6±1.75	123.4±3.01	72.9±2.11	120.4±3.62
Average	84.5±8.71	123.3±4.16	72.2±5.29	113.68±5.90

(B) Amplitudes of onset and offset FVEP features.

Subject	Onset FVEP		Offset FVEP	
	$N2_{onset}$	$P2_{onset}$	$N1_{offset}$	$P1_{offset}$
I	-1.13±0.77	7.20±1.13	-1.35±0.55	1.68±0.74
II	-2.08±1.05	4.69±1.54	-1.12±0.45	1.34±0.51
III	-3.24±0.68	7.19±1.16	-1.47±0.93	3.74±0.93
IV	-2.20±0.56	1.67±0.62	-0.41±0.25	1.84±0.67
V	-1.34±0.48	6.66±0.54	-1.89±0.48	2.21±0.57
Average	-1.99±0.72	5.48±2.18	-1.25±0.64	2.16±0.93
Average	Amp_{onset}=7.47±2.47		Amp_{offset}=3.41±1.01	

Table 2. The latencies and amplitudes of the $N2_{onset}$, $P2_{onset}$, $N1_{offset}$, and $P1_{offset}$ peaks induced from the 25 flickering channels.

Subject	Input results (wrong underlined)	Total time (sec)	Accuracy ($N_{correct}/N_{total}$)	CTI (sec/command)	ITR (bits/min)
I	0287513694E	48	11/11 (100%)	4.36	49.26
II	0287513694E	56	11/11 (100%)	5.09	42.20
III	028751236794E	81	11/13 (84.6%)	6.23	23.08
IV	028751376 94E	70	11/12 (91.7%)	5.83	29.69
V	027875136934E	79	11/13 (84.6%)	6.07	24.04
Average		66.8	92.18%	5.52	33.65

Table 3. Results of producing the string '0287513694E' from five subjects.

4. Discussion

FVEP has been a popular clinical index to monitor anesthesia level during surgery (Raitta et al., 1979; Uhl et al., 1980), to diagnose prechiasmal and retrochiasmal lesions (Carlin et al.,

1983; Kriss et al., 1982; Markand et al., 1982; Wilson, 1978), to indicate intracranial pressure induced by head injury (McSherry et al., 1982), and to alarm brain death (Reilly et al., 1978; Trojaborg & Jorgensen 1973). FVEP can be measured in patients who have very poor visual acuity (Spehlmann, 1985), and some studies also reported that the FVEP can be measured in patients who can see flashes clearly but not pattern stimuli owing to their partial deficiencies in optical fiber connections between retina and visual cortex (Kriss et al., 1982; Wilson, 1978). These studies suggest that the FVEP is a widely measurable biosignal which has also been used as a control signal for BCI systems (Lee et al., 2005; Lee et al., 2006; Sutter, 1992).

The visual 'Flash offset' responses have been investigated in the single-neuron recording (Duysens et al., 1996; Brooks & Huber , 1972) and electroretinogram (ERG) (Kondo et al., 1998) studies. It has been reported that at least one-third of the cortical cells in visual area (area 17 and 18) produced the visual 'Flash offset' responses that were sensitive to the duration of preceding light stimulus (Duysens et al., 1996). In particular, the amplitudes of such visual 'Flash offset' responses were proportional to the duration of preceding light stimuli (Duysens et al., 1996; Brooks & Huber, 1972). In our study, the visual 'Flash offset' responses were not only clearly observed (Fig. 5), but also preserved the characteristics of central magnification similar to onset FVEP, which was in line with the Duysens et al.s' results in which the presence of offset-FVEP central magnification in offset FVEP was suggested to be generated at cortical level rather than the input from the Y-OFF cells in LGN (Duysens et al., 1996), since the visual 'Flash offset' responses from Y-OFF cells in LGN should be specially prominent with peripheral fields (Ferster, 1990). Duysens et al. (1996) further pointed out that the visual 'offset' response was duration-dependent which may be caused by "cortical disinhibition", meaning a release from the inhibition of other surrounding cortical cells over the same region after long-duration light stimulation.

The flickering sequences in this study were generated by random ON and OFF durations. Each ON or OFF state in the flickering sequence was a concatenation of one fixed length (116.7 ms) and a variable length (uniformly distributed between 0 ms and 233.3 ms). The fixed duration was designed to prevent the major visual response of current onset or offset FVEP overlapped with the incoming offset or onset FVEP, and the random duration was used to generate temporal independence among different flickering sequences. The ensemble average FVEPs evoked by flash onsets (or offsets) can be viewed as sums of two stimulus-driven responses: the time-locked FVEPs induced from the target flickering sequence and the non-time-locked visual responses from other flickering sequences. The same ensemble averaging process also attenuates noise, random VEPs and the endogenous EEG. In order to further examine the uncorrelation among different flickering sequences, the correlation coefficients between any two flickering sequences with different temporal lengths (N), from 1000 frames to 100000 frames, were computed. The formula of correlation coefficient is given by $Coef(X,Y) = \dfrac{E[(X-\overline{X})\cdot(Y-\overline{Y})]}{(E[(X-\overline{X})^2])^{1/2}\cdot(E[(Y-\overline{Y})^2])^{1/2}}$, where $E[\cdot]$ represents the operator of expected value, X and Y are two different flickering sequences, and $\overline{X}$ and $\overline{Y}$ are the mean (expected) values of X and Y, respectively. For pairs of flickering stimulus sequences of lengths 1000, 10000, 20000, 30000, 40000, 50000, 60000, 70000, 80000, 90000, and 100000, we tested the hypothesis that the mean correlation coefficient between any two sequences was greater than r_c, where r_c is the critical value of Coef(X,Y) for a one-tailed test with $p < .01$ (e.g., r_c. value is 0.0734 for stimulus sequence of lengths 1000). In every case, we rejected the hypothesis that the observed Coef(X,Y) exceeded r_c.

The mean ITR (33.65 bits/min) and accuracy (92.18%) of the proposed BCI can be further improved in the following two ways. First, advanced signal processing techniques can be applied to extract the FVEPs with higher SNR so that much fewer epochs are used in the averaging process for suppressing peripheral visual responses. For example, the independent component analysis (ICA) (Hyvarinen & Oja, 1997) can be used to extract the FVEP in a single trial (Lee et al., 2003; Jung et al., 2001; Tang et al., 2002). Since the FVEP is time-locked and phase-locked, the gaze-FC can be identified by examining the latencies of central FVEP and thereby higher ITR may be achieved with few averaged epochs. Second, effective classifiers, such as artificial neural network (ANN) (Haselsteiner & Pfurtscheller, 2000; Palaniappan et al., 2002), support vector machine (SVM) (Meinicke et al., 2003) and linear discriminate analysis (LDA) (Donchin et al., 2000; Hinterberger et al., 2003) can be adopted for accuracy improvement. Cheng et al. (2006) have improved the mean ITR of their SSVEP-based BCI from 27.15 bits/min to 43 bits/min by designing an optimal bipolar measurement with the use of ICA. Meinicke et al. (2003) took the advantage of SVM and have increased the mean ITR of their P300-based BCI from 12 bits/min to 50.5 bits/min. Based on the ICA and advanced classifiers, the performance improvement of our BCI system can be expected.

Comparing the proposed FVEP-based BCI system with other SSVEP-based (including the gaze-dependent SSVEP and attention-regulated SSVEP) or FMFVEP-based systems, both the flickering design and the translation algorithm in these three categories are different. In our system, mutually independent flickering sequences were designed to induce onset and offset FVEPs and the temporally-encoded stimulus onsets and offsets were used to segment FVEPs followed by averaging and comparison for the detection of gazed stimulus. In contrast, the SSVEP-based system was a frequency-encoded method which encoded flickering sequences in distinct frequencies, that is, each visual stimulus was designed to have its own flickering frequency, and the gazed target was identified by finding the stimulus that contributed maximum power of SSVEP at Fourier spectrum. In the FMFVEP-based system, it presumed identical response of FVEP across all trials and used such an "expected response" as the template in correlation computation (Sutter, 1992). The flickering sequence that produced the maximal correlation was determined as the target stimulus. Of note is that the computational complexities for SSVEP system and FMFVEP system were orders of $M \cdot \log 2M$ (M=512) and M^2 (M=300, at 250 Hz sampling rate and 10/sec flickering activation rate), respectively, where M was number of data points in data processing. By taking the advantage of the design of mutually independent random sequences, the proposed system only requires simple averaging, leading to computation complexity no larger than order of N (N=10), where N is the number of epoch used in averaging.

The proposed study utilizes focal stimulus light to induce cortical FVEPs. Intraocular light scattered in ocular media and reflected from ocular surfaces may evoke photoreceptors on peripheral visual fields and induce stray light responses (Sandberg et al., 1996; Shimada & Horiguchi, 2003; Stenbacka & Vanni, 2007), which are mainly contributed from rod cells owing to their nondirectional sensitivity (Sandberg et al., 1996). Since the stray light responses are induced by the light which has been reflected and nondirectionally scattered for multiple times, the stray light responses have delayed and weaker responses compared to those evoked from fovea region (Sandberg et al., 1996; Shimada & Horiguchi, 2003). Nevertheless, in this study, the stray light responses are not clearly observed (see Fig. 2, 4 and 5). Possible reasons are as follows. First, the data were recorded in a dimly illuminated room instead of a completely dark environment so that the sensitivity of peripheral photoreceptors to stray light is reduced (Stenbacka & Vanni, 2007). Second, our study utilizes multiple flickering stimuli presented simultaneously on a screen. The flickering states of each FC are determined by a self-generated random function and independent of the flickering of other FCs. Due to the property of mutual independence among different FCs, it keeps approximately half of FCs in ON state and the other half of FCs in OFF states which results in no large change in net luminance modulation and the stray light in the periphery is not largely modulated (Riemslag et al., 1985; Fry & Bartley, 1935). Third, since the interferences of FVEP from non-gazed FC have been successfully suppressed using averaging technique in this study and the responses of stray light from peripheral visual fields are usually delayed and weaker than FVEPs induced from central visual fields, we can speculate that the interference of stray light responses induced from non-gazed FCs can be suppressed as well after applying the averaging process. However, the responses of the visual system are dependent on spatial and temporal parameters, such that periphery may sometimes dominate the central response even when the stimuli are central in some practical applications. The issues of precise contribution from periphery are beyond the scope of current study and will be investigated in future work.

It is noted that operations of both the gaze-dependent VEP-based BCI system and the popular eye tracker systems are associated with eye motions. Eye tracking systems require constant light sources, such as infrared light, and a stationary environment with tolerance of minor head movements (Duchowski, 2003). Although eye trackers have been well-developed, some physiological or spatial calibration issues still limit its applications in practical use. First, eye trackers are operated based on image analysis to detect retro-reflectivity of two reference points, e.g., reflection from pupil center and the corneal of a stationary light source. As a consequence, eye tracking systems require stationary environments to prevent influence of glint from surrounding false objects (Duchowski, 2003). Second, available visual angles for eye tracking systems are usually operating within ±45° so that the boundaries of iris or cornea can be well captured. Third, the velocities of eye saccade can be up to 700°/sec within a duration as short as 20ms (Carpenter, 1988), and thereby most video-based eye trackers are equipped with costly high-speed video capture systems (>250 Hz) (Duchowski, 2003). In contrast, the VEP-based BCI aims to develop a user-friendly and low-cost system but with the compromised response time of 1 ~ 4 seconds (Cheng et al., 2002; Cheng et al., 2006; Kelly et al., 2005; Lee et al., 2005; Lee et al., 2006; Middendorf et al., 2000; Sutter 1992; Trejo et al., 2006), which requires only an EEG and an EOG channels.

5. Conclusion

In this study, a gaze-dependent FVEP-based BCI with ITR of 33.65 bits/min has been proposed. Subjects can shift their gazes at target flashing digits or letters to generate a string for communication purposes. The salient features of the proposed system include (1) FVEP is a reliable neuroelectric signal with fast response that can be used to achieve high ITR, (2) mutually random sequences are designed to suppress inter-flickering-channel interferences via simple averaging which is suitable for real-time processing, (3) the mutually independent sequences consisting of ON and OFF states can be used to induce onset and offset FVEPs at the timing of stimulus onsets and offsets for increasing the detection rates of gazed stimulus, (4) the central magnification of offset FVEP was confirmed in this study and has been used to incorporate with onset FVEP for defining more reliable feature

Amp_{onset}+Amp_{offset} in identifying gazed stimulus, (5) the mean ITR using Amp_{onset}+Amp_{offset} achieves 33.65 bits/min, which is higher than the maximum ITR (~25 bits/min) in classical BCI systems (Walpow et al., 2002), with satisfactory mean detection rate 92.18%

6. References

Birbaumer, N.; Flor, H.; Ghanayim, N; Hinterberger, T.; Iverson, I.; Taub, E.; Kotchoubey, B.; Kubler, A. & Perelmouter, J. (1999). A spelling device for the paralyzed. *Nature,* Vol. 398, 297 - 298.

Blankertz, B.; Dornhege, G.; Krauledat, M.; Muller, K. R. & Curio, G. (2007). The non-invasive Berlin brain- computer interface: fast acquisition of effective performance in untrained subjects. *NeuroImage,* Vol. 37, No. 2, 539-550.

Brooks, B. & Huber, C. (1972). Evidence for the role of the transient neural "off-response" in perception of light decrement. A psychophysical test derived from neuronal data in the cat. *Vision Research,* Vol. 12, No. 7, 1291-1296.

Carlin, L.; Roach, E. S.; Riela, A.; Spudis, E. & McLean, W. T. (1983). Juvenile metachromatic leukodystrophy: Evoked potentials and computed tomography. *Annals of Neurology,* Vol. 13, No. 1, 105-106.

Carpenter, R. H. S. (1988). *Movements of the eyes, 2nd edition,* Pion, ISBN 9780850861099, London.

Cheng, M.; Gao, X.; Gao, S. & Xu, D. (2002). Design and implementation of a brain-computer interface with high transfer rates. *IEEE Transactions on Biomedical Engineering,* Vol. 49, No. 10, 1181-1186.

Donchin, E.; Spencer, K. M. & Wilesinghe, R. (2000). The mental prosthesis: Assessing the speed of a P300-based braincomputer interface. *IEEE Transactions on Rehabilitation Engineering,* Vol. 8, No. 2, 174 - 179.

Duchowski, A. T. (2003). *Eye tracking methodology: theory and practice.* Springer-Verlag, ISBN 978-1846286087, London.

Duysens, L.; Orban, G. A.; Cremieux, J. & Maes, H. (1985). Visual cortical correlates of visible persistence. *Vision Research,* Vol. 25, No. 2, 171-178.

Duysens, L.; Maes, H. & Orban, G. A. (1987). The velocity dependence of direction selectivity of visual cortical neurones in the cat. *Journal of Physiology,* Vol. 387, June, 95-113.

Duysens, J.; Schaafsma, S. J. & Orban, G. A. (1996). Cortical off response tuning for stimulus duration. *Vision Research,* Vol. 36, No. 20, 3243-3251.

Ferster, D. (1988). Spatially opponent excitation and inhibition in simple cells of the cat visual cortex. *Journal of Neuroscience,* Vol. 8, 1172-1180.

Fisch, B. J. & Spehlmann, R. (1999). Spatial analysis of the EEG. In: *Fisch and Spehlmann's EEG primer: basic principles of digital and analog EEG.,* Fisch, B. J., 73-92, Elsevier, ISBN 9780444821485, Amsterdam.

Fry, G. A. & Bartley, S. H. (1935). The relation of stray light in the eye to the retinal action potential. *The American Journal of Physiology,* Vol. 111, 335-340.

Haselsteiner, E. & Pfurtscheller, G. (2000). Using time-dependent neural networks for EEG classification. *IEEE Transactions on Rehabilitation Engineering,* Vol. 8, No. 4, 457-463.

Hyvarinen, A. & Oja, E. (1997). A fast fixed-point algorithm for independent component analysis. *Neural Computing,* Vol. 9, No. 7, 1483-1492.

Jung, T. P.; Makeig, S.; Westerfield, M.; Townsend, J.; Courchesne, E. & Sejnowski, J. T. (2001). Analysis and visualization of single-trial event-related potentials. *Human Brain Mapping,* Vol. 14, No. 3, 166-185.

Kelly, S. P.; Lalor, E. C.; Reilly, R. B. & Foxe, J. J. (2005). Visual spatial attention tracking using high density SSVEP data for independent brain-computer communication. *IEEE Transactions on Neural Systems and Rehabilitation Engineering,* Vol. 13, No. 2, 172-178.

Hinterberger, T.; Kubler, A.; Kaiser, J.; Neumann, N. & Birbaumer, N. (2003). A brain-computer interface (BCI) for the locked-in: comparison of different EEG classifications for thought translation device. *Clinical Neurophysiology,* Vol. 114, No. 3, 416-425.

Kondo, M.; Miyake, Y.; Horiguchi, M.; Suzuki, S & Tanikawa, A. (1998). Recording multifocal electroretinogram on and off responses in humans. *Investigative Ophthalmology & Visual science,* Vol. 39, No. 3, 574-580.

Kriss, A.; Carroll, W. M.; Blumhardt, L. D. & Halliday, A. M. (1982). Pattern and flash evoked potential changes in toxic (nutritional) optic neuropathy. *Advances in Neurologly,* Vol. 32, 11-19.

Lee, P. L.; Wu, Y. T.; Chen, L. F.; Chen, Y.S; Cheng, C. M.; Yeh, T. C.; Ho, L. T.; Chang, M. S. & Hsieh, J. C. (2003). ICA-based spatiotemporal approach for single-trial analysis of postmovement MEG beta synchronization. *Neuroimage,* Vol. 20, No. 4, 2010-2030.

Lee, P. L.; Wu, C. H.; Wu, Y. T.; Chen, L. F.; Yeh, T. C. & Hsieh, J. C. (2005). Visual evoked potential (VEP) - actuated brain computer interface: A brain-actuated cursor system. *Electronics Letters,* Vol. 21, No. 15, 832-834.

Lee, P. L., Hsieh, J. C.; Wu, C. H.; Yeh, T. C. & Wu, Y. T. (2006) The brain computer interface using flash visual evoked potential and independent component analysis. *Annals of Biomedical Engineering,* Vol. 34, No. 10, 1641-1654.

Markand, O. N.; Garg, B. P.; DeMyer, W. E. & Warren, C. (1982). Brain stem auditory, visual and somatosensory evoked potentials in leukodystrophies. *Electroencephalography and Clinical Neurophysiology,* Vol. 54, No. 1, 39-48.

Mason, S. G. & Birch, G. E. (2000). A brain-controlled switch for asynchronous control applications. *IEEE Transactions on Biomedical Engineering,* Vol. 47, No. 10, 1297 - 1307.

McSherry, J. W.; Walters, C. L. & Horbar, J. D. (1982). Acute visual evoked potential changes in hydrocephalus. *Electroencephalography and Clinical Neurophysiology,* Vol. 53, No. 3, 331-333.

Meinicke, P.; Kaper, M.; Hoppe, F.; Heumann, M. & Ritter, H. (2003). Improving transfer rates in brain computer interfacing: a case study. *Advances In Neural Information Processing Systems,* Vol. 15, 1131-1138.

Middendorf, M.; McMillan, G.; Calhoun, G. & Jones, K. S. (2000). Brain-computer interface based on the steady-state visual-evoked response. *IEEE Transactions on Rehabilitation Engineering,* Vol. 8, No. 2, 211-214.

Muller-Putz, G. R.; Scherer, R.; Neuper, C. & Pfurtscheller, G. (2006). Steady-state somatosensory evoked potentials: suitable brain signals for brain-computer interface? *IEEE Transactions on Neural Systems and Rehabilitation Engineering,* Vol. 14, No. 1, 30-37.

Odom, J. V.; Bach, M.; Barber, C.; Brigell, M.; Marmor, M. F.; Tormene, A. P.; Holder, G. E. & Vaegan. (2004). Visual evoked potentials standard. *Documenta Ophthalmologica,* Vol. 108, 115 - 123.

Palaniappan, R.; Paramesran, R.; Nishida, S. & Saiwaki, N. (2002). A new brain-computer interface design using fuzzy ARTMAP. *IEEE Transactions on Neural Systems and Rehabilitation Engineering,* Vol. 10, No. 3, 140-148.

Pfurtscheller, G.; Neuper, C.; Guger, C.; Harkam, W.; Ramoser, H.; Schlogl, A.; Obermaier, B. & Pregenzer, M. (2000). Current trends in Graz brain-computer interface (BCI) research. *IEEE Transactions on Rehabilitation Engineering,* Vol. 8, No. 2, 216-219.

Raitta, C.; Karhunene, U.; Seppalainen, A. M. & Naukkarinen, M. (1979). Changes in the electroretinogram and visual evoked potentials during general anaesthesia. *Graefe's Archive for Clinical and Experimental Ophthalmology,* Vol. 211, No. 6, 139-144.

Reilly, E. L.; Kondo, C.; Brunberg, J. A. & Doty, D. B. (1978). Visual evoked potentials during hypothermia and prolonged circulatory arrest. *Electroencephalography and Clinical Neurophysiology,* Vol. 45, No. 1, 100-106.

Riemslag, F.C.; Ringo, J.L.; Spekreijse, H. & Verduyn Lunel, H.F. (1985). The luminance origin of the pattern electroretinogram in man. *Journal of Physiology,* Vol. 363, June, 191-209.

Salmelin, R. & Hari, R. (1994). Characterization of spontaneous MEG rhythms in healthy adults. *Electroencephalography and Clinical Neurophysiology,* Vol. 91, No. 4, 237-248.

Sandberg, M.A.; Pawlyk, B.S & Berson, E.L. (1996). Isolation of focal rod electroretinograms from the dark-adapted human eye. *Investigative ophthalmology and visual science,* Vol. 37, No. 5, 930-934.

Shimada, Y. & Horiguchi, M. (2003). Stray light - induced multifocal electroretinograms. *Investigative ophthalmology and visual science,* Vol. 44, 1245-1251.

Spehlmann, R. (1985). The transient VEP to diffuse light simuli. In: *Evoked potential primer,* Spehlmann, R., 135-142, Butterworth Heinemann, ISBN 0750673338, Stoneham.

Stenbacka, L. & Vanni, S. (2007). Central luminance flicker can activate peripheral retinotopic representation. Neuroimage, Vol. 34, No. 1. 342-348.

Sutter, E.E. (1992). The brain response interface: communication through visually-induced electrical brain responses. *Journal of Microcomputer Applications,* Vol. 15, No. 1, 31-45.

Tang, A.C.; Pearlmutter, B.A.; Malaszenko, N.A. & Phung, D.B. (2002). Independent components of magnetoencephalography: single-trial response onset times. *Neuroimage,* Vol. 17, No. 4, 1773-1789.

Trejo, L.J.; Rosipal, R. & Matthews, B. (2006). Brain-computer interfaces for 1-D and 2-D cursor control: designs using volitional control of the EEG spectrum or steady-state visual evoked potentials. *IEEE Transactions on Neural Systems and Rehabilitation Engineering,* Vol. 14, No. 2, 225-229.

Trojaborg, W. & Jorgensen, E.O. (1973). Evoked cortical potentials in patients with "isoelectric" EEGs. *Electroencephalography and Clinical Neurophysiology,* Vol. 35, No. 3, 301-309.

Uhl, R.R.; Squires, K.C.; Bruce, D.L. & Starr, A. (1980). Effect of halothane anesthesia on the human cortical visual evoked response. *Anesthesiology,* Vol. 53, No. 4, 273-276.

Wang, Y.; Wang, R.; Gao, X.; Hong, B. & Gao, S. (2006). A practical VEP-based brain-computer interface. *IEEE Transactions on Neural Systems and Rehabilitation Engineering,* Vol. 14, No. 2, 234-240.

Wilson, W.B. (1978). Visual-evoked response differentiation of ischemic optic neuritis from the optic neuritis of multiple sclerosis. *American journal of ophthalmology,* Vol. 86, No. 4, 530-535.

Wolpaw, J.R.; Birbaumer, N.; McFarland, D.J.; Pfurtscheller, G. & Vaughan, T.M. Brain-computer interfaces for communication and control. *Clinical Neurophysiology,* Vol. 113, No. 6, 767-791.

6

Usability of Transient VEPs in BCIs

Natsue Yoshimura[1] and Naoaki Itakura[2]
[1]*Tokyo Institute of Technology,*
[2]*The University of Electro-Communications*
Japan

1. Introduction

Among non-invasive Brain Computer Interfaces (BCIs), electroencephalogram (EEG) has been the most commonly used for them because EEG is advantageous in terms of its simplicity and ease of use, which meets BCI specifications when considering practical use. In general, EEG signals (EEGs) can be classified into two categories, spontaneous EEGs and stimulus evoked EEGs. Focusing on stimulus evoked EEGs, signals called P300 and Visual Evoked Potentials (VEPs) are often utilized for BCIs. Both types of BCIs extract the intention of users by detecting which target on the PC monitor users are gazing at (Sellers & Donchin, 2006; Sellers, et al., 2006).

While P300 signals are thought to be derived from the thoughts of users, VEPs are simply derived from physical reaction to visual stimulation. In that sense, VEP-based BCIs are thus known as the simplest BCIs.

Most VEP-based BCIs utilize so-called "steady-state VEPs" (SSVEPs) which are generated in reaction to high-speed blinking light (Allison, et al., 2008; Cheng, et al., 2002). Because SSVEPs are characterized by sinusoidal-like waveforms whose frequencies are synchronized with the frequency of blinking light, the gazing target of users can be identified by using frequency analysis of SSVEPs from among several visual targets with different blinking frequencies.

On the other hand, there is another type of VEP called a "transient VEP." Transient VEPs are generated in reaction to low-speed blinking light (i.e., blinking frequency of less than 3.5 Hz), and they can be characterized with a negative peak of around 75 ms and a positive peak of around 100 ms (N75 and P100 in Fig. 1). Unlike SSVEPs, transient VEPs are rarely used for BCIs because it is considered that they need longer detection time than SSVEPs.

However, there are several issues which need to be addressed regarding the use of SSVEP-based BCIs. The first issue is discomfort caused by blinking light. When gazing at high-speed blinking light, some people exhibit symptoms similar to optically stimulated epileptic seizure such as annoyance, headache, or nausea (Graf, et al., 1994; Guerrini & Genton, 2004). Most of the subjects in the authors' study group actually felt discomfort caused by the blinking stimuli. The second issue is that SSVEPs are not detected in all people. One of the reasons for this is considered to be that some people unconsciously refuse to gaze at discomfort targets, and the authors' group included some users in which SSVEPs were not detected. SSVEP-based BCIs cannot be practically used for such kind of users.

Considering these issues, the authors have proposed a transient VEP-based BCI which reduces discomfort caused by gazing at high-speed blinking light (Yoshimura & Itakura,

2009). If long detection time of transient VEPs can be shortened, there is a possibility that the proposed BCI may be put into practical use, especially for users who are easily annoyed with high-speed blinking light. To accomplish this, the proposed BCI employs bipolar derivation to reduce unwanted signals. Moreover, our BCI utilizes non-direct gazed visual stimuli to further reduce discomfort.

In this chapter, a new usability of transient VEPs is introduced, and the possibility that the transient VEP-based BCI can be used as a substitute for SSVEP-based BCIs is shown.

2. Visual Evoked Potentials (VEPs)

VEPs are one of evoked potentials which can be recorded from scalp. Retinal photoreceptor cells located in the retina are discharged by visual stimuli such as light, and discharged electrical signals are transferred to the visual cortex via the visual pathway. The consequential response signals are referred to as VEPs.

VEPs are used in the field of clinical medicine to examine the function of optic nerves and visual cortex. As visual stimuli for the inspection, pattern reversal stimuli which use a switching black-and-white lattice pattern, or flicker stimuli which use blinking LED or flash light, are commonly used. This is because neurons in the visual cortex show high sensitivity to patterns which have a clear shape or contrast, while these neurons show low sensitivity to uniform irradiation to the retina.

VEPs can be categorized into transient VEPs or SSVEPs according to waveform patterns. While transient VEPs occur in reaction to visual stimuli which blink at a frequency of less than 3.5 Hz, SSVEPs occur in reaction to stimuli of higher blinking frequency. Transient VEPs, which are recorded from the occipital area, show triphasic waveforms as shown in Fig. 1, and a positive peak referred to as P100 appears stably at about 100 ms after stimulation.

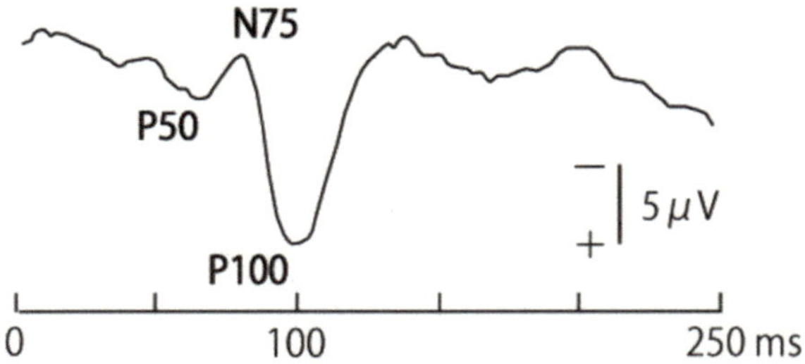

Fig. 1. A typical waveform of transient VEPs. Two positive peaks, P50 and P100, and a negative peak referred to as N75 are shown at about 50, 100, and 75 ms after visual stimulation, respectively (Watanabe, 2004). Waveforms are plotted negative-up in this and all subsequent figures.

On the other hand, sinusoidal-like waveforms are shown in SSVEPs instead of triphasic waveforms as shown in Fig. 2, because signals generated in reaction to single stimulation interfere with other signals which are caused by subsequent stimulation. It is known that frequencies of the waveforms are synchronized with repetition frequency of the stimulation. Therefore, the phenomenon can be referred to as synchronization phenomenon. SSVEP-based BCIs are interfaces based on this synchronization phenomenon.

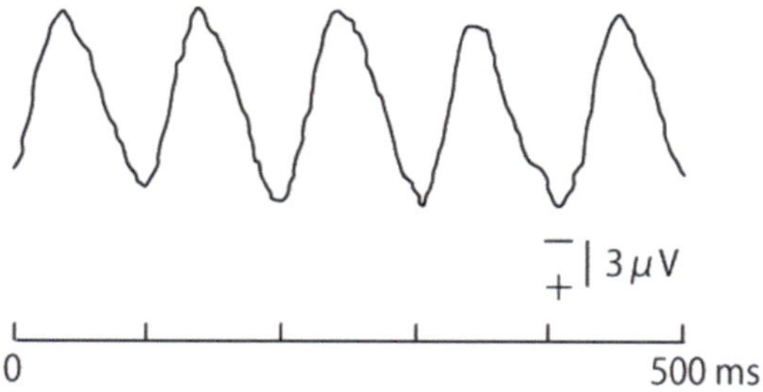

Fig. 2. An example of sinusoidal-like waveforms shown in SSVEPs using 5 Hz blinking visual stimulation (Watanabe, 2004). Frequencies of SSVEPs are synchronized with the frequency of visual stimuli.

3. Availability of transient VEPs

The most important reason transient VEPs are rarely used for VEP-based BCIs may be due to their long detection time. There are two reasons for a long detection time.

One reason is due to the low-blinking frequency of visual stimuli. There is a limit on the shortening blinking interval of visual stimuli because a precedence response and a subsequent response might interfere with each other in the case of a shorter blinking interval, which may result in generating SSVEPs. The other reason is due to the number of epochs which are required for signal averaging. In general, 100-200 epochs are required for signal averaging to detect clear transient VEPs.

Due to these two reasons, it is considered that transient VEPs cannot offer higher performance for BCIs than SSVEPs can in terms of performance on extracting information in a short time. However, considering the issue that there are some users who experience discomfort by looking at high-speed blinking visual stimuli, establishment of a substitute system might be required for such users. If transient VEPs can be recorded in a short time and especially by using non-direct gazed visual stimuli, there is a possibility for providing more comfortable BCIs.

Therefore, as a preliminary experiment, the authors examined the possibility of bipolar derivation and non-direct gazed visual stimuli. While non-direct gazed visual stimuli are expected to reduce discomfort during use, bipolar derivation is expected to reduce unwanted signals such as background noise and signals caused by eye blinking, and thus it will reduce the number of epochs used for signal averaging.

3.1 Short-distance bipolar derivation

There are two methods of recording EEGs, monopolar derivation and bipolar derivation. While monopolar derivation measures the potential between biological reference (i.e. ear lobe) and a measurement point, bipolar derivation measures potential subtraction between two measurement points.

In the field of clinical medicine, bipolar derivation is used to record VEPs, but two distantly-positioned measurement points, one at the midfrontal area and the other at the occipital area, are generally used. This is why about 100 epochs are needed for signal averaging to eliminate background noise.

In this study, therefore, short-distance bipolar derivation using two nearly-positioned occipital measurement points was employed to reduce the number of epochs for signal averaging (see Fig. 4). Although the amplitude of VEPs tends to decrease with the shortening of the distance of measurement points, in-phase signals (i.e. artifacts such as AC noise or eye blinking) cancel each other out, and out-of-phase signals between two measurement points (i.e. VEPs) are expected to be enhanced. Furthermore, it is considered that the number of epochs for signal averaging is surely reduced by locating two electrodes at the right and the left occipital area when considering paradoxical lateralization (Barrett, et al., 1976).

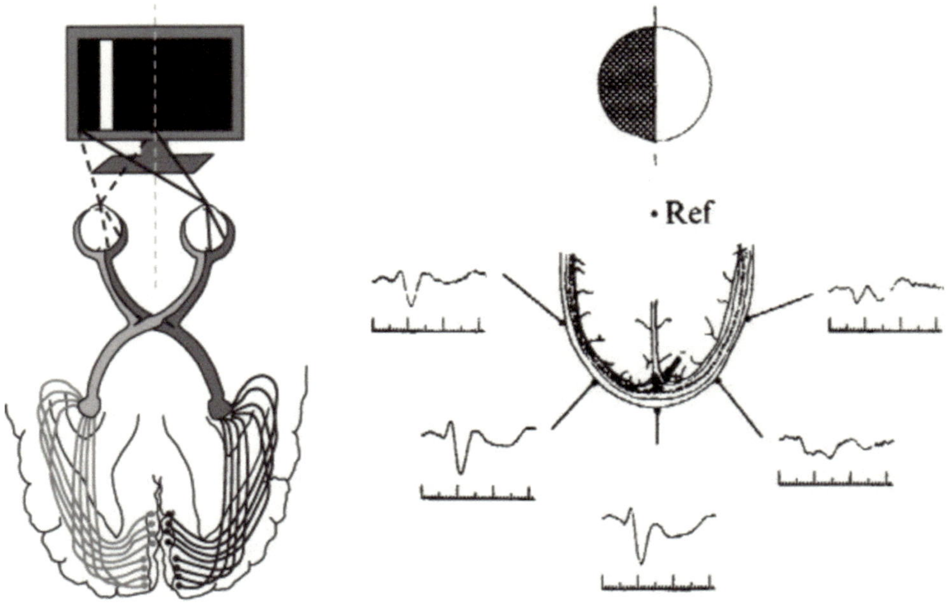

(a) (b)

Fig. 3. (a) The pathways from the retina to the visual cortex undergo partial decussation in the chiasma, so that information presented to the left of the visual field passes to the right hemisphere (Watanabe, 2004). (b) Paradoxical lateralization. Stimulation of one half field produces an evoked response which is maximal over the ipsilateral hemisphere, whereas the maximal response is predicted to be recorded over the contralateral hemisphere (Barrett, et al., 1976).

It is known that the VEPs of a half visual field stimulation are recorded maximally from electrodes over the midline and the hemisphere ipsilateral to the field of stimulation, whereas the VEPs on the contralateral side show a comparatively flat or reversed polarity signal. This phenomenon is called paradoxical lateralization (See Fig. 3). Considering this study case, in the case of left visual field stimulation, bipolar records using a right occipital electrode and a left occipital electrode may show difference potential which is subtraction of N100 recorded from the right occipital area from P100 recorded from the left occipital area, resulting in summation of absolute amplitude values of the P100 and the N100. This may alleviate the problem of small amplitudes in the case of bipolar derivation, and characteristic peaks of transient VEPs are expected to be recorded even if the number of epochs for signal averaging is small.

To the best of the authors' knowledge, there have been no studies except that of the authors' which have shown averaged transient VEPs by using a small number of epochs and which investigated evoked response patterns by a half visual field stimulation in the case of bipolar recording using a right occipital electrode and a left occipital electrode (Yoshimura & Itakura, 2008a). Briefly, the experiment is explained in the next subsection. The experiment was performed to verify the possibility of whether the stimulated visual field could be distinguished by VEPs.

3.2 Experiment

(a) Protocol

Signals were amplified with a gain of 94 dB and 0.08-100 Hz bandpass filtered using an electrode input box JB-620J and an amplifier AB-610J (Nihon-Kohden Corporation, Tokyo, Japan). An A/D converter PCI-3153 (Interface Corporation, Hiroshima, Japan) with a 12-bit resolution was set at a sampling frequency of 1 kHz. Three subjects were seated facing a 19-inch PC monitor at a viewing distance of 63 cm under a normal room condition with fluorescent lights and were asked to gaze at a fixation cross point on the monitor.

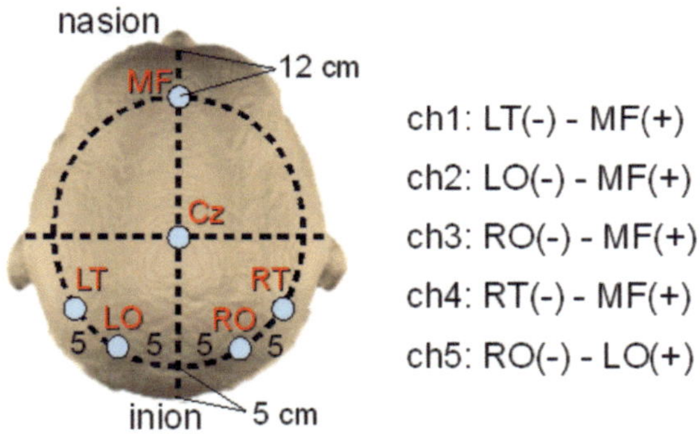

Fig. 4. Electrode positions and channel configuration. Six electrodes were placed over the midfrontal (MF), central (Cz), temporal (LT and RT) and occipital (LO and RO) areas. LO and RO were located 5 cm apart from the position which is located 5 cm above the inion. For channel configuration of bipolar derivation, LT, LO, RO, RT were connected to the minus input, and MF and LO were connected to the plus input. Cz was used as a ground electrode.

Ag/AgCl electrodes were placed over the midfrontal area (MF), the temporal area (LT and RT), the occipital area (LO and RO) and the central area (Cz of the international 10-20 system) as shown in Fig. 4. Cz was used as a ground electrode. Electrode combinations for bipolar derivation are also shown in Fig. 4. A general combination used in clinical medicine was set at ch1-ch4, and a short-distance combination was set at ch5.

As seen in Fig. 5, a white slit was displayed on a black-background PC monitor as pattern-onset stimulation. The most important feature is that subjects were asked not to gaze at the white slit but instead to gaze at a fixation cross point displayed at the center of the monitor. Although responses tended towards higher amplitude in the case of using pattern-reversal stimulation (Torok, et al., 1992), the pattern-onset stimulation was employed to verify whether the response could be recorded under such an adverse condition. The white slit was displayed at several visual angles to investigate the effect on responses.

Epochs were extracted in reference to stimulus onset (spanning +300 ms from a slit display). The mean was subtracted from each epoch, and 15 epochs were used to calculate an averaged signal. The averaged signal was low-pass filtered with a cutoff frequency of 30 Hz.

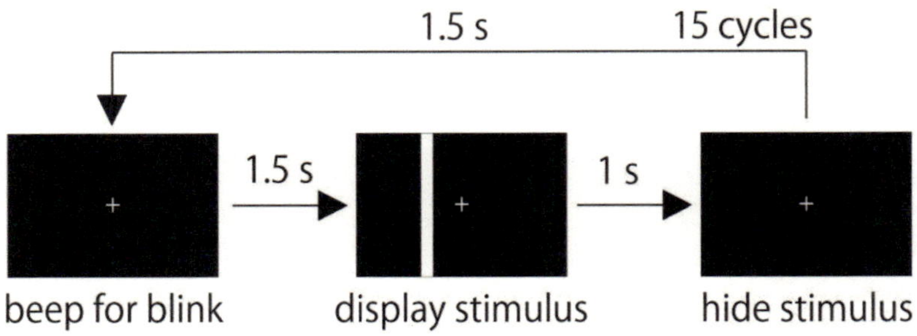

Fig. 5. Experimental sequence. A fixation cross point was placed at the center of the monitor. A non-direct gazed visual stimulus (a white slit with the visual angles of 2.5 degrees horizontally and 24.5 degrees vertically at a view distance of 63 cm) was displayed for 1 s on the left or the right of the fixation cross point with the visual angles of 1.25, 3.75, 6.25 and 13.75 degrees, respectively. The subjects were asked to blink along to a beep sound to avoid extra blinking while the slit was being displayed.

(b) Results

Comparing the averaged signals between different channels, signals of RO-LO (ch5) showed a reproducible pattern in which the differences of the stimulated visual fields can be recognized as shown in Fig. 6.

According to paradoxical lateralization, it is predicted that the maximal signal is recorded from RO-MF (ch3) in the case of the right visual field stimulation and a reversed polarity signal with small amplitude is recorded from LO-MF (ch2). However, signals of LO-MF and RO-MF shown in Fig. 6(b) did not show the predicted signals because of the small number of epochs for signal averaging and non-direct gazed visual stimulation in this experiment. This also happened in the case of the left visual field stimulation (Fig. 6(a)).

In the case of RO-LO (ch5), two characteristic peaks with latencies of around 75 ms and 120 ms were shown even when using non-direct gazed stimulation and a small number of epochs for signal averaging (the vertical dotted lines in Fig. 6). Furthermore, as expected, the polarities of the two peaks were reversed between the right and the left visual field stimulation. For example, the peak with 75 ms latency had a positive peak in the case of the right visual field stimulation (Fig. 6(b)), whereas it had a negative peak in the case of the left visual field stimulation (Fig. 6(a)). This tendency was seen for all visual angles of the slit display position and for all subjects. Therefore, it was considered that RO and LO was the best combination for a BCI. Hereafter the two characteristic peaks are referred to as N/P75 and P/N100 because these peaks seemed to represent N75 and P100 of typical transient VEPs.

To identify which peak, N/P75 or P/N100, was applicable for discriminating gazing direction, grand mean latencies and grand mean amplitudes of these peaks were calculated as shown in Fig. 7. Despite lower amplitudes, N/P75 showed a significantly smaller variation of latencies than P/N100 did. These results seem to indicate that a classification algorithm for gazing direction could be established using data around N/P75.

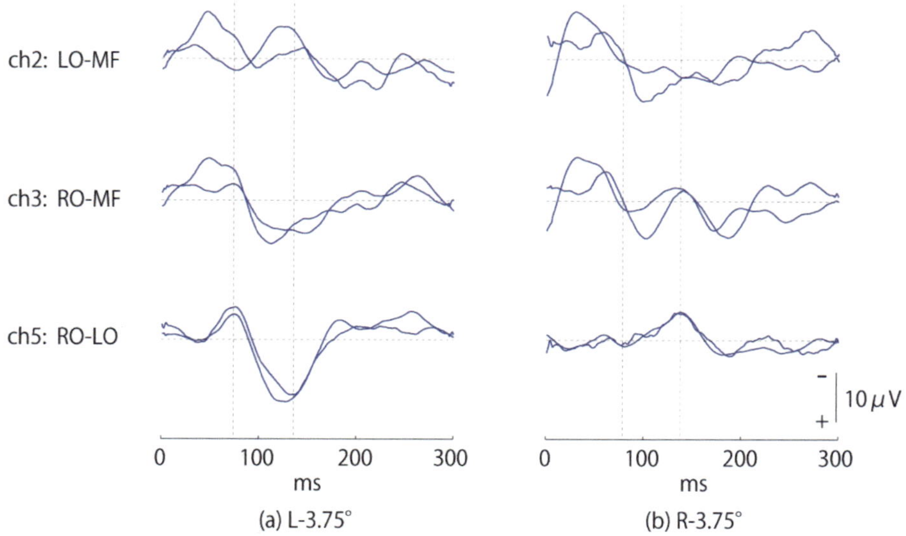

Fig. 6. Examples of signals recorded from ch2 (LO-MF), ch3 (RO-MF), and ch5 (RO-LO). Two examples of signals, in the case of the left (a) and the right (b) visual field stimulation with 3.75 degrees of visual angle, were overwritten. Signals of ch5 (RO-LO) showed reproducible peaks with latencies of 75 ms (N/P75) and 120 ms (P/N100). (modification by (Yoshimura & Itakura, 2008a)

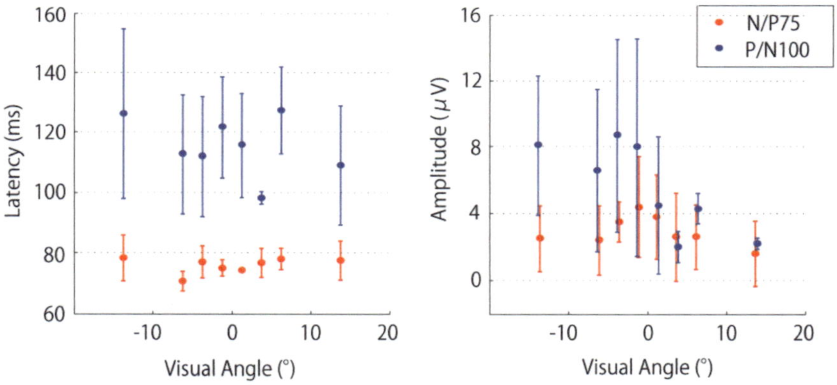

Fig. 7. Grand mean latencies and grand mean amplitudes of N/P75 and P/N100. Latencies of N/P75 showed a significantly smaller variation in comparison to that of P/N100, although amplitudes of N/P75 were relatively small. (Yoshimura & Itakura, 2008a)

In this section, the following results were suggested.

1. VEPs could be detected even when using non-direct gazed visual stimuli.
2. Characteristic peaks of transient VEPs (N/P75 and P/N100) were reproducibly-observed with only 15 epochs of signal averaging when using short-distant bipolar derivation of two electrodes located in the right and the left occipital areas (RO-LO).
3. RO-LO signals showed positive N/P75 and negative P/N100 in the case of the right visual field stimulation, whereas they showed negative N/P75 and positive P/N100 in the case of the left visual field stimulation.

4. Comparing N/P75 and P/N100 in terms of interfaces development, it was found that N/P75 would be applicable to a classification algorithm for gazing direction because N/P75 had smaller variation of latencies.

These results suggested that transient VEPs recorded by conditions shown in this section can be used for a BCI. In the next section, therefore, two kinds of BCIs are proposed, and their patterns of responses are investigated.

4. Comfortable BCIs using non-direct visual stimuli

4.1 Proposed BCIs

Two types of BCIs (Type I and Type II) were proposed as shown in Fig. 8. Both of them have characteristic specifications in which low-speed reversal stimulation and non-direct gazed visual stimuli were used.

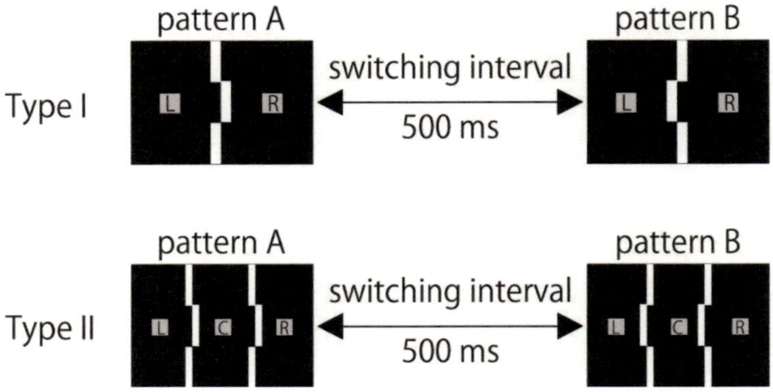

Fig. 8. Schematic diagrams of the proposed BCIs. Type I (above): A white lattice pattern, pattern A and pattern B, is displayed alternately on a black background of a 19-inch PC monitor as visual stimuli. The pattern has the visual angles of 2.5 degrees horizontally and 24.5 degrees vertically at a viewing distance of 63 cm. Square-shaped visual targets with the visual angles of 1.5 degrees (L or R) are displayed at 9 degrees to the left or right side of the pattern (Yoshimura & Itakura, 2008b). Type II (below): A pair of two white lattice patterns, pattern A and pattern B, is displayed on the PC monitor as visual stimuli. The pattern has the visual angles of 2 degrees horizontally and 24.5 degrees vertically at a viewing distance of 63 cm. Square-shaped visual targets with the visual angles of 1 degrees (L, C or R) are displayed at the center of the screen (C) and at 7 degrees to the left (L) or right (R) side of the pattern (Yoshimura & Itakura, 2009).

(a) Type I

A white lattice pattern, pattern A or pattern B, is displayed on a black background of a 19-inch PC monitor as a visual stimulus. The pattern switches between pattern A and pattern B at switching intervals of 500 ms. Subjects were asked to gaze at a gray visual target indicated by the black letter L or R located at the left or the right side of the switching pattern. This specification was determined with the aim of classifying subjects' gazing direction, right-gazing or left-gazing, according to the difference of N/P75 peaks mentioned in section 3. For example, in the case of subjects gazing at the right target, characteristic peaks of left side stimulation are expected because the switching pattern is displayed at the left visual field of the subjects.

(b) Type II
While it is assumed that subjects always gaze at the right or the left side of the monitor in Type I, Type II was designed based on the assumption of real-time classification which works with movement of gazing direction. Therefore, a specification requiring subjects to change their gazing direction from the center (center-gazing) to the left (left-gazing) or the right (right-gazing) was proposed.
A pair of two white lattice patterns, pattern A or pattern B, is displayed alternately on a black background of the PC monitor as visual stimuli. The switching intervals were also set at 500 ms. The biggest difference between Type I is that Type II has two switching patterns to divide the screen into three sections. This specification maintains the comfortable feature because subjects do not have to gaze at the switching pattern directly even during center-gazing. In addition, the widths of the lattice patterns and the visual targets were smaller than those of Type I considering the smaller areas of split screens.
When subjects gaze at the center target in Type II, visual stimulation is given from both visual fields, the right visual field and the left visual field. If VEPs in response to the stimulation in Type II follow the theory of paradoxical lateralization, signals during center-gazing are predicted to become relatively flat by canceling out responses from the dual stimuli. On the other hand, when subjects move their gazing direction to the right or the left, the responses are expected to become larger because the dual stimulation is provided from the same direction with different visual angles.
(c) Common features of Type I and II
The sizes of the lattice patterns are not usual for VEP recordings in the field of clinical medicine (Torok, et al., 1992). Although it was reported that amplitudes of responses differed according to differences of stimuli patterns (Suttle & Harding, 1999; Torok, et al., 1992), the tendency might be different between subjects. Especially in this research, because the number of epochs used for signal averaging is quite smaller than that of other research, it is considered that the influences of individual difference might be greater than that of patterns differences. Therefore, the sizes of the patterns were determined based on feedback from subjects in terms of reducing discomfort.
Furthermore, the positions of the visual targets, visual angles of 9 degrees, were also determined based on feedback from subjects despite responses with possible larger amplitudes and smaller variation of latencies when setting the visual targets close to the center of the screen (as seen in Fig. 7). Keeping the targets away from the center of the screen may lead to another advantage in terms of subjects not being bothered by the switching stimuli.
Several improvements were made to the experiment as discussed in section 3. First, the type of stimulation was changed from pattern-onset to pattern-reversal to minimize the stimulation interval as much as possible. Second, a beep sound for the eye blink was discontinued to make the interface suitable for practical use, and the number of pattern switchings in one trial was increased from 15 times to 20 times to sufficiently cancel artifacts of eye blinking by signal averaging.
The advantage of the proposed interfaces is that discomfort of blinking stimuli could be reduced by low-frequency of pattern switching and non-direct gazed visual stimuli. The possibility of the BCIs was validated by the following experiment (Yoshimura & Itakura, 2008b; Yoshimura & Itakura, 2009).

4.2 VEP patterns of the proposed BCIs

(a) Experimental protocol

Six healthy subjects (3 male and 3 female), between 33 and 39 years of age, participated in the experiment. All subjects had normal or corrected-to-normal vision and were right-handed. Electrodes were placed as shown in Fig. 9. Besides RO and LO shown in Fig. 4, PLO, PRO, CLO and CRO were also investigated to identify the best position for each subject.

The system configuration was the same as described in section 3.2(a). Each subject performed 20 trials consisting of 10 each for the right and the left gazing directions in random order. Epochs were extracted in reference to stimulus onset (spanning +300 ms from a pattern switching). The mean was subtracted from each epoch, and 20 epochs were used to calculate an averaged signal. The averaged signal was low-pass filtered with a cutoff frequency of 30 Hz. Detailed protocol of one trial for Type I and Type II is described below.

1. Type I:
   Subjects were asked to gaze at either of the visual targets (L or R) on the monitor and to maintain the gazing direction for about 10 s until the lattice pattern switched 20 times.
2. Type II:
   A trial began after the subjects started gazing at the visual target with the letter C in Fig. 8 (i.e., center-gazing). When the letter C changed to another letter, L (left) or R (right), after 10 occurrences of pattern switching (about 5 s), the subjects changed their gazing direction from the center to the left (i.e., left-gazing) or to the right (i.e., right-gazing) according to the letter L or R. Then their gazing direction was maintained for another 20 occurrences of pattern switching (about 10 s). Signal averaging was performed by using 20 of the most recent epochs, except for the first 19 epochs which used all epochs recorded from the beginning of a trial.

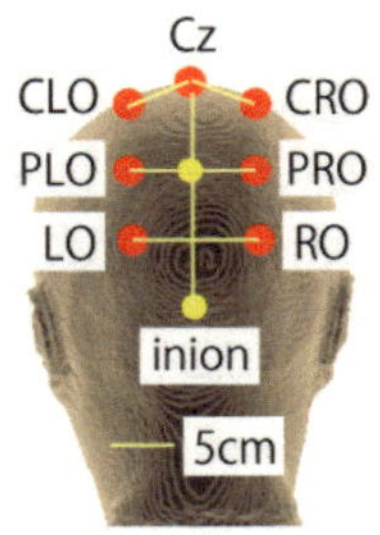

Fig. 9. Electrode positions. Three pairs of electrodes over the occipital (LO and RO), parietal (PLO and PRO), and central (CLO and CRO) regions were used to construct three channels of bipolar derivation. LO, PLO, and CLO were connected to the plus input, and RO, PRO, and CRO were connected to the minus input. A ground electrode was applied over Cz.

(b) Results

Fig. 10 shows examples of VEPs in the case of Type I. While N/P75 was shown to be similar to that in Fig. 6 in section 3, P/N100 was not clearly shown to be similar. This may have been because the display interval of stimuli was shortened from 3 sec to 500 ms.

Next, waveform examples in the case of Type II are shown in Fig. 11. In the case of left-gazing (a red line), N/P75 and P/N100 were shown, but N/P75 was not shown in the case of right-gazing (a blue line). Moreover, the waveform of center-gazing did not show a flat peak contrary to expectation. These results seemed to indicate that transient VEPs were detected in Type II, but that the waveforms became complicated due to the dual stimuli from different visual angles. Especially in the case of center-gazing, the dual stimuli were provided from different directions, left and right, and thus responses to these stimulations might not have become flat but complicated by interfering with each other.

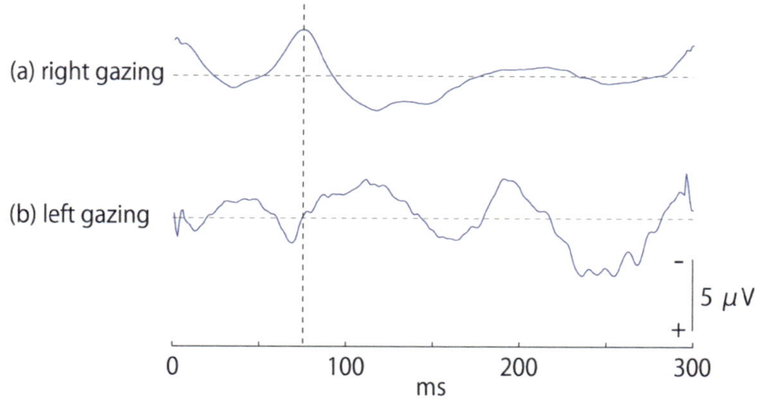

Fig. 10. Examples of transient VEPs in Type I during right-gazing (a) and left-gazing (b). Characteristic peaks appeared at around 75 ms (a vertical dotted line). A negative peak was shown in the case of right-gazing, whereas a positive peak was shown in the case of left-gazing.

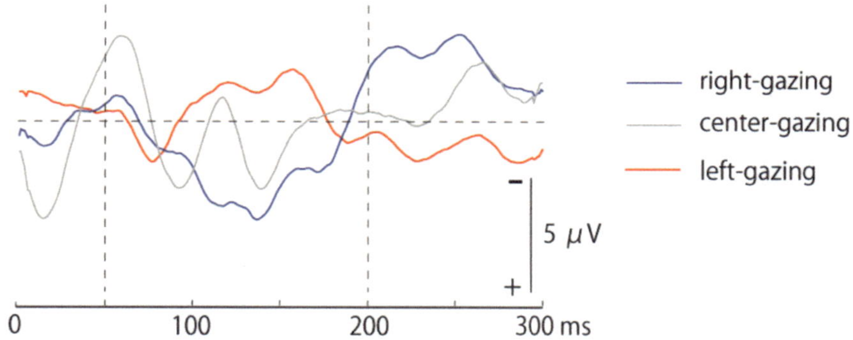

Fig. 11. Examples of waveforms for three gazing directions in Type II. Although N/P75 and P/N100 were not clearly shown, a waveform between 50 to 200 ms (between two vertical dotted lines) shifted to negative voltages when the subject changed the gazing direction from the center to the left, while the waveforms shifted to positive voltages when changing the gazing direction was changed from the center to the right.

4.4 Results: classification of gazing direction in Type II

In the case of Type I, the gazing direction of the left or the right was found to be classified with a 90% mean accuracy by using data around 75 ms from the pattern switching (Yoshimura & Itakura, 2008b). In order to aim for more practical BCIs, classification of gazing directions in Type II was also investigated, and an 84.2% mean accuracy was obtained by using shifts of the waveforms between 50 to 200 ms (Yoshimura & Itakura, 2009). Briefly, the classification method is explained below.

When signals of left- or right-gazing were compared with the center-gazing signal shown in Fig. 11, it was found that signals between 50 to 200 ms shifted to negative voltages during left-gazing and to positive voltages during right-gazing. Focusing on the shift, the areas surrounded by signals between 50 to 200 ms and x-axis were calculated using quadrature by parts, and the areas were compared between the gazing directions as shown in Fig. 12. It was suggested that changing the direction of gazing could be classified by comparing the area between center-gazing and right-gazing or left-gazing. There are minus values because the total areas were calculated by subtracting areas of plus voltage from areas of minus voltage.

In addition to the method above, we also employed another method in the same manner but using the waveforms between 50 to 100 ms because some subjects showed larger shifts in the range of the waveforms. A calibration step was used to select an appropriate method and an appropriate pair of electrodes for each subject, and real-time classification accuracies of gazing direction were obtained as shown in Fig. 13. The accuracies were improved when

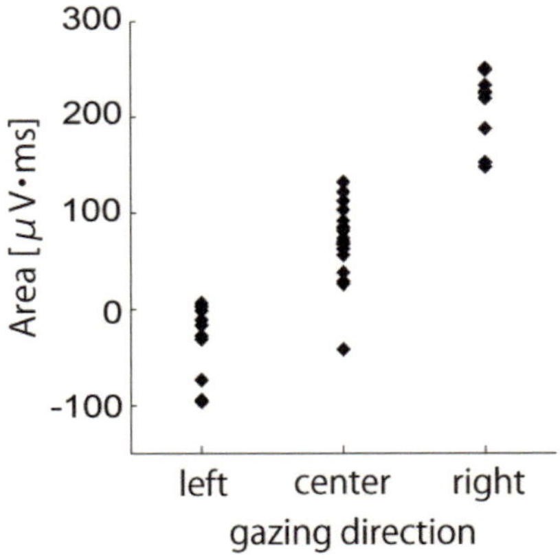

Fig. 12. Comparison of areas between different gazing directions (Yoshimura & Itakura, 2009). Areas of left-gazing tend to be smaller than those of center-gazing, whereas areas of right-gazing tend to be larger than those of center-gazing.

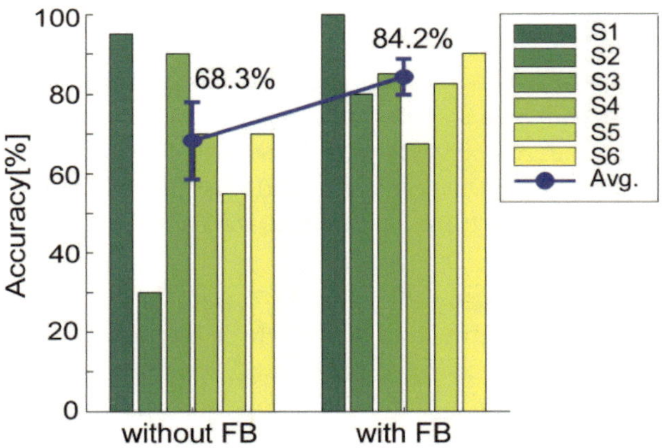

Fig. 13. Real-time classification accuracies of 2 gazing directions, left- and right- gazing (Yoshimura & Itakura, 2009). Accuracies became higher when subjects were given tentative classification feedback of gazing direction in the middle of each session (indicated as "with FB" in the figure).

using the midstream feedback (FB) which gave a classification result to subjects in the middle of a trial as feedback. The FB might help subjects to control the final classification results to be consistent with actual gazing directions.

These results suggest that a more comfortable BCI could be established based on transient VEPs using non-direct gazed visual stimuli. In the next section, the possibility of a machine learning approach was investigated in order to obtain higher classification accuracies.

5. Machine learning approach

5.1 Comparison of classification accuracies

To discern future potential of the proposed BCI, classification accuracies were compared between the classical method introduced in section 4 and a method called support vector machine (SVM). SVM is one of the most popular machine learning methods, and it has often been used for BCIs. A two-class or a three-class nonlinear SVM was conducted using LIBSVM, an SVM software package (Chang & Lin, 2001). A radial basis function was used for the SVM kernel. Data obtained in real-time classification without FB (Fig. 13) were used to compare accuracy rates with the classical method in section 4. Fig. 14(a) shows accuracy rates of a 2-class classification (two moving directions of gazing, from the center to the right or to the left), and Fig. 14(b) shows accuracy rates of 3-class classification (center-gazing, right-gazing, or left-gazing). Although the classical method required 20 epochs (10 seconds gazing after moving the gazing direction) for signal averaging to obtain the mean accuracy of 68.3 %, SVM obtained higher accuracy rates even using only 10 epochs (5-second gazing data) or 5 epochs (2.5-second gazing data).

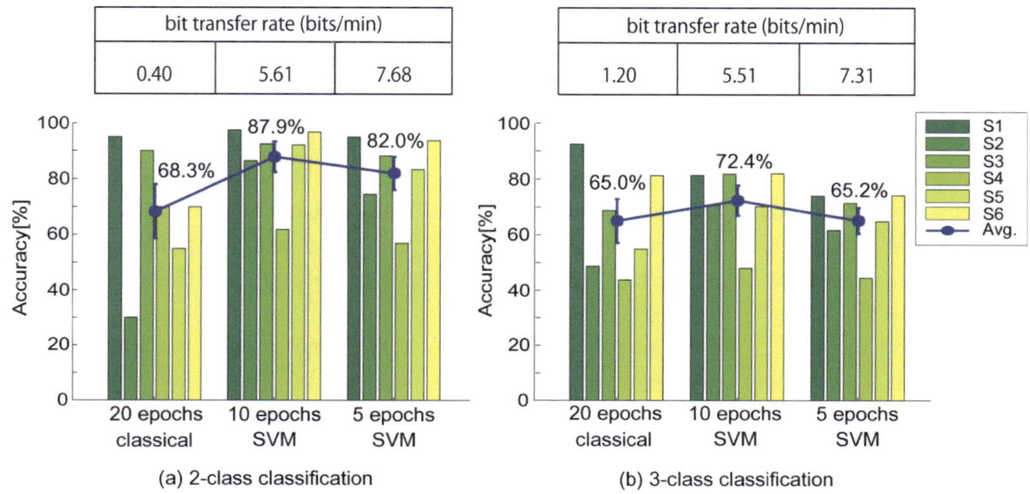

Fig. 14. Comparison of classification accuracies between classical approach and SVM (offline classification). (a) Comparison in the case of 2-class classification, left- and right- gazing.
(b) Comparison in the case of 3-class classification, left-, center-, and right-gazing.

Furthermore, SVM showed a higher mean accuracy in the case of the 3-class classification using 10 epochs (72.4 %) than the classical method in the case of the 2-class classification using 20 epochs (68.3 %) even though the 3-class classification showed overall lower accuracies than the 2-class classification. Therefore, it was suggested that performance of the BCI could be enhanced more using the machine learning method.

5.2 Comparison of bit transfer rate

The concept of bit transfer rate (BTR) is commonly used to validate BCI performance. BTR indicates the amount of information input per unit time and can be calculated using the following formula (1) (McFarland, et al., 2003),

$$\text{BTR (bits/min)} = (\log_2 N + P \log_2 P + (1-P)\log_2[(1-P)/(N-1)]) * 60/T \quad (1)$$

where N is the number of possible targets, P is the accuracy rate, and T is the required time for 1 command in a second.

BTRs of the proposed BCI were calculated as shown in Fig. 14. The highest BTR was found to be obtained in the case of SVM 2-class classification using 5 epochs, and SVM 3-class classification using 5 epochs also showed a relatively high BTR despite its low accuracy. These BTRs are not higher than BTRs shown in other research (Cheng, et al., 2002), but still they can be said to be as practicable BTRs as a BCI, therefore these results suggested the possibility of the proposed BCI using transient VEPs.

6. Conclusion and future research

This research proposed a new approach showing that transient VEPs could be used not only in the field of clinical medicine but also for BCIs, and it showed the possibility of the new approach through several experiments. Transient VEP-based BCIs may have an advantage when compared to SSVEP-based BCIs because low-speed blinking frequencies less than 3.5 Hz are used for detecting transient VEPs, which could suppress specific discomfort symptoms often seen in people who gaze at high-speed blinking visual stimuli. Furthermore, this research achieved a more comfortable feature by incorporating non-direct gazed visual stimuli into the proposed BCI.

The proposed BCI showed practicable performance as a BCI (more than 7 bits/min of BTR), and also could incorporate a worthwhile feature which might classify a situation in which subjects do not gaze at either of two visual targets but instead gaze at the center of the screen.

However, the number of visual targets (commands) is still much less than that of other published BCIs, so there are several issues which need to be addressed to make the proposed BCI more practicable. As a future work, it will be necessary to increase the number of visual targets by incorporating features of classifying not only using several horizontal positions but also using several vertical positions of visual targets.

7. References

Allison, B. Z., McFarland, D. J., Schalk, G., Zheng, S. D., Jackson, M. M., & Wolpaw, J. R. (2008). Towards an independent brain-computer interface using steady state visual evoked potentials. *Clinical Neurophysiology,* Vol. 119, No. 2, (Feb,2008), pp. 399-408, 1388-2457

Barrett, G., Blumhardt, L., Halliday, A. M., Halliday, E., & Kriss, A. (1976). PARADOX IN LATERALIZATION OF VISUAL EVOKED-RESPONSE. *Nature,* Vol. 261, No. 5557, (May,1976), pp. 253-255, 0028-0836

Chang, C., & Lin, C. (2008). *LIBSVM: a library for support vector machines (Version 2.89).* Software available at
http://www.csie.ntu.edu.tw/~cjlin/libsvm

Cheng, M., Gao, X. R., Gao, S. G., & Xu, D. F. (2002). Design and implementation of a brain-computer interface with high transfer rates. *Ieee Transactions on Biomedical Engineering,* Vol. 49, No. 10, (Oct,2002), pp. 1181-1186, 0018-9294

Graf, W. D., Chatrian, G. E., Glass, S. T., & Knauss, T. A. (1994). VIDEO GAME-RELATED SEIZURES - A REPORT ON 10 PATIENTS AND A REVIEW OF THE LITERATURE. *Pediatrics,* Vol. 93, No. 4, (Apr,1994), pp. 551-556, 0031-4005

Guerrini, R., & Genton, P. (2004). Epileptic syndromes and visually induced seizures. *Epilepsia,* Vol. 45, No. s1, (Jan,2004), pp. 14-18, 0013-9580

McFarland, D. J., Sarnacki, W. A., & Wolpaw, J. R. (2003). Brain-computer interface (BCI) operation: optimizing information transfer rates. *Biological Psychology,* Vol. 63, No. 3, (Jul,2003), pp. 237-251, 0301-0511

Sellers, E. W., & Donchin, E. (2006). A P300-based brain-computer interface: Initial tests by ALS patients. *Clinical Neurophysiology,* Vol. 117, No. 3, (Mar,2006), pp. 538-548, 1388-2457

Sellers, E. W., Krusienski, D. J., McFarland, D. J., Vaughan, T. M., & Wolpaw, J. R. (2006). A P300 event-related potential brain-computer interface (BCI): The effects of matrix size and inter stimulus interval on performance. *Biological Psychology,* Vol. 73, No. 3, (Oct,2006), pp. 242-252, 0301-0511

Suttle, C. M., & Harding, G. F. A. (1999). Morphology of transient VEPs to luminance and chromatic pattern onset and offset. *Vision Research,* Vol. 39, No. 8, (Apr,1999), pp. 1577-1584, 0042-6989

Torok, B., Meyer, M., & Wildberger, H. (1992). THE INFLUENCE OF PATTERN SIZE ON AMPLITUDE, LATENCY AND WAVE FORM OF RETINAL AND CORTICAL POTENTIALS ELICITED BY CHECKERBOARD PATTERN REVERSAL AND STIMULUS ONSET-OFFSET. *Electroencephalography and Clinical Neurophysiology,* Vol. 84, No. 1, (Jan-Feb,1992), pp. 13-19, 0013-4694

Watanabe, C. (Ed.). (2004). *Brain Evoked Potentials measurment handbook* (3rd ed.). Tokyo: Medical System Institute Co., Ltd.

Yoshimura, N., & Itakura, N. (2008a). A Study on Brain-Computer Interface Using Transient Visual Evoked Potentials. *Transactions of Japanese Society for Medical and Biological Engineering,* Vol. 46, No. 2, (Apr,2008a), pp. 202-211, 1347-443X

Yoshimura, N., & Itakura, N. (2008b). Study on transient VEP-based brain-computer interface using non-direct gazed visual stimuli. *Electromyogr Clin Neurophysiol,* Vol. 48, No. 1, (Jan-Feb,2008b), pp. 43-51, 0301-150X

Yoshimura, N., & Itakura, N. (2009). A transient VEP-based real-time brain-computer interface using non-direct gazed visual stimuli. *Electromyogr Clin Neurophysiol,* Vol. 49, No. 8, (Nov-Dec,2009), pp. 323-335, 0301-150X

7

Visuo-Motor Tasks in a Brain-Computer Interface Analysis

Vito Logar and Aleš Belič
Faculty of Electrical Engineering, University of Ljubljana,
Tr□aška 25, SI-1000 Ljubljana
Slovenia

1. Introduction

The neurophysiological studies covered by the subject of Brain-Computer Interfaces (BCIs) (del R. Millán et al., 2004; Lebedev & Nicolelis, 2006; Wolpaw et al., 2002) represent a promising, but so far rather undiscovered, area of research. What is perhaps the most interesting part of BCI research is the idea of understanding the information coding in the brain and its use when performing different predefined actions or commands. Recent reports have proposed various techniques for the development of BCIs, based either on the electroencephalographic (EEG) non-invasive (Birbaumer et al., 1999; Wolpaw & McFarland, 2004), invasive (Taylor et al., 2002; Wessberg et al., 2000), magnetoencephalographic (MEG) (Georgopoulos et al., 2005; Mellinger et al., 2007) or other (fMRI, PET, optical imaging) measurements. Since all of these, except EEG, still represent technically demanding and expensive methods, the EEG-based BCIs tend to prevail. Modern BCIs are often classified into several groups based on the electrophysiological signals used, i.e., the different brain potentials (evoked visual, slow cortical, P300 evoked), the mu and beta rhythms, the activities of single cortical neurons, etc. (Wolpaw et al., 2002).

The human brain can be considered as a system of highly interconnected groups of neurons, where each neuron or group acts as an oscillator. When the brain is in a certain mode or state, different groups of these neurons synchronize themselves to a certain physiological frequency. In order to achieve a large-scale neuronal synchronization that is detectable, for instance, when using an EEG, several tens of thousands of neurons need to fire at approximately the same time with respect to a neuronal population that has approximately the same spatial orientation. It is believed that the theory of oscillations represents one of the essential mechanisms of brain operation, as studies have shown that every single process in the brain is probably within the neuronal system mediated by means of the electric oscillations of the neuronal populations (Engel et al., 2001). These oscillations or oscillatory activity can be classified into different frequency bands and are referred to as the brain rhythms ($[0.5-3Hz]$ – delta, $[4-7HZ]$ – theta, $[8-12Hz]$ – alpha, $[13-30Hz]$ – beta, $[30-50Hz]$ – gamma). It is suggested that the synchronization of the oscillatory activity carries out the brain's functionality, cognition and behavior, which are based on distributed, parallel information processing and exchange between anatomically not necessarily connected neuronal populations (Ivanitsky et al., 2001; Manganotti et al., 1998; Pfurtscheller & Andrew, 1999). When a collaboration of neuronal populations is necessary to

perform a cognitive task, the information exchange between these regions is mediated through a synchronized oscillatory activity (Schnitzler & Gross, 2005) that is believed to be an integral aspect of the brain function (Engel et al., 2001). The synchronized connection between the separated areas is also referred to as the neuronal coupling or binding (Classen et al., 1998).
Besides the mechanisms of oscillations, synchronization and binding, the newest insight into the brain's informational exchange and coding suggests a mechanism that could represent a general information-coding scheme and is based on the phase coding of the content in the oscillatory activity (Lisman, 2005). The theory of phase coding has already been explored in working-memory processes (Huxter et al., 2008; Jensen, 2001; 2005; Mormann et al., 2005); however, it is assumed that similar coding patterns are present during other cognitive actions too. Briefly, the idea behind the phase coding is that the phase characteristics of the synchronized oscillations in the brain that originate from two or more different brain areas could carry the information relevant to the completion of a certain task currently being performed (Buzsáki & Draguhn, 2004; Jensen & Lisman, 2005). Therefore, if we combine the mechanisms of oscillatory activity and neuronal coupling with the proposed mechanism of phase coding, it may be possible that the content that is coded in the oscillations is transferred between the synchronized regions of the cooperating neuronal populations as the phase modulated content. Consequently, it is reasonable to anticipate that using phase-decoding techniques, such as phase demodulation, it may be possible to decode at least some parts of the exchanged information that are relevant to the current action in the brain.
The study presented in this chapter investigates an alternative approach to the development of a non-invasive, EEG-based, beta-rhythm BCI. The EEG signals used for the study were measured on several subjects performing different types of visuo-motor tasks. As is generally known, many proposed BCIs need extensive training for the subjects so that they can gain control over their brain rhythms in order to properly use the BCI (Neuper & Pfurtscheller, 2001; Wolpaw et al., 1991). However, the approach presented in this paper deviates from the subject-training ideas and is instead based on EEG data pre-processing and fuzzy classification, which does not need any preliminary subject training (Logar, Belič, Koritnik, Brežan, Zidar, Karba & Matko, 2008; Logar, Škrjanc, Belič, Brežan, Koritnik & Zidar, 2008). The proposed methodology, which is capable of interpreting the measured EEG information in a certain predefined action, uses different beta brain-rhythm filters, phase demodulation and a principal component analysis for the signal pre-processing. The signals processed in this manner are then used in a Takagi-Sugeno (Takagi & Sugeno, 1985) fuzzy inference system (Kosko, 1994; Wang & Mendel, 1992; Ying, 1997), which serves as a classifier for the BCI's output activity. The goal of the presented BCI is to use the processed EEG signals, measured during different visuo-motor tasks, as inputs to the BCI to estimate (predict) the course of the given motor action (gripping force and wrist movements).

2. Materials and Methods

2.1 Visuo-motor tasks

For this study two different types of visuo-motor tasks (VM) were performed by the subjects, i.e., a static visuo-motor task (sVM) and a dynamic visuo-motor task (dVM). When performing the sVM task the EEG signals and the gripping force were measured as the subjects performed the task with their right and the left hands. The sVM task required the subjects to observe a sine-wave signal, representing the amplitude of the desired gripping force on the screen, and follow its shape by applying a force to the sensor with the index finger and the thumb as precisely as possible, as shown in figure 1. The thin and the thick lines were not displayed to the subject during the performance of the task in order to prevent any possible estimation of the course of a forthcoming signal. The subject could only see the two dots in the middle of the screen, representing the actual and the desired gripping force. Each task was divided into 20 blocks, of which the first part was active and lasted 25*s* and the second part was a pause that lasted 25*s*. For this study the data from all five tasks were used.

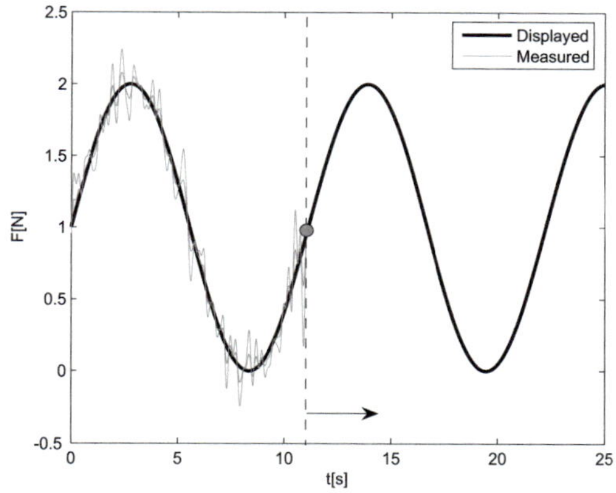

Fig. 1. Static visuo-motor task

When performing the dVM task the EEG signals and the wrist movements were measured simultaneously as the subjects performed the task with their right hands. The dVM task required the subjects to observe a randomly generated continuous signal, representing the amplitude of the desired joystick movement on the screen and following its shape by applying the wrist shift to the joystick as precisely as possible, as shown in figure 2. The grey and the black lines were not shown to the subject during the experiment in order to prevent any prediction of the forthcoming movement. Only the two dots in the middle, which indicated the desired and the actual wrist (joystick) shift, were displayed to the subject during the performance of each task. The wrist shifts that needed to be applied were limited to 70% of the joystick's maximum shift so as to prevent any possible hardware non-linearities, while the upper frequency limit of the target signal was $0.15Hz$. Each task was divided into 10 blocks, of which the first part was active and lasted 30 seconds and the second part was a pause that lasted 30 seconds.

The main difference between the static and the dynamic VM tasks is related to the target signal to be followed by the subjects. While the sVM task uses sine-wave target signals with constant amplitude and frequency, the dVM task uses randomly generated continuous signals with variable amplitude and frequency, which are different for each task repetition. The dVM target signal, which is thought to be harder to predict, could prevent the brain's learning process and probably represents a more complex task for the brain.

2.2 Subjects and EEG sessions

In the case of the static VM task we used electroencephalographic data from three healthy, right-handed subjects: two male, one female, aged 26, 27 and 29 years. The EEG recording sessions took place in a dark, quiet and electromagnetically shielded room. The subjects were placed on a bed with an elevated headrest to minimize the tension of the neck muscles. The tasks were displayed on an LCD screen, 80 centimetres in front of the subject, using *Matlab* 5.3

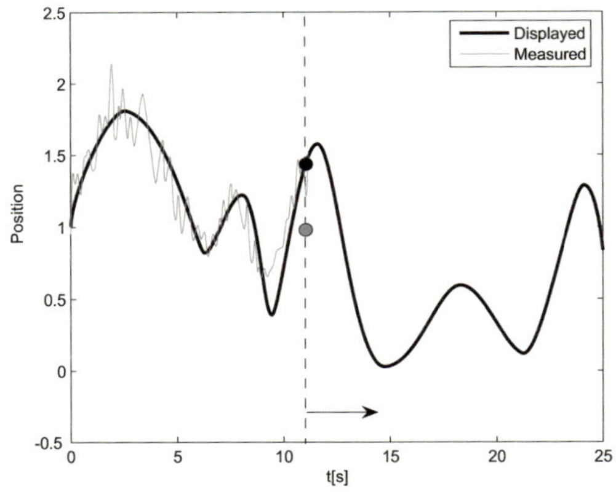

Fig. 2. Dynamic visuo-motor task

software. The subjects performed the tasks with their right or left hands, gripping the force sensor with an index finger and a thumb.

For the needs of the dynamic VM task we used electroencephalographic data from four healthy, right-handed subjects: all male, aged 24, 27, 32 and 37 years. The EEG recording sessions took place in a dark, quiet and electromagnetically shielded room. The subjects sat on a chair with elevated leg and hand rests in order to minimize any muscle tension. The subjects performed the tasks with their right hands, moving the joystick, which was placed on a desk in front of the subject, back and forth. The tasks were displayed on an LCD screen, 80 centimetres in front of the subject, using *Matlab* 7 software.

In both types of tasks the amplitude of the target signals subtended approximately 10 degrees of the visual angle. None of the participating subjects had any previous experience with such cognitive tasks nor had any of them ever participated in an EEG-related study.

2.3 EEG and motor action data

For the study, two types of measurements were performed simultaneously, i.e., the EEG measurements and the motor action data. To obtain the electroencephalographic activity two similar EEG systems were used.

In order to be able to measure the EEG data when performing the sVM task we used a Medelec system (Profile Multimedia EEG System, version 2.0, Oxford Instruments Medical Systems Division, Surrey, England) with a 10–20 electrode montage system, linked-ear reference, low- ($< 0.5Hz$) and high-pass ($> 70Hz$) filters and a $256 - Hz$ sampling frequency. The electrode impedance was retained below 5kΩ. In order to record the gripping-force data an analog force sensor was used and connected to a PC through a 12-bit PCI-DAS1002 card (Measurement Computing Corp. Middleboro, USA). Both recordings were mutually synchronized through the signal sent from the PC and recorded with the EEG system. The force data were acquired using *Matlab* software. The gripping-force signal was sampled with a $100 - Hz$ sampling frequency.

To measure the EEG data when performing the dVM task we used the Brain Products system (Brain Products GmbH, Germany) with a 10–20 electrode montage system, a common average reference, low- ($< 0.15Hz$) and high-pass ($> 100Hz$) filters and a $512 - Hz$ sampling frequency. The electrode impedance was retained below $5k\Omega$. The wrist-movement data were acquired using a joystick connected to a PC via a USB port. The wrist movements were performed in the up/down (forth/back) joystick direction. Both recordings were synchronized through the signal that was sent from the PC and recorded with the EEG system. *Matlab* software was used for the wrist-movement acquisition. The wrist-movement signal was sampled with a $50 - Hz$ sampling frequency.

2.4 Software tools

The numerical analysis of the obtained measurements was performed using *Matlab* 7 with its fuzzy logic, signal processing and statistics toolboxes. To extract the required brain-rhythm intervals from the raw EEG data and to prevent a potential signal-drift when using phase demodulation, 5th-order band-pass and 3rd-order high-pass (0.025Hz) Butterworth filters were applied. When processing the sVM task data, zero-phase filters were used, i.e., *Matlab*'s *□lt□lt* function, in order to preserve the phase characteristics of the signals. When processing the dVM task data ordinary filters were used, i.e., *Matlab*'s *□lter* function, in order to achieve a real-time data-processing ability. The EEG signals were phase demodulated using *Matlab*'s *demod* function, and the principal component analysis was applied using *Matlab*'s *prepca* function.

2.5 Signal processing

Although the signal-processing methods are very alike for both types of VM task performed, there are a few important differences that allow the dVM methodology to be used for the on-line, real-time BCI data processing, while the sVM methodology can only be used for off-line signal analysis. The obtained EEG measurements underwent several combinations of signal-processing procedures, parameter fitting and fuzzy-model options in order to find the methodology constellation that yields the optimal gripping-force or wrist-movement estimations for the forthcoming task trials.

When processing the sVM task data the following signal-processing algorithm was applied. First, a zero-phase band-pass filter was applied to the original EEG signal so as to obtain the frequency band of the beta brain rhythm ($[13 - 30Hz]$). Afterwards, since the phase characteristics of the signals supposedly play an important role in the information exchange (Buzsáki & Draguhn, 2004; Jensen & Lisman, 2005), the signals were phase demodulated. This phase demodulation was calculated with the *demod* function, which uses the Hilbert transformation for the calculations. The carrier-wave frequency for the demodulation was chosen experimentally in such a way that the transformed signals exhibited no drift. The frequency was approximately the same for all three subjects and both tasks (left/right hand), i.e., around $20Hz(+/-1Hz)$. After the phase demodulation we used a principal components analysis (PCA) transformation. The PCA is normally used to convert the original variables into new, uncorrelated variables, which are called the principal components, and represent linear combinations of the original variables, lie along the directions of maximum variance and carry the same amount of information as the original variables. When processing the EEG data, there are two reasons for using the PCA. The first is to transform the data in a reduced coordinate system, where only the directions of the eigenvectors with the main variance are taken into account; meaning that the dimensionality of the primary data can be considerably reduced - in this study from 29 electrode signals to 5 principal components, which according to the calculations carry 95% of the original information. The second reason lies in the linear independence of the principal components, which is significant for problem-less training and the validation of the fuzzy model.

Afterwards, the pre-processed signals were used as the input data for the fuzzy model for predicting the gripping force. The designed model was trained and validated using the data from each task repetition separately, i.e., one period (25*s*) of activity was used for the training, and the successive period of activity, which was not a part of the training data set, was used for validating the model. The model calculated the estimated force in every time sample using the pre-processed EEG data for the non-delayed input/output signal without any output to the input feedback connections.
The block diagram of the signal-processing methods for the gripping-force prediction used in this study is shown in figure 3.

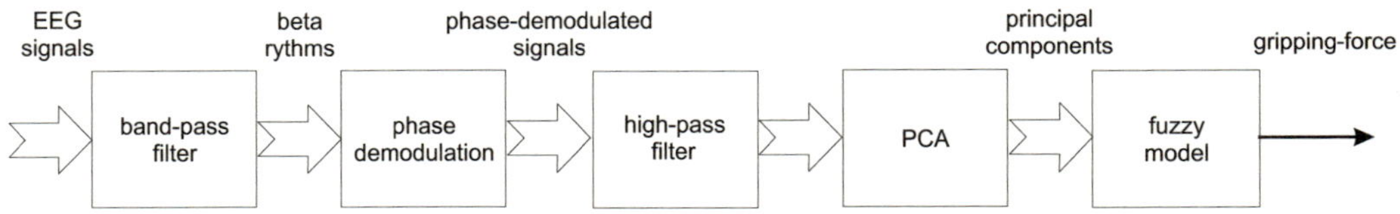

Fig. 3. Schematic representation of the data processing for sVM task data

When processing the dVM task data, the following signal-processing algorithm was applied. First, the raw EEG data were duplicated to produce two identical sets. Then, each data set was sliced into intervals of interest, i.e., 30-second activity periods, and band-pass filtered (ordinary filter), each with its own frequency interval to obtain two different areas of the beta rhythms, i.e., $\approx [12 - 16Hz]$ and $\approx [18 - 22Hz]$. Afterwards, each set was phase demodulated with a different carrier-wave frequency using Matlab's *demod* function (Hilbert transform), i.e., $\approx 14Hz$ and $\approx 20Hz$. Finally, the PCA transformation was applied to both sets. The main difference in the application of the PCA procedure to the dVM task data in comparison to the sVM task data is the following: for the dVM task we computed the PCA transformation matrix in the model-training period and then applied it to the EEG data in the model-validation period. In this way the causality (real-time processing) of the method is achieved, which enables on-line data processing. Otherwise, the reason for using the PCA was the same as for the sVM tasks, i.e., to reduce the dimensionality of the input data and to achieve a linear independence of the signals. The study showed that also for the dVM task, it is possible to describe 95% of the signals' variance using five principal components. Therefore, two data sets, each composed of the first five PCA scores, were used for the further analysis, thus producing ten different inputs to the prediction model. The dVM-task data processing scheme is shown in figure 4.

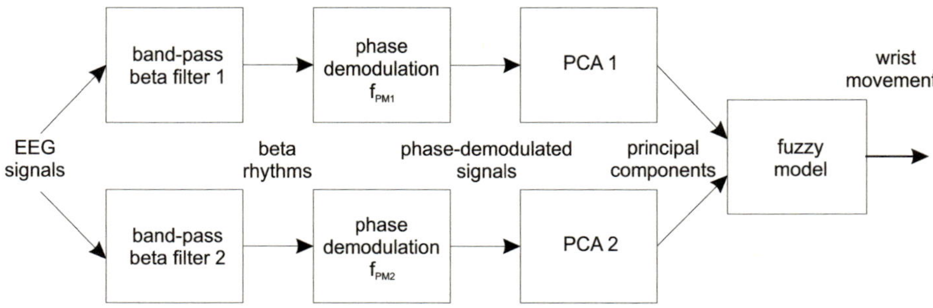

Fig. 4. Schematic representation of the data processing for dVM task data

As already mentioned, for each VM task (sVM or dVM) the trained model was validated using the EEG and gripping-force or wrist-movement activity data from the forthcoming signal periods, which were not selected as a part of the training-data set.
The main difference in the signal-processing methodology between both VM tasks is the possibility for the dVM methodology to process the data in real time. This was achieved by using ordinary (non-zero-phase) Butterworth filters and by applying the PCA transformation matrix to the validation (prediction) period, which has already been obtained in the previous (training) period of the data processing. In this way the dVM methodology is more complex and requires more time to process the data; however, in contrast to the sVM methodology it is usable for the development of the BCI.

2.6 Fuzzy estimator

In the presented study, the motor-action-estimation model was built using a fuzzy inference system in the Takagi-Sugeno (TS) form, which approximates a nonlinear system by smoothly interpolating affine local models (Takagi & Sugeno, 1985). Each local model contributes to the global model in a fuzzy subset of the space characterized by a membership function.
We assume a set of input vectors $X = [x_1, x_2, \dots, x_n]^T$ and a set of corresponding outputs that is defined as $Y = [y_1, y_2, \dots, y_n]^T$.
A typical fuzzy model (Takagi & Sugeno, 1985) is given in the form of rules:

$$R_i : \; if \; x_k \; is \; A_i \; then \; \hat{y}_k = \phi_i(x_k) \quad i = 1, \dots, c \tag{1}$$

where the vector x_k denotes the input or variables in premise, and the variable $\hat{y}_k$ is the output of the model at time instant k. The premise vector x_k is connected to one of the fuzzy sets $(A_1, \dots, A_c)$ and each fuzzy set A_i ($i = 1, \dots, c$) is associated with a real-valued function $\mu_{A_i}(x_k)$ or $\mu_{ik} : \mathbb{R} \rightarrow [0, 1]$, that produces the membership grade of the variable x_k with respect to the fuzzy set A_i. The functions $\phi_i(\cdot)$ can be arbitrary smooth functions in general, although linear or affine functions are normally used.
The affine Takagi-Sugeno model can be used to approximate any arbitrary function with any desired degree of accuracy (Kosko, 1994; Ying, 1997). The generality can be proven with the Stone-Weierstrass theorem (Goldberg, 1976), which suggests that any continuous function can be approximated by a fuzzy basis function expansion (Lin, 1997).
For generating an initial fuzzy inference system (FIS) we used the fuzzy subtractive clustering method. When given separate sets of input (EEG) and output (motor action) data, this method generates an initial FIS or the model training by applying fuzzy subtractive clustering of the data. This is accomplished by extracting a set of rules that models the data behavior. The rule-extraction method first determines the number of rules and antecedent membership functions and then uses a linear least-squares estimation to determine each rule's consequent equations. A combination of the least-squares and the backpropagation-gradient-descent methods were used to train the initial FIS membership function parameters to model a given set of input/output data.

2.7 BCI signal processing

As has already been mentioned, the dVM task methodology allows processing of the EEG and motor-action data in real time, thus enabling its usage in a BCI. The methodology used for the sVM data processing is non-causal, meaning that its use in a real-time data analysis is not possible, as the zero-phase filters and the PCA transformation cannot process the data sample-by-sample. The filters are non-causal because the filtering is done in both directions of the signal simultaneously in order to preserve the phase, while the PCA procedure is non-causal because it is done by means of a singular value decomposition, which also transforms the signals all at once and not sample-by-sample. Thus, both of these methods need the complete EEG data set at once in order to process it properly. Therefore, to achieve an on-line data-processing ability several experiments were performed. In the end, the best results were achieved when replacing the zero-phase with ordinary Butterworth filters and when using the same PCA transformation matrix for training and validating the fuzzy model. Thus, the EEG data from the preceding activity period were used to obtain the transformation matrix, which was then applied to the EEG data in the succeeding activity period. Since the phase-demodulation method itself is already causal, its structure remained the same. In this way the algorithm for real-time, online data processing exploits the advantages of the methodology to train the BCI in the resting period when an activity period has just finished and then validates it with the forthcoming activity period. The algorithm should re-train and re-validate the BCI in each task repetition.

3. Results

The following section presents the results of the proposed methodology for EEG data processing when using measurements from the sVM and dVM tasks. To achieve the best possible motor-action estimation, numerous attempts, with different brain-rhythm combinations as the model inputs, were made; however, satisfactory results were achieved with beta-filtered, phase-demodulated and PCA-transformed EEG signals, and these are described below.

3.1 sVM task

The following section presents the gripping-force estimation obtained by the presented fuzzy-inference model using the EEG measurements processed according to the described sVM methodology. In the subsequent figures the thin line represents the measured gripping force as applied by the subject in the activity period, while the thick line is the estimated gripping force of the fuzzy model for the following period of activity. In figures 5 to 7 the left-hand side panel shows the measured and estimated result when the task was performed with the left hand, and the right-hand side panel represents the measured and estimated result when the task was performed with the right hand.

As shown in figures 5 to 7 the gripping-force predictions are successful for all three subjects and both types of VM task (left and right hands), which indicates the suitability of the proposed signal-processing and modeling approach for handling the VM-task EEG measurements.

Since the fuzzy estimator predicts the gripping-force signal of a sine-wave shape, there could be an assumption or a doubt that the identified model is merely a sine-wave generator using the EEG signals as inputs. On the other hand, if the predicted output signal really is the applied gripping force, the estimated output signal should not contain any sine waveforms when validating the model using resting period (no motor action) EEG data. Therefore, the trained estimation model was validated using the EEG signals obtained during the subject 1 rest period, and the results are presented in figure 8.

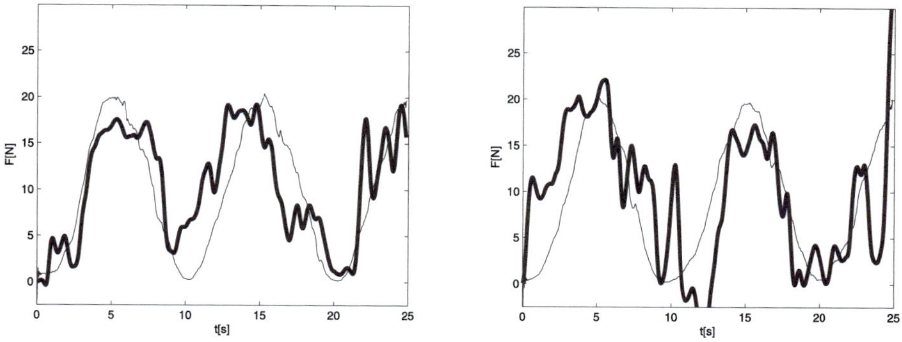

Fig. 5. Comparison of the gripping-force predictions for one period of activity for subject 1; left panel: sVM task performance with the left hand; right panel: sVM task performance with the right hand

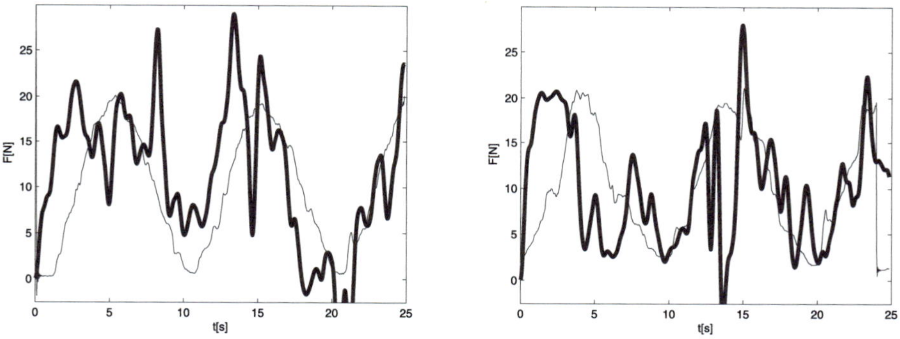

Fig. 6. Comparison of the gripping-force predictions for one period of activity for subject 2; left panel: sVM task performance with the left hand; right panel: sVM task performance with the right hand

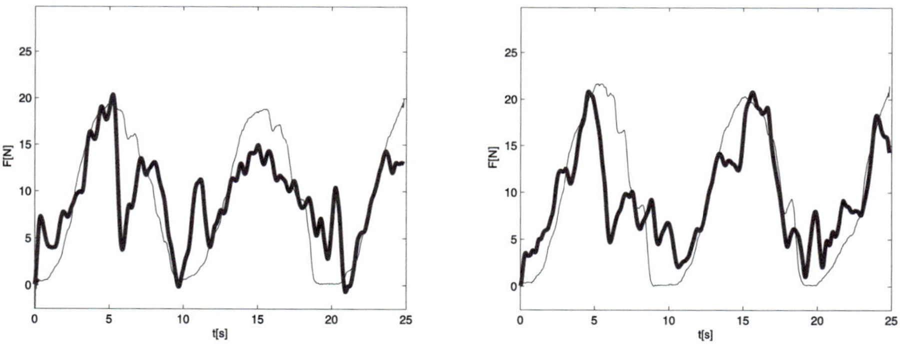

Fig. 7. Comparison of the gripping-force predictions for one period of activity for subject 3; left panel: sVM task performance with the left hand; right panel: sVM task performance with the right hand

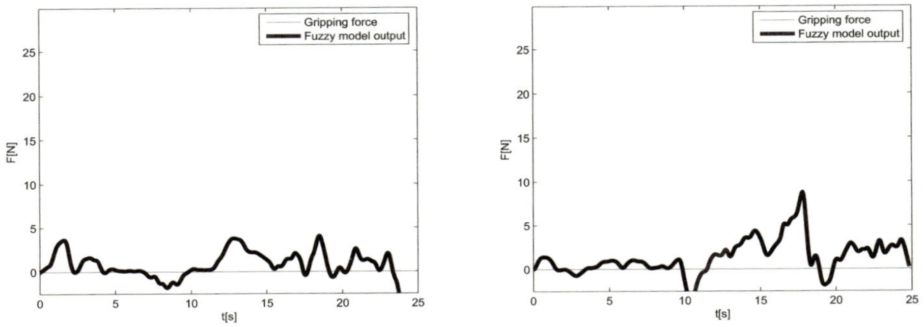

Fig. 8. Comparison of the gripping-force predictions for two periods of rest for subject 1

As figure 8 shows, the gripping-force estimation for the rest periods does not include any sine waveforms, opposed to the prediction results in figures 5 to 7, which excludes the possibility of any force prediction in the activity periods being the result of a random event or a characteristic of the given fuzzy estimator.

Furthermore, the study also revealed, that satisfactory gripping-force predictions could be obtained when cross-validating the identified model, meaning that the model was trained using one subject's EEG data and validated using the the other two subjects's data. Figure 9 shows the model-estimated force response.

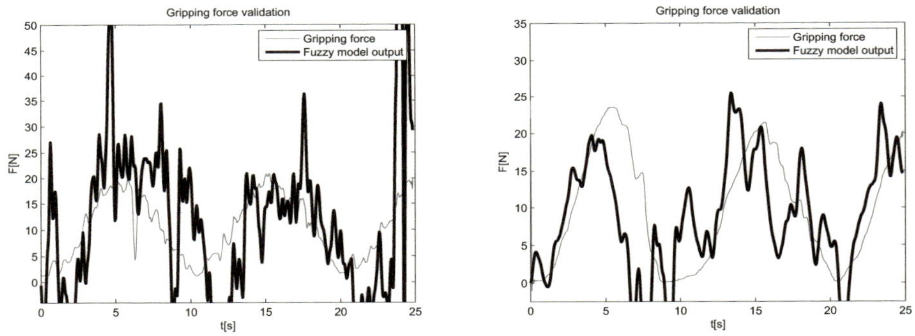

Fig. 9. Cross-validation of the identified fuzzy estimator

Figure 9 shows the satisfactory cross-validation result of the identified fuzzy model, which suggests that similar coding patterns of information are present during the performance of the visuo-motor task between the three examined subjects.

3.2 dVM task

The following section presents the wrist-movement estimation obtained by the fuzzy inference model using the EEG measurements processed according to the described dVM methodology. In the subsequent figures the thin line represents the measured wrist movement as applied to the joystick by the subject in the activity period, while the thick line represents the estimated wrist movement of the fuzzy model for the same period of activity. Figures 10 to 13 show the results for four successive periods of activity for all four subjects.

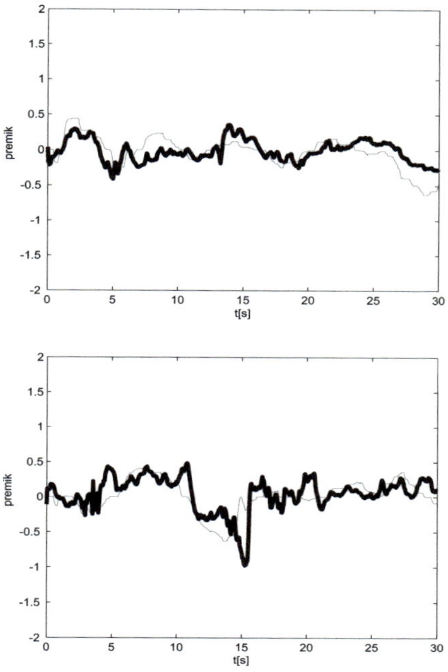

Fig. 10. Wrist-movement predictions for four successive periods of activity for subject 1, when performing a dVM task

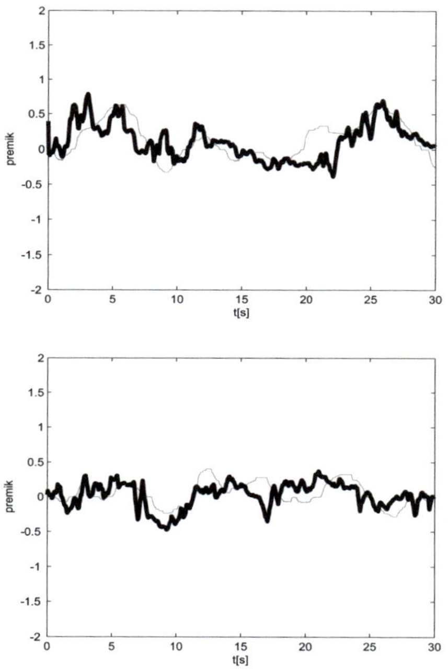

Fig. 11. Wrist-movement predictions for four successive periods of activity for subject 2, when performing a dVM task

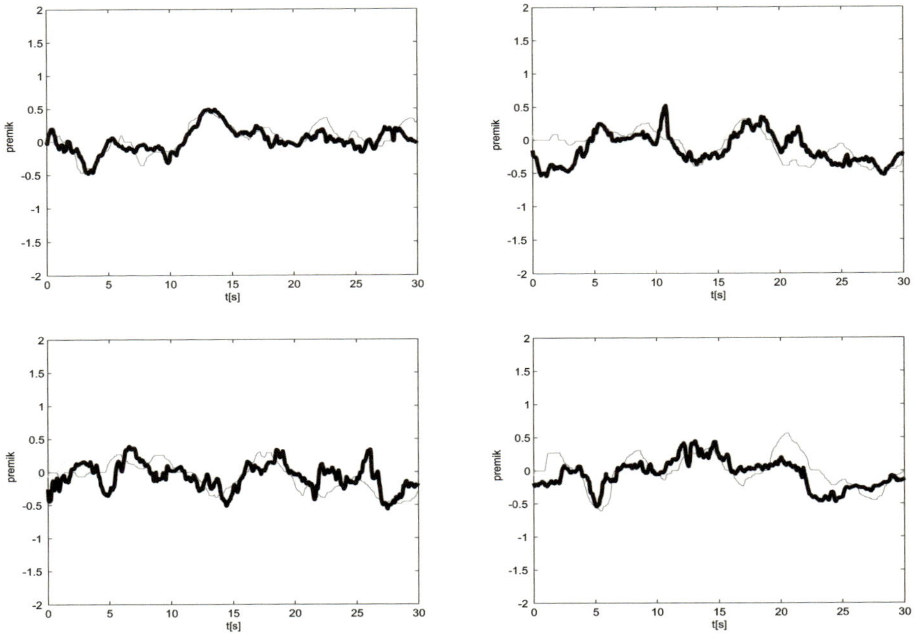

Fig. 12. Wrist-movement predictions for four successive periods of activity for subject 3, when performing a dVM task

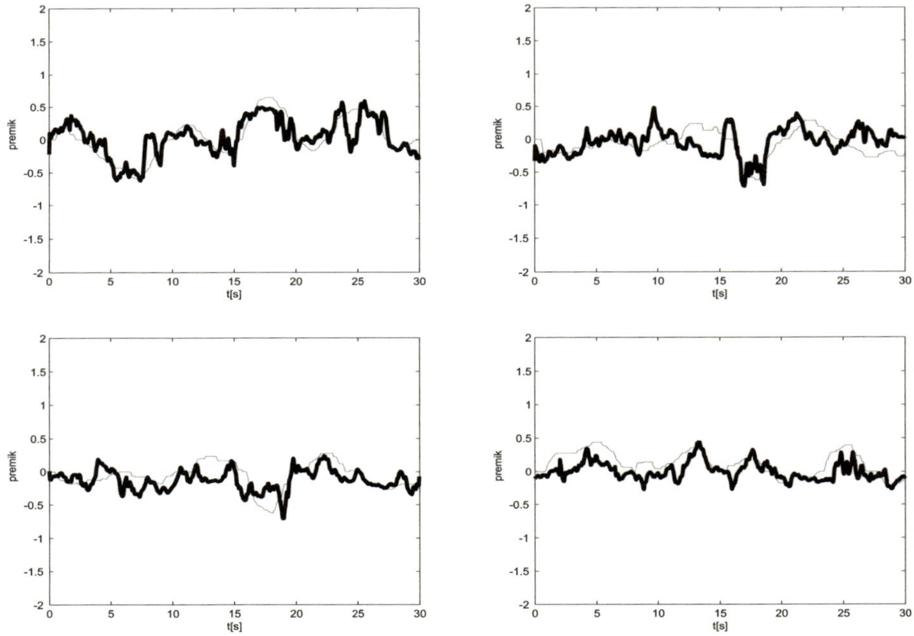

Fig. 13. Wrist-movement predictions for four successive periods of activity for subject 4, when performing a dVM task

As is clear from figures 10 to 13 the fuzzy model successfully predicts the wrist movements from the EEG signals for all four subjects and all the periods of activity, which demonstrates the adequacy of the proposed signal-processing and modeling approach. When comparing the dVM task results to the sVM task results it is clear that both models output motor-action predictions of approximately the same quality; however, to achieve the same level of quality for the dVM task, a greater level of complexity in the signal processing is needed. This could be the consequence of several factors, e.g., greater task complexity, different information coding, prevention of the brain-learning process, etc.

4. Discussion

In the chapter we presented a fuzzy estimation of the brain-code during simple gripping-force and more complex wrist-movement control tasks. As is clear from the results, by using the appropriate signal-processing approach, which is similar for both types of VM task, a fuzzy model can successfully predict the course of the motor actions from the brain's activity measured by EEG. The obtained results show the high prediction ability of the model and suggest that the proposed methodology of the signal processing and the fuzzy-prediction models are suitable for decoding some parts of the information, which is supposedly transferred between the active regions of the brain when performing both types of VM task. Thus far the methodology that successfully decodes the brain information consists of filtering different bands of brain rhythms, phase demodulation and a principal component analysis. All of these methods are relatively simple; however, to find the optimal methodology constellation that yields the optimal gripping-force or wrist-movement estimations for the forthcoming task trials, the EEG measurements underwent several combinations of signal-processing procedures, parameter fitting, optimization and fuzzy model options. Similar methods of signal processing have proved to be suitable for extracting the EEG information from working-memory tasks (Logar, Belič, Koritnik, Brežan, Zidar, Karba & Matko, 2008), and now we have shown that they can also, with some modifications, be used for extracting the information from VM tasks.

In order to use such a methodology for the information decoding of VM tasks the required modifications include a replacement of the model's parameters to comply with the theory of the brain's visuo-motor integration. Therefore, for the needs of a different cognitive task, the filtering intervals and carrier-wave frequencies need to be adapted to meet the needs of a motor task instead of a working-memory task. Briefly, this means that all the frequency parameters that were placed in the theta frequency band (Logar, Belič, Koritnik, Brežan, Zidar, Karba & Matko, 2008) had to be shifted to the beta frequency band and precisely re-fitted. Parameter re-fitting proved to suit the needs of the static VM task data processing; however, to handle the data of a more complex dVM task an extension of the data processing had to be performed. Therefore, the EEG data were duplicated and the signal-processing methods were applied twice with different processing parameters. There are a few possible reasons why the results obtained with double signal processing are better, compared to a single signal processing. The first of them could be the more complex dVM task that had to be performed. Since the target signal to be followed is a randomly generated continuous signal, which is more information-rich than a sine wave, its tracking could elicit more complex brain processes. These processes could be encoded differently or maybe carry different information about the wrist movements. Another possible reason also arises from the randomly generated target signal. Since the signal is newly generated for each task repetition it could prevent the so-called learning process, which is usually initiated when a certain task is repeated several times, e.g., the static VM task. Naturally, there are other plausible reasons like, e.g., a non-deterministic signal that codes the neuronal information, moving a wrist represents a more complex task than gripping a force sensor, achieving causality of the filters and the PCA worsen the prediction ability of single signal processing, etc.

Nonetheless, the results have shown that the proposed methodology can be used in a real-time brain-computer interface that is able to decode the brain code supposedly transferred between the visual and motor areas of the human brain during the VM tasks. The main difference between the proposed methodology and the existing BCI systems lies in the mode of its use and in the signal-processing complexity. While the existing BCIs mostly need extensive training for the subjects to adapt to the BCI and to master the control of their brain rhythms, the proposed approach does not need any previous subject training as it uses the EEG signals as they are. Therefore, signal-processing methods try to extract the encoded information about the motor actions. However, such methods represent a more complex system, which needs efficient hardware and constant re-training of the fuzzy classifier to retain the necessary input/output data mapping for an optimal movement estimation. However, considering the obtained results, showing the high prediction ability of the introduced approach, it appears that the phase characteristics of the brain waves together with different bands of beta rhythms play an important role in the brain's informational coding and transfer and can also be used for the development of a non-invasive, brain-computer interface.

5. Conclusion

This chapter shows that in spite of the fact that measured brain signals represent a superposition of nearly all the active neurons, it is, using appropriate signal-processing methods, possible to identify and predict the motor-action information encoded in the person's EEG. Supposedly, this information is encoded in the phase characteristics of the brain oscillations and transferred between the active regions of the brain when the cooperation of these regions is necessary to accomplish the task (sVM or dVM). This study had revealed that during gripping-force or wrist-movement performance the informational coding prevails in the beta frequency range, which also supports the ascertains of (Pfurtscheller et al., 2003), who suggest that beta synchronization plays an important role in motor control.

To conclude, the study revealed that relatively simple signal-processing methods can be used to identify a person's brain code and use it to estimate the course of gripping force or wrist movements in simulated or real time. The methodology already proved to be adequate for reading the working-memory task brain code and now we have shown that it can also, with some modifications, be used for VM task signal processing. However, a more complicated methodology has to be used when decoding dVM task data, in comparison to the sVM task data, to obtain satisfactory results, which most probably indicates the greater complexity of the dVM task.

6. References

Birbaumer, N., Flor, H., Ghanayim, N., Hinterberger, T., Iverson, I., Taub, E., Kotchoubey, B., Kübler, A. & Perelmouter, J. (1999). A brain-controlled spelling device for the completely paralyzed, *Nature* 398: 297–298.

Buzsáki, G. & Draguhn, A. (2004). Neuronal oscillations in cortical networks, *Science* 304(5679): 1926–1929.

Classen, J., Gerloff, C., Honda, M. & Hallet, M. (1998). Integrative visuomotor behaviour is associated with interregionally coherent oscilations in the human brain, *Journal of Neurophysiology* 79: 1567–1573.

del R. Millán, J., Renkens, F., Mouriño, J. & Gerstner, W. (2004). Non-invasive brain-actuated control of a mobile robot by human EEG, *IEEE Transations on Biomedical Engineering* 51: 1–2.

Engel, A. K., Fries, P. & Singer, W. (2001). Dynamic predictions: oscillations and synchrony in top-down processing, *Nature reviews. Neuroscience* 2(10): 704–716.

Georgopoulos, A. P., Langheim, F. J. P., Leuthold, A. C. & Merkle, A. N. (2005). Magnetoencephalographic signals predict movement trajectory in space, *Experimental Brain Research* 167(1): 132–135.

Goldberg, R. R. (1976). *Methods of Real Analysis*, John Wiley and Sons Inc., New York.

Huxter, J. R., Senior, T. J., Allen, K. & Csicsvari, J. (2008). Theta phase-specific codes for two-dimensional position, trajectory and heading in the hippocampus, *Nature Neuroscience* 11(5): 587–594.

Ivanitsky, A. M., Nikolaev, A. R. & Ivanitsky, G. A. (2001). Cortical connectivity during word association search, *International Journal of Psychophysiology* 42: 35–53.

Jensen, O. (2001). Information transfer between rythmically coupled networks: reading the hippocampal phase code, *Neural computation* 13: 2743–2761.

Jensen, O. (2005). Reading the hippocampal code by theta phase-locking, *Trends in Cognitive Sciences* 9(12): 551–553.

Jensen, O. & Lisman, J. E. (2005). Hippocampal sequence-encoding driven by a cortical multi-item working memory buffer, *Trends in Neurosciences* 28(2): 67–72.

Kosko, B. (1994). Fuzzy systems as universal approximators, *IEEE Transactions on Computers* 43(11): 1329–1333.

Lebedev, M. A. & Nicolelis, M. A. L. (2006). BrainŰmachine interfaces: past, present and future, *Trends in Neurosciences* 29(9): 536–546.

Lin, C. H. (1997). Siso nonlinear system identification using a fuzzy-neural hybrid system, *International Journal of Neural Systems* 8(3).

Lisman, J. (2005). The theta/gamma discrete phase code occuring during the hippocampal phase precession may be a more general brain coding scheme, *Hippocampus* 15(7): 913–922.

Logar, V., Belič, A., Koritnik, B., Brežan, S., Zidar, J., Karba, R. & Matko, D. (2008). Using ANNs to predict a subject's response based on EEG traces, *Neural Networks* 21(7): 881–887.

Logar, V., Škrjanc, I., Belič, A., Brežan, S., Koritnik, B. & Zidar, J. (2008). Identification of the phase code in an EEG during gripping-force tasks: A possible alternative approach to the development of the brain-computer interfaces, *Arti□cial Intelligence in Medicine* 44(1): 41–49.

Manganotti, P., Gerloff, C., Toro, C., Katsuta, H., Sadato, N., Zhuang, P., Leocani, L. & Hallett, M. (1998). Task-related coherence and task-related spectral power changes during sequential finger movements, *Electroencephalography and clinical Neurophysiology* 109: 50–62.

Mellinger, J., Schalk, G., Braun, C., Preissl, H., Rosenstiel, W., Birbaumer, N. & Kübler, A. (2007). An MEG-based brain-computer interface (BCI), *Neuroimage* 36(3): 581–593.

Mormann, F., Fell, J., Axmacher, N., Weber, B., Lehnertz, K., Elger, C. E. & Fernandez, G. (2005). Phase/amplitude reset and theta-gamma interaction in the human medial temporal lobe during continuous word recognition memory task, *Hippocampus* 15(7): 890–900.

Neuper, C. & Pfurtscheller, G. (2001). Event-related dynamics of cortical rhythms: frequency specific features and functional correlates, *International Journal of Psychophysiology* 43(1): 41–58.

Pfurtscheller, G. & Andrew, C. (1999). Event-related changes of band power and coherence: methodology and interpretation, *Journal of clinical neurophysiology* 16: 512–519.

Pfurtscheller, G., Woertz, M., Supp, G. & Lopes da Silva, F. (2003). Early onset of post-movement beta electroencephalogram synchronization in the supplementary motor area during self-paced finger movement in man, *Neuroscience Letters* 339(2): 111–114.

Schnitzler, A. & Gross, J. (2005). Normal and pathological oscillatory communication in the brain, *Nature Reviews/Neuroscience* 6: 285–296.

Takagi, T. & Sugeno, M. (1985). Fuzzy identification of systems and its applications to modelling and control, *IEEE Transactions on Systems, Man, and Cybernetics* 15: 116–132.

Taylor, D. A., Tillery, S. I. H. & Schwartz, A. B. (2002). Direct cortical control of 3d neuroprosthetic devices, *Science* 296: 1829–1832.

Wang, L. X. & Mendel, J. M. (1992). Fuzzy basis functions, universal approximation, and orthogonal least-squares learning, *IEEE Transactions on Neural Networks* 3(5): 807–814.

Wessberg, J., Stambaugh, C. R., Kralik, J. D., Beck, P. D., Laubach, M., Chapin, J. K., Kim, J., Biggs, S. J., Srinivasan, M. A. & Nicolelis, M. A. L. (2000). Real-time prediction of hand trajectory by ensembles of cortical neurons in primates, *Nature* 408(6810): 361–365.

Wolpaw, J. R., Birbaumer, N., McFarland, D. J., Pfurtscheller, G. & Vaughan, T. M. (2002). BrainŰcomputer interfaces for communication and control, *Clinical Neurophysiology* 113(6): 767–791.

Wolpaw, J. R. & McFarland, D. J. (2004). Control of a two-dimensional movement signal by a noninvasive brain-computer interface in humans, *Proceedings of the National Academy of Sciences* 101(51): 17849–17854.

Wolpaw, J. R., McFarland, D. J., Neat, G. W. & Forneris, C. A. (1991). An eeg-based brain-computer interface for cursor control, *Electroencephalography and Clinical Neurophysiology* 78(3): 252–259.

Ying, G. H. (1997). Necessary conditions for some typical fuzzy systems as universal approximators, *Automatica* 33: 1333–1338.

8

A Two-Dimensional Brain-Computer Interface Associated With Human Natural Motor Control

Dandan Huang[1], Xuedong Chen[2], Ding-Yu Fei[1] and Ou Bai[1]
[1]*EEG & BCI Laboratory, Virginia Commonwealth University*
[2]*State Key Laboratory of Digital Manufacturing Equipment and Technology, Huazhong University of Science and Technology*
[1]*USA*
[2]*P. R. China*

1. Introduction

1.1 Target groups of brain-computer interfaces (BCIs)

Amyotrophic lateral sclerosis (ALS) is a progressive neurodegenerative disease that affects nerve cells which are responsible for controlling voluntary movement. Primary lateral sclerosis (PLS) is a variant of ALS that affects the corticospinal upper motor neurons, limiting movement. ALS/PLS patients, as well as patients disabled from other degenerative diseases or brain injuries, have difficulty with everyday motor behaviors such as moving, swallowing, and speaking. In the later stages of disease, some patients may completely lose motor function and become totally 'locked-in' (Hayashi and Oppenheimer, 2003). Loss of motor function significantly affects patients' quality of life (QoL) (Mockford et al., 2006; Bromberg, 2008; Williams et al., 2008; Lule et al., 2009) and increases the financial burden for the cost of care (Mutsaarts et al., 2004). One important component of quality of life being addressed repeatedly by patients, specifically as the disease progresses, is the ability to communicate. A brain-computer interface (BCI) or brain-machine interface (BMI), has been proposed as an alternative communication pathway, bypassing the normal cortical-muscular pathway (Joseph, 1985; Kennedy et al., 2000). BCI is a system that provides a neural interface to substitute for the loss of normal neuromuscular outputs by enabling individuals to interact with their environment through brain signals rather than muscles (Wolpaw et al., 2002; Daly and Wolpaw, 2008). Recent years have featured a rapid growth of BCI research and development owing to increased societal interest and appreciation of the serious needs and impressive potential of patients with severe motor disabilities (Birbaumer and Cohen, 2007; Daly and Wolpaw, 2008). The majority of BCI-related publications have studied performance in healthy volunteers and focused on the development of signal processing/computational algorithms to improve BCI performance (Bashashati et al., 2007). Practical BCI clinical applications for the potential patient users, however, are still limited (Birbaumer, 2006a).

1.2 Worldwide research on Electroencephalography (EEG)-based BCI

The BCIs using invasive signal methods to record intracortical neuronal activities have shown great promise in direct brain control of external devices in primates, for example, to restore self-feeding by controlling a 3-D robotic arm (Velliste et al., 2008). However, due to the technical concerns such as associated surgical risks as well as unclear long-term benefit and robustness, non-invasive signal methods, mainly EEG, have been extensively explored because of its lower clinical threshold as well as the ease of use. Although EEG mainly supports one dimensional control (Krusienski *et al.*, 2007; McFarland and Wolpaw, 2003), successful two-dimensional BCI has been achieved. Wolpaw's group used two channels of bipolar EEG from the two hemispheres to provide vertical and horizontal cursor control (Wolpaw and McFarland, 2004). In contrast to invasive methods, non-invasive methods feature an extremely low signal-to-noise (s/n) ratio, which is a major challenge in EEG-based BCI development. Conventionally, s/n ratio can be improved by repeated averaging, for example, as in event-related potentials (ERPs), which can be obtained by averaging across trials time-locked to the stimuli. However, due to the requirement for repeated measurements, the communication speed is greatly reduced. An alternative method to improve s/n ratio for reliable BCI control is to train users to regulate their brain activity, such as by modulation of the slow-cortical potentials (SCP) (Birbaumer et al., 2000) or the 8–12 Hz sensorimotor Mu rhythm (Wolpaw and McFarland, 1994). Once people learn to effectively regulate their brain activity, reduction of the variance in the EEG signal can be expected and as a result, the s/n ratio is increased. However, due to the variance of spontaneous activity in EEG, long-term training is usually required for users to achieve effective and accurate regulation of either SCPs or sensorimotor Mu rhythms. The long-term training may require a couple of months to 1 or 2 years (Wolpaw and McFarland, 2004; Iversen et al., 2008b). Moreover, users may be easily fatigued from the sustained attention that is required to regulate their brain activities and as a result, render the BCI control unreliable.

1.3 What challenges practical applications of EEG-BCI?

Fatigue becomes serious in severely paralyzed patients who demonstrate not only reduced physical but also mental endurance (Sykacek et al., 2003; Birbaumer, 2006b). Recent pilot studies of BCI feasibility for ALS patients shows that they may not be able to learn the skills for effective regulation of brain activities because they are too weak to tolerate long-term training and/or active regulation with focused attention (Kubler et al., 1999, 2001; Hill et al., 2006). Though healthy persons or less severely paralyzed patients may operate current EEG-based BCIs efficiently (Birch et al., 2002; Blankertz et al., 2007), the performance of current BCIs in severely paralyzed patients with degenerative diseases such as ALS, however, was much lower because they were easily fatigued or could not tolerate long-term training. The accuracy was just over the random level for ALS patients, in contrast to the 90% accuracy level achieved in healthy subjects (Sellers and Donchin, 2006; Iversen et al., 2008a). Therefore, the inconvenience in operation may prevent current BCIs from practical clinical applications for severely paralyzed patients who are the users most in need of direct brain control of external devices to restore function.

1.4 Sensorimotor Rhythm-based 2D cursor control in EEG&BCI Lab VCU

Sensorimotor rhythms (SMR) decrease (event-related desynchronization or ERD) with movement or preparation for movement and increase (event-related synchronization or ERS) in the post-movement period or during relaxation, based on which our 2D BCI strategy was established. We have identified that the human volition to move or cease to move associated with natural motor behavior can be reliably decoded online from EEG signals, where users do not need to learn vast training to regulate brain activities. We found that the discrimination of ERD from ERS was much more reliable than the discrimination of ERD from background activities in conventional BCI methods (Bai et al., 2008; Kayagil et al., 2009). A short-lasting burst of EEG oscillation, termed as beta rebound or beta-ERS, has been observed in beta band (16–30 Hz) over human sensorimotor area after subjects produce a self-paced movement (Salmelin et al., 1995; Pfurtscheller and Lopes da Silva, 1999; Neuper and Pfurtscheller, 2001). Though the beta rebound has been postulated as the result of afferent input (Cassim et al., 2001), other studies show that the beta rebound does not necessarily depend on motor cortex output and muscle activation, and it may reflect a short-lasting state of deactivation or inhibition of the motor cortex (Pfurtscheller, 1992; Pfurtscheller et al., 1996). The feasibility of the beta rebound for BCI application derives from the fact that beta rebound may not only occur with real physical movement but also presents with motor imagery (Pfurtscheller et al., 2005). This comes into consideration since the patients who lose their voluntary muscle contraction may only imagine movement instead of producing real movement (Bai et al., 2008). The beta rebound results in a strong synchronization, i.e. higher amplitude of rhythmic activities in beta band than background activities. As ERD features lower amplitude beta band activities, the discrimination of beta rebound or beta-ERS from beta-ERD is presumably more accurate than the discrimination of ERD from background activity. Furthermore, the beta rebound also features strict somatotopic organization (Salmelin et al., 1995), allowing for potential discrimination of different limb movements spatially according to human somatotopy. In 2008, our group implemented a synchronous sequencial binary controls approach to decode EEGs to provide 2D control of a cursor on a computer screen, with simple threshold-based binary classification of band power readings taken over pre-defined time windows during subject right hand movement/motor imagery (Bai et al., 2008). The following study, using spatial feature of the beta rebound, supports a multi-dimensional BCI by reliable decoding of intentions to move individual limbs (Huang et al., 2009). The beta-ERD and beta-ERS features associated with human natural motor control has also been further tested on six ALS or PLS patients in sequential binary control for 2D cursor control, and two patients further participated in direct two-dimensional cursor control in a single visit (Bai et al., 2010).

2. Physiological rationale for the proposed two-dimensional BCI

Human somatotopic organization indicates that human limbs are controlled by contralateral brain hemispheres. Many neurophysiological and neuroimaging studies have confirmed the nature of contralateral control (Bai *et al.*, 2005; Rao *et al.*, 1993; Stancak and Pfurtscheller, 1996). Therefore, reliably decoding the movement intention of right and left hand, which are associated with different spatiotemporal patterns of event-related desynchronization (ERD), i.e. oscillation amplitude attenuation, and event-related synchronization (ERS), i.e. oscillation amplitude increase, may provide additional degrees-of-freedom for control. During physical and motor imagery of right and left hand movements, beta band brain activation (15-30 Hz) ERD occurs predominantly over the contralateral left and right motor areas. The brain activity associated with ceasing to move, the post movement ERS, can also be found over the contralateral motor areas. It suggests that the brain activity associated with four natural motor behaviors (thus, not requiring extensive training) may potentially provide four reliable features for a discrete two-dimensional control, e.g. left-hand ERD to command move to the left, left-hand ERS to command move up, right-hand ERD to command move to the right, and right-hand ERS to command move down. As the spatial distribution of post movement beta rebound (ERS) is more focal than ERD distribution, the detection of ERS might be potentially more reliable than ERD detection only (Pfurtscheller and Solis-Escalante, 2009). As a result, the proposed method to discriminate spatial distribution of ERD and ERS might provide more accurate classification than previous methods relying on the detection of ERD only (Neuper *et al.*, 2005; Naeem *et al.*, 2006). Evidence has demonstrated separate spatial patterns of ERD and ERS with physical movement, it is also important to know about the hemispheric patterns during motor imagery of limb movement which is essential for achieving purely mental control without involvement of muscle activity.

3. Experimental paradigms

3.1 Data acquisition and online processing system

We used the typical BCI system setting (Fig. 1). Participants were presented with stimuli and required to perform specific mental tasks while the electrical activity of the brains was being recorded by EEG. Relevant EEG features were extracted and then fed back to the user by so-called closed-loop BCI.

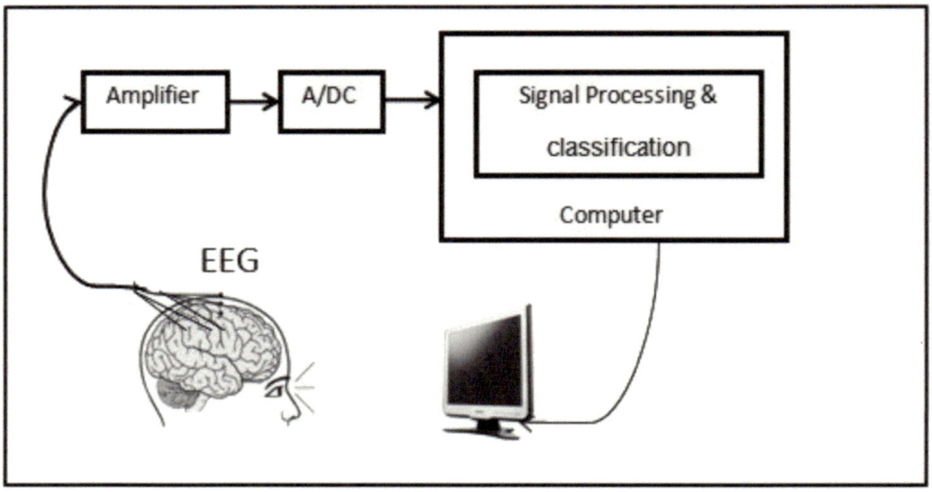

Fig. 1. Experimental system. EEG signals were picked up from scalp and amplified, then were digitized through A/D convertor and sent to the computer for signal processing.

We recorded EEG signals from 27 (tin) surface electrodes (Fig. 2) attached on an elastic cap (Electro-Cap International, Inc., Eaton, OH, U.S.A.) according to the international 10-20 system (Jasper and Andrews, 1938), with reference from the right ear lobe and ground from the forehead. Surface electromyography (EMG), which was used to monitor the movement and bipolar electrooculogram (EOG) above left eye and below right eye were also recorded. The analog signals were amplified, and then digitized through A/D convertor. The digital signal was then sent to a computer for online processing. Signals from all the channels were amplified using a 64 channel g.USBamp-System (g.tec GmgH, Schiedlberg, Austria), filtered (0.1-100 Hz) and digitized (sampling frequency was 250 Hz).

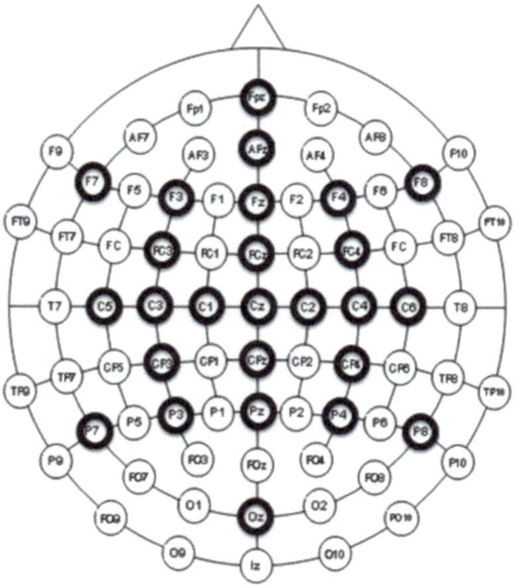

Fig. 2. Placement of 27 electrodes on the cap, marked by solid bold circles. They were F3, F7, PC3 (C3A), C1, C3, C5, T3, CP3 (C3P), P3, P7 (T5), F4, F8, PC4 (C4A), C2, C4, C6, T4, CP4 (C4P), P4, T6, FPZ, FZ, PCZ (FCZ), CZ, CPZ (CZP), PZ, OZ and AFz was used as the ground.

3.2 Binary and four-directional control paradigms for 2D control

A text box was provided in the center of the computer monitor. The text message was either a blue 'Yes' or 'No' (the first cue) as illustrated in Fig. 3. Subjects were instructed to start a motor task with motor execution or motor imagery of repetitive wrist extension when they perceived the blue text message of either 'Yes' or 'No'. Subjects kept performing the motor task in the Condition window of 2.5 s until the color of the text message changed from blue to green (the second cue). In the 'Yes' case, subjects were instructed to continue the motor task of either motor execution or motor imagery until the text message disappeared. In the 'No' case, subjects were asked to stop the motor task and relax as soon as possible. The duration of the Detection window from text color change to text removal was also 2.5 s. Because of the response delay, the signal from 1 s after color change to the end of the Detection window was extracted for classification. After an inter-trial interval randomly from 4 to 6 s, the next text message was provided. The detailed paradigm was provided in a previous study (Bai et al., 2008; Kayagil et al., 2009). Patients participated in both motor execution and motor imagery sessions. The purpose of the motor execution session was 2-fold: the patients are more comfortable with the paradigms, and the investigators could check whether patients performed the instructions properly by monitoring their motor output from EMG. One important factor was that patients need to relax as soon as possible at the beginning of the 'Detection' window in order to induce a transient feature of ERS for BCI detection. ERD was expected when subjects performed the active motor task during the Detection window, whereas ERS was expected when subjects stopped the motor task in the Detection window. This paradigm would yield a more accurate classification between ERD and ERS compared with that between ERD and baseline activity.

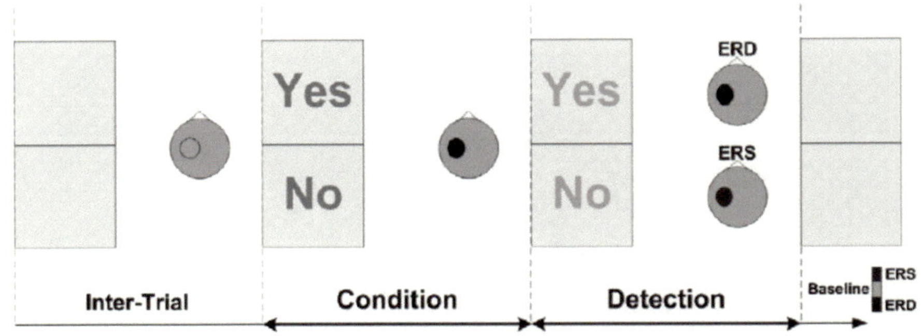

Fig. 3. Binary control paradigm. Subject started motor tasks of motor execution or motor imagery when they perceived the first color text message of either 'Yes' or 'No'. When the color of text message changed from blue to green (less dark in grey scale), subjects sustained the motor tasks in case of 'Yes' or ceased the motor tasks and relaxed in case of 'No'. EEG signal in the Detection window was extracted to determine 'Yes' from ERD activity or 'No' from ERS activity. Therefore, subjects was able to make binary control of either 'Yes' or 'No' intentionally by sustaining or ceasing motor tasks time-locked to the cues (see Bai et al., 2010).

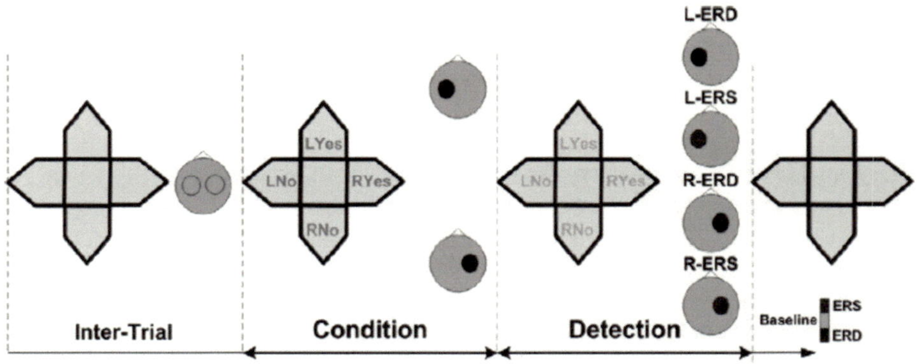

Fig. 4. Four-directional cursor control paradigm. Subjects started motor execution or motor imagery of right hand movement upon perceiving the blue text message (in Condition window) of 'RYes' or 'RNo', or left hand movement when perceiving 'LYes' or 'LNo'. They would continue the movement after text color change in cases of 'RYes' or 'LYes', or stop moving and relax in cases of 'RNo' or 'LNo'. Computer extracted EEG signal in the Detection window and decoded 'RYes', 'RNo', 'LYes' and 'LNo' from ERD and ERS over the left hemisphere, or ERD and ERS over the right hemisphere correspondingly (see Bai et al., 2010).

Each of the four text messages 'RYes', 'RNo', 'LYes' and 'LNo' was assigned to one of the four directions of a computer cursor, provided in the center of the computer monitor (Fig. 4). One of four text messages in the corresponding cursor direction was provided each time. The message text was a blue color at first; in the cases of 'RYes' or 'RNo', subjects started to perform motor execution or motor imagery of their right wrist in the form of repetitive extension; and in the cases of 'LYes' or 'LNo', subjects started to perform motor execution or motor imagery of their left wrist in the form of repetitive extension. Subjects kept performing the motor task until the color change of the text message. In the Detection window after the color change, subjects were instructed to continue the motor task of right wrist extension or left wrist extension with text messages of 'RYes' or 'LYes', respectively. Subjects were asked to cease the motor task as soon as possible and relax when they saw the messages of 'RNo' or 'LNo'. The durations of the Condition and Detection window were both 2 s. The signal between 1 s after the text color change and the end of the Detection window was extracted for classification. The detailed paradigm can be found in (Huang et al., 2009). In the Detection window, the four motor tasks of 'RYes', 'RNo', 'LYes' and 'LNo' were associated with four spatial patterns of ERD over the left hemisphere, ERS over the left hemisphere, ERD over the right hemisphere and ERS over the right hemisphere according to human somatotopy of hand control. The spatial distribution of the four patterns provided the basis for the classification of 'RYes', 'RNo', 'LYes' and 'LNo' to achieve control of the four directions of the computer cursor.

3.3 Online two-dimensional cursor control game

A computer game of virtual computer cursor control using BCI was developed to facilitate subjects' interest and active involvement for BCI development (Kayagil et al., 2009). Subjects were asked to control the cursor movement in a two-dimensional space on the computer monitor (see Fig. 5) by performing motor tasks with either motor execution or motor imagery. The binary control of two-dimensional cursor movement was achieved by consecutive binary classification to determine one of up, down, right and left directions. Subjects were instructed to move the cursor (the dark square box) towards the target (the circle) with minimal cursor movements in the grids, and at the same time, avoid the trap (the black ghost). The initial position of the cursor as well as the target and trap position were randomly generated by the computer. Fig. 5 shows screen shots of a binary control in the up row. As the target was in the upper left direction of the cursor, the subjects would select either up or left cursor, i.e. 'No' directions. Similar to the binary control paradigm, subjects started motor task with either motor execution or motor imagery when the four text boxes were provided. Because the 'No' direction was closer to the target, subjects would stop the motor task when the cursor color changed to green so that the ERS activity was

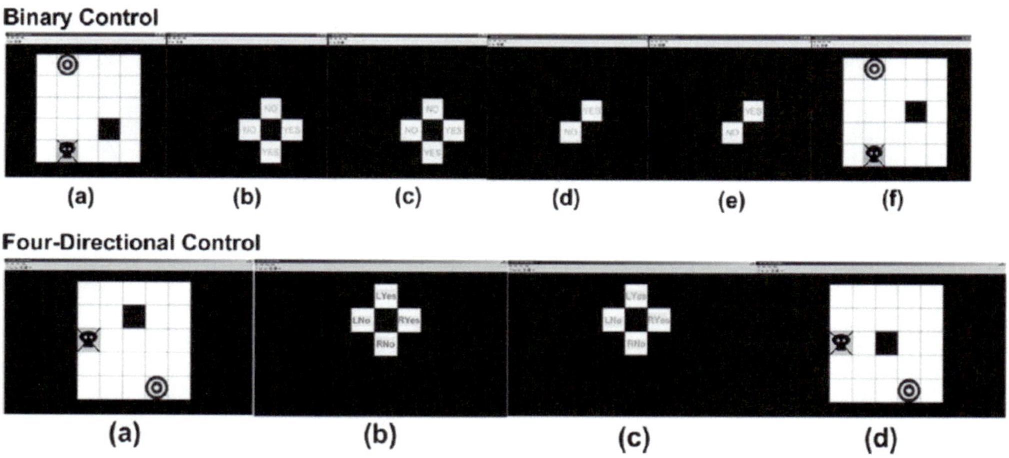

Fig. 5. Consecutive binary control and four-directional control of two-dimensional computer cursor movement: an online computer game to test the performance of binary control and four-directional control paradigms (see detail in the text).

voluntarily produced. The computer determined whether the subjects intended to move to 'Yes' or 'No' direction according to the extracted EEG signal, i.e. ERS, with respect to the computer model created from the data obtained from binary control paradigm. The two 'Yes' directions were removed when the computer detected ERS signal. The two 'No' directions were changed to one 'Yes' direction and one 'No' direction, and the subjects performed the motor task to voluntarily 'tell' the computer which direction they wanted to move to. In the illustrated sample, the subjects performed a sustained movement, and the computer determined the 'Yes' direction and move the cursor upward. Similarly, subjects would control the cursor movement until it reached the target. The detailed explanation of the binary cursor control game was described in the previous study (Kayagil et al., 2009). The scheme of the four-directional control of two-dimensional cursor movement was similar to that of binary cursor control. Because one of the possible four directions was able to be determined from one of 'RYes', 'RNo', 'LYes' and 'LNo', which were provided in four-directional control paradigm, the consecutive two binary classification was reduced to one classification from four options as shown in the lower row in Fig.5. The detailed explanation of the four-directional cursor control game was described in (Huang et al., 2009).

3.4 Center-out two-dimensional cursor control paradigm

A trial began when a target (dark) appeared at one of the four locations on the periphery of the screen, together with three non-target objects on the other three sides (Fig. 6a). A target location was pseudo-randomized (i.e. each occurred the same times in one block). In both parts (physical movement and motor imagery), there were four hint words in the task paradigm (a), 'RYes', 'RNo', 'LYes', and 'LNo' ('R' indicating right hand task, and 'L' for left hand task) on the four directions of the central cursor, which was set in green initially. Subjects were instructed to begin real or imagined repetitive wrist extensions of the right arm, if the target was on the direction of 'RYes' or 'RNo'; if the target was on the direction of

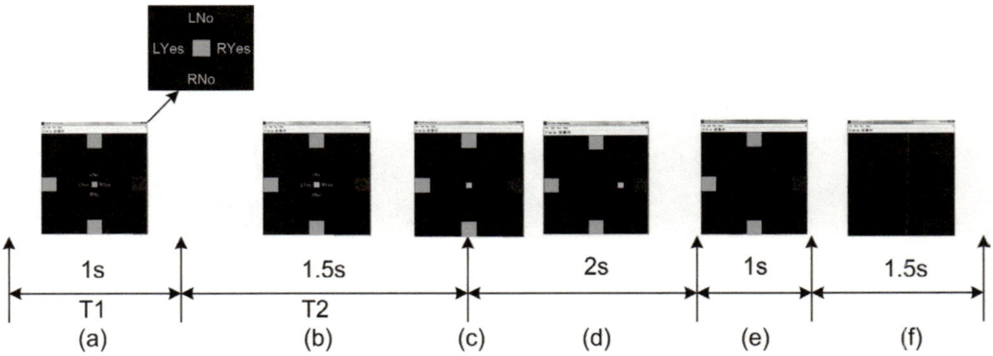

Fig. 6. Online 2D center-out cursor control paradigm. (a) A trial began. The target (dark) was pseudo-randomly chosen from the four positions along the edges; the cursor was in green. Subject started motor task for 1 s. (b) The cursor turned to cyan, at which point subject stopped and relaxed in 'No' case, or performs sustained movement in 'Yes' case for 1.5s. (c) The hint words disappeared. Subject stopped the task. (d) The cursor moved steadily towards the classified direction for 2 s. (e) The target flashed for 1 s when it was hit by the cursor. If the cursor missed the target, the screen was blank for 1 s. (f) The screen was blank for a 1.5s interval before next trail started.

'LYes' or 'LNo', they performed real or imagined repetitive wrist extensions of the left arm. After a period of 1s, the central cursor changed color to blue (b), when the subject was instructed to continue real or imagined movement with the 'Yes' case or abruptly relax and stop moving with the 'No' case. After displaying for a period of 1.5s, the configuration disappeared, indicating that subject needed to stop the task, and the screen was blank for 4.5s (f). Next trial began from (a).

4. Signal processing and computational methods

4.1 Pre-processing

EEG signal in the Detection window was extracted for modeling and classification. Signals from 27 channels were spatially filtered by surface Laplacian derivation (SLD), i.e. signal from each electrode was referenced to the averaged potentials from the nearby four orthogonal electrodes (Hjorth, 1975). The temporal filtering was achieved by power spectral estimation with Welch method. A 4 Hz frequency resolution with segment length of 0.25 s and 50% overlapping was determined for spectral estimation (Bai et al., 2007).

4.2 Feature extraction

Empirical feature reduction: assuming that movement intention associated cortical activities occur over the motor cortex, we reduced the channel number from 27 to 14, which covered both left and right motor areas. Furthermore, as we did not expect relevant activities in the delta, theta or gamma band, only alpha and beta band (8–30 Hz) activities were extracted for modeling and classification. Thus, the total number of extracted features were 8 (frequency bins) * 14 (channels) = 112 features.

Bhattacharyya distance: Bhattacharyya distance provides an index of feature separability for binary classification, which is proportional to the inter-class mean difference divided by intra-class variance (Chatterjee et al., 2007). The empirically extracted features were ranked by the Bhattacharyya distance for further classification.

Genetic algorithm: Genetic algorithm (GA)-based feature selection is a stochastic search in the feature space guided by the concept of inheriting, where at each search step, good properties of the parent subsets found in previous steps are inherited. Ten fold cross-validation was used with a Mahalanobis Linear Distance (MLD) classifier for feature evaluation (Li and Doi, 2006). In this approach, the population size we used was 20, the number of generations was 100, the crossover probability was 0.8, the mutation probability was 0.01, and the stall generation was 20.

4.3 Classification

ROC: A receiver operating characteristics (ROC) was generated from the feature with the largest Bhattacharyya distance, i.e. the one providing the largest inter-class separability. The working point was determined from the ROC curve that was the closet point to 100% true positive with 0% false positive.

GA-MLD: The sub-optimal feature subset was selected by genetic algorithm (GA) with Mahalanobis Linear Distance (MLD) as the evaluation function. Then, the selected features providing the best cross-validation accuracy were applied to a Mahalanobis Linear Distance Classifier. The number of features for the subset was four, which was determined from the cross-validation accuracy with feature numbers of 2, 4, 6, 8 and 10.

SVM: the support vector machine (SVM) was employed as the evaluation function. We employed a SVM approach provided in LIBSVM (Fan et al., 2005). The radial basis function was used as the SVM kernel function as it can provide similar classification outcome compared with other kernels (Keerthi and Lin, 2003). As the performance of SVM depends on the regulation parameters or hyper-parameters C and the width of the kernel r (Chang and Lin, 2001; Muller et al., 2001), 10-fold cross-validation was performed; 2^K, K from -5 to 15 with step of 2 for the penalty parameter and 2^K, K from -15 to 5 with step of 2 for the spread parameter. These parameters were determined by the training dataset only.

4.4 Flow chart of online calibration and two-dimensional cursor control games

Fig.7 illustrates the general procedures for online calibration and online 2D cursor control games. In calibration step, data was first spatially filtered using surface Laplacian derivation (SLD), and then was temporally filtered by estimation of the power spectral density. Through offline neurophysiological analysis, 0.5-1.5 s after T2 window started was selected to obtain strongest ERD/ERS. We applied Welch method with Hamming window, and kept the frequency resolution 4 Hz, the same as previous study, with 50% overlap of the segments. For either physical movement or motor imagery, parameters and features were determined from the training data to make a model, used for decoding the movement intention in online tests. We performed empirical feature reduction by empirical feature reduction of channel and frequency band restrictions. GA-MLD and DTC were used to generate models. The online data also went through spatial filtering, temporal filtering, channels and frequency bands restriction. The cursor was moved to the classified direction. For the center-out paradigm, where we performed model adaptation, trials were combined with the old ones, keeping the data pool updated. New models would be generated using MLD and DTC, the one with higher accuracy would be used as the classifier in next trial. If the block was completed, the features were re-selected by genetic algorithm, and new models were generated by GA-MLD and DTC. Next block began with the same procedures.

4.5 Offline cross-validation

The offline performances were evaluated from 10-fold cross-validation; 90% of the data pool was used for training, and the other 10% was used for validation so that the validation dataset was independent from the training dataset. In the online game, the features for decoding the movement intention was extracted and classified using the parameters determined from the training datasets.

4.6 Data processing for neurophysiological analysis

Offline data analysis was performed to investigate the neurophysiology following the tasks of 'Yes' and 'No' for binary classification, and 'RYes', 'RNo', 'LYes' and 'LNo' for four-directional classification. The calibration datasets were used for analysis. Data processing was performed using MATLAB Toolbox: BCI2VR (Bai et al., 2007). Epoching was done with windows of -2 s to 7 s with respect to the first cue onset. Any epochs contaminated with artifacts were rejected. ERD and ERS were calculated for each case. Epochs were linearly de-trended and divided into 0.25 s segments. The power spectrum of each segment was calculated using FFT with Hamming window resulting in a bandwidth of 4 Hz. ERD and ERS were obtained by averaging the log power spectrum across epochs and having baseline corrected with respect to -2 s to 0 s.

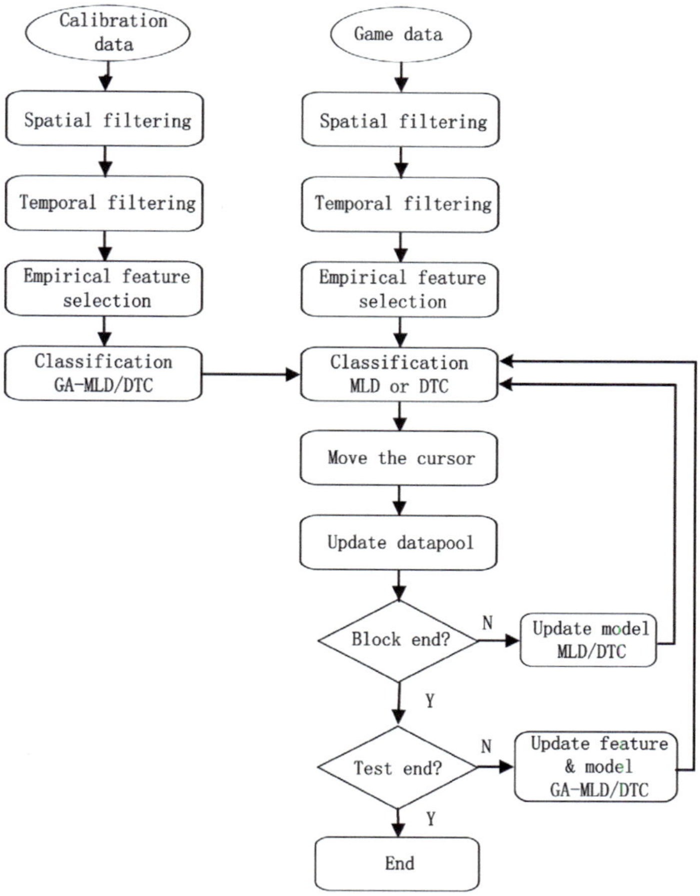

Fig. 7. Flow chart of online calibration and two-dimensional cursor control games. Calibration data went through spatially filtering, temporally filtering and empirical feature selection. In classification, genetic-algorithm based Mahalanobis linear discrimination (MLD) classifier and decision tree classifier (DTC) were used to generate models for online game. During the online test, data was spatially filtered, temporal filtered, and empirical features were selected. Then the model generated in calibration step, giving a better prediction result was used to classify the movement intention, and the cursor was moved. For the later study with center-out 2D paradigm, after data pool was updated, the model was updated consequently, using MLD and DTC, and the one giving a higher result was used as the model for classification in next trial; if the block ended, features would be re-selected by genetic algorithm. If all the blocks were completed, the procedure ended.

5. Observations and experiment results

5.1 ERD/ERS in healthy subjects and in ALS/PLS patients

For ERD/ERS patterns in ALS/PLS patients during binary control in order to realize 2-D control, results were shown in (Bai et al., 2010). We selected to present results of healthy and ALS1/PLS1 patients in four-directional control, which included patterns from all four motor tasks.

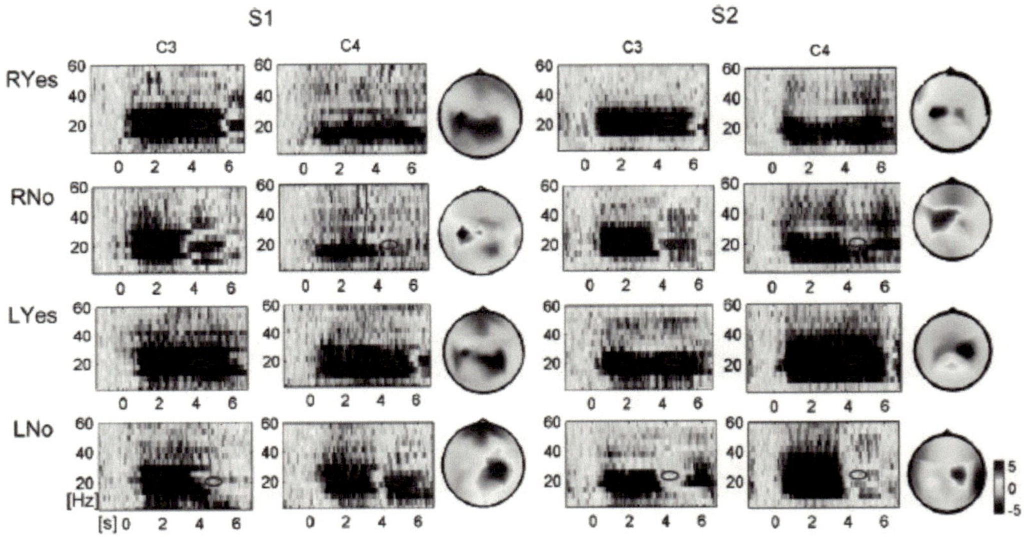

Fig. 8. Time-course and topography of ERD and ERS during motor execution following the calibration paradigm for healthy subjects S1and S2. Blue color stands for power decrease or ERD; red stands for power increase or ERS (see original color picture in Huang et al., 2009). The T1 window is from 0 s to 2.5 s and the T2 window is from 2.5 s to 5 s. ERD was observed in the T2 window on the left hemisphere during sustained right-hand movement; ERS was observed in the T2 window on the left hemisphere when the subjects ceased to move right-hand movement. During left-hand movement, ERD was observed in the T2 window on the right hemisphere during sustained movement and ERS on the right hemisphere when the subjects ceased to move left hand. ERD and ERS in each case were marked by pink circles in the time-course plot. The head topography corresponding to the pink marked time period was provided next to the time-course plots.

Fig.8 shows an example of time-frequency plots, head topographies of ERDs or ERSs for motor execution with physical movement, from two healthy subjects. For each subject, time-frequency plots of channel C3 over the left sensorimotor cortex and C4 over the right hemisphere are illustrated in the left two columns and head topography of ERD or ERS to their right, containing each of the four situations: 'RYes', 'RNo', 'LYes' and 'LNo'. In the time- frequency plot, 0 s stands for the first cue (green in the visual paradigm) occurrence. ERD (blue color) was observed from around 0.5–1 s after the cue onset due to the response delay; for S1, S2 and S3, ERD in both alpha and beta bands from 10–30 Hz was observed over motor areas contralateral to the hand moved. The ERS in red color was mainly observed in the beta band centered around 20 Hz over the contralateral motor areas. Compared with ERD patterns, ERS was shortlasting in time but highly distinguishable. Therefore, the ERD and ERS on either left or right hemisphere provided four spatial patterns to detect 'RYes', 'RNo', 'LYes' and 'LNo' intentions.

Fig.9 shows the time-frequency plots and head topography of ERD and ERS associated with motor imagery. Similar to the patterns associated with physical movement, ERD associated with motor imagery was observed in both alpha and beta bands on the contralateral hemisphere with the hand moved, although ERD amplitude was smaller than that of physical movement. ERS in the T2 window was observed on the contralateral hemisphere in beta band (13–24 Hz) only, and its amplitude was smaller than that of physical movement.

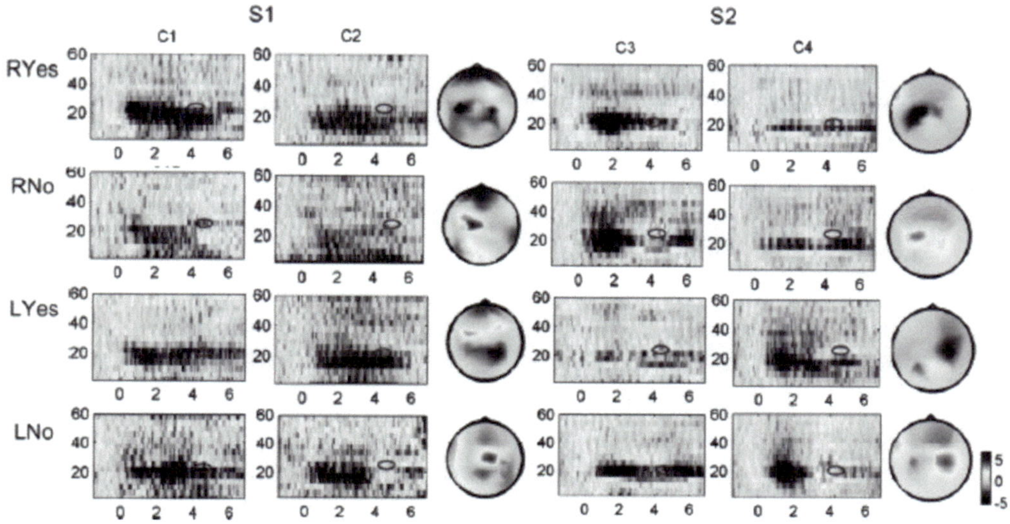

Fig. 9. Time-course and topography of ERD and ERS during motor imagery following the calibration paradigm for healthy subjects S1 and S2. For both S1 and S2, ERD is obtained in the time window with sustained motor imagery and ERS with termination of motor imagery. ERDs appear in both alpha and beta bands, bilateral, whereas ERSs appear only in the alpha band on the contralateral hemisphere. ERD and ERS in each case were marked by pink circles in the time-course plot. The head topography corresponding to the pink marked time period is provided next to the time-course plots (see original color picture in Huang et al., 2009).

During left hand motor imagery for S1 ('LYes'), ERD in the T2 time window was also observed on the left hemisphere. The ERD and ERS associated with motor imagery also provided four spatially differentiable patterns; however, the smaller amplitudes of ERD and ERS with motor imagery may result in less effective detection in single trials.

In the further study with patients, ALS1 and PLS1 participated in the additional session of four-directional control. ERD and ERS associated with motor execution were presented over left and right hemispheres corresponding to right hand and left hand movements as illustrated in Fig. 10. ERD was observed over contralateral hemispheres to the right and left hand for both subjects. Similar to the ERD pattern in binary control paradigm, ipsilateral ERD was also seen in ALS1 during the active motor task. The contralateral ERS after active motor task was clearly seen in PLS1, whereas ERS pattern was not distinguishable in ALS1. In the motor imagery experiment, ALS1 was not able to cease the motor task as soon as the color was changed. The subject reported that the muscle stiffness delayed her relaxation response. The time-frequency analysis was not presented because the ERD and ERS patterns were not distinguishable.

5.2 Feature selection and classification

The best frequency bands and channels for classifying movement intentions were determined from the calibration data sets. Fig.11 shows the spatial-frequency feature analysis indexed by the Bhattacharyya distance for S1 and S2 during motor execution with physical movement and motor imagery. All the channels over the whole head were used for plot. The first column for each subject illustrates the channel-frequency plot of the

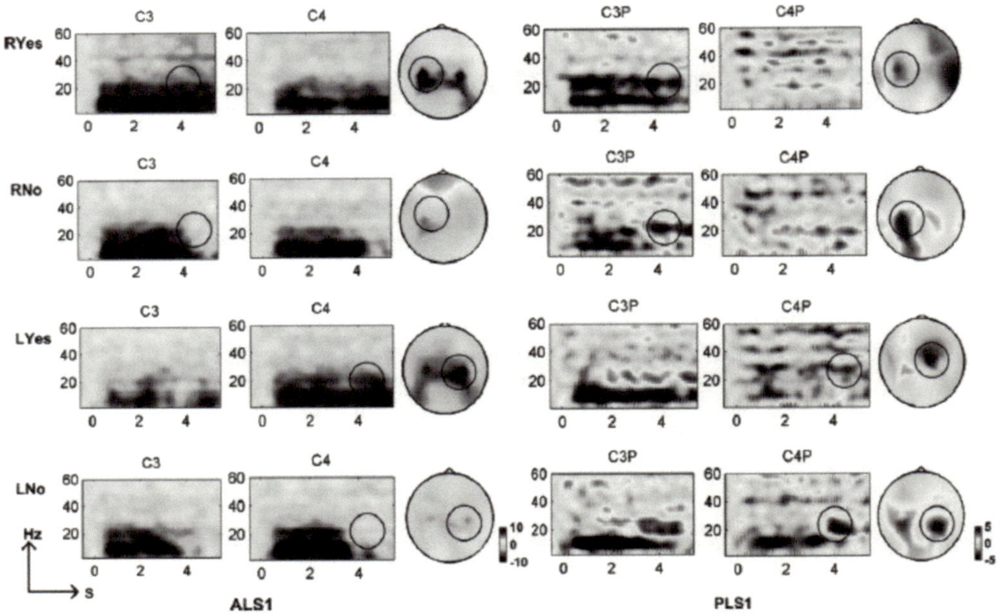

Fig. 10. Example of ERD and post-beta ERS activity over left and right motor areas associated with motor execution of right and left hand movement in the four-directional control paradigm for patients ALS1 and PLS1. ERD was detected over the motor area contralateral to the hand moved in both ALS1 and PLS1: ERD on the left hemisphere contralateral to right hand moved in case of 'RYes', and ERD on the right hemisphere contralateral to left hand moved in case of 'LYes'. Contralateral ERS to hand moved was distinguishable in PLS1: ERS on the left hemisphere contralateral to right hand moved in case of 'RNo', and ERS on the right hemisphere contralateral to left hand moved in case of 'LNo'. However, post-beta ERS in ALS1 was not recognizable (see original color picture in Bai et al., 2010).

Bhattacharyya distance, and the second column is the topography of the Bhattacharyya distance of the best frequency band. In the Bhattacharyya distance plot, the dark red color shows the higher Bhattacharyya distance standing higher separability to classify movement intentions from single trial EEG signal. In the channel-frequency plot for S1, the higher Bhattacharyya distance value for right-hand physical movement was observed in beta band ranging from 17 to 24 Hz in the channels located on the left hemisphere over the sensorimotor area. The high separability between ERD and ERS in the beta band was consistent with the time-frequency analysis in time-frequency plot. The topography of the Bhattacharyya distance around 17-24 Hz shows that the best EEG spatial channels for the classification of 'RYes' and 'RNo' were in the contralateral left hemisphere over the sensorimotor area since ERS presented on contralateral left hemisphere only, although ERD occurred bilaterally in time-frequency plot. A higher Bhattacharyya distance value for left-hand physical movement was also seen in the beta band on the contralateral right hemisphere. For S2, the distribution of Bhattacharyya distance values was similar to that of S1, except that for either right hand or left hand, the 'Yes' case showed high separability only on the contralateral hemisphere, which can be seen in the topography of the Bhattacharyya distance. Compared with physical movement, separability of mental tasks in motor imagery was weaker, indicated by lighter red area in the right two columns. Figure 7 shows feature analysis for S1 and S2 with motor imagery. The highest Bhattacharyya distance values were in the beta band and on the channels over contralateral hemisphere for both right and left-hand motor imagery.

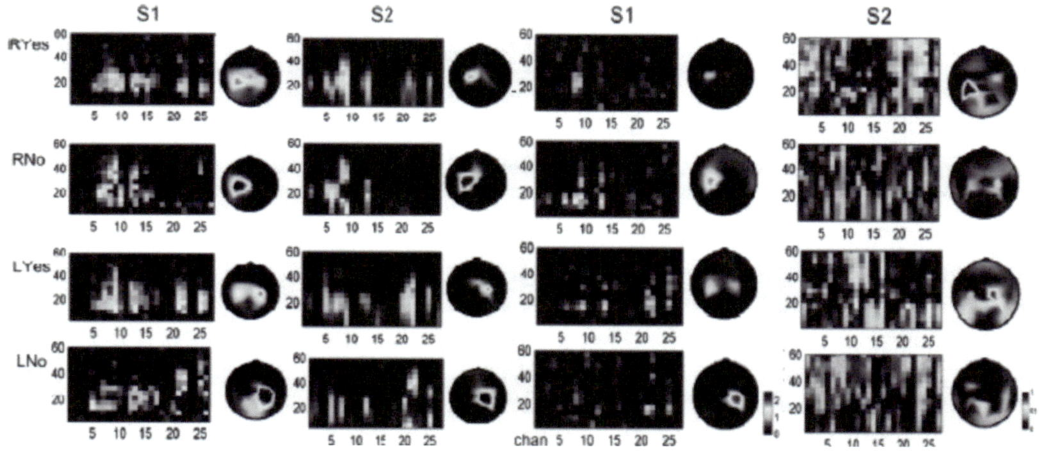

Fig. 11. Feature visualization indexed by Bhattacharyya distance for healthy subjects S1 and S2 in physical movement (left two columns) and in motor imagery (right two columns) following the calibration paradigm. The best frequency band with the highest separability was found in beta band, and the best channel was found on sensorimotor areas (see original color picture in Huang et al., 2009).

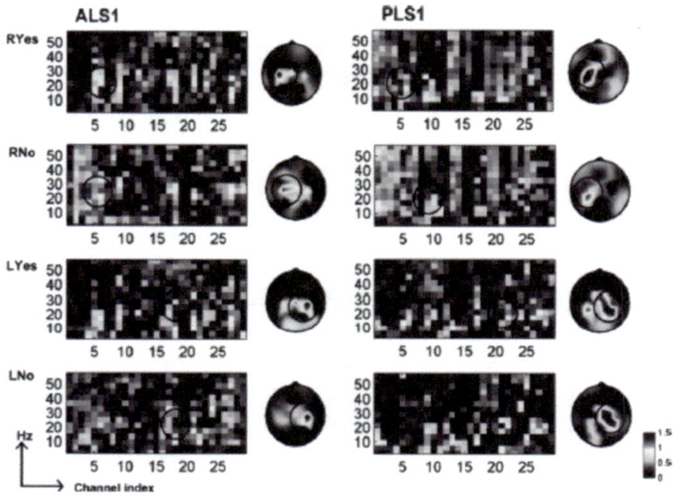

Fig. 12. Bhattacharyya distance for patient ALS1 and PLS1 in selecting better spatiotemporal features for four-directional classification. The frequency power features over left motor areas in beta band provided better detection of 'RYes' and 'RNo' associated with right hand movement, whereas the frequency power features over right motor areas in beta band provided better detection of 'LYes' and 'LNo' associated with left hand movement (see original color picture in Huang et al., 2009).

Subject	MLD(%)	GA-MLD(%)	DTC(%)	SVM(%)
S1	63.1 ± 4.51	87.7 ± 1.29	87.8 ± 1.47	87.8 ± 1.31
S2	79.5 ± 6.21	93.0 ± 1.97	85.5 ± 3.87	90.0 ± 3.12
S3	67.3 ± 3.04	85.2 ± 0.95	84.5 ± 2.30	88.9 ± 1.04
S5	71.0 ± 2.18	87.2 ± 0.58	87.7 ± 1.75	85.8 ± 2.13
Average	70.2 ± 6.97	88.3 ± 3.33	86.4 ± 1.64	88.1 ± 1.79

Table 1. 10-fold cross-validation accuracy. MLD, Mahalanobis linear discrimination; GA-MLD, genetic algorithm-based Mahalanobis linear discrimination; DTC, decision tree classifier; SVM, support vector machine classifier.

The Bhattacharyya distance was also analyzed from the activity associated with four-directional control paradigm. Fig. 12 shows the Bhattacharyya distance values in ALS1 and PLS1 who performed motor execution. In consistence with the ERD and ERS patterns presented in Fig. 10, the better features to classify one of four directions from the other three directions were the activities in the beta band over the motor cortex contralateral to the hand moved. The EEG activities over central-medial area in PLS1 also provided good discrimination of 'LYes' and 'LNo'.

For study with five healthy subjects, Table 1 provides the comparison of offline 10-fold cross-validation accuracies using MLD, GA-MLD, DTC and SVM methods for S1, S2, S3 and S5 during physical movement. Since ERD and ERS patterns were not strong enough for S4, we excluded it from further exploration of classification methods. MLD has a mean value of 70.2%; after applying genetic algorithm in feature selection, GA-MLD provides an improved mean value of 88.3%. A paired *t*-test suggested that GA-MLD had a significant improvement of the classification accuracy over the MLD (t = 7.64, df = 3, p-value < 0.01*). Similarly, we also compared DTC and SVM performance with that of MLD and found that DTC and SVM outperformed MLD significantly while they two had no great difference. Since there was no significant difference among the intensive methods, the DTC method was employed for the online 2D cursor control game. Except for S4, all the other four subjects were successful in controlling the cursor moving to the target by physical movement and the average online game performances for S1, S2, S3 and S5 were 92%, 85%, 81% and 84%, with the overall performance of 85.5% ± 4.65%. S1 and S2 participated in the second session performing motor imagery tasks. The offline classification accuracy for S1 was 73% ± 5.97%, and for S2 was 59.2% ± 3.63%, which were lower than those of cursor control with physical movement. The two subjects reported good concentration throughout the recording, except that S2 felt sleepy in a short period in the middle. Online 2D cursor control game using motor imagery was performed by S1 and S2. S1 was able to move the cursor to the target. However, S2 performed less well than S1. The performance was consistent with the classification results for motor imagery.

To further investigate the performance of proposed 2D BCI, the four-directional classification result for ALS1 and PLS1 was provided in Table 2. The four-direction classification accuracy was about 60% for motor execution, which was much higher than the random level of 25% in the case of 4-class discrimination. The subjects also reported that it was more difficult to imagine wrist movement of the non-dominant left hand than the dominant right hand. An appropriate training to teach effective motor imagery maybe necessary for this motor imagery task. The online game provided a better accuracy than that of offline analysis of data recorded using the four-direction control paradigm. A possible

	Motor Execution			Motor Imagery		
	Offline Cross-Validation		Online	Offline Cross-Validation		Online Game*
	GA-MLD	GA-SVM	GA-MLD	GA-MLD	GA-SVM	GA-MLD
ALS1	**52.5±6.4**	47.3±4.4	52.0	**42.1±4.7**	39.1±4.5	59.7
PLS1	**67.1±2.6**	61.5±5.6	71.0	**43.9±3.6**	31.0±6. 9	55.3
Average	**59.8±10.3**	54.4±10.0	61.5	**43.0±1.3**	35.1±5.7	58.0

Table 2. Decoding four-directional movement intention from lateral ERD and beta-ERS associated with human natural motor behavior. *Estimated from cursor trajectory towards target.

reason might be that subjects were more actively involved with the interactive game than the paradigm without performance feedback. Further, subjects might be able to adapt to the computer model for the classification from the cursor movement feedback.

5.3 Information transfer rate of the BCI

The BCI performance can be evaluated from both the decoding rate and accuracy (Wolpaw *et al* 2002). Wolpaw *et al* introduced the information transfer rate (ITR) for a BCI as bits per minute (bpm) as a good measurement for both decoding rate and accuracy (Wolpaw *et al* 2000). In our study of 2D control for healthy subjects, accuracies for physical movement ranged from 85.2% to 93.0% (given by GA-MLD, although not significantly better than DTC and SVM), with the average of 88.3%; for a fourclass mental task, ITR was from 1.16 bits per trial, to 1.37 bits per trial, with the average 1.29 bits per trial. For motor execution with physical movement, the total duration of T1 and T2 windows was 5 s, i.e. 12 trials per minute. Therefore, the ITR was 13.9–16.5; the average was 15.5 bits per minute. Similarly, for motor imagery, the ITR was 4.15 bits per minute to 8.03 bits per minute. The cueing period T1 is important as it left enough time for the subjects to prepare for the movement. The results were comparable in terms of both accuracy and decoding rate with previous studies (see review in Wolpaw *et al* (2002)). In the study where center-out paradigm was adopted, T1 window was further shortened and the subjects can still make rapid response, and as a result, the ITR was further improved. As we also consider that the control performance/accuracy is very important in practical BCI application since BCI is intended for patients having limited motor function which features extremely slowness in motor control, it may be appropriate to have limited communication speed, whereas the accuracy needs to be high enough so that the users may avoid frustration when using BCI.

6. Conclusion

We analyzed ERD and ERS activity from EEG associated with human natural motor control in healthy people and ALS/PLS patients. ERD associated with active motor control and post beta-ERS associated with cessation of active motor control were preserved in four out of five healthy subjects and all six ALS and PLS patients participating in this study. ERD and ERS occurred not only with motor execution with physical movement, but also with motor imagery without overt movement. The amplitudes of ERD and ERS were less with motor imagery than during motor execution. In this study, we verified that the difference between ERS and ERD provided better contrast than the difference between idle state or baseline activities and ERD in not only healthy subjects but also ALS and PLS patients. The better contrast provided better classification rate by reducing the inter-class pattern overlapping. Under the proposed ERD and ERS-based paradigm, subjects achieved a high accuracy of binary control (80–90% for motor execution/motor imagery) despite not receiving extensive training. The accuracy for four-directional control was also much higher than the random level, though further training of effective motor imagery of right and left hand might be required.

The successful test on the ERD and ERS-based method associated with human natural motor control will promote the development of a practical user-friendly BCI because long-term training becomes unnecessary. This is important for severely affected patients who are unable to tolerate prolonged training. Further, users may not need to keep sustained attention to regulate EEG rhythm in the proposed BCI associated with human natural motor control.

7. References

Bai O, Lin P, Huang D, Fei DY, Floeter M.K. (2010) Towards a user-friendly brain-computer interface: initial tests in ALS and PLS patients. *Clin Neurophysiol* 121: 1293-303.

Bai O, Lin P, Vorbach S, Floeter MK, Hattori N, Hallett M (2008) A high performance sensorimotor beta rhythm-based brain-computer interface associated with human natural motor behavior. *J Neural Eng* 5: 24-35

Bai O, Lin P, Vorbach S, Li J, Furlani S, Hallett M (2007) Exploration of computational methods for classification of movement intention during human voluntary movement from single trial EEG. *Clin Neurophysiol* 118: 2637-2655

Bai O, Mari Z, Vorbach S and Hallett M (2005) Asymmetric spatiotemporal patterns of event-related desynchronization preceding voluntary sequential finger movements: a high-resolution EEG study *Clin Neurophysiol* 116 1213-21

Bashashati A, Fatourechi M, Ward RK, Birch GE (2007) A survey of signal processing algorithms in brain-computer interfaces based on electrical brain signals. *J Neural Eng* 4: R32-57

Birbaumer N, Kubler A, Ghanayim N, Hinterberger T, Perelmouter J, Kaiser J, Iversen I, Kotchoubey B, Neumann N, Flor H (2000) The thought translation device (TTD) for completely paralyzed patients. *IEEE Trans Rehabil Eng* 8: 190-193

Birbaumer N, Cohen LG (2007) Brain-computer interfaces: communication and restoration of movement in paralysis. *J Physiol* 579: 621-636

Birbaumer N (2006b) Breaking the silence: brain-computer interfaces (BCI) for communication and motor control. *Psychophysiology* 43: 517-532

Birbaumer N (2006a) Brain-computer-interface research: coming of age. *Clin Neurophysiol* 117: 479-483

Birch GE, Bozorgzadeh Z, Mason SG (2002) Initial on-line evaluations of the LF-ASD brain-computer interface with able-bodied and spinal-cord subjects using imagined voluntary motor potentials. *IEEE Trans Neural Syst Rehabil Eng* 10: 219-224

Blankertz B, Dornhege G, Krauledat M, Muller KR, Curio G (2007) The non-invasive Berlin Brain-Computer Interface: fast acquisition of effective performance in untrained subjects. *Neuroimage* 37: 539-550

Bromberg MB (2008) Quality of life in amyotrophic lateral sclerosis. *Phys Med Rehabil Clin N Am* 19: 591-605, x-xi

Cassim F, Monaca C, Szurhaj W, Bourriez JL, Defebvre L, Derambure P, Guieu JD (2001) Does post-movement beta synchronization reflect an idling motor cortex? *Neuroreport* 12: 3859-3863

Chang CC, Lin CJ (2001) Training nu-support vector classifiers: theory and algorithms. *Neural Comput* 13: 2119-2147

Chatterjee A, Aggarwal V, Ramos A, Acharya S, Thakor NV (2007) A brain-computer interface with vibrotactile biofeedback for haptic information. *J Neuroeng Rehabil* 4: 40

Daly JJ, Wolpaw JR (2008) Brain-computer interfaces in neurological rehabilitation. *Lancet Neurol* 7: 1032-1043

Hayashi H, Oppenheimer EA (2003) ALS patients on TPPV: totally locked-in state, neurologic findings and ethical implications. *Neurology* 61: 135-137

Hill NJ, Lal TN, Schroder M, Hinterberger T, Wilhelm B, Nijboer F, Mochty U, Widman G, Elger C, Scholkopf B, Kubler A, Birbaumer N (2006) Classifying EEG and ECoG signals without subject training for fast BCI implementation: comparison of nonparalyzed and completely paralyzed subjects. *IEEE Trans Neural Syst Rehabil Eng* 14: 183-186

Hjorth B (1975) An on-line transformation of EEG scalp potentials into orthogonal source derivations. *Electroencephalogr Clin Neurophysiol* 39: 526-530

Huang D, Lin P, Fei DY, Chen X, Bai O (2009) Decoding human motor activity from EEG single trials for a discrete two-dimensional cursor control. *J Neural Eng* 6: 46005

Iversen IH, Ghanayim N, Kubler A, Neumann N, Birbaumer N, Kaiser J (2008b) A brain-computer interface tool to assess cognitive functions in completely paralyzed patients with amyotrophic lateral sclerosis. *Clin Neurophysiol* 119: 2214-2223

Iversen I, Ghanayim N, Kubler A, Neumann N, Birbaumer N, Kaiser J (2008a) Conditional associative learning examined in a paralyzed patient with amyotrophic lateral sclerosis using brain-computer interface technology. *Behav Brain Funct* 4: 53

Jasper HH, Andrews HL (1938) Electro-encephalography. III. Normal differentiation of occipital and precentral regions in man. *Arch Neurol Psychiat* 39: 95-115

Joseph AB (1985) Design considerations for the brain-machine interface. *Med Hypotheses* 17: 191-195

Kayagil TA, Bai O, Henriquez CS, Lin P, Furlani SJ, Vorbach S, Hallett M (2009) A binary method for simple and accurate two-dimensional cursor control from EEG with minimal subject training. *J Neuroeng Rehabil* 6: 14

Keerthi SS, Lin C (2003) Asymptotic behaviors of support vector machines with Gaussian kernel. *Neural Computation* 15: 1667-1689

Kennedy PR, Bakay RA, Moore MM, Adams K, Goldwaithe J (2000) Direct control of a computer from the human central nervous system. *IEEE Trans Rehabil Eng* 8: 198-202

Krusienski D J, Schalk G, McFarland D J and Wolpaw J R (2007) A mu-rhythm matched filter for continuous control of a brain-computer interface *IEEE Trans Biomed Eng* 54 273-80

Kubler A, Neumann N, Kaiser J, Kotchoubey B, Hinterberger T, Birbaumer NP (2001) Brain-computer communication: self-regulation of slow cortical potentials for verbal communication. *Arch Phys Med Rehabil* 82: 1533-1539

Kubler A, Kotchoubey B, Hinterberger T, Ghanayim N, Perelmouter J, Schauer M, Fritsch C, Taub E, Birbaumer N (1999) The thought translation device: a neurophysiological approach to communication in total motor paralysis. *Exp Brain Res* 124: 223-232

Li Q, Doi K (2006) Analysis and minimization of overtraining effect in rule-based classifiers for computer-aided diagnosis. *Med Phys* 33: 320-328

Lule D, Zickler C, Hacker S, Bruno MA, Demertzi A, Pellas F, Laureys S, Kubler A (2009) Life can be worth living in locked-in syndrome. *Prog Brain Res* 177: 339-351

McFarland D J and Wolpaw J R (2003) EEG-based communication and control: speed-accuracy relationships *Appl Psychophysiol Biofeedback* 28 217-31

Mockford C, Jenkinson C, Fitzpatrick R (2006) A Review: carers, MND and service provision. *Amyotroph Lateral Scler* 7: 132-141

Muller KR, Mika S, Ratsch G, Tsuda K, Scholkopf B (2001) An introduction to kernel-based learning algorithms. *IEEE Trans Neural Netw* 12: 181-201

Mutsaarts M, Steenbergen B, Meulenbroek R (2004) A detailed analysis of the planning and execution of prehension movements by three adolescents with spastic hemiparesis due to cerebral palsy. *Exp Brain Res* 156: 293-304

Naeem M, Brunner C, Leeb R, Graimann B and Pfurtscheller G (2006) Seperability of four-class motor imagery data using independent components analysis *J Neural Eng* 3 208-16

Neuper C, Scherer R, Reiner M and Pfurtscheller G (2005) Imagery of motor actions: differential effects of kinesthetic and visual-motor mode of imagery in single-trial EEG *Brain Res Cogn Brain Res* 25 668-77

Neuper C, Pfurtscheller G (2001) Evidence for distinct beta resonance frequencies in human EEG related to specific sensorimotor cortical areas. *Clin Neurophysiol* 112: 2084-2097

Pfurtscheller G and Solis-Escalante T (2009) Could the beta rebound in the EEG be suitable to realize a "brain switch"? *Clin Neurophysiol* 120 24-9

Pfurtscheller G, Neuper C, Brunner C, da Silva FL (2005) Beta rebound after different types of motor imagery in man. *Neurosci Lett* 378: 156-159

Pfurtscheller G, Lopes da Silva FH (1999) Event-related EEG/MEG synchronization and desynchronization: basic principles. *Clin Neurophysiol* 110: 1842-1857

Pfurtscheller G, Stancak A, Jr., Neuper C (1996) Post-movement beta synchronization. A correlate of an idling motor area? *Electroencephalogr Clin Neurophysiol* 98: 281-293

Pfurtscheller G (1992) Event-related synchronization (ERS): an electrophysiological correlate of cortical areas at rest. *Electroencephalogr Clin Neurophysiol* 83: 62-69

Rao S M, Binder J R, Bandettini P A, Hammeke T A, Yetkin F Z, Jesmanowicz A, Lisk L M, Morris G L, Mueller W M, Estkowski L D and et al. (1993) Functional magnetic resonance imaging of complex human movements *Neurology* 43 2311-8

Salmelin R, Hamalainen M, Kajola M, Hari R (1995) Functional segregation of movement-related rhythmic activity in the human brain. *Neuroimage* 2: 237-243

Sellers EW, Donchin E (2006) A P300-based brain-computer interface: initial tests by ALS patients. *Clin Neurophysiol* 117: 538-548

Sykacek P, Roberts S, Stokes M, Curran E, Gibbs M, Pickup L (2003) Probabilistic methods in BCI research. *IEEE Trans Neural Syst Rehabil Eng* 11: 192-195

Velliste M, Perel S, Spalding MC, Whitford AS, Schwartz AB (2008) Cortical control of a prosthetic arm for self-feeding. *Nature* 453: 1098-1101

Williams MT, Donnelly JP, Holmlund T, Battaglia M (2008) ALS: Family caregiver needs and quality of life. *Amyotroph Lateral Scler* 9: 279-286

Wolpaw JR, McFarland DJ (2004) Control of a two-dimensional movement signal by a noninvasive brain-computer interface in humans. *Proc Natl Acad Sci U S A* 101: 17849-17854

Wolpaw JR, Birbaumer N, McFarland DJ, Pfurtscheller G, Vaughan TM (2002) Brain-computer interfaces for communication and control. *Clin Neurophysiol* 113: 767-791

Wolpaw J R, Birbaumer N, Heetderks W J, McFarland D J, Peckham P H, Schalk G, Donchin E, Quatrano L A, Robinson C J and Vaughan T M (2000) Brain-computer interface technology: a review of the first international meeting *IEEE Trans Rehabil Eng* 8 164-73

Wolpaw JR, McFarland DJ (1994) Multichannel EEG-based brain-computer communication. *Electroencephalogr Clin Neurophysiol* 90: 444-449

9

Advances in Non-Invasive Brain-Computer Interfaces for Control and Biometry

Nuno Figueiredo, Filipe Silva, Pétia Georgieva and Ana Tomé
Department of Electronics, Telecommunications and Informatics
Institute of Electronic Engineering and Telematics of Aveiro (IEETA)
University of Aveiro
Portugal

1. Introduction

During the last decade many advances in a number of fields have supported the idea that a direct interface between the human brain and an artificial system, called Brain Computer Interface (BCI), is a viable concept, although a significant research and development effort has to be conducted before these technologies enter routine use. The conceptual approach is to model the brain activity variations and map them into some kind of actuation over a target output through the use of signal processing and machine learning methods. In the meantime, several working BCI systems have been described in the literature using a variety of signal acquisition methods, experimental paradigms, pattern recognition approaches and output interfaces, and requiring different types of cognitive activity (Allison *et al.*, 2008; Bashashati *et al.*, 2007; Berger *et al.*, 2008; Leeb *et al.*, 2007; Millán, 2008; Müller-Putz & Pfurtscheller, 2008). Nowadays, the principal reason for the BCI research is the potential benefits to those with severe motor disabilities, such as brainstem stroke, amyotrophic lateral sclerosis or severe cerebral palsy (Bensch *et al.*, 2007; Birbaumer *et al.*, 2007; Nijboer *et al.*, 2008; Pfurtscheller *et al.*, 2008). However, the most recent advances in acquisition technology and signal processing assert that controlling certain functions by neural interfaces may have a significant impact in the way people will operate computers, wheelchairs, prostheses, robotic systems and other devices.
A very effective way to analyze the brain physiological activity is the electroencephalogram (EEG) measurements from the cortex whose sources are the action potentials of the nerve cells in the brain. The theoretical and the application studies are based on the knowledge that the EEG signals are composed of waves inside the 0-60 Hz frequency band and on the fact that different brain activities can be identified based on the recorded oscillations (Niedermayer & Lopes da Silva, 1999). Over the last years, the interest in extracting knowledge hidden in the EEG signals is rapidly growing, as well as their applications. EEG-based BCIs for motor control and biometry are among the most recent applications in the computational neuro-engineering field. Despite the proof of concept and many encouraging results achieved by some research groups (Marcel & Millán, 2007; Millán *et al.*, 2004; Palaniappan & Mandic, 2007; Pineda, 2005; Pfurtscheller *et al.*, 2006; Vidaurre *et al.*, 2006), additional efforts are required in order to design and implement efficient BCIs. For example, reliable signal processing and pattern recognition techniques able to continuously extract meaningful information from the very noisy EEG is still a high challenge.

The project behind this chapter aims to initiate a long-term multidisciplinary research by combining developments in relevant fields, such as computational neuro-engineering, signal processing, pattern recognition, brain imaging and robotics. In the middle-term, the main objective has been the design and development of BCIs to exploit the benefits of advanced human-machine interfaces for control and biometry. In this line of thought, this chapter will present recent advances towards the development of two BCI systems that analyzes the brain activity of a subject measured through EEG. The former tries to find out the user's intention and generates output commands for controlling an appropriate output device (Bento *et al.*, 2008). The later explores the possibility of using the brain electrical activity during visual stimuli for implementing an EEG biometric system (Ferreira *et al.*, 2010).

The remainder of the chapter is organised as follows: Section 2 presents an overview of the activity at the IEETA (Institute of Electronic Engineering and Telematics of Aveiro) research unit. Section 3 explores the application of beamforming techniques in EEG source analysis from a simulated dataset. Section 4 describes the main advances in the development of an EEG-based BCI for biometry. Section 5 concludes the chapter and outlines the perspectives of future research.

2. Framework of the research at IEETA

The development of non-invasive BCIs for control and biometry are the research focus of the IEETA Computational Neuro-engineering research group and among the most recent applications based on personal EEG data. In spite of sharing the same basic components, a BCI to provide an alternative control channel for acting on the environment and a biometric system for identification or authentication reveal significant differences. While the BCI technology has been focused on interpreting brain signals for communication and control, the requirements of an EEG-based biometric system are entirely different: they require no interpretation of the brain signals, but use the unique brain´s response to stimuli as the identification method. The identified person is exposed to a stimulus (usually visual or auditory) for a certain time and the EEG data collected over this time is input to the biometry system. It has been shown in previous studies (Paranjape *et al.*, 2001; Poulos *et al.*, 1999) that the EEG can be used for building personal identification systems due to the unique brain-wave patterns of every individual. At the same time, the frequency band segmentation is a key concept in the area of EEG-based BCIs. Current implementations for motor control are based on the special frequency range termed sensorimotor rhythm mu which is related with imagery subject movements. As for the EEG-based biometry, the concept of Evoked Potentials (EP) and Visual Evoked Potentials (VEP) of the brain electrical activity play a major role. EP are transient EEG signals generated in response to a stimulus (*e.g.*, motor imagery or mental tasks) and VEP are EP produced in response to visual stimuli generating activity within the gamma band.

From the viewpoint of brain-computer interfacing for control, a major concern has been considered to structure the research, which is: how to improve the BCI's performance by solving the EEG inverse problem for the localization of the brain activities underlying recorded EEG. Source-based BCIs have been exploited with encouraging results by achieving improved spatial accuracy, as well as by providing additional biophysical information on the origin of the signals (Grave de Peralta *et al.*, 2005; Grosse- Wentrup *et al.*, 2009; Kamousi *et al.*, 2005; Noirhomme *et al.*, 2008; Qin *et al.*, 2004). In line with this, the problems of head models in EEG source analysis, the generation of the simulated datasets, the estimation of original sources signals using beamforming and the optimization of certain parameters with influence in the system's performance will be addressed as the central topics of this chapter. The insights gained with this study can be relevant when optimizing the design and implementation of a practical source-based BCI.

In what concerns the EEG-based biometrical scenario, we aim at focusing on several open problems related with: i) design a feature model that belongs to a certain person and design a personal classifier with a respective owner, ii) study on the type and the duration of the evoked potentials (visual or auditory) that would enhance the identification/authentication capacity; iii) post-processing techniques on the classifier output as averaging or sporadic error correction would improve the identification/authentication capacity, and iv) optimization of the evoked potential duration (EPD) in order to implement the paradigm in an on-line scheme.

3. Beamforming in brain-computer interfaces

In brain imaging, the EEG inverse problem can be formulated as follows: using the measurements of electrical potential on the scalp recorded from multi-sensors, the idea is to build a reconstruction system able to estimate the time course of the original source signals or some of them with specific properties. The problems of reconstructing the original source waveforms from the sensor array, without exploiting the *a priori* knowledge about the transmission channel, can be expressed as a number of related blind source separation (BSS) problems. Choi *et al.* (2005) present a review of various blind source separation and independent component analysis (ICA) algorithms for static and dynamic models and their applications.

Nowadays, beamforming has also become a popular analysis procedure for non-invasive recorded electrophysiological data sets (Baillet et al., 2001; Fuchs, 2007). The goal is to use a set or recording sensors and combine the signals recorded at individual sites to increase the signal-to-noise ratio, but focusing on a certain region in space (region-of-interest, ROI). In that sense, beamforming uses a different approach to image brain activity: the whole brain is scanned point by point. In general, when this approach is applied to EEG recordings the objective is to estimate the magnitude, locations and directions of the neural brain sources, by applying a spatial filter to the data. This spatial filter is designed to be fully sensitive to activity from the target location, while being as insensitive as possible to activity from other brain regions. This is achieved by constructing the spatial filter in an adaptive way, i.e., by taking into account the recorded data. More concretely, the beamforming is carried out by weighting the EEG signals, thereby adjusting their amplitudes such as that when added together they form the desired source signal.

The primary motivation for our study is the potential of application of beamforming in brain-computer interfaces. In spite of some encouraging results (Grosse- Wentrup *et al.*, 2009; Kamousi *et al.*, 2005; Noirhomme *et al.*, 2008; Qin *et al.*, 2004), only recently the concept of source-based BCI was adopted in literature. Therefore, additional research efforts are needed to establish a solid foundations aiming at uncovering the driving force behind the growth of source-based BCI as a research area and to expose its implications for the design and implementation of better systems.

This section proceeds as follows: first, an EEG dataset is created by simulating the neural activity in specific locations modelled as current dipoles. The spatiotemporal patterns that would be measured by the recording system are the superposition of these brain sources. Second, some basic concepts on beamforming are presented before the EEG dataset used to estimate the source activity is processed. Finally, several simulations are performed in order to evaluate how certain parameters affect the performance of the reconstruction system.

3.1 Simulating the electric activity in the brain

The human brain consists of neuron cells that communicate by means of short bursts of electrical activity called action potentials. Neurons that have relatively strong potentials at any given time tend to be clustered in the brain. Thus, the total electric potentials at any given time in such an activated region may be large enough to be detected on the scalp by EEG electrodes. Bearing this in mind, the current distribution in an activated region will be modelled by an equivalent current dipole within the conductive brain tissue. Further, the EEG dataset is simulated assuming that the electrical activity of the brain, at any given time, can be modelled by only a small number of dipoles.

A three-concentric spherical model consisting of a central sphere for the brain and two spherical shells for the skull and scalp was used to approximate the head volume. This is a simplification that preserves some important electrical characteristics of the head, while reducing the mathematical complexity of the problem. The different electric conductivities of the several layers between the brain and the measuring surface need to be known. The skull is typically assumed to be more resistive than the brain and scalp that, in turn, have similar conductivity properties (Lai *et al.*, 2005).

Once defined the source and head models, the computation of the scalp potentials given by known electrical dipoles sources requires the solution of the forward problem. If there are M active dipoles and N sensors, the measured activity at the sensors $x(t)$ is the sum of the individual contributions of each individual dipole $y_m(t)$ as follows:

$$x(t) = \sum_{m=1}^{M} L_m y_m(t) \tag{1}$$

Here, $L_m \in R^{N\times 3}$ is the lead field matrix for dipole m. In the spherical three-layer model, an analytical expression for the forward model can be derived as function of the dipole location, electrodes positions and head geometry (Salu *et al.*, 1990). The three columns in the forward model contain the activity that will be measured at the sensors due to a dipole source with unity moment in the x, y, and z directions, respectively, and zero moment in the other directions. The development of a forward model is also the first step in building the beamformer filter. This model is needed because its inverse describes how the brain activity can be estimated from sensor measurements, which is the purpose of beamforming.

Throughout this section, all simulations are based on the following assumptions: (1) the scalp electrodes record the superposition of both brain sources and non-brain sources related to, for example, movements of muscles, (2) the reference is at an infinite distance with zero potential, (3) the location of the target dipoles are known; (4) the distribution of the electrodes on the scalp is made by selecting spherical coordinates θ and ϕ from uniform distributions. Fig. 1 illustrates a realistic head model and the hemisphere model (top view) where an array of 64-electrodes is arranged. Their coordinates are defined with respect to a reference frame whose origin is located at the centre of the sphere.

3.2 Beamforming: generic concepts

The basic idea behind beamforming is to estimate the time course of a current dipole $y(t)$ at location r and direction d using the measurements of electrical potential on the scalp recorded from N sensors located at the surface of the head. The beamformer filter consists of weight coefficients w_m that when multiplied by the electrode measurements give an estimate of the dipole moment:

$$y(t)= w_m^T x(t) \quad (2)$$

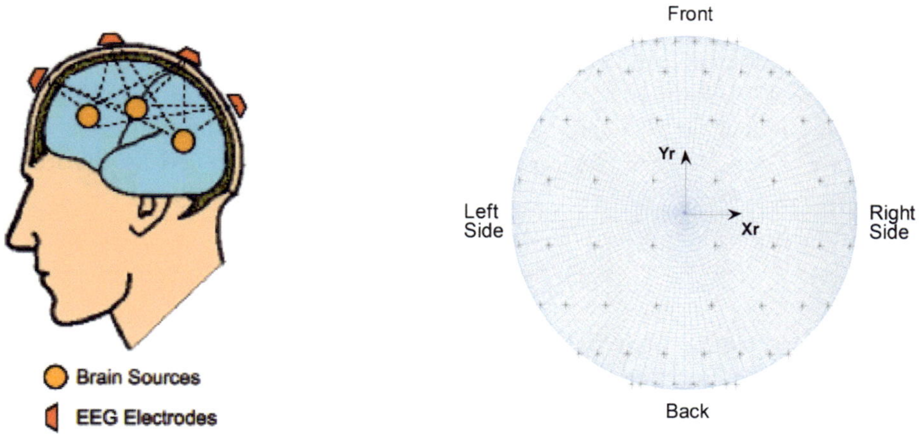

Fig. 1. The realistic head shape (left) is approximated by three concentric spherical shells; the referece coordinate frame has its origin at the centre of the spheres (right)

The choice o the beamformer weights w_m is based on the statistics of the signal vector $x(t)$ received at the electrodes. Basically, the objective is to optimize the beamformer response with respect to a prescribed criterion, so that the output $y(t)$ contains minimal contribution from noise and interference. There are a number of criteria for choosing the optimum weights. The method described above represents a linear transformation where the transformation matrix is designed according to the solution of a constrained optimization problem (the early work is attributed to Capon, 1969). The basic idea is the following: assuming that the desired signal and its direction are both unknown, one way of ensuring good signal estimation is to minimize the output signal variance. To ensure that the desired signal is passed with a specific gain, a constraint may be used so that the response of the beamformer to the desired signal is:

$$w_m L_m(r) = I \quad (3)$$

where L_m is the lead field matrix of a unit source at target location r and I is the unit matrix. Minimization of contributions to the output due to interference is accomplished by choosing the weights to minimize the variance of the filter output:

$$Var\{y\} = tr\{w_m^T R_x w_m\} \quad (4)$$

Here, $tr\{\ \}$ is the trace of the sub-matrix of the bracketed expression and R_x is the covariance matrix of the EEG signals. In practice, the covariance matrix R_x will be estimated from the EEG signals during a given time window. Therefore, the filter is derived by minimizing the output variance subject to the constraint defined in (3). This constraint ensures that the desired signal is passed with unit gain. Finally, the optimal solution can be derived by constrained minimization using Lagrange multipliers (Van Veen, *et al.*, 1997) and it can be expressed as:

$$w_m^{opt} = R_x^{-1} L_m (L_m^T R_x^{-1} L_m)^{-1} \quad (5)$$

The response of the beamformer is often called the linearly constrained minimum variance (LCMV) beamformer. The LCMV provides not only an estimate of the source activity, but also its orientation, reason why is classified as vector beamforming. The differences and similarities among beamformers based on this criterion for choosing the optimum weights are discussed in Huang *et al.* (2004). It is also shown that the output power P of the beamformer, for a specific brain region at location r, can be computed by the following equation:

$$Var\{y\} = tr\left\{\left[L_m^T R_x^{-1} L_m\right]^{-1}\right\} \quad (6)$$

This is known as the Neural Activity Index (NAI) and it can be calculated for over the whole head at each grid point (Van Veen *et al.*, 1997).

3.2.1 Two dipole simulation

The performance of the beamformer algorithm in determining the magnitude and direction of the source is evaluated in a specific scenario. First, two uncorrelated sources are defined based on sinusoidal waveforms with amplitudes 0.1 and frequencies 10 Hz and 15 Hz. The dipole moments are oriented along the z-axis and they are located at the following coordinates: $d_1:(x,y,z)=(-4,4,1)$ cm and $d_2:(x,y,z)=(4,-4,1)$ cm. The radii of the three concentric hemispheres are 8.7, 9.2 and 10 cm. The corresponding conductivity values are 0.33, 0.0165 and 0.33 $S \cdot m^{-1}$. The scalp electrodes are distributed on a regular grid of 64-electrodes covering the entire hemisphere. Second, white noise is added into the EEG representing the effect of external sources not generated by brain activity, but by some disturbance. The noise power was defined in such a way that the maximum signal-to-noise ratio (SNR) among the electrodes never exceeds 10. It is assumed that the EEG recording system operates with a 1kHz sampling rate.

Fig. 2 shows the original and the estimated waveforms, giving an idea of the achieved accuracy provided by the LCMV algorithm. It must be emphasised that the reconstruction is performed considering that the location of one dipole is known, while the other represents an unknown interference source (single-source beamformer). The method is able to reconstruct the original signal and suppress the interfering source activity, though both estimates are noisy. The considerable noise gain can be reduced by subspace projection: the measurement space is separated into a signal and noise space by applying an eigenspace decomposition of the covariance matrix R_x. The dimensionality is reduced to the subspace defined by the eigenvectors whose eigenvalues are significantly bigger than zero. This eigenspace-based LCMV is able to strongly suppress the interfering source, as well as to provide a low noise gain (Fig. 3). However, the condition (3) is not preserved affecting slightly the amplitude of the output signal. In the simulations, the mean square error (MSE) is used to quantify the difference between the estimated source moments (beamformer output) and the reference signals.

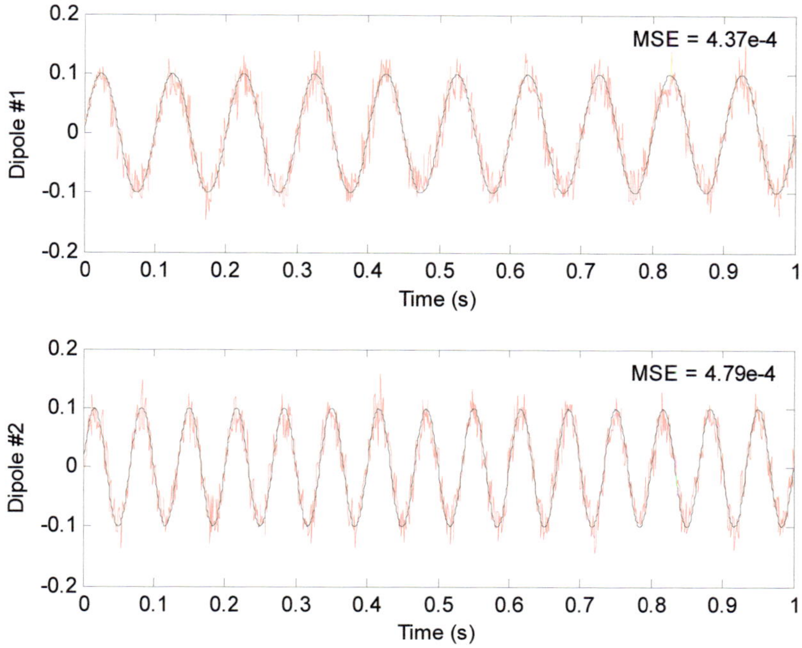

Fig. 2. The original and estimated source waveforms represented together for dipole 1 (top) and dipole 2 (bottom) using the LCMV beamformer

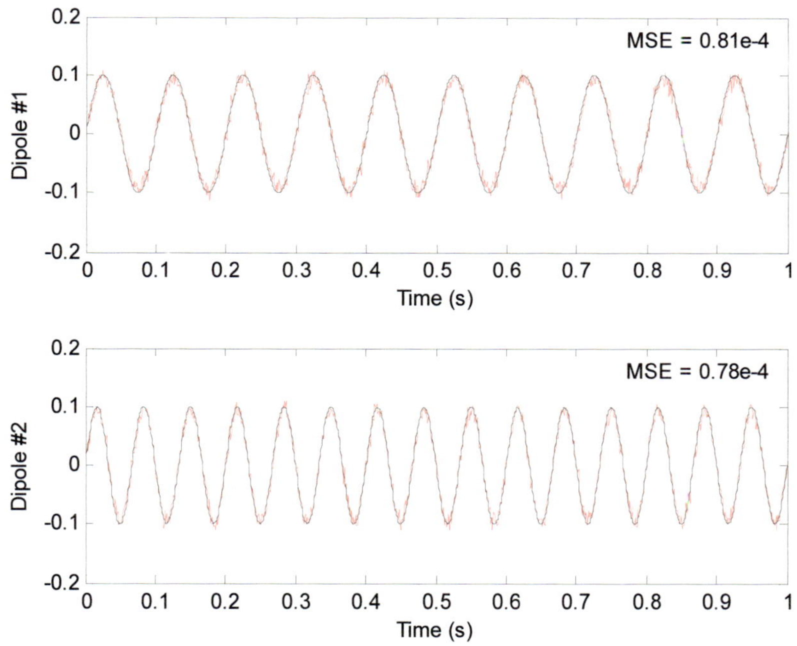

Fig. 3. The original and estimated source waveforms represented together for dipole 1 (top) and dipole 2 (bottom) using the eigenspace-based LCMV beamformer

3.2.2 Performance limitations

The distance and correlation among sources are two factors that may lead to degradation in the beamforming algorithm. Van Veen *et al.* (1997) pointed out these limitations by calculating the neural activity index in brain areas over a certain time interval. On the one hand, sources that are close to each other tend to merge. On the other hand, when the sources are correlated it is difficult to detect distinct source locations. A number of techniques have attempted to address the problem of correlated sources, such as a dual beamformer (Herdman *et al.*, 2003) or using only half of the sensor array (Popescu *et al.*, 2008). The idea of a multiple-source beamforming is to account for the activity from possibly correlated brain regions: the calculation contains not only the leadfield matrix of the source at the target location, but also those of possible sources whose interference is to be minimized. For example, this allows for source separation of highly correlated bilateral activity in the two hemispheres that commonly occurs during motor imagery tasks (a common control paradigm in BCI). Anyway, localising potentially correlated sources remains an open problem and it is not addressed along this chapter. Instead, the sources are assumed uncorrelated and relatively distant. Fig. 4 shows the contour plot of the global neural activity measured in a horizontal cross section for two uncorrelated dipoles, as defined in the previous subsection.

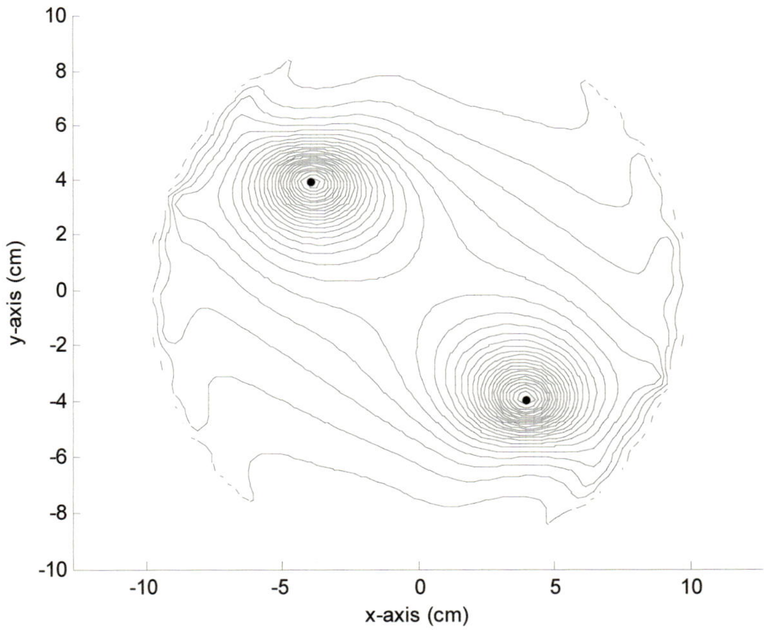

Fig. 4. Contour plot of the neural activity index in a horizontal cross section 1 cm above the centre of the sphere where the two dipoles are localized

3.3 Number and localization of the electrodes

One of the questions about applying beamforming techniques to BCIs is the choice of the number and localization of the electrodes. Here, the goal is to understand how the performance of the LCMV beamformer is influenced by these two factors, for example: (1) to what extend the number of electrodes can be reduced and (2) what is the optimal distribution of the electrodes on the scalp. In line with this, the MSE between reference and estimated waveforms is evaluated for different number of electrodes and distributions. The electrodes form a grid of points covering a variable percentage of the total hemisphere surface area (see Fig. 5). In this study, the electrodes are located, symmetrically, around a specific point in the scalp considering two different situations: a first in which this point has coordinates $(x,y)=(0,0)$ and a second in which the point has coordinates $(x,y)=(-5,0)$ cm (exactly where the dipole vector points). The parameters associated with the head and dipole models remain unchanged, but the dipole locations: $d_1:(x,y,z)=(-5,0,1)$ cm and $d_2:(x,y,z)=(5,0,1)$ cm. The additive noise power is assumed to be the same throughout the simulations.

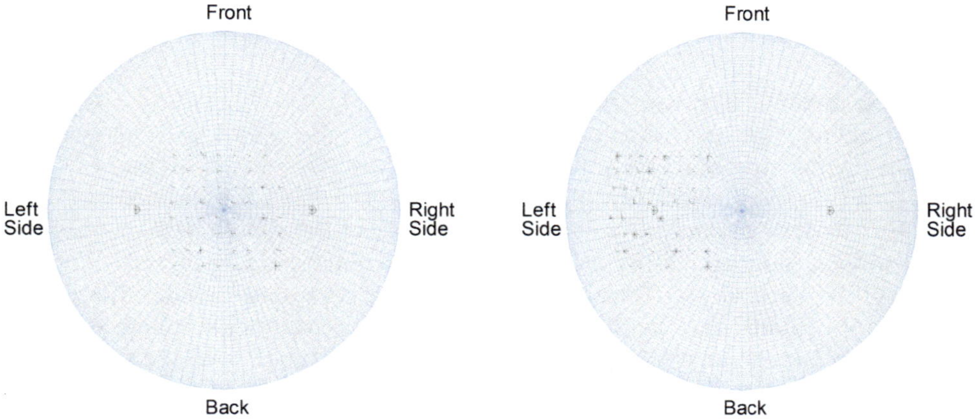

Fig. 5. Top view of the hemisphere with the locations of two dipoles and 64-electrodes (with a normalized area of 0.062); the electrodes are located, symmetrically, around a point with coordinates $(x,y)=(0,0)$ cm (left) and a point with coordinates $(x,y)=(-5,0)$ cm (right)

Fig. 6 shows the achieved results for dipole 1 in terms of MSE as function of the normalized area. The two graphics were obtained by superimposing the curves for $N=\{4,9,16,32,64\}$ electrodes. The first observation is the quite modest performance with only 4 electrodes. However, for $N=9$, the second arrangement (closer to the target dipole) is able to achieve improved results, especially by increasing the surface area. When the number of electrodes increases, the curves give a good indication of the required area and number of electrodes from which no improvements are achieved. At the same time, the second distribution leads to only a slightly better performance than the first one, observable at higher areas.

In conclusion, when fewer electrodes are more suitable (*e.g.*, BCI applications), an optimal local distribution seems to be essential to reduce the number of electrodes, while maintaining an acceptable performance from the viewpoint of source reconstruction. However, the extrapolation of these results for other scenarios is more difficult since they are the direct consequence of the selected dipoles, as well as the time course of the signal-to-noise ratio.

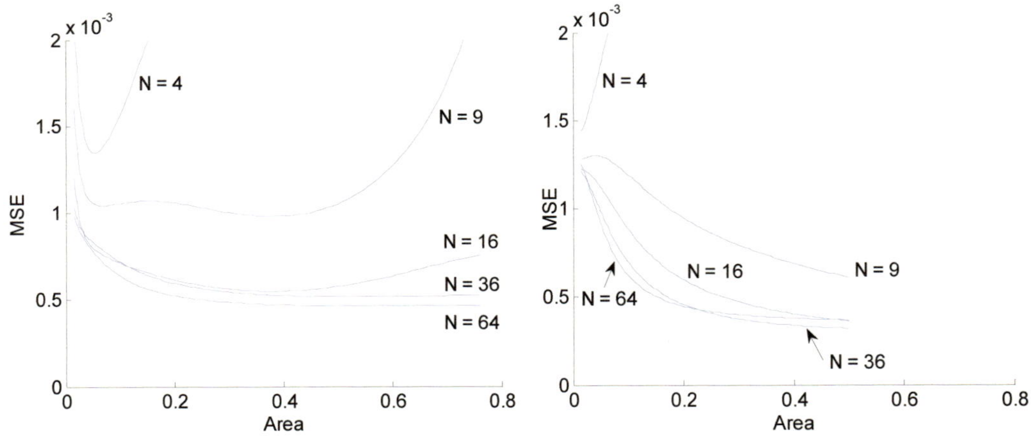

Fig. 6. Mean-square error for dipole 1 as function of the normalized area using N electrodes

3.4 Sensitivity analysis to errors in the forward model

In this subsection, we will discuss the sensitivity of the reconstruction system to uncertainties in the mathematical model. More precisely, we intend to study how the uncertainties in the parameters of the forward model can affect the performance of the beamformer. The forward model is derived as function of the dipole location, electrodes positions and head geometry. Here, the attention is devoted to parameters related with the localization of the electrodes and the *a priori* estimation of the source location. The objective is to execute the model repeatedly for a combination of parameter values with some probability distribution. In the first case, the error in the location of each electrode is represented by the radius R_c of a circumference centred at the original electrodes' locations. Every electrode moves the same distance from the original position, but with a random direction. In Fig. 7, the MSE as function of radius are plotted for the two dipoles.

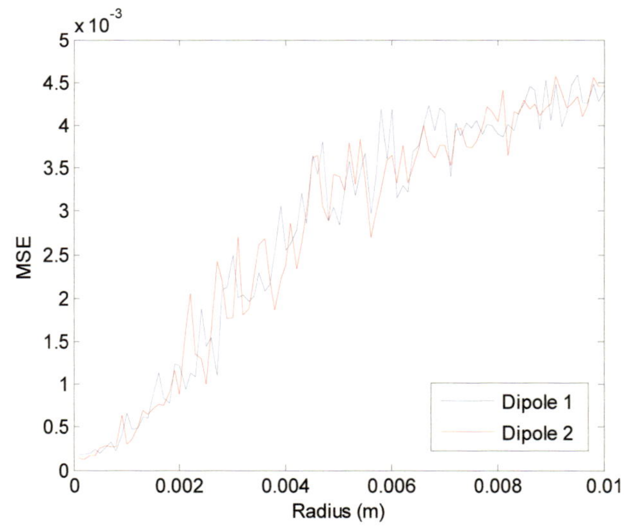

Fig. 7. Mean-square error for the two dipoles as function of radius R_c

In this simulation, the dipole locations are $d_1 : (x,y,z) = (-5,0,1)$ cm and $d_2 : (x,y,z) = (5,0,1)$ cm, while the simulated EEG is generated using 36 measurement electrodes distributed over the whole head. Then, the LCMV beamformer algorithm estimates the sources based on a leadfield matrix that incorporates the random errors. As expected, the MSE tends to increase with the radius, but with random fluctuations. A small increase in R_c does not necessarily signify a degradation of the system's performance due to the random orientation applied in each electrode. In some way, this procedure represents well a real scenario involving the placement of electrodes in the scalp. A similar analysis is performed when small deviations between the real and the estimated dipole's locations occur. Fig. 9 shows the MSE degradation when the location of dipole 1 is not correctly estimated in the directions defined by the x-, y- and z-axis in the reference coordinate frame.

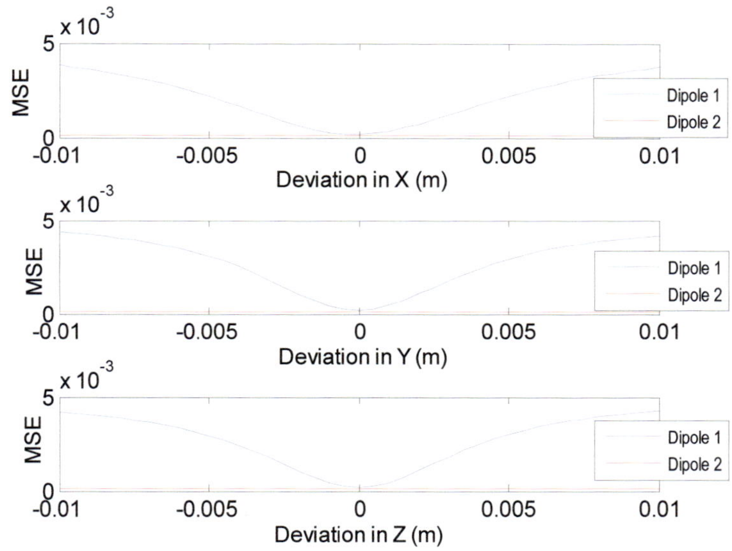

Fig. 8. Mean-square error for the two dipoles as function of deviation in the dipole 1

3.5 Adaptive algorithm

The simulations performed so far use the complete dataset to calculate the filter weights and then to estimate the time course of the target source. However, in a practical situation the EEG signals are not known and a nonstationary (time-varying) environment can be anticipated. To evaluate the performance of the spatial filter as a function of the amount of available data the following procedure is employed: first, in the static mode, the beamformer weights are computed once using a given segment of data and they are applied to new data without further update. The beamformer algorithm uses estimates of the covariance matrix based on the available EEG data. Further, this matrix needs to be inverted and, in certain circumstances, it can be close to singular. Theoretically, the number of observations must greater than number of sensors to avoid singularities. Fig. 9 shows the influence of the number of observations on the MSE of the dipole 1 with 36 sensors. Independently of the SNR, a number of 400 independent observations should be used to estimate the covariance matrix (dashed line).

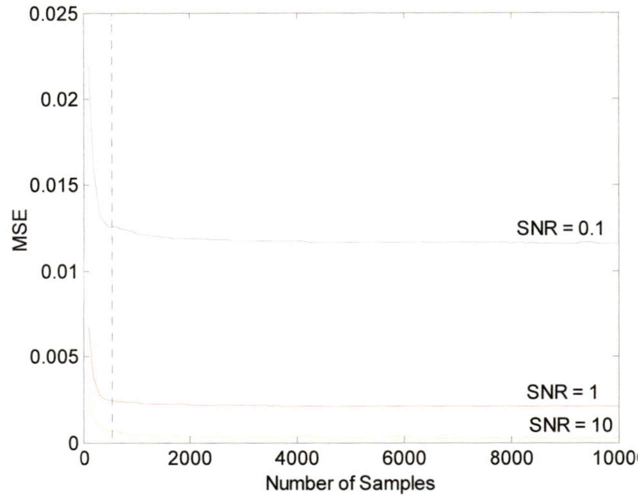

Fig. 9. Mean-square error for dipole 1 as function of the number of samples used to estimate the covariance matrix when varying the noise power

Second, an adaptive algorithm is continually updating the weight vector to meet the new requirements imposed by the varying conditions. This need to update the weight vector without *a priori* information leads to the expedient of obtaining estimates of the covariance matrix in a finite observation interval and then using these estimates to obtain the optimum weight vector. This is a block-adaptive approach where statistics are estimated from successive temporal windows. In the present simulation, the source waveform is a damped sinusoid and the EEG acquisition uses a sampling rate of 512 Hz with 36-electrodes. Fig. 10 allows the comparison between the static and block-adaptive approaches.

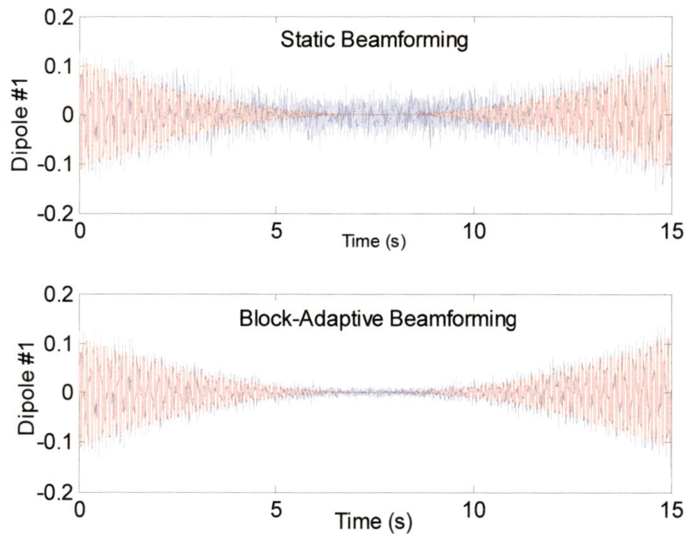

Fig. 10. The original and estimated source waveforms represented together for dipole 1 using static beamforming (top) and block-adaptive beamforming (bottom)

In block-adaptive beamforming the optimal weights are recomputed from time windows of 1 second. As can be observed, the adaptive approach outperforms the static approach when the amplitude of the source waveform reduces significantly. This suggests its potential utility to deal with dynamic changes in the source brain activity.

4. EEG-based biometry

Like the BCIs discussed in the previous sections, the EEG based biometry provides an alternative communication channel between the human brain and the external world. There is very little research work published using brain signals as biometric tools to identify individuals (Poulos et al., 1999; Paranjape, et al., 2001; Palaniappan & Mandic, 2007). Nevertheless, in these studies it was suggested that the brain-wave pattern of every individual is unique and, therefore, the EEG can be used for building personal identification or authentication systems. The identification attempts to establish the identity of a given person out of a closed list of persons (one from many), while the authentication aims to confirm or deny the identity claimed by a person (one to one matching), Marcel & Millan, 2007. The identified person is exposed to a stimulus (usually visual or auditory) for a certain time and the EEG signals coming from a number of electrodes spatially distributed over the subject's scalp are collected and input to the biometry system. The EEG signals induced by mental or perception tasks related with visual stimuli are known as Visually Evoked Potentials (VEP).

The raw EEG signals are too noisy and variable to be analyzed directly. Therefore, the EEG signals need to go through a sequence of processing steps: i) Data acquisition, storage and format transforming; ii) Filtering (removal of interferences from other unwanted sources, as for example physiological artifacts or baseline electrical trends); iii) Feature extraction and classification; iv) Feedback generation and visualization.

The identification/authentication systems built so far differ basically in filtering and classification components (Palaniappan & Mandic, 2007; Marcel & Millán, 2007). However, our initial study (Ferreira et al., 2010) has shown that the discrimination process is slightly dependent on the specific filter and classifier. Critical issues related with building an efficient EEG based biometry system are briefly discussed below.

Biometry as a modeling problem. The EEG recordings are unique for each person and the problem of EEG-based biometry can be interpreted as a modelling problem, *i.e.*, design a feature model that belongs to a certain person and design a personal classifier with a respective owner. The trained identification model has to identify the subject from a data base of personal profiles and the authentication system has to confirm or not that the subject being evaluated is who he claims to be.

Stimulus. Study on the type and the duration of the evoked potentials (visual or auditory) that would enhance the identification/authentication capacity. Preliminary tests have demonstrated that the type of the stimulus (for example mental task, motor task, image presentation or a combination of them) is crucial for reliable extraction of personal characteristics. It seems that some mental tasks are more appropriate than others. At the same time, experiments with combination of stimuli appear to be more advantageous for the personal uniqueness of the EEG patterns.

Post-processing. Ongoing research suggests that post-processing techniques on the classifier output as instant error correction and averaging would improve the identification/ authentication capacity.

Real-time biometry. Optimization of the evoked potential duration (EPD) in order to implement the paradigm in an on-line scheme. Current study has shown that both two short or too long EPD worsen the biometrical system (Ferreira *et al.*, 2010). The compromise can be learned by cross validation during the classifier training.
This section is organized as follows: Subsection 4.1 presents the experimental setup for the present study. In subsections 4.2 to 4.5 the main modules of the EEG biometry system are discussed, namely the feature extraction, the classification and the post-processing procedure. Finally, in subsection 4.6 the effect of the EPD is analyzed.

4.1 Experimental setup

VEP signals were extracted from thirteen female subjects (20-28 years old). All participants had normal or corrected to normal vision and no history of neurological or psychiatric illness. Neutral, fearful and disgusting faces of 16 different individuals (8 males and 8 females) were selected, giving a total of 48 different facial stimuli. Images of 16 different house fronts to be superimposed on each of the faces were selected from various internet sources. This resulted in a total of 384 grey-scaled composite images (9.5 cm wide by 14 cm high) of transparently superimposed face and house with equivalent discriminability.
Participants were seated in a dimly lit room, where a computer screen was placed at a viewing distance of approximately 80 cm coupled to a PC equipped with software for the EEG recording. The images were divided into two experimental blocks. In the first, the participants were required to attend to the houses (ignoring the faces) and in the other they were required to attend to the faces (ignoring the houses). The participant's task was to determine, on each trial, if the current house or face (depending on the experimental block) is the same as the one presented on the previous trial. Stimuli were presented in sequence, for 300ms each and were preceded by a fixation cross displayed for 500 ms. The inter-trial interval was 2000 ms.
EEG signals were recorded from 20 electrodes (Fp1, Fp2, F3, F4, C3, C4, P3, P4, O1, O2; F7, F8, T3, T4; P7, P8, Fz, Cz, Pz, Oz) according to the 10/20 International system (see Fig. 11). EOG (Electrooculogram - eye movemen) signals were also recorded from electrodes placed just above the left supraorbital ridge (vertical EOG) and on the left outer canthus (horizontal EOG). VEP were calculated off-line averaging segments of 400 points of digitized EEG (12 bit A/D converter, sampling rate 250 Hz). These segments covered 1600ms comprising a pre-stimulus interval of 148 ms (37 samples) and post-stimulus onset interval of 1452 ms. Before processing, EEG was visually inspected and those segments with excessive EOG artifacts were manually eliminated. Only trials with correct responses were included in the data set. The experimental setup was designed by Santos *et al.* (2008) for their study on subject attention and perception using VEP signals.

4.2 Feature extraction

The neuro-engineering theoretical and application studies related with the EEG signals are based on the knowledge that the EEG signals are composed of waves inside the 0-60 Hz frequency band and that different brain activities can be identified based on the recorded oscillations. For example, signals within the delta band (below 4 Hz) correspond to a deep sleep, theta band (4-8 Hz) signals are typical for dreamlike state, alpha frequencies (8-13 Hz) correspond to relaxed state with closed eyes, beta band (13-30 Hz) are related with waking activity and gamma frequencies (30-50 Hz) are characteristics for mental activities as perception and problem solving. The relationship between the EEG and the brain functions is well documented in Niedermayer and Lopes da Silva (1999).

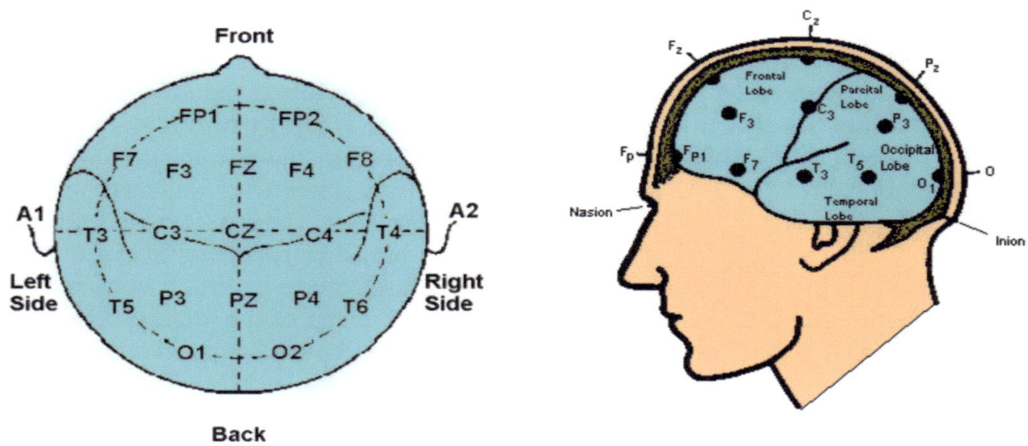

Fig. 11. Spatial location of the EEG electrodes over the frontal, central and parietal areas

For the present study the gamma-band spectral power of the VEP signals was computed by the Welch's periodogram method. The temporal segments, over which one value of the spectral power matrix is computed, correspond to one trial (around 1600 ms), *i.e.*, the samples collected during one image presentation. The normalized gamma-band spectral power for each channel was computed. It is a ratio of the spectral power of each channel and the total gamma-band spectral power of all channels. The level of perception and memory access among individuals are different and this reflects in significant difference between the gamma-band spectral power ratios of the subjects which is the key for the VEP based individuals identification.

4.3 Classifiers

Two strategies of training multiple binary classifiers for classification of the VEP spectral power ratios were implemented, Tan (2006): i) Support Vector Machine - One Against Other (SVM_OAO) and ii) Support Vector Machine - One Against All (SVM_OAA). Each strategy creates a set of binary classifiers that are afterwards combined to output the final labeling. Linear or nonlinear functions are comparatively tested as the SVM feature space mapping functions. Radial Basis Function (RBF) is selected for the nonlinear SVM case. The SVM-OAO creates P(P-1)/2 binary classifiers where P is the number of the persons identified. The classification principle is the max-wins voting strategy, in which every classifier assigns the instance to one of the two classes, the class with most votes determines the instance classification. The SVM-OAA creates P binary classifiers with the classification principle - the winner-takes-all and the binary classifier with the highest output function assigns the class.

Two training scenarios were considered:

- **Scenario 1**: The classifier is trained with data set coming from one experimental block (subject has to attend to the faces ignoring houses) and tested with data from the other experimental block (subject has to attend to the houses and ignore the faces).

- **Scenario 2**: The classifier is trained with data coming from both experimental blocks and tested with unseen data from the same blocks.

4.4 Principal component analysis (PCA)

A possible way to increase the signal to noise ratio is to accompany the feature extraction step with the principal component analysis (PCA). For the case considered, the PCA was designed first to extract only principal components of the normalized gamma-band spectral power (the feature space) that accumulates 95% of the signal energy (this is equivalent to feature space reduction). Then, it follows a step to reconstruct the feature space with the same dimensionality. The performance of both SVM classifiers was evaluated with or without PCA processing in the framework of the two scenarios. The results, summarized in Table 1 and Table 2, suggest that while the PCA is aimed at capturing the main EEG patterns, the individual specificity is lost and the classification accuracy is worsen. A possible interpretation is that the energy in the 30-50 Hz band of the original data set is already attenuated due to an embedded filtering process of the EEG acquisition apparatus. The PCA processing additionally reduces the VEP power spectral density and, therefore, all classifiers studied exhibit worse generalization performance (Table 1).

4.5 Post processing (PP) procedure

Both classifiers perform a static (memoryless) classification that does not consider explicitly the temporal nature of the VEP signals. Time accounting classifiers, as for example Recurrent Neural Networks (NNs), Time Lag NNs or Reservoir Computing, have the disadvantage to require complex training procedures that not always converge.

In order to keep low complexity of the biometrical system, we propose here an empirical way to introduce memory into the classifiers. During a post processing (PP) procedure, a moving window of a sequence of n past classifier outputs (personal labels) is isolated and following a predefined strategy the labels are corrected. For example, during the first PP step a window of the last three labels is defined (n=3) and, in case the first and the last labels are the same but different from the central one, this label is corrected to be equal to the others. The window dimension of the second PP step is increased with one (n=4). If the first and the last elements have the same label, but the two central elements are different from each other and from the lateral elements they are corrected. It was observed that increasing the dimensionality of the moving window (third PP step with n=5; fourth PP step with n=6; fifth PP step with n=7) the overall performance of both classifiers improved. The strategy of each next step is to increase the number of central elements and to correct them in case they are different from the equal lateral elements of the moving (with one sample) window. After the fifth PP step the performance started to decrease, therefore five PP steps were subsequently implemented in the EEG-based biometry system (see Table 1 and Table 2 below). In Fig. 12 an example of classifier response for 5 classes with a sequence of 10 samples per class is depicted. Though the classifier recognizes in general the different persons correctly some of the responses are incorrect and the aim of the PP procedure is to correct these wrong guesses. The incorrect responses of the classifier decrease after each subsequent PP step.

4.6 Evoked potential duration

The effect of the Evoked Potential Duration (EPD) was particularly studied since it defines the viability of the biometry system. If the identified person has to be exposed too long time

With PCA		Classifier	1st PP step	2nd PP step	3rd PP step	4th PP step	5th PP step
SVM_ OAO (One Against One)	Linear (Scenario 1)	65,94	63,10	60,01	59,71	59,79	59,61
	Linear (Scenario 2)	56,42	51,58	48,05	47,12	46,25	45,57
	Nonlinear (Scenario 1)	44,53	37,26	31,24	27,95	26,19	24,07
	Nonlinear (Scenario 2)	**36,43**	**28,00**	**22,08**	**19,01**	**17,41**	**14,49**
SVM_ OAA (One Against All)	Linear (Scenario 1)	58,65	54,24	50,64	49,88	49,34	48,60
	Linear (Scenario 2)	59,79	56,55	54,42	53,42	52,36	51,24
	Nonlinear (Scenario 1)	43,78	36,76	31,12	28,03	24,93	23,33
	Nonlinear (Scenario 2)	**35,99**	**27,60**	**21,24**	**18,67**	**16,44**	**15,17**

Table 1. Average classification error with PCA feature selection

Without PCA		Classifier	1st PP step	2nd PP step	3rd PP step	4th PP step	5th PP step
SVM_ OAO (One Against One)	Linear (Scenario 1)	38,21	35,36	33,43	31,89	31,63	30,37
	Linear (Scenario 2)	29,98	24,88	23,19	23,55	22,77	21,54
	Nonlinear (Scenario 1)	26,42	20,31	17,42	16,87	15,97	14,95
	Nonlinear (Scenario 2)	**15,67**	**10,16**	**8,32**	**6,95**	**5,54**	**5,10**
SVM_ OAA (One Against All)	Linear (Scenario 1)	30,57	25,02	23,56	22,58	21,27	20,26
	Linear (Scenario 2)	26,84	21,17	17,87	16,45	14,52	13,71
	Nonlinear (Scenario 1)	26,99	21,54	18,32	16,70	15,16	14,49
	Nonlinear (Scenario 2)	**17,43**	**12,05**	**9,78**	**8,49**	**6,96**	**6,62**

Table 2. Average classification error without PCA feature selection

to a stimulus in order to be identified, it would make the system not quite practical and difficult to realize in real time. Therefore, the length of the ERP time series required for person identification needs to be reasonably short. The results of this study are summarized in Fig. 13 to Fig. 15 where the average classification error (ACE) is depicted as a function of the training segment length (N° of trails). This analysis was done for the two studied SVM classifiers: SVM_OAO (Fig. 13), SVM_OAA (Fig. 14) and confirmed also for the k-Nearest

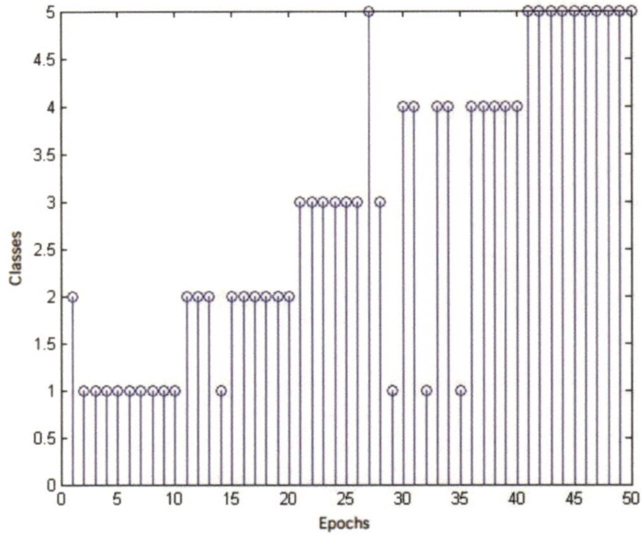

Fig. 12. Example of classifier response for 5 classes with a sequence of 10 samples per class

Neighbor (k-NN) basic classifier (Fig. 15) with k=3 and k=5. Note that for all classifiers there is a number of trails for which the ACE is minimized and longer time exposure does not suggest better person's discrimination. These results are averaged over the total number of identified subjects (13 persons) and an interval of 25-30 trials is determined as the optimal duration. Each trial corresponds to 400 samples with duration of about 1.5 s. Subsequently, 40-45 s is going to be the expected times for stimulus expose before the classifier identify one person with the highest probability to make a correct guess. Though the conclusions go beyond of what can be analytically proved, the intuition behind is that too long time exposure to visual stimuli leads to accommodation and tiredness, thus the personal specificity encoded in the ERPs is vanishing and the classifier error increases.

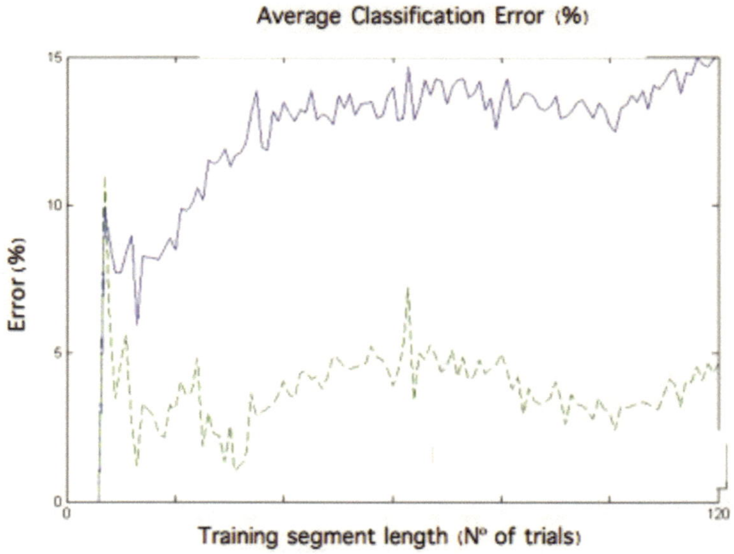

Fig. 13. SVM_OAO: ACE without PP (bold line) & after the 5th PP step (dashed line)

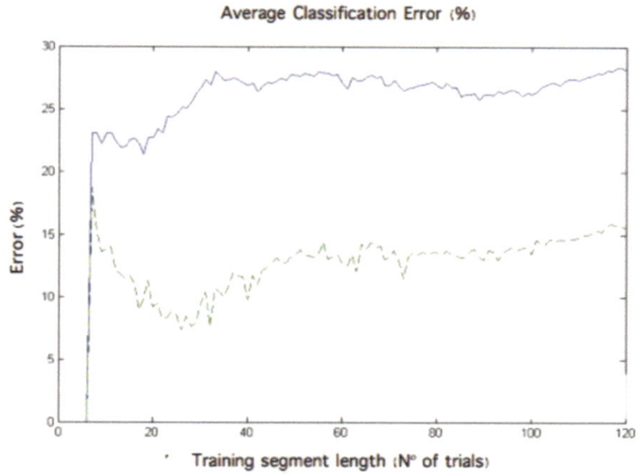

Fig. 14. SVM_OAA: ACE without PP (bold line) & after the 5th PP step (dashed line)

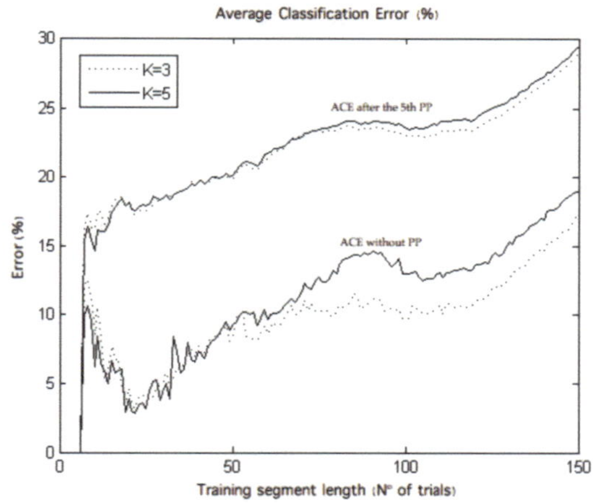

Fig. 15. k-NN: ACE without PP (bold (K=5) and dashed (K=3) lines below) & after the 5th PP step (bold (K=5) and dashed (K=3) lines above)

5. Conclusion

This chapter described recent efforts towards the development of EEG-based brain computer interfaces for control and biometry. In the first part, the chapter focuses upon an introduction of the principles underlying the use of beamforming to reconstruct the brain activity. Completely different problems in developing BCI systems and in their applications arise when moving from electrode-based domain to source-based scale. The goal of this source-based approach is to obtain knowledge about our brain activity and to answer fundamental questions about interacting regions. Beamforming techniques for source-based estimation are being proposed and recent research efforts demonstrate potential as a new direction in BCI design.

In this line of though, the first study was dedicated to source signal estimation based on vectorised beamformers and to the optimization of certain parameters that have influence in the system's performance. For example, the problem of the localization and number of measurement electrodes was addressed, as well as how modelling errors in the constraint matrix or imprecise dipole locations can result in signal attenuation. LCMV beamforming does not require the *a priori* knowledge about the number of active sources. Instead, it provides an adaptive filter in which the degrees of freedom are used so that the activity from the target location is accepted, while being as insensitive as possible to activity from other brain regions.

The insights gained with this study can be relevant when optimizing the design and implementation of a practical source-based BCI. However, there are a number of open issues to be investigated in the near future. For example, defining a real-time model paradigm in an EEG-fMRI environment provides, in theory, new perspectives to achieve innovative designs. At the same time, the inverse solution is constructed from the forward or lead-field matrix which makes the system greatly underdetermined considering that the solution space consists typically of thousands of source locations. Regularisation and smoothing methods need to be applied to create a unique solution. Finally, on-line and off-line experiments are essential to full access the advantages and limitations of beamforming in BCI applications when compared with other alternative approaches.

The present study also confirmed the feasibility of the EEG-based person identification. Although the results are only for 13 person subject pool, it does provide evidence of stability and uniqueness in the EEG shapes across persons. However, the classification accuracy of the EEG biometry currently cannot compete with the conventional biometrics (such as fingerprint, iris or palm recognition systems) and in general the EEG person identification modality can be seen just as a supplement ("a second opinion").

Nevertheless, our long term goal is to use the principles of EEG-based biometry to detect abnormal scenarios, *i.e.*, scenarios where a person is not acting as it would normally do in similar circumstances. Cognitive functions, such as attention, learning, visual and audio perception and memory, are critical for many human activities (for example driving) and they trigger numerous brain activities. Assuming that those brain activities follow a pattern for each person in normal circumstances (reference pattern), they are likely to change when the person is stressed, fatigued (physically, visually or mentally), or under the influence of several substances (alcohol, stimulants, drugs, etc.) (deviation pattern). In this context, the EEG-based biometry would be particularly effective in health care applications, where it could be used not only to verify a patient's identity in medical records, prior to drug administration or other medical procedures but also to detect early in advance abnormal physiological or mental states of the patient.

In all, we expect several potential applications to emerge in the future. Control of the classified access into restricted areas security systems, illnesses or health disorder identification in medicine, gaining more understanding of the cognitive human brain processes in neuroscience are among the most appealing.

6. Acknowledgments

The first author is supported by the Portuguese Foundation for Science and Technology under grant SFRH/BD/48775/2008.

7. References

Baillet, S., Mosher, J.C., Leahy, R.M. (2001). Electromagnetic Brain Mapping. *IEEE Signal Processing Magazine*, 18: 14-30.

Bashashati, A., M. Fatourechi, R.K. Ward and G.E. Birch, "A survey of signal processing algorithms in brain-computer interfaces based on electrical brain signals", *J. Neural Engineering*, 4: R32-R57, 2007.

Bensch, M., A. Karim, J. Mellinger, T. Hinterberger, M. Tangermann, M. Bogdan, W. Rosenstiel and N. Birbaumer, "Nessi: an EEG-controller web browser for severely paralyzed patients", *Intelligence Neuroscience*, (2): 1-10, 2007.

Bento, V., J.P. Cunha and F. Silva, "Towards a Human-Robot Interface Based on the electrical Activity of the Brain", *Proc. IEEE-RAS International Conference on Humanoid Robots*, pp. 85-90, Daejon, South-Korea, 2008.

Berger, T.W., J.K. Chapin, G.A. Gerhardt, D.J. McFarland, J.C. Princípe, W.V. Soussou, D.M. Taylor and P.A. Tresco, *Brain-Computer Interfaces: An International Assessment of Research and Development Trends*, Springer, 2008.

Birbaumer, N. and L. Cohen, "Brain-computer interfaces (BCI): communication and restoration of movement in paralysis", *J. Physiology*, January, 2007.

Capon, J. (1969). "High-resolution Frequency Wavenumber Spectrum Analysis", *Proceedings of the IEEE*, 57: 1408-1418.

Choi, S., Cichocki, A., Park, H-M. and Lee, S-Y. (2005). "Blind Source Separation and Independent Component Analysis: A Review", *Neural Information Processing*, 6(1): 1-57.

Ferreira A., Almeida, C., Georgieva, P., Tomé, A., Silva, F. (2010). Advances in EEG-based Biometry, In: Lecture Notes in Computer Science (LNCS) series, A. Campilho & M. Kamel (Eds.), 287-295, ICIAR 2010, Part II, LNCS 6112, Springer, Heidelberg.

Fuchs, A. (2007). Beamforming and Its Applications to Brain Connectivity, In: *Handbook of Brain Connectivity*, V.K. Jirsa and A.R. McIntosh, (Ed.), 357-, 378, Springer-Verlag, Berlin.

Grave de Peralta, R., S.G. Andino, L. Perez, P.W. Ferrez and J.R. Millán, "Non-invasive Estimation of Local Field Potentials for Neuroprosthesis Control", *Cognitive Process*, Vol. 6, pp. 59-64, 2005.

Gross, J., Kujala, J., Hamalainen, M., Timmermann, L., Schnitzler, A., Salmelin, R. (2001). Dynamic Imaging of Coherent Sources: Studying Neural Interactions in the Human Brain. *Proceedings of the National Academy of Sciences USA*, 98: 694-699.

Grosse-Wentrup, M., C. Liefhold, K. Gramann and M. Buss, "Beamforming in Non-Invasive Brain-Computer Interfaces", *IEEE Transactions on Biomedical Engineering*, 56(4): 1209-1219, 2009.

Herdman, A.T., Wollbrink, A., Chau, W., Ishii, R., Ross, B., Pantev, C. (2003). Determination of Activation areas in the Human Auditory Cortex by Means of Synthetic aperture Magnetometry. *Neuroimage*, 20: 995-1005.

Huang, M-X., Shih, J.J., Lee, R.R., Harrington, D.L., Thoma, R.J., Weisend, M.P., Hanion, F., Paulson, K.M., Li, T., Martin, K., Miller, G.a., Canive, J.M. (2004). "Commonalities and Differences Among Vectorized Beamformers in Electromagnetic Source Imaging", *Brain Topography*, 16: 139-158.

Kamousi, B, Z. Liu and B. He, "An EEG Inverse Solution Based Brain-Computer Interface", *The International Journal of Bioelectromagnetism*, 7(2): 292-294, 2005.

Lai, Y., Van Drongelen, W., Ding, L, Hecox, K.E., Towle, V.L., Frim, D.M., He, B. (2005). Estimation of in Vivo Human Brain-Skull Conductivity Ratio from Simultaneous Extra- and Intra-Cranial Electrical Potential Recordings. *Clinical Neurophysiology*, 116: 456-465.

Leeb, R., F. Lee, C. Keinrath, R. Scherer, H. Bischof and G. Pfurtscheller, "Brain computer communication: motivation, aim and impact of exploring a virtual apartment", *IEEE Transactions on Neural Systems and Rehabilitation Engineering*, 15(4): 473-482, 2007.

Marcel, S., José del R. Millán, "Person authentication using brainwaves (EEG) and maximum a posteriori model adaptation", *IEEE Transactions on Pattern Analysis and Machine Intelligence*, 29(4), 743-752, 2007.

Millán, J. del R., F. Renkens, J. Mouriño and W. Gerstner "Brain-Actuated Interaction", *Artificial Intelligence*, 159: 241-259, 2004.

Millán, J. del R., "Brain-controlled robots", *IEEE Intelligent Systems*, 2008.

Müller-Putz, G.R. and G. Pfurtscheller, "Control of an electrical prosthesis with an SSVEP-based BCI", *IEEE Transactions on Biomedical Engineering*, 55(1): 361-364, 2008.

Niedermeyer, E. and F. Lopes da Silva, *Electroencephalography*. Lippincott Williams and Wilkins, 1999.

Nijboer, F., E. Sellers, J. Mellinger, M. Jordan, T. Matuz, A. Furdea, S. Halder, U. Mochty, D. Krusienski and T. Vaughan, "A P300-based brain computer interface for people with amyotrophic lateral sclerosis", *Clinical Neurophysiology*, 119(8): 1909-1916, 2008.

Noirhomme, Q., R.I. Kitney and B. Macq, "Signle-Trial EEG Source Reconstruction for Brain-Computer Interface", *IEEE Transactions on Biomedical Engineering*, 55(5): 1592-1601, 2008.

Palaniappan, R., D. P. Mandic, "Biometrics from Brain Electrical Activity: A Machine Learning Approach", *IEEE Transactions on Pattern Analysis and Machine Intelligence*, 29(4), 2007.

Paranjape, R.B., J. Mahovsky, L. Benedicenti, and Z. Koles, "The Electroencephalogram as a Biometric", *Proc. CCECE*, vol. 2, pp.1363-1366, 2001.

Pfurtscheller, G., G.R. Muller-Putz, A. Schlogl, B.A. Graimann, R.A. Scherer, R.A. Leeb, C.A. Brunner, C.A. Keinrath, F.A. Lee, G.A. Townsend, C.A: Vidaurre, and C.A. Neuper, "15 years of BCI research at graz university of technology: current projects", *IEEE Transactions on Neural Systems and Rehabilitation Engineering*, 14: 205-210, 2006.

Pfurtscheller, G., G.R. Muller-Putz, R.A. Scherer and C.A. Neuper, "Rehabilitation with brain-computer interface systems", *Computer*, 41(10): 58-65, 2008.

Pineda, J.A., "The functional significance of mu rhythms: translating 'seeing' and 'hearing' into 'doing'", *Brain Res Rev*, 50:57-68, 2005.

Popescu, M., Popescu, E.A., Chan, T., Blunt, S.D., Lewine, J.D. (2008). Spatio-temporal Reconstruction of Bilateral Auditory Steady-state Responses using MEG Beamformers. *IEEE Transactions on Biomedical Engineering*, 55: 1092-1102.

Poulos, M., M. Rangoussi, V. Chrissikopoulos, and A. Evangelou, "Person identification based on parametric processing of the EEG", *Proc. IEEE ICECS*, vol. 1, pp. 283-286, 1999.

Qin, L., L. Ding and B. He, "Motor Imagery Classification by Means of Source Analysis for Brain Computer Interface Applications", *Journal of Neural Engineering*, Vol. 1, pp. 133-141, 2004.

Rush, S, Driscoll, D. (1969). EEG Electrode Sensitivity - An Application of Reciprocity. IEEE Transactions on Biomedical Engineering, 16(1):15-22.

Salu, Y., Cohen, L.G., Rose, D., Sato, S., Kufta, C., Hallet, M. (1990). An Improved Method for Localizing Electric Brain Dipoles. *IEEE Transactions on Biomedical Engineering*, 37: 699-705.

Santos, I.M., J. Iglesias, E. I. Olivares, A.W. Young, "Differential effects of object-based attention on evoked potentials to fearful and disgusted faces", *Neuropsychologia*, 46(5), 1468-1479, 2008.

Tan, P.-N., M. Steinbach and V. Kumar, *Introduction to Data Mining*, 2006.

Van Veen, B.D., van Drongelen, W., Yuchtman, M., Suzuki, A. (1997). "Localization of Brain Electrical Activity via Linearly Constrained Minimum Variance Spatial Filtering", *IEEE Transactions on Biomedical Engineering*, 44(9):867-880

10

State of the Art in BCI Research: BCI Award 2010

Christoph Guger[1], Guangyu Bin[2], Xiaorong Gao[2], Jing Guo[2], Bo Hong[2], Tao Liu[2], Shangkai Gao[2], Cuntai Guan[3], Kai Keng Ang[3], Kok Soon Phua[3], Chuanchu Wang[3], Zheng Yang Chin[3], Haihong Zhang[3], Rongsheng Lin[3], Karen Sui Geok Chua[4], Christopher Kuah[4], Beng Ti Ang[5], Harry George[6], Andrea Kübler[6], Sebastian Halder[7], Adi Hösle[7], Jana Münßinger[7], Mark Palatucci[8], Dean Pomerleau[8], Geoff Hinton[8], Tom Mitchell[8], David B. Ryan[9], Eric W. Sellers[9], George Townsend[10], Steven M. Chase[11], Andrew S. Whitford[12], Andrew B. Schwartz[11], Kimiko Kawashima[13], Keiichiro Shindo[13], Junichi Ushiba[13], Meigen Liu[13] and Gerwin Schalk[14]

[1]*g.tec medical engineering GmbH/Guger Technologies OG, Graz*
[2]*Department of Biomedical Engineering, School of Medicine, Tsinghua University, Beijing*
[3]*Institute for Infocomm Research, A*STAR*
[4]*Tan Tock Seng Hospital*
[5]*National Neuroscience Institute*
[6]*Department of Psychology I, University of Würzburg*
[7]*Institute of Medical Psychology and Behavioural Neurobiology, University of Tübingen*
[8]*Carnegie Mellon University, Intel Labs, University of Toronto*
[9]*East Tennessee State University*
[10]*Algoma University BCI Lab*
[11]*Dept. of Neurobiology, University of Pittsburgh*
[12]*Dept. of Bioengineering, University of Pittsburgh*
[13]*Keio University*
[14]*Wadsworth Center, Albany*
[1]*Austria*
[2]*China*
[3,4,5]*Singapore*
[6,7]*Germany*
[8,9,11,12,14]*USA*
[10]*Canada*
[13]*Japan*

1. Introduction

The possibility of brain-computer communication based on the electroencephalogram (EEG) has been discussed almost four decades ago (Vidal, 1973). In another pioneering work, Farwell and Donchin described the use of evoked potentials for communication (Farwell, 1988). Up to the early 2000s, no more than 5 groups were active in brain-computer interface (BCI) research. Now, about 200-300 laboratories are focused on this work. This dramatic growth has been driven by high performance and low cost of computing power and related instrumentation, increased understanding on normal and abnormal brain function, and improved methods for decoding brain signals in real time. As a result, the performance and usability of BCI systems have advanced dramatically over the past several years.
BCI systems can be described by the following characteristics: (i) invasive (electrocorticogram (ECoG), spikes) or non-invasive (EEG, NIRS (near infrared-spectroscopy), fMRI (functional magnetic resonance imaging), MEG (magnetoencephalogram)) systems (Leuthardt, 2004, Owen, 2008, Velliste, 2008, Wolpaw 2003, Pfurtscheller 2010a, 2010b), (ii) portable (EEG) or stationary (fMRI, ECoG, spikes), (iii) according to application area (spelling, wheelchair control, brain painting, research,…) (Sellers, 2010, Galán, 2008, Kübler, 2008), (iv) type of BCI principle used (P300, SSVEP (steady-state visual evoked potential)), steady state evoked potential (steady-state somatosensory evoked potential)), motor imagery, slow cortical potentials (Bin, 2009, Birbaumer, 2000, Pfurtscheller, 2010, Krusienski, 2006) (v) speed and accuracy, (vi) training time and reliability, (vii) synchronous and asynchronous, (viii) low cost (EEG, NIRS) and high costs (MEG, fMRI, spikes), (ix) degrees of freedom. A detailed review can be found in Allison (Allison, 2007). Over the last years the importance of specific properties changed, new technologies were developed that enabled new applications or made BCI systems affordable. For example, in the late 90s there were just a few real-time systems worldwide. At present, almost every lab is equipped with real-time BCI systems.
To highlight these trends and developments of BCI technology, g.tec began to sponsor an annual BCI Award in 2010. The prize, endowed with 3,000 USD, is an accolade to recognize outstanding and innovative research in the field of brain-computer interface research and application. Each year, a renowned research laboratory is asked to judge the submitted projects and to award the prize. The jury consists of world-leading BCI experts recruited by the awarding laboratory. g.tec is a leading provider of BCI research equipment and has a strong interest in promoting excellence in the field of BCI to make BCIs more powerful, more intelligent and more applicable. The competition is open to any BCI group worldwide. There is no limitation or special consideration for the type of hardware or software used in the submission. This year, the jury was recruited by its chair Dr. Gerwin Schalk of the Wadsworth Center in Albany, New York. It consisted of world-leading experts in the BCI community: Theresa Vaughan, Eric Sellers, Dean Krusienski, Klaus-Robert Mueller, Benjamin Blankertz, and Bo Hong.
The jury scored the submitted projects on the basis of the following criteria:

- does the project include a novel application of the BCI?
- is there any new methodological approach used compared to earlier projects?
- is there any new benefit for potential users of a BCI?
- is there any improvement in terms of speed of the system (e.g., bits/min)?
- is there any improvement in system accuracy?
- does the project include any results obtained from real patients or other potential users?

- is the used approach working online/in real-time?
- is there any improvement in terms of usability?
- does the project include any novel hardware or software developments?

We received a total of 57 high quality submissions. Out of these submissions, the jury nominated the 10 top-ranked candidates for the BCI Research Award in April 2010 (see Table 1). The following sections describe each project in more detail.

Name and institution	Title of BCI project
Guangyu Bin, Xiaorong Gao, Shangkai Gao	A high-speed word spelling BCI system based on code modulated visual evoked potentials
Cuntai Guan, Kai Keng Ang, Kok Soon Phua, Chuanchu Wang, Zheng Yang Chin, Haihong Zhang, Rongsheng Lin, Karen Sui Geok Chua, Christopher Kuah, Beng Ti Ang	Motor imagery-based brain-computer interface robotic rehabilitation for stroke
Jing Guo, Shangkai Gao, Bo Hong	An active auditory BCI for intention expression in locked-in
Tao Liu, Shangkai Gao, Bo Hong	Brain-actuated Google search by using motion onset VEP
Harry George, Sebastian Halder, Adi Hösle, Jana Münßinger, Andrea Kübler	Brain Painting - "Paint your way out"
Mark Palatucci, Dean Pomerleau, Geoff Hinton, Tom Mitchell	Thought recognition with semantic output codes
David B. Ryan and Eric W. Sellers	Predictive spelling with a P300-base BCI: increasing communication rate
George Townsend	Innovations in P300-based BCI stimulus presentation methods
Steven M. Chase, Andrew S. Whitford, Andrew B. Schwartz	Operant conditioning to identify independent, volitionally-controllable patterns of neural activity
Kimiko Kawashima, Keiichiro Shindo, Junichi Ushiba, Meigen Liu	Neurorehabilitation for chronic-phase stroke using a brain-machine interface

Table 1. Nominees of the BCI Award 2010.

2. Nominated projects

Project 1: A high-speed word spelling BCI system based on code modulated visual evoked potentials

Guangyu Bin, Xiaorong Gao, Shangkai Gao

A high-speed word spelling brain-computer interface (BCI) based on code modulated visual evoked potentials (c-VEPs) was developed. The c-VEP BCI uses a binary pseudorandom sequence for stimulus modulation (Sutter, 1992, Bin, 2009). In the system, the stimuli were set to two states: "light" and "dark", and so a binary sequence can be used as modulation sequence. "Light" and "dark" represented "1" and "0" in the modulation sequence. For instance, the stimulus modulated by a sequence "100010001000..." represented 15 Hz flickering, when the refresh rate of the monitor was 60Hz.

The targets of the stimuli are distributed as an array and the number of targets can be selected to be either 16 (4x4), 32 (4x8) or 64 (8x8). Figure 1A shows a c-VEP based BCI system with 16 targets. Each target was periodically modulated by a binary m-sequence. Except for a fixed time lag between two consecutive targets, the used modulation sequences in one period were the same. As an example, Figure 1B presented the modulation sequences of a c-VEP system with sixteen targets. In the system, a binary m-sequence with 63 elements and its time shift sequences are used as the modulation signals, and there is a four-frame lag between two consecutive targets.

A template matching method is used for target identification. In the training stage, the user is instructed to fixate on one of the targets (such as target "10", the training target), and the template of the training target is obtained. According to the time lag, templates of all targets are generated. In the online application, the correlation coefficient between EEG data and every template is calculated. If the coefficient remains above a certain threshold and is larger than all the others for a certain amount of time, then the corresponding target is considered to be the selected one.

The stimulus was presented on a CRT monitor with 60Hz refresh rate and EEG data were recorded with a g.USBamp amplifier (g.tec medical engineering GmbH, Austria). The parallel port is used to synchronize EEG data acquisition with the stimulus. The system is implemented with EEGOnline, which is a general-purpose system for real-time EEG signal processing developed by Tsinghua University. EEGOnline provides a comprehensive framework of functionalities that allows the user to focus on the implementation of his application specific module. It can be used for EEG data acquisition, brain-computer interface research and brain monitoring applications.

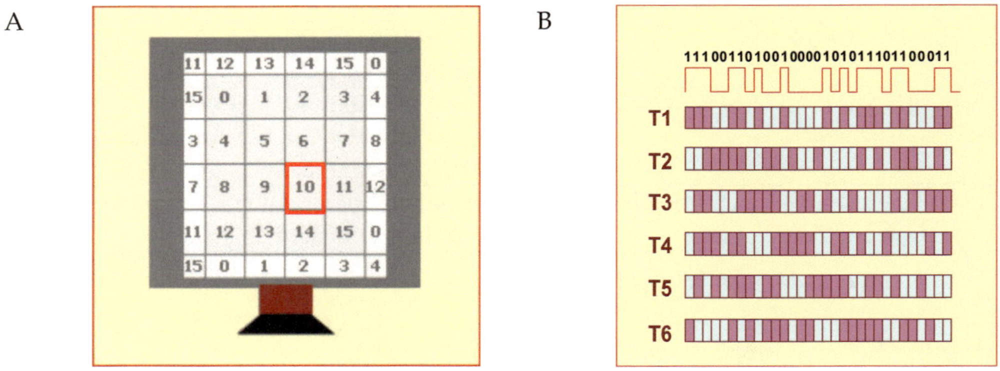

Fig. 1. (A) The target arrangement of the c-VEP based BCI. The sixteen targets are distributed in a 4x4 array surrounded by a border to eliminate the effect of the array boundary. When the border fields are stimulated according to the wrap-around principle, all targets have equivalent neighbours. Thus, the responses obtained when the subject fixated on different targets were practically identical. (B) The modulation sequences of the targets in one stimulation cycle. Each sequence is from a binary m-sequence. There is a four-frame lag between two consecutive sequences. All targets were activated simultaneously, and the stimulation cycle was repeated constantly.

For the 16 targets system, twelve healthy right-handed adults with normal or corrected-to-normal vision served as volunteers after giving informed consent. The information transfer rate (ITR) averaged more than 92.8bits/min. Moreover, a system with 32 possible selections was used for spelling. These thirty-two possible selections corresponded to the 26 characters of the alphabet and another six keys (SPACE, DELETE, ENTER, three punctuators) are presented on the screen. This system was tested with many users and the achieved spelling speed was approximately 15-20 characters per min.

The main advantages of the c-VEP based BCI system include high-speed communication, more targets, and lower user variation.

Project 2: Motor imagery-based brain-computer interface robotic rehabilitation for stroke

Cuntai Guan, Kai Keng Ang, Karen Sui Geok Chua, Beng Ti Ang, Kok Soon Phua, Christopher Kuah, Chuanchu Wang, Zheng Yang Chin, Haihong Zhang, Rongsheng Lin

Stroke is the leading cause of severe disabilities in the developed world (Beers, 2000). Each year, there are around 15 million new stroke cases worldwide. About 30% of stroke survivors need various forms of rehabilitation. Among these, upper limb weakness and loss of hand function are among the most devastating types of disabilities. Despite optimal acute medical treatment and modern rehabilitation, 45% of the patients do not achieve complete recovery of their bodily functions. In addition, 85% to 90% of stroke survivors with upper limb impairment do not regain full functional use of their upper extremities. Limitations in current physiotherapy and occupational therapy techniques include: (i) difficulties in rehabilitation for the severely paralyzed arm and hand which are often treated with passive modalities, (ii) difficulties in achieving intensive rehabilitation and high repetitions in those with moderate to severe upper extremity paralysis, (iii) problems in motivating and sustaining patient interest in repetitive exercises, (iv) therapy is often perceived to be boring due to lack of immediate biofeedback.

Recently, robot-aided rehabilitation has been clinically investigated worldwide to try to address these issues. Despite continuous improvements and progress in the field, there is a strong request from rehabilitation clinicians to call for more efficacious and more target-specific approaches to address the aforementioned issues.

Given recent progress in BCI technologies, there is an increased interest in applying BCI to stroke rehabilitation (Daly, 2008, Wolpaw, 2002, Ang, 2009, Ang, 2010), as BCIs provide a direct and real-time link between the human brain (in particular, cortical area) to external devices (Birbaumer, 2006, Ang, 2008). With this motivation, we embarked on this project from April 2007 to Oct 2009. Our hypotheses for this project were as follows:

1. A BCI provides an effective guide and visual feedback to motivate patients
2. BCI guides patients to improve the excitation of the motor cortex
3. Mechanical stimulation provides movement training, as well as motor/sensory feedback to the patient
4. Combination of BCI and mechanical stimulations could provide an effective guided training system

The system was developed and evaluated with patients as depicted in Figure 2. It consisted of a BCI and a robotic arm (MANUS from InMotion). The patient was asked to perform motor imagery (instead of movement, in order to prevent possible use of compensated movements due to mal-adaptation after stroke insult). Once the BCI detected motor imagery (with a technique developed in our group, which is the winning algorithm in BCI Competition IV 2008, dataset II (Calautti, 2003)), it triggered the robotic arm to move the patient's arm to a designated direction. The direction was randomly selected by the training protocol.

A clinical trial (Registration number NCT00955838 in ClinicalTrials.gov) was then performed to assess the effects. As a reference, we also recruited patients to use the MANUS alone for rehabilitation. 26 patients were recruited, and randomized into two groups (15 in MANUS group, 11 in BCI group).

Patients performed rehabilitation training for 4 weeks, 3 sessions per week, and each session lasted around 1 hour. The clinical evaluation was done at the beginning of the training (week 0), mid of the training (week 2), and at the end of the training (week 4). A follow-up assessment was performed at week 12. However, due to the nature of the training process, patients in the MANUS group performed 960 repetitions, while the BCI group only performed 160 repetitions, i.e., a 1:6 difference in intensity.

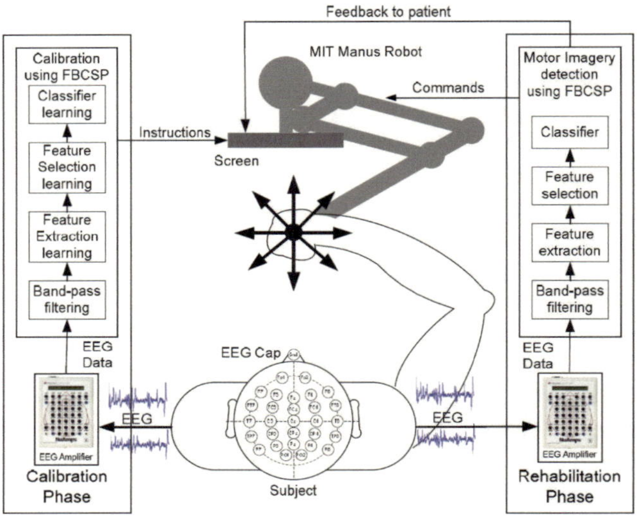

A

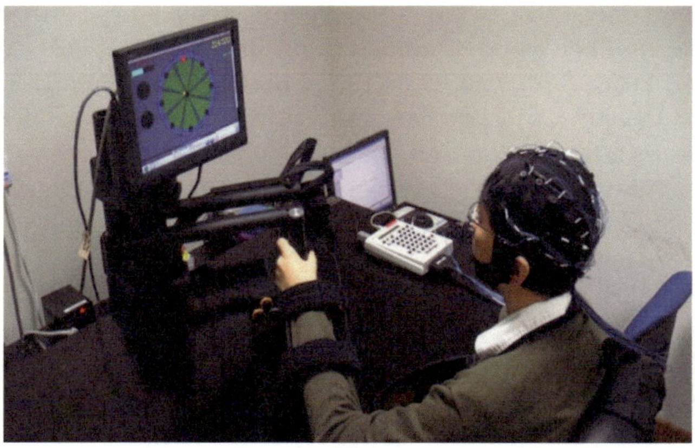

B

Fig. 2. (A) Block diagram of the motor imagery BCI with robotic rehabilitation. (B) Actual system tested in hospital by patients.

Table 1 summarizes the outcome of our study and reports the Fugl-Meyer Assessment (FMA) score. The FMA score demonstrates an overall recovery of motor impairment. The results show that, at week 4 & 12, the improvements for the BCI and the MANUS groups are statistically significant. Encouragingly, for both groups, it seems that the improvement is maintained after 12 weeks - a suggestion for sustainability of the rehabilitation training. There is no significant difference in improvement between the two groups.

	BCI group				MANUS group			
	Week 0	Week 2	Week 4	Week12	Week 0	Week 2	Week 4	Week12
Mean FMA score±STD	26.3±10.3	27.4±12.0	30.8±13.8	31.5±13.5	26.6±18.9	29.9±20.6	32.9±21.4	33.9±20.2
Improvement ±STD	-	1.1±4.1	4.5±6.1	5.3±6.3	-	3.2±4.5	6.2±6.3	7.3±9.4
t-test p value	-	0.402	0.032	0.020		0.020	0.003	0.013

Table 1. Mean FMA score, improvement related to week 0 and paired t-test for BCI and MANUS groups.

In this project, we evaluated the feasibility of using a BCI for stroke rehabilitation. Some of the results are summarized as follows:

- There is evidence from this study to suggest that motor imagery rehabilitation for stroke using the BCI is as effective and comparable to robotic rehabilitation, while the BCI group needs much less intensity compared to robotic training (a factor of 6).
- Stroke patients are able to use BCI to perform rehabilitation (we did a pre-screening with 54 patients; around 89% of the patients, who were all naïve users, can operate a BCI with an accuracy better than chance level).
- BCI based on automatic feature selection and band-pass filtering was proven to be reliable across various patients.
- The combination of the BCI and the robotic arm seemed a feasible setup.

Invaluable experience was gained throughout the project and it must be noted that not much literature exists about BCI and stroke. The following important issues will be considered in our follow-up study:

- BCI is considered as a guide for patients. However, what is the best way to detect motor activities?
- Should the detection make use of the whole brain EEG or just from the lesion hemisphere?
- Should the detection strategy change over time when patients get more recovery?
- How to balance the detection accuracy and patients' motivation, especially at the early stage of the training, when the patient is not good at exercising motor imagery?
- Which types of patients are most suitable to use the BCI (versus robotic, etc.)?

Project 3: An active auditory BCI for intension expression in locked-in

Jing Guo, Shangkai Gao, Bo Hong

An intention expression system using event-related potentials (ERP) elicited by sound stimulus is presented. It allows subjects to express their intentions by mentally selecting a target among a random sequence of sound options. BCIs based on visual modalities have proved to be highly effective, but too limited for those locked-in patients who have compromised vision. Since hearing is usually preserved in severely paralyzed patients, a novel auditory BCI paradigm using subjects' active mental response is implemented in this study.

An auditory stimulus was given in form of a sequence of 5 spoken digits in Chinese, i.e., 1,2,3,4,5, presented randomly and repeatedly. Each digit can be used to represent one possible option of intentions. The gender of the voices was random. A segment of the voice sequence is shown in Figure 3. The subject operated this system by focusing on the target digit voices and silently telling whether the target digit was a male or female voice. The subject' voluntary mental response to target digit voices elicited a distinct ERP over the centro-parietal cortex, which was quite different from that of the non-targets.

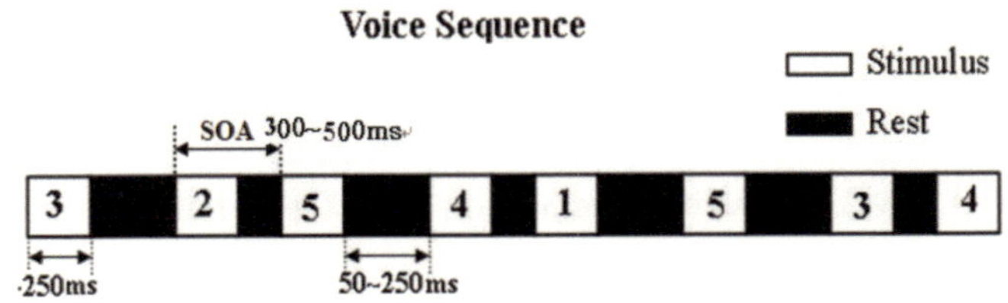

Fig. 3. Auditory BCI scheme with voice sequence design

Figure 4 shows twelve subjects' grand averaged temporal waveform and amplitude topographic maps. It revealed a negative deflection (N2) with latency of 100-300ms and peak at 120ms, which displays more negativity in the target item. A broad late positive component (LPC) between 400-700ms was elicited by the target with a parietal topography maximum around Pz, and was absent in response to non-target stimuli.

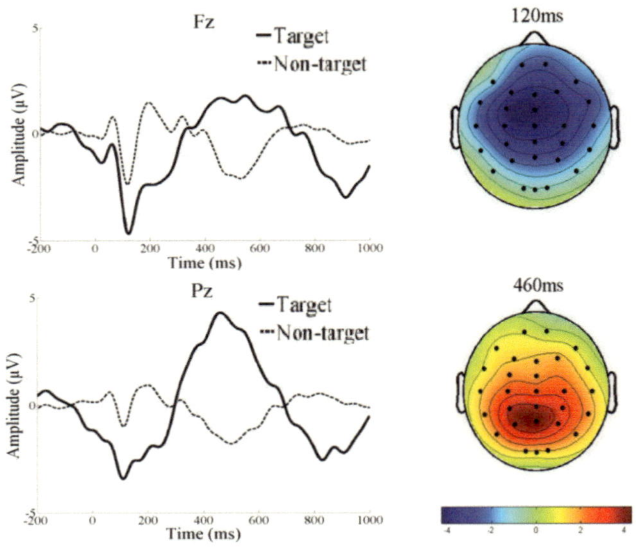

Fig. 4. Averaged temporo-spatial pattern of the ERP.

The proposed paradigm shares some of its features with P300-based BCIs, e.g., the 'oddball' design of the stimulus sequence. However, in the current paradigm, voluntary mental tasks were employed to enhance the LPC response, which may involve more 'active' mental processes than the P300 paradigm.

Fig. 5. BCI system configuration

The auditory stimulus in the online system is still a spoken Chinese digits of 1-5, which is used to represent five possible options of intentions, e.g., "cold", "hot", "eat", "drink" and "sit". After signal processing and target detection of the ERP, the system returns the subject's choice result visually and verbally, to help the subject express his current intentions. The illustration of online application system is shown in Figure 6. The voice sequence is presented to the subject by headphones. EEG is recorded from less than 3 electrodes (optimally selected for individuals) using the g.USBamp amplifier (g.tec medical engineering GmbH, Austria). The whole system is running under MATLAB.

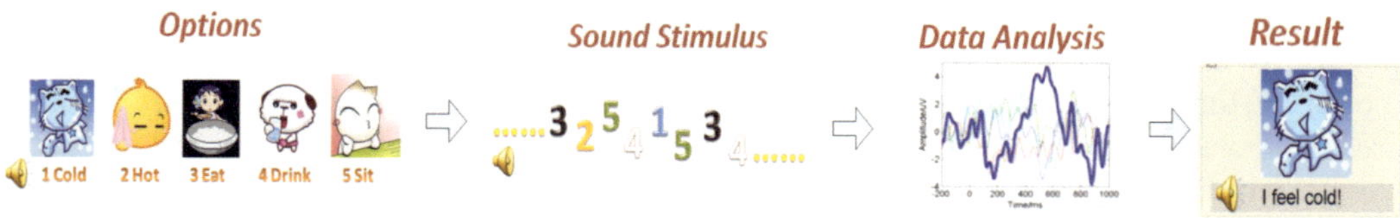

Fig. 6. Principle of the BCI system

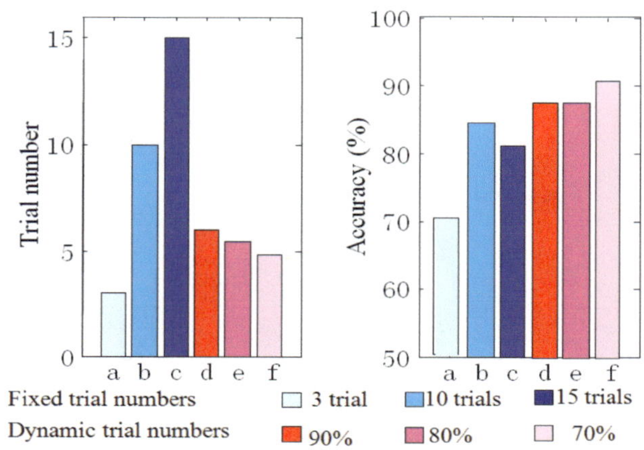

Fig. 7. Accuracy of BCI systems

In our system, a statistical approach is proposed to adaptively adjust the number of trials to be averaged for a decision. The discriminant function is computed with a support vector machine algorithm at each sample; its result was converted into probabilities of each BCI choice being the target. If the highest probability among all BCI choices reached a pre-defined threshold that was estimated from training accuracy, the adaptive algorithm terminated and selected the target with the highest probability.

Figure 7 depicts the averaged online results of 8 subjects, using fixed or dynamic trial numbers. The trial numbers of the fixed method were set to 3, 10 and 15. The thresholds of the dynamic method were set as 90%, 80% and 70% of training accuracy. There were about 4-6 trials to reach the equivalent accuracy of 15-trial averaging, demonstrating the advantage of this adaptive approach.

This adaptive active auditory BCI system allows the subjects to express their intentions, which is potentially helpful for the locked-in patients with compromised vision or the ALS patients.

Project 4: Brain-actuated Google search by using motion onset VEP

Tao Liu, Shangkai Gao, Bo Hong

The motion-onset VEP (mVEP), a scalp potential from the higher visual system for visual motion processing, is promising for BCI applications due to its large amplitude, stable latency, and immunity to low contrast and illumination. In this study, mVEP was used to implement a single-channel brain-computer interface system for brain-actuated Google search. With a flexible and non-flashing interface, mVEP-based BCI system was embedded into screen elements, such as menus and buttons, to achieve a better human computer interaction.

First a vertical bar appears in sequence and moved leftwards in each of the virtual buttons (Figure 8). Users focus on the vertical bar in the desired button to operate the system. The motion of the vertical bar elicits the mVEP over the temporo-occipital and parietal cortex, areas responsible for visual motion processing. Figure 8A shows a virtual keypad interface, composed of 6 virtual buttons, to type in the search terms. With the dynamic menu in the virtual keypad, 26 letters together with another 10 symbols were divided into 6 groups, thus making character selection a two-step process. Furthermore, the web browser was modified with an embedded virtual command toolbar (Figure 8B) to enable the user to directly

Fig. 8. Screen shot from the BCI system to operate Google.

interact with the web contents and accomplish web-browsing tasks, such as "Back", "Forward", and "Enter".

The grand average temporal waveform of the mVEP and its amplitude topographic maps are shown in Figure 9. Similar to previous findings, it is characterized by a negative N2 component with asymmetrical occipito-temporal topography around 200ms and a positive complex of P2 and P3 component, which has a similar spatial distribution with N2 component, but with an additional broader parietal distribution at 325ms.

Using motion-onset VEP, the proposed BCI system requires no flashing or sudden change of visual objects, which poses no discomfort and less visual fatigue on BCI users. Additionally, because of the tolerance to a large contrast range, the mVEP is a steady and robust signal for a highly adaptable BCI system that could work in various applications. Furthermore, the localized spatial distribution of the mVEP (Figure 9) allows to perform the target selection with fewer channels. By contrast, in the previous P300-based BCI systems, the involvement of more channels is needed to improve the classification accuracy due to the relatively broad distribution of P300 component. In a practical online BCI system, fewer channel means less preparation time and lower system cost.

To minimize the number of required EEG channels, the squared Pearson product-moment coefficient (r^2) between the EEG channel and the task was calculated. Then we sorted the channels by their r^2 value. Since the EEG features relevant to the motion stimuli are localized, we selected only the channel with highest r^2 value for each subject (typically at P3, P7 or O1 electrode).

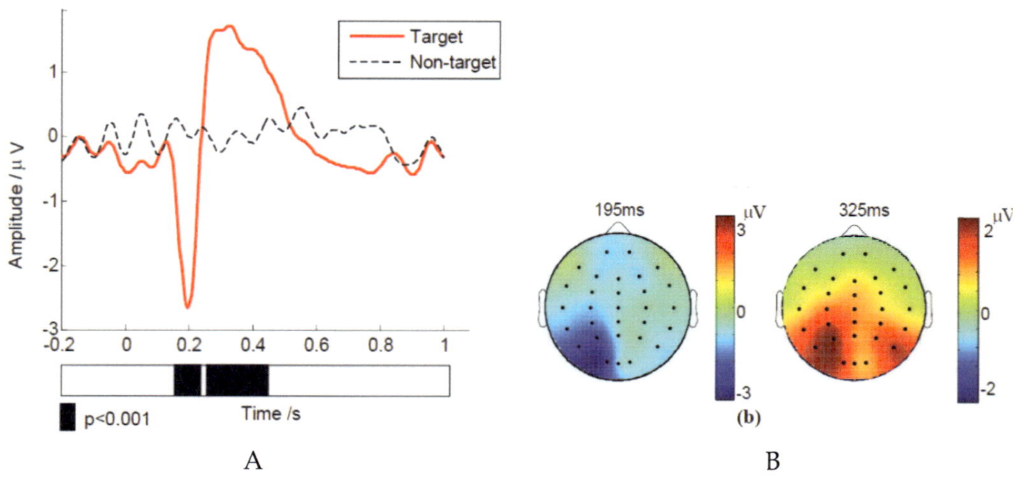

Fig. 9. Temporal (A)–spatial (B) patterns of mVEP

12 subjects were instructed to input the search the term "BCI", then search and select the desired link. The EEG epochs from 'best' electrodes were windowed from 100ms to 500ms following the motion-onset and down-sampled to 20Hz to form a 9-point feature vector. The support vector machine was used for the target detection in the online application. The system has been tested with both the g.tec and Neuroscan amplifiers. As shown in Table 2, all the subjects could successfully operate this system, and completed the task in a reasonable time ranging from 50.9s to 234.2s. A mean ITR of 42.1 bits/min was achieved by 12 subjects, with an average accuracy of 91%.

Subject	Operations	Trials/ Operation	Accuracy (%)	Time(sec)
S1	14	2.4	92	79.4
S2	10	4.3	100	77.3
S3	18	5.6	89	164
S4	26	5.5	77	234.2
S5	22	6.0	86	210.1
S6	18	5.3	89	159.6
S7	11	2.4	91	61.6
S8	14	4.7	93	114.6
S9	11	2.9	91	68.2
S10	14	3.2	93	91.5
S11	10	1.9	100	50.9
S12	14	4.9	93	117.9
Average	**15.1**	**4.1**	**91**	**119.1**

Table 2. BCI Accuracy

The first online BCI system using non-flashing VEP is presented here. The Google search application was successfully implemented and tested on 12 subjects with only 1 EEG channel.

Project 5: Brain painting – BCI meets patients and artists in the field

Harry George, Sebastian Halder, Adi Hösle, Jana Münßinger, Andrea Kübler

Current BCI systems have primarily been developed to replace the lost abilities of patients diagnosed with motor-neuron diseases such as amyotrophic lateral sclerosis (ALS). Of these lost abilities, the most important seems to be that of communication, represented by the increasing volume worldwide of research and development into such applications. Another valuable element of human life, however, is that of creative expression. Through modification of the P300-BCI communication system it was possible to create an application that provides the ability for such expression. We call this Brain Painting.

The P300-Brain Painting application is a new online BCI-application created from the collaboration between artist Adi Hösle and the Universities of Würzburg and Tübingen. Based on the P300 elicited by a rare event in an oddball paradigm (Farwell, 1988), it enables users to express themselves, not only verbally, but also creatively through picture painting. Replacement of the matrix of the P300-Spelling application with a new painting matrix containing functions such as cursor control, shape, object size, grid size and color selections guarantees individual selection of objects and placement on the canvas. While the rows and columns of the matrix start flashing in random order, the user has to concentrate on the symbol of the desired function, which elicits a P300 that is detected and translated by the device. Different objects can be "drawn" on a virtual canvas to produce images of an abstract nature (see Figure 10).

A first evaluation of the P300-Brain Painting application (Muenssinger, 2010) demonstrated a high accuracy in ALS-patients (above 89% in two of the three patients) when reproducing existing paintings. This accuracy was even higher than in healthy controls. This is outstanding because other research found paralyzed patients to show lower performance in P300-BCI use than healthy controls (Piccione, 2006). Moreover, we further increased the accuracy by implementing a black and white matrix for painting that turned out to be less distracting than the colored matrix. Accuracy of the P300 black and white Brain Painting matrix equalled that achieved using the P300-Spelling application (spelling: 93.20% (*SD* ± 7.50); painting: 92.60% (SD ± 5.70); (Muenssinger, 2010) in healthy subjects.

Qualitative responses from patients using the system were very positive and enthusiastic and they confirmed that they experience satisfaction and are entertained while using the application. They display a strong repeated desire to re-use the system; one patient reported that she was so excited about painting that she spent the whole night planning her next picture. To date, patients using the system have produced numerous images from independent sittings lasting upwards of 1.5 - 3.5 hours. Patients have demonstrated a high motivation, exceeding 8.5 on a visual analogue scale (VAS) ranging from 1 to 10 before and after painting sessions. This serves as an indication that participants like the application, find it intuitive, highly user-friendly, and enjoy working with it.

Applied as leisure time activity, the P300-Brain Painting application provides patients with the ability to be productive again and to participate in prolific society through art exhibitions of their paintings such as that taken place in the Künstlerbund in Tübingen (a German artist association) in November 2007 (Kübler, 2008). Recently Brain Painting has been showcased to several healthy prominent German artists as an assessment by healthy subjects. The application was received enthusiastically, demonstrated and evaluated for further improvements.

The Brain Painting application serves to satisfy some basic human needs, providing a positive, useful difference and great enthusiasm to ALS-patients but also as an advanced tool and research platform whereby new technological prototypes and developments in stimulus presentation, online data processing and prototype classifying techniques may be effectively trialled using motivated ALS-patients as subjects. Moreover, pictures produced by ALS-patients and healthy subjects alike have clearly demonstrated that Brain Painting is a new dimension of art that represents a real chance to minimise the gap between healthy subjects and patients through collaborative work in the field of art.

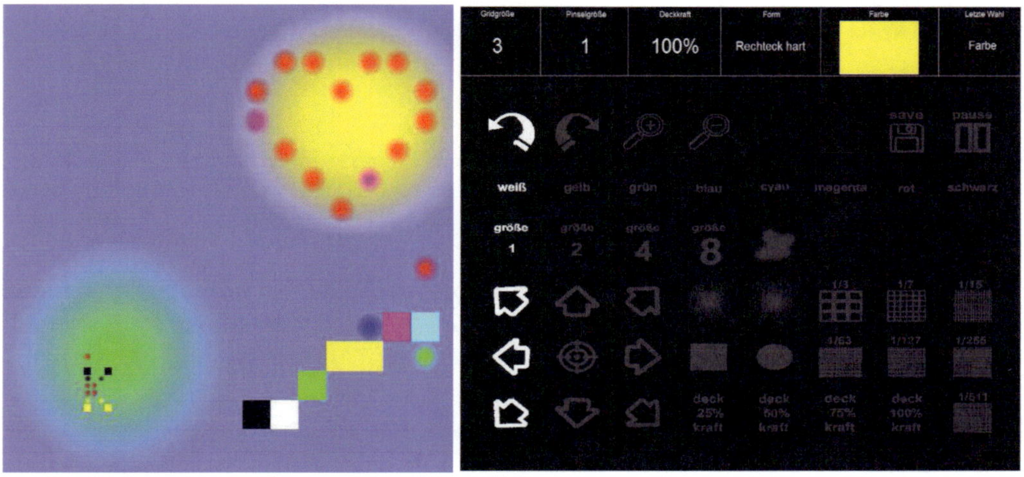

Fig. 10. Image produced by an ALS patient using the P300-Brain Painting application. Left: The painter dedicated the heart in the upper right corner to his wife. Right: Spelling matrix.

Project 6: Thought recognition with semantic output codes

Mark Palatucci, Dean Pomerleau, Geoff Hinton, Tom Mitchell

Our research focuses on thought recognition, where the objective is to determine the word that a person is thinking about from a recorded image of that person's neural activity. While most BCI work to date has focused on control problems using EEG or implanted electrodes, our work focuses on identifying specific words a person is thinking about using higher-resolution brain scanners like fMRI and MEG. Our goal is to develop a vocal prosthesis that would allow a person to speak without any movement of his/her body. This could have a major impact, not only on the way people interact with computers, but also on the quality of life of disabled persons.

While machine learning and pattern recognition methods have already made a large impact on this field, most prior work has focused on word category studies with small numbers of categories and moderate amounts of training data. In our research, however, we focus on thought recognition in a limited data setting, where there may not be training examples for every possible word we might want to classify, and the number of possible words can be in the thousands.

Our most recent work was recently published at the Neural Information Processing Systems (NIPS) conference in Vancouver (Palatucci, 2009). In this work, we've made two significant advances to the field of thought recognition and brain-computer-interfaces:

1. Our work has shown that it is possible to predict specific words a person is thinking about with accuracy far above the chance level, even when the classifier is forced to choose from a very large set (e.g. 1,000) of possible words. Thus, we have shown that it is possible to predict a person's mental state at a granularity much higher than previously thought.
2. We have shown that it is not necessary to have training examples for every word we wish to classify. We achieved this by developing a technique known as zero-shot learning with semantic output codes which we expect will have a major impact on the broader fields of pattern recognition and brain-computer-interfaces.

Bear	**Foot**	**Screwdriver**	**Train**	**Truck**	**Celery**	**House**	**Pants**
(1)	(1)	(1)	(1)	(2)	(5)	(6)	(21)
bear	*foot*	*screwdriver*	*train*	jeep	beet	supermarket	clothing
fox	feet	pin	jet	*truck*	artichoke	hotel	vest
wolf	ankle	nail	jail	minivan	grape	theater	t-shirt
yak	knee	wrench	factory	bus	cabbage	school	clothes
gorilla	face	dagger	bus	sedan	*celery*	factory	panties

Table 3. The top five most likely words predicted for a held-out fMRI image collected for the word in bold. The number in the parentheses contains the rank of the correct word selected from 941 concrete nouns in English. Note that no training images for the held-out word appeared in the training set.

The problem of thought recognition sits at the intersection of brain-computer interfaces and computational neuroscience. These fields are deeply interrelated, and we believe our research to date has already made contributions to each of these areas.

Regarding brain-computer-interfaces, we have taken steps towards a non-invasive, high-bandwidth, brain-computer-interface (BCI). Our results in Table (3) show that we can often predict a specific word that a person is thinking about from a large set of 941 words. This is a much higher granularity of word classification than previously thought possible. Another major feature of this result is that we are able to predict words even when we never saw examples of those words during classifier training.

The key insight that made these results possible was the notion of a semantic output code. The idea is that the brain encodes meaning of words and objects according to semantic properties such as: is it big? can it be held? does it provide shelter? is it edible? Rather than trying to predict words directly, we try to predict the semantic properties of a word given a fMRI image of neural activity recorded while the person is thinking about the word (see Figure 11). Given a prediction of semantic properties, we can look up in a knowledge base which words have the closet semantic properties to the prediction. A key benefit of this approach is that we no longer need to have training examples for every word we wish to classify. We only need enough training examples in order to classify the individual semantic properties.

We have used computational methods to evaluate different sets of semantic properties for neural activity and believe our findings have made important contributions to the field of computational neuroscience as well.

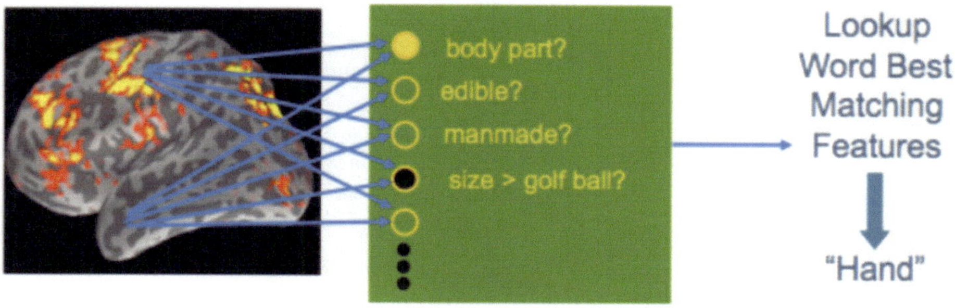

Fig. 11. Example of a Semantic Output Code for the word hand. Rather than predicting words directly, we try to predict semantic properties of the word a person is thinking about given a fMRI image of neural activity. We can then compare the prediction of semantic properties to known words in a semantic knowledge base for many words.

Project 7: Predictive spelling with a P300-based BCI: Increasing communication rate

David B. Ryan, Eric W. Sellers

Brain-computer interface (BCI) technology can be valuable for people with severe neuromuscular disabilities. The P300-BCI uses the electroencephalogram (EEG), and can return communication to people locked-in by ALS (Townsend, 2010, Sellers 2007, 2010); it requires little training (Guger, 2009) and speed/accuracy is relatively high compared to other BCI systems. However, current communication rate is still a major factor that is limiting widespread BCI use. The current study examines the affect of predictive spelling on P300-BCI performance in terms of output speed/accuracy, and waveform morphology.

Twenty-four subjects participated in the study. None had prior predictive spelling experience. All subjects performed a session with a predictive spelling program and a session without predictive spelling, counter-balanced. Using an 8x9 matrix of alphanumeric characters and commands, the subjects' task was to accurately (i.e., correcting errors) copy a sentence that consisted of 58 items. Each session began with a no-feedback calibration phase of 36 item selections to serve as training data for a step-wise linear discriminant analysis (SWLDA) (Krusienski, 2008) that was then applied online for character classification during the copy task. Items were flashed in quasi-random groups (Townsend, 2010) of six for 62.5

ms and there was 62.5 ms between each flash. During calibration, 120 flashes were used for each item (10 targets). Written Symbol Rate (Furdea, 2009) optimized the number of flashes used for the online copy task.

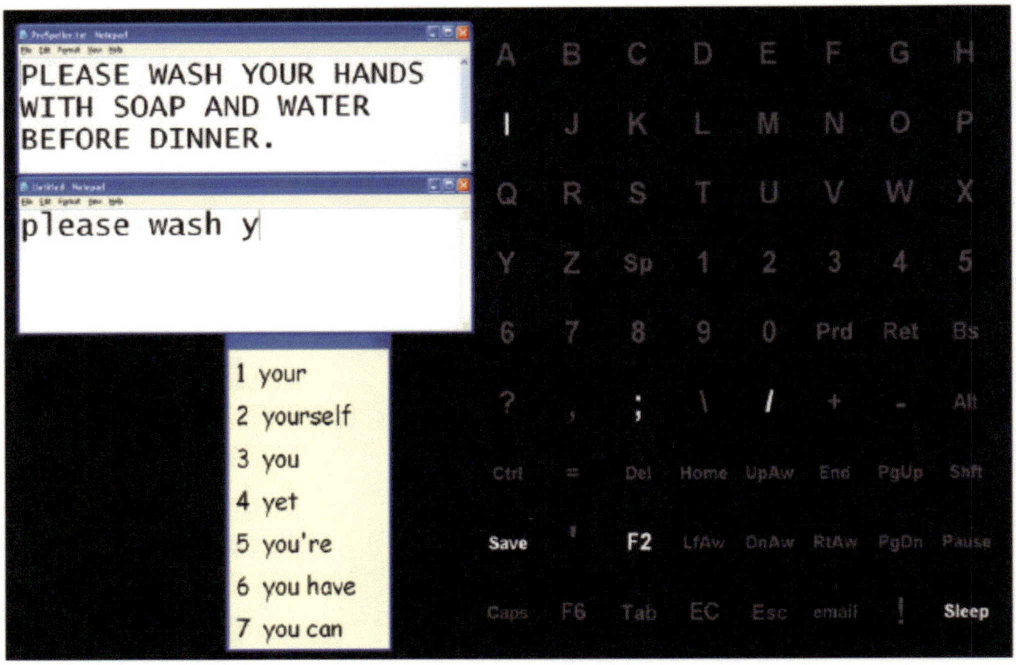

Fig. 12. The 8x9 matrix and additional windows used during the online spelling phase of the experiment. Right: the flashing matrix used to make item selections. Left top: the sentence target window. Left middle: the sentence output window. Left bottom: the predictive spelling window used in the predictive speller condition

During the copy task, a Notepad window (target window) adjacent to the matrix showed the sentence to copy (Fig.12). Selections were made by attending to the matrix (Fig.12 right) and counting how many times the desired item flashed. Output was presented in a second Notepad window (output window, Fig.12 middle left) that was located directly below the target window (Fig.12 top left). In the condition without the predictive speller, subjects selected items, evaluated output, and determined what item to choose next; the next item or Backspace. In the predictive speller condition, the predictive speller application program window was directly below the output window. After each selection, the predictive speller program would populate a numbered list of seven words. Subjects evaluated feedback in the predictive speller program window to determine if the desired word was listed; if so, the subject attended to the number in the matrix corresponding to the desired word on the next selection; when a number is selected the predictive speller program sends a word and space to the output window. If an incorrect number is selected, the participant can select Escape from matrix on the next selection, which returns the output window to its prior state, thus, eliminating multiple backspaces.

Table 4 (columns 1 and 2) shows that the non-predictive speller condition provided significantly higher accuracy than the predictive speller condition, 90% and 85%, respectively ($t(23) = 2.15$, $p = 0.04$, $d = 0.40$).

Subject	Predictive Accuracy	Non-predictive Accuracy	Predictive Bit Rate	Non-predictive Bit Rate	Predictive Theoretical BR	NonPredictive Theoretical BR
1	96.88	95.31	23.70	28.26	39.33	56.09
2	88.89	87.50	19.93	19.54	32.62	32.38
3	70.00	88.16	11.48	16.46	17.11	24.58
4	79.59	89.86	18.78	20.41	33.52	33.82
5	91.89	92.65	17.71	15.39	26.33	21.50
6	87.18	95.31	21.73	22.58	38.70	37.39
7	91.67	100.00	21.21	24.85	34.96	41.13
8	81.13	87.50	15.79	21.72	24.66	38.86
9	80.95	70.83	17.35	17.60	28.64	35.05
10	82.35	98.33	22.28	29.98	44.12	59.45
11	80.00	91.18	12.11	14.91	16.87	20.79
12	77.59	82.50	11.55	12.69	16.10	17.70
13	82.22	93.94	17.61	22.00	28.91	36.45
14	94.29	77.17	22.01	14.57	36.00	22.81
15	91.18	95.31	19.10	20.51	29.70	32.05
16	94.29	85.25	18.52	15.62	27.51	23.29
17	72.50	77.23	8.18	11.45	10.48	15.98
18	91.89	100.00	26.69	31.12	52.65	61.70
19	100.00	100.00	25.00	24.85	41.13	41.13
20	96.88	91.18	21.25	19.00	33.01	29.70
21	86.67	91.43	16.06	14.95	23.92	20.82
22	57.58	83.67	5.02	15.13	6.19	22.62
23	67.07	96.77	11.80	16.55	18.46	23.06
24	94.44	84.15	20.27	15.28	31.54	22.82
Average	84.88	89.80	17.71	19.39	28.85	32.13
Stand. Dev.	10.59	7.78	5.38	5.39	10.95	12.83
Stand. Error	2.16	1.59	1.10	1.10	2.24	2.62

Table 4. Online test phase accuracy, bit rate, and theoretical bit rate for the predictive speller and non-predictive speller.

In contrast, output selections/min, 5.3, was significantly higher in the predictive speller condition than in the non-predictive speller condition, 3.8 selections/min ($t (23) = 6.05$, $p < .001$, $d = 0.78$) (Table 5 columns 3 and 4). Moreover, the total time to complete the task was significantly less in the predictive speller condition, 12.4min, than in the non-predictive speller condition, 20.2min ($t (23) = 7.52$, $p < .001$, $d = 0.84$) (Table 5 columns4 and 5). P300 amplitude at Pz was significantly higher in the non-predictive condition. Reduced amplitude in the predictive speller condition may be due to additional workload (Kramer, 1983).

Subject	Predictive Sets Per Seq.	NonPredictive Sets Per Seq.	Predictive Completion (min)	NonPredictive Completion (min)	Predictive Sel (min)	NonPredictive Sel (min)	Output Chars (min)
1	3.00	2.00	7.80	12.70	4.10	5.04	7.44
2	3.00	3.00	9.00	17.90	4.00	4.02	6.44
3	4.00	4.00	24.00	22.70	3.33	3.35	2.42
4	2.50	3.00	10.92	17.15	4.49	4.02	5.31
5	4.00	5.00	11.00	23.58	3.36	2.88	5.27
6	2.50	3.00	8.67	15.90	4.50	4.03	6.69
7	3.00	3.00	8.90	14.40	4.04	4.03	6.52
8	3.50	2.50	14.47	16.10	3.66	4.47	4.01
9	3.00	2.00	10.40	23.90	4.04	5.02	5.58
10	2.00	2.00	10.10	11.90	5.05	5.04	5.74
11	5.00	5.00	19.15	23.70	2.87	2.87	3.03
12	5.00	5.00	20.20	27.90	2.87	2.87	2.87
13	3.00	3.00	11.25	16.40	4.00	4.02	5.16
14	3.00	3.50	8.75	25.20	4.00	3.65	6.63
15	3.50	3.50	9.25	17.50	3.68	3.66	6.27
16	4.00	4.00	10.40	18.20	3.37	3.35	5.58
17	5.00	5.00	17.75	35.25	2.25	2.87	3.27
18	2.00	2.00	7.30	11.50	5.07	5.04	7.95
19	3.00	3.00	7.65	14.40	4.05	4.03	7.58
20	3.50	3.50	8.70	18.60	3.68	3.66	6.67
21	4.00	5.00	13.40	24.45	3.36	2.86	4.33
22	3.50	4.00	16.95	29.30	1.95	3.34	3.42
23	3.50	5.00	22.45	21.60	3.65	2.87	2.58
24	3.50	4.00	9.80	24.50	3.67	3.35	5.92
Mean	3.42	3.54	12.43	20.20	3.71	3.76	5.28
Stand. Dev.	0.830	1.062	4.963	5.978	0.745	0.749	1.666
Stand. Error	0.169	0.217	1.013	1.220	0.152	0.153	0.340

Table 5. Online test phase sets per sequence, time to complete the sentence, and selections per minute in the predictive speller and non-predictive speller paradigms, and the predictive output in characters per minute.

Accuracy was lower in the predictive speller condition than in the non-predictive speller condition. Nonetheless, the predictive speller saved 7.4min as compared to the same overall output in the non-predictive speller. Over a period of one hour this translates to 92 extra selections. Accuracy in the predictive speller was 85%; it is unclear if similar savings are possible with lower accuracy. These results suggest that a predictive speller can dramatically improve P300-BCI performance.

Support: NIH/NIBIB & NINDS (EB00856); NIH/NIDCD (R21 DC010470-01); NIDCD, NIH (1 R15 DC011002-01).

Project 8: Innovations in P300-based BCI presentation methods

George Townsend

Since its original inception by Farwell and Donchin in 1988, the P300-based interface has always flashed in rows and columns. Disassociating the physical rows and columns of the target matrix from the way targets are grouped to flash in the P300 interface brings about a number of advantages. Supported by the Wadsworth BCI group (Wolpaw, 2003), the Algoma University BCI Laboratory introduced the "checkerboard" paradigm in which targets are grouped in rows and columns in two "virtual matrices" taken from the white and from the black squares of a checkerboard that is overlaid on the physical matrix (see Figure 13).

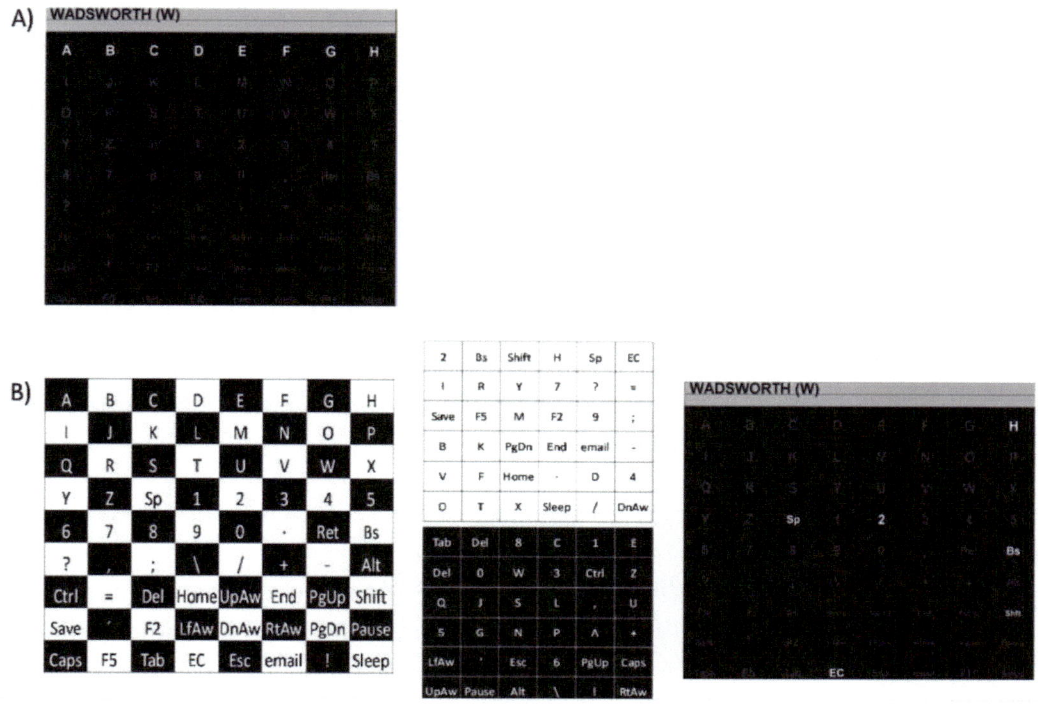

Fig. 13. A: The Row-Column paradigm (RCP) for the 8x9 matrix, with one row flashing. B: The Checkerboard paradigm (RCP) for the 8x9 matrix. On the left is the checkerboard pattern. In the middle are the two virtual 6x6 matrices derived from the checkerboard. On the right is the matrix as presented to the participant with the top row of the white matrix flashing.

This innovative approach eliminated the troublesome "double flash" problem and mitigated the "adjacency distraction" problem that plagued the original P300 implementation. Subsequent studies have shown this version to provide an increase in both speed and accuracy over the traditional implementation. The approach has been studied online in real time with both able-bodied subjects as well as disabled individuals.

Perhaps most important is the success that this new approach has had with those who suffer from ALS. The "checkerboard" interface was featured on CBS's primetime news program "60 minutes," where it was demoed by both the commentator as well as the ALS patient Scott Mackler. http://www.cbsnews.com/video/watch/?id=5228109n&tag=related; photovideo. The flashing pattern used in the demonstration was the one developed by the Algoma University Lab. There was a dramatic improvement experienced by the ALS patients tested on the new interface in a preliminary study.

These improvements are only the beginning of what might be possible. The disassociation of the "flash groups" from the physical matrix is now being taken further and the flash groups become purely "abstract" bearing no relationship to rows or columns either physical or virtual. Our experience with the "checkerboard" has brought us to realize that performance-based constraints rather than physical constraints should be used to guide the organization of flash groups in the P300-based BCI. Once the shackles of physical constraints are cast off, we realize that there are C(n,k) ways in which to flash k target flashes in amongst n total

flashes per sequence, or n!/(k!(n-k)!). In a sequence of 36 flashes in which each target flashes five times, there are 376,992 ways in which this can be accomplished. In the case of a target matrix in which there are only 72 items, this leads to a high degree of flexibility allowing for imposing many constraints designed to improve the performance of the interface. This includes those already addressed by the original checkerboard design as well as many others such as minimizing the number of flashes that a target has in common with other targets. We are currently working on new paradigms based on these ideas.
As this research begins to push the limits of the P300 interface, issues with the timing limitations associated with computer video monitors have begun to surface and we have developed a self contained LED based display compatible with the BCI2000 platform to address these issues. This new specialized hardware is currently under testing and shows promising results when used in conjunction with these new paradigms based on performance guided flash organizations. Participants involved in the studies have expressed a preference for the new paradigms and the new LED based display demonstrating a clear improvement in the usability of the interface.

Project 9: Operant conditioning to identify independent, volitionally-controllable patterns of neural activity

Steven M. Chase, Andrew S. Whitford, Andrew B. Schwartz

One of the most exciting applications of brain-computer interface (BCI) devices is the restoration of hand and arm function to individuals who have lost that ability. This is also one of the most challenging applications: a human hand and arm have more than 20 independently controllable degrees of freedom (DoFs) that must be coordinated to achieve even simple tasks. To date, the most successful application of a BCI toward functional arm restoration has been the demonstration of a monkey using a 4 DoF robotic arm to feed itself (Velliste, 2008). While a remarkable achievement, this is still well below the number of controllable DoFs required to replace the capability of a lost limb.
One of the major difficulties in establishing high dimensional control is the problem of calibration: when recording from a network of sensors, how should the patterns of activity in the sensor array be mapped to the controllable degrees of freedom in the device? A number of different approaches have been used to solve this problem. One method is to perform the calibration on natural arm movements (Ganguly, 2009, Wessberg, 2000). This technique is clearly inappropriate in a clinical setting when the subject cannot move his natural arm. Another approach is to instruct the subject to produce imagined movements while recording the sensor activity (Velliste, 2008, Taylor, 2002, Hochberg, 2006, Schalk, 2008). While this technique has proven successful in many experimental settings, it relies on there being a clear representation of the imagined movement in the recorded sensors. If the sensors are recording neural activity that represents other movements or volitional signals than the instructed movement, this information will be missed. A third possibility is to use operant conditioning to discover the volitionally controlled signals that affect the recorded population. This technique, first performed on single neurons by Fetz (Fetz, 1969), has been tried with some success in low dimensional BCI devices (Moritz, 2008, Birbaumer, 1999). However, without modification this technique cannot be extended to the control of high numbers of dimensions, for the following reasons. First, mapping a single neuron or sensor to a single DoF can be noisy; a preferable approach would reduce noise by averaging across multiple neurons or sensors. Second, Fetz' approach cannot constrain multiple neurons to be

mutually uncorrelated, and so cannot be extended to gain multiple dimensions of control. The technique we propose here allows us to (1) find a pattern of correlated sensor or neural activity that can be used to control a single DoF, and (2) find multiple patterns of such activity that are mutually uncorrelated. Furthermore, because the technique relies on biofeedback, it need not be assumed that the recorded neural activity represents a particular movement; in principle, any latent volitionally controllable signal that affects the recorded activity can be uncovered.

The procedure for identifying orthogonal patterns of brain activity is as follows. The monkey sits in a primate chair facing a monitor that displays two concentric rings: a blue target ring and a green feedback ring. The radius r of the feedback ring is controlled by the subject's neural activity, through the equation $r=a\mathbf{f}^*\mathbf{w}$. Here, $\mathbf{f}=[f1,\ldots,fn]$ is the vector containing the sampled firing rate from n neurons (or equivalently, activity from n sensors), $\mathbf{w}=[w1,\ldots wn]^T$ is the weight vector that determines how each neuron contributes to the radius, and a is a normalizing constant. The goal of the task is for the subject to control his neural activity such that the feedback ring hits the target ring. After hitting two target rings (an outer ring and an inner ring) consecutively, within a timeout period, a reward is given. We start with the standard Fetz task (Fetz, 1969), where we use the firing rate of only one neuron to control the radius of the feedback ring. We've found that the subject can learn, by trial and error, to achieve volitional control over approximately >50% of the recorded neurons within ~2 minutes, at least for neurons with sufficiently high baseline rates (Fig. 14A). Once volitional control has been established with one neuron, we pick another and use it to drive the ring. This procedure continues for a small sample of cells, typically between 2 and 10, taking between 5 and 20 minutes. During single-unit control there is significant correlation in the population response, even though the other units do not contribute to control. This suggests that if we were to average over the population appropriately, we might uncover cleaner, less noisy control signals. We extract the first pattern of neural activity by performing a principal components analysis (PCA) on the neural data. Specifically, we create a data matrix F that contains all of the firing rate samples from the successful trials so far observed ($F=[f_1^T,\ldots,f_m^T]$, where m is the number of successful trials). We then perform PCA on this data matrix to find the single vector that explains the most variance in the data. Mathematically, we solve $\mathbf{w}_{PC1} = \mathrm{argmax}_w\{\mathrm{Var}(w^T F)\}$, subject to the constraint that $||\mathbf{w}|| = 1$. We then use this vector to control the feedback ring. Control with the first PC is typically very good (Fig. 14B); noisiness that can result when sampling a single neuron is reduced when projecting the firing rates from the entire population onto the first PC. To find the next orthogonal pattern of controllable activity, we combine all of the data we have taken to this point (both data from when single neurons were in control and from when the first PC was used for control) into a data matrix F_{total}. We then project this data into the space orthogonal to the first PC, through the equation $F=F_{total}-\mathbf{w}_{PC1}\mathbf{w}_{PC1}^T F_{total}$. Essentially, we take every vector of firing rates we've observed and subtract off the component that lies along $\mathbf{w}_{PC1}$. We then again perform PCA, to find the single vector that explains the maximum amount of variance in $F\perp$. By construction, this vector is guaranteed to be orthogonal to $\mathbf{w}_{PC1}$. We then apply this vector as the weight vector that controls the feedback ring. This procedure can be iterated until the subject can no longer control the ring, or until there are as many components as there are neurons. We find that with recordings consisting of only 30 neurons, we can reliably find ~5 orthogonal components that can be volitionally controlled (Fig. 14C).

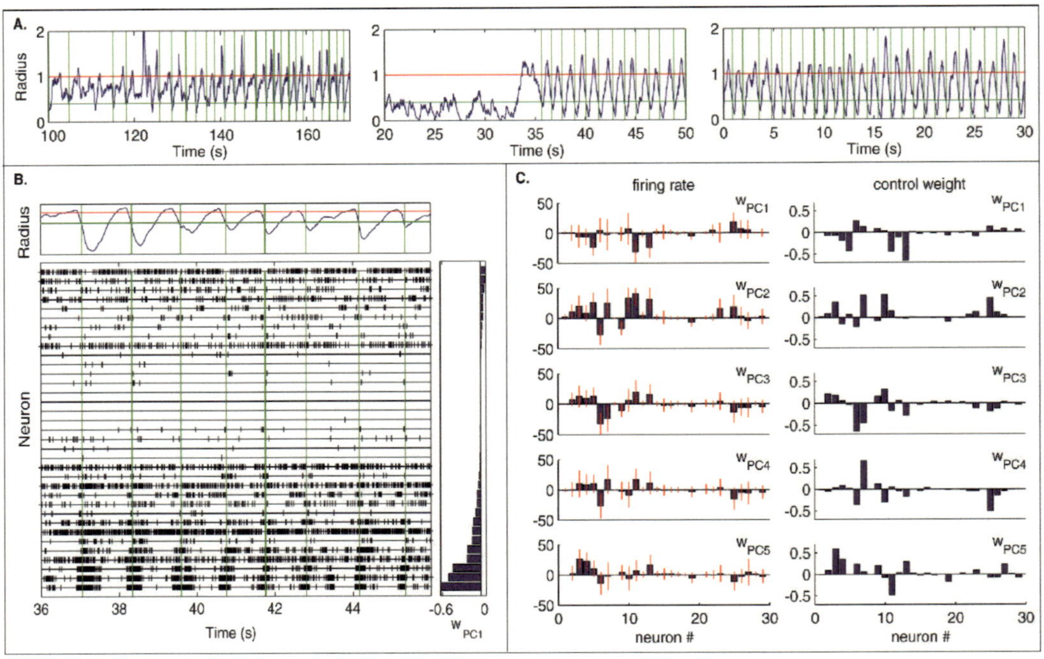

Fig. 14. Patterns of neural activity revealed through operant conditioning. A. Three examples of control with single neurons. The plots show the radius of the feedback ring as a function of time since the neuron was put in control of the ring. The first two plots show examples of the subject learning, through trial and error, volitional control of the ring. The third shows an example where the control was immediate, because the control neuron was correlated with the neuron previously in control. Red and green horizontal lines denote outer and inner target ring positions, respectively; green vertical lines denote successes. B. Raster plot during control with wPC1. Units are sorted according to their contribution to the PC, shown on the right. C. The left column displays histograms of the difference in firing rate between the outer and inner targets for all neurons; each plot shows control with a different PC. Red bars display +/- 1 SD. The corresponding PC weights are shown on the right.

Often, the biggest problem with achieving high dimensional control with a BCI device is training. The training procedure has two components: first, a mapping between the neural activity and the control of each device DoF must be established; second, given a particular mapping, the subject must learn how to shape his neural activity to achieve the desired movement. In our experience, subjects have little ability to control a device when an arbitrary mapping is applied between the neural activity and the device (data not shown). On the other hand, humans have little trouble learning to control a computer cursor with a cyber glove, even when the joint angles in the glove are arbitrarily mapped to cursor movements (Liu, 2008, Mosier, 2005). The difference is that the cyber glove maps independent volitional signals to cursor movements, while arbitrary mappings of the neural activity do not preserve the independence of the volitional signals. Using our procedure, the underlying latent volitional signals can be recovered and mapped to particular device DoFs while maintaining their independence. In addition to reduced training times and a consistent framework in which to calibrate the operation of multiple BCI devices, the procedure we have developed has a number of basic science applications. In particular, it allows us to explore the fundamental limits on learning and adaptation, by probing a subject's ability to sculpt the correlations in a network of neurons. Ultimately, using models of the volitional control signals and the functional connectivity of the network, we hope to predict the behavior of the network in response to different behavioral challenges.

Project 10: Neurorehabilitation for chronic-phase stroke using a brain-machine interface

Kimiko Kawashima, Keiichiro Shindo, Junichi Ushiba, Meigen Liu

Spelling devices or robotic-arm control with BCIs have been widely developed for the purpose to substitute lost motor function in patients with spinal cord injury and neuromuscular diseases. In addition to such 'functional compensation with BCI', rather a new concept of 'neurorehabilitation with BCI', in facilitation of neural sensory-motor activity using volitionally controlled motor-driven orthosis, might also be valuable in rehabilitation.

To test the feasibility of the concept of BCI neurorehabilitation, we recruited two patients with hemiplegic stroke due to sub-cortical lesions (Patient A (PAT-A): corona radiata infarction, Patient B (PAT-B): putaminal hemorrhage) for this study, which was approved by the local ethics committee, and the patients gave informed consent. The scores of Stroke Impairment Assessment Set (SIAS) finger function test were 1A in both patients, meaning no observable volitional finger movement. Spasticity was present in fingers and wrist flexors, and paralyzed fingers and arms were flexed and supinated in a typical Wernicke-Mann posture. More than one year had passed since the stroke, and thus further functional recovery was not expected.

Our BCI was designed to activate a motor-driven orthosis that was attached to the paretic hand in response to the motor intention of the patient's hand (Figure 15a). Using Ag/AgCl scalp electrodes (φ = 10 mm), the EEG was recorded over the sensorimotor cortex of both hemispheres (C3 and C4, with four neighbor Laplacian) and digitized at 256 Hz using an EEG amplifier (g.tec Guger Technologies, Graz, Austria). The amplitude of the event-related desynchronization (ERD) within 8–35 Hz was calculated every 300 ms with a time-sliding window of 1 s, as a feature that represents the participant's motor intention [4]. The magnitude of ERD in both hemispheres was classified with linear discriminant analysis to judge whether the patient was at rest or was intending hand opening. The orthosis was triggered to move after a motor intention of 2–5 s (which was set depending on patient's proficiency), if the accuracy of the EEG classification exceeded 50% (Fig.15b). This protocol was repeated for 1 hour once or twice a week over a period of 4 to 7 months.

An evaluation of the BCI neurorehabilitation demonstrated an enhancement of ERD with motor imagery. Comparison of the results of pre- and post-BCI training revealed that the ERD values significantly decreased over both hemispheres (Fig. 15c), and was more prominent in ipsi-lesional side. Enhancement of ERD resulted in a higher accuracy of BCI (Patient A: 38% -> 97%, Patient B: 55% -> 63%). Surface electromyography (EMG) recorded from finger extensors (extensor digitorumcommunis) showed improvement of volitional changes in amplitude (Fig.15d). Reappearance of EMG with a long-term use of BCI is outstanding because previous research found changes of cortical activity only [Daly &Wolpaw 2008].

Also, qualitatively the results were very positive; enthusiastic comments from the patients suggested that they had experienced raised awareness of the paretic hand. This should stimulate them to use their paretic hand in their daily activities. In addition, the increase in the EMG suggests the possible use of other therapeutic methods such as EMG-triggered electrical stimulation, in which minimal voluntary muscle control is needed, for further rehabilitation.

BCI training may have induced EEG changes over the sensorimotor cortices, thereby improving muscle control and increasing the efficiency of rehabilitation. In the future, BCI technology might be a promising tool to restore more effective motor control in patients with stroke.

This study was partially supported by the Strategic Research Program for Brain Sciences (SRPBS) from the Ministry of Education, Culture, Sports, Science and Technology, Japan.

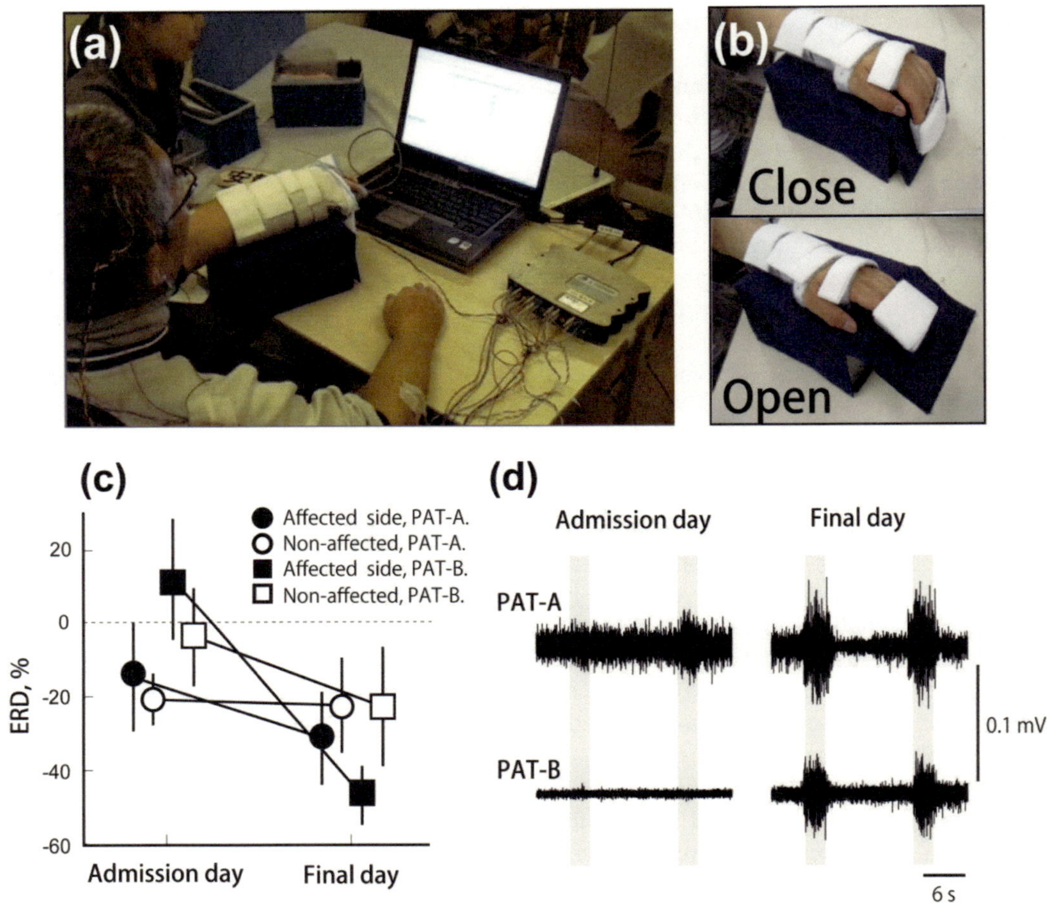

Fig. 15. Experimental setup and changes of ERD and EMG by BCI neurorehabilitation. (A) Overview of the experiment. (B) Action of the motor-driven hand orthosis. (C) ERD changes by BCI neurorehabilitation. Bar indicates standard deviation. (D) EMG changes by BCI neurorehabilitation. Shaded period indicates when patients were intending finger extension.

3. Discussion

Out of 57 high quality submissions, the jury nominated the 10 top-ranked candidates for the BCI Research Award in April 2010. The jury then selected the winner of the 2010 BCI Award at the BCI 2010 conference in Monterey, California, in June 2010. The winning team was Cuntai Guan, Kai Keng Ang, Kok Soon Phua, Chuanchu Wang, Zheng Yang Chin, Haihong Zhang, Rongsheng Lin, Karen Sui Geok Chua, Christopher Kuah, Beng Ti Ang (A*STAR, Singapore), and their project was "Motor imagery-based Brain-Computer Interface robotic rehabilitation for stroke". This project represents a study with 26 subjects that combines current understanding of neurophysiology, rehabilitation, computer science, and signal processing to realize one of the most impressive studies in the rapidly growing area of brain-computer interfacing for stroke rehabilitation.

Table 5 shows a categorization of the BCI Award 2010 nominees into utilized control signals and application areas. The majority of 8 projects used EEG as input signal and 6 utilized the P300/N200 response. This has several reasons: (i) the EEG P300 response is easy to measure and a non-invasive method, (ii) it requires just a few minutes of training, (iii) works with the majority of subjects and (iv) gives a goal-oriented control signal that is especially suited for spelling and control application where no continuous control signal is needed (e.g., Internet surfing, painting). Actually, all the spelling/Internet/art applications were controlled with the N200/P300 strategy. Two projects used motor imagery (MI) in order to generate a continuous control signal. Both MI projects used the BCI system for the activation of the sensori-motor cortex for stroke rehabilitation that cannot be done with N200/P300- or SSVEP-based BCI systems. No SSVEP-based BCI systems were nominated for the BCI Award. This is surprising, because SSVEP-based systems achieve high accuracies and information transfer rate and can be operated by the majority of people. The reason could be that for goal-oriented control, the P300 principle is better suited because it gives more options by using standard computer screens. SSVEP-based systems required LED stimulators but can also use computer screens. Especially in the latter case, it is complicated to realize a high number of different frequencies. But it becomes more difficult for a high number of LEDs compared to arranging 50-100 icons on the screen for a P300 speller.

One fMRI- and one spike-based project were nominated. fMRI-based BCIs are more complicated to operate but have the big advantage of the good spatial resolution which allows to read out different control signals compared to EEG-based systems. Instead of selecting single characters, fMRIs can be used to extract, e.g., the semantic output code to form words and sentences, to play tennis, or to navigate in your home (Owen, 2008, Palatucci, 2009). Action potentials give the highest spatial and temporal resolution, but are require implantation of electrodes within the cortex. Nevertheless, spikes allow a very accurate control of BCI systems and can even be used for robotic control with high accuracy [Velliste, 2008].

Table 6 lists different properties of all the 57 projects submitted to the BCI Award 2010. Of particular interest is the high percentage of real-time BCI implementations that exist nowadays. Motor imagery is still the mostly used strategy to control a BCI, followed by P300 and SSVEP. It is also not surprising that mostly EEG-based BCI systems are used because they are easier to handle and are cheaper. The mostly implemented application is spelling, ahead of general control (the papers did not mention a certain application) and stroke rehabilitation, wheelchair/robot or Internet control. 12.3 % of the submission introduced a BCI platform or certain improvements of technology.

Title	Control signal					Application		
	fMRI	Spikes	N200/P300	SSVEP	MI	Stroke	Spelling/ internet/art	Algorithm development
A high speed word spelling BCI system based on code modulated visual evoked potentials			X				X	
Motor imagery-based Brain-Computer Interface robotic rehabilitation for stroke					X	X		
An active auditory BCI for intention expression in locked-in			X				X	
Brain-actuated Google search by using motion onset VEP			X				X	
Brain Painting – "Paint your way out"			X				X	
Thought Recognition with Semantic Output Codes	X						X	
Predictive Spelling with a P300-based BCI: Increasing Communication Rate			X				X	
Innovations in P300-based BCI Stimulus Presentation Methods			X				X	
Operant conditioning to identify independent, volitionally-controllable patterns of neural activity		X						X
Neurorehabilitation for Chronic-Phase Stroke using a Brain-Machine Interface					X	X		
Total	1	1	6		2	2	7	1

Table 5. Categorization of the BCI Award nominees.

Property	Percentage (N=57)	Property	Percentage (N=57)
Real-time BCI	65.2	Stroke	7.0
Off-line algorithms	17.5	Spelling	19.3
P300	29.8	Wheelchair/Robot	7.0
SSVEP	8.9	Internet/VR	8.8
Motor imagery	40.4	Control	17.5
EEG	75.4	Platform/Technology	12.3
fMRI	3.5		
ECoG	3.5		
NIRS	1.8		

Table 6. Properties of the submissions to the BCI Award 2010

4. Conclusion

The BCI Award 2010 was the first international Award for BCI system development. The submissions highlight the current status of BCI technology. It is important to identify the most promising technologies and application areas for a faster grow of the community. g.tec plans to continue the BCI Award on an annual basis. This should provide annual snapshots of the progress of BCI research and its exciting new applications.

5. Acknowledgements

We are grateful to the members of the jury of the BCI Award 2010: Gerwin Schalk, Theresa Vaughan, Eric Sellers, Dean Krusienski, Klaus-Robert Müller, Benjamin Blankertz, Bo Hong. We also thank Aysegul Gunduz and Peter Brunner for their assistance with the evaluation process. Finally, we thank Theresa Vaughan and Jon Wolpaw for organizing the BCI conference 2010 as platform for the BCI Award 2010. The work was funded by the EC projects Decoder, Brainable, Better.

6. References

Allison, B.Z., Wolpaw, E.W., Wolpaw, J.R. (2007). Brain-computer interface systems: progress and prospects. Expert Rev. Med. Devices 4(4). 463-474.

Ang, K.K., Chin, Z.Y., Zhang, H., and Guan, C. (2008). Filter Bank Common Spatial Pattern (FBCSP) in Brain-Computer Interface, in Proc. IJCNN'08, pp. 2391-2398.

Ang, K.K., Guan, C., Chua, K.S.G., Ang, B.T., Kuah, C.W.K., Wang, C., Phua, K.S., Chin, Z.Y., and Zhang, H. (2009). A clinical study of motor imagery-based brain-computer interface for upper limb robotic rehabilitation, in Proc. EMBC, pp. 5981-5984.

Ang, K.K., Guan, C., Chua, K.S.G., Ang, B.T., Kuah, C.W.K., Wang, C., Phua, K.S., Chin, Z.Y., and Zhang, H. (2010). Clinical study of neurorehabilitation in stroke using EEG-based motor imagery brain-computer interface with robotic feedback", 32nd Annual International Conference of the IEEE Engineering in Medicine and Biology Society (EMBC), Buenos Aires, Argentina, 1- 4 September.

Beers, M.H., and Berkow, R. (2000). The Merck Manual of Geriatrics," 3rd ed New Jersey: Merck Research Laboratories.

Bin, G., Gao, X., Yan, Z., Hong, B., & Gao, S. (2009). An online multi-channel SSVEP-based brain–computer interface using a canonical correlation analysis method. Journal of Neural Engineering , 6pp.

Birbaumer N, Ghanayim N, Hinterberger T, Iversen I, Kotchoubey B, Kübler A, Perelmouter J, Taub E, Flor H. (1999). A spelling device for the paralysed. Nature, 398(6725), 297-8.

Birbaumer, N., Kubler, A., Ghanayim, N., Hinterberger, T., Perelmouter, J., Kaiser, J., Iversen, I., Kotchoubey, B., Neumann, N., Flor, H. (2000). The thought translation device (TTD) for completely paralyzed patients. IEEE Trans. Rehabil. Eng, 8(2): p. 190-193.

Birbaumer, N. (2006). Brain-computer-interface research: Coming of age, Clin. Neurophysiol., vol. 117(3), pp. 479-483.

Calautti C., and Baron, J.C. (2003). Functional Neuroimaging Studies of Motor Recovery After Stroke in Adults: A Review, Stroke, vol. 34(6), pp. 1553-1566.

Daly J.J. and Wolpaw, J.R. (2008). Brain-computer interfaces in neurological rehabilitation, The Lancet Neurology, vol. 7(11), pp. 1032-1043.

Farwell L.A., and Donchin, E. (1988). Talking off the top of your head: toward a mental prosthesis utilizing event-related brain potentials. *Electroencephalogr. Clin.* Neurophysiol., 70, 510-523.

Fetz EE. (1969). Operant conditioning of cortical unit activity. Science. 163(870), 955-8.

Furdea, A. *et al. (2009).* An auditory oddball (P300) spelling system for brain-computer interfaces. Psychophysiology 46, 617-625, doi:PSYP783 [pii] 10.1111/j.1469-8986.2008.00783.x.

Galán F, Nuttin M, Lew E, Ferrez PW, Vanacker G, Philips J, Millán J del R. (2008). A brain-actuated wheelchair: asynchronous and non-invasive Brain-computer interfaces for continuous control of robots. Clin Neurophysiol. 119(9), pp.2159-69. Epub 2008 Jul 14.

Ganguly K, Carmena JM. (2009). Emergence of a stable cortical map for neuroprosthetic control. PLoS Biol, 7(7):e1000153. Epub 2009 Jul 21.

Guger, C. *et al. (2009).* How many people are able to control a P300-based brain-computer interface (BCI)? Neuroscience Letters, 462, 94-98, doi:S0304-3940(09)00819-2 [pii] 10.1016/j.neulet. 2009.06.045.

Hochberg LR, Serruya MD, Friehs GM, Mukand JA, Saleh M, Caplan AH, Branner A, Chen D, Penn RD, Donoghue JP. Neuronal ensemble control of prosthetic devices by a human with tetraplegia. Nature, 442(7099), 164-71.

Kramer, A. F., Wickens, C. D. & Donchin, E. (1983).An analysis of the processing requirements of a complex perceptual-motor task. Hum Factors, 25, 597-621.

Krusienski, D.J., Sellers, E.W., Cabestaing, F., Bayoudh, S., McFarland, D.J., Vaughan, T.M., and Wolpaw, J.R. (2006).A comparison of classification techniques for the P300 Speller. J.NeuralEng, 3(4), 299-305.

Krusienski, D. J., Sellers, E. W., McFarland, D. J., Vaughan, T. M. & Wolpaw, J. R. (2008). Toward enhanced P300 speller performance. J Neurosci Methods, 167, 15-21, doi:S0165-0270(07)00370-6 [pii] 10.1016/j.jneumeth. 2007.07.017.

Kübler, A.,Halder, S.,Furdea, A.,Hösle, A. (2008). Brain painting - BCI meets art, Proceedings *of the 4th International Brain-Computer Interface Workshop and Training Course,* 361-366.

Leuthardt, E.C., Schalk, G., Wolpaw, J.R., Ojemann, J.G., and Moran, D.W. (2004). A brain-computer interface using electrocorticographic signals in humans. J Neural Eng. 1, pp.63-71.

Liu X, Scheidt RA. (2008). Contributions of online visual feedback to the learning and generalization of novel finger coordination patterns. J Neurophysiol, 99(5), pp.2546-57.

Martens, S. M., Hill, N. J., Farquhar, J., Scholkopf, B. (2009).Overlap and refractory effects in a brain-computer interface speller based on the visual P300 event-related potential. J Neural Eng 6, 026003, doi:S1741-2560(09)96900-2 [pii] 10.1088/1741-2560/6/2/026003.

Moritz CT, Perlmutter SI, Fetz EE. (2008). Direct control of paralysed muscles by cortical neurons. Nature, 456(7222), 639-42.

Mosier KM, Scheidt RA, Acosta S, Mussa-Ivaldi FA, (2005). Remapping hand movements in a novel geometrical environment. J Neurophysiol., 94(6), pp.4362-72.

Münßinger J, Halder S, Kleih SC, Furdea A, Raco V, Hoesle A and Kubler A (2010). Brain Painting: First Evaluation of a New Brain–Computer Interface Application with ALS-Patients and Healthy Volunteers. Front. Neurosci. doi: 10.3389/fnins.2010.00182

Münßinger, J.I., Halder, S., Kleih, S.C., Furdea, A., Raco, V., Hösle, A., Kübler, A. (in revision). Brainpainting: Evaluation of a newbrain-computer interface application with ALS-patients and healthy volunteers, Frontiers in Neuroprosthetics.

Nijboer, F., Sellers, E., Mellinger, J., Matuz, T., Furdea, A., Halder, S., Mochty, U., Jordan, M.,Krusienski, D.,Wolpaw, J.R., Birbaumer, N., Kübler, A. (2008). A P300-based brain-computer interface for people with amyotrophic lateral sclerosis, Clinical Neurophysiology, pp. 1909-1916.

Owen, A.M., Coleman, M.R. (2008). Using neuroimaging to detect awareness in disorders of consciousness. Funct Neurol. 23(4), 189-94.

Palatucci, M., et al. (2009).Zero-shot learning with semantic output codes. Neural Information Processing Systems. NIPS.

Pfurtscheller G, Bauernfeind G, Wriessnegger SC, Neuper C. (2010) Focal frontal (de)oxyhemoglobinresponses during simple arithmetic. Int J Psychophysiol, 76(3), pp.186-92.

Pfurtscheller, G., Allison, B.Z., Brunner, C., Bauernfeind, G., Solis-Escalante, T., Scherer, R., Zander, T.O., Mueller-Putz, G., Neuper, C., Birbaumer, N. (2010). The Hybrid BCI. Front Neurosci, 4, 42.

Piccione, F., Giorgi, F., Tonin, P., Priftis, K., Giove, S., Silvoni, S., Palmas, G., Beverina, F. (2006). P300-based brain computer interface: Reliability and performance in healthy paralyzed participants, Clinical Neurophysiology, pp. 531-537.

Townsend, G. T. et al. (2010). A novel P300-based brain-computer interface stimulus presentation paradigm: moving beyond rows and columns, Clinical Neurophysiology, 121, 1109-1120.

Schalk G, McFarland DJ, Hinterberger T, Birbaumer N, Wolpaw JR. (2004). BCI2000: a general-purpose brain-computer interface (BCI) system. IEEE Trans Biomed Eng. 51(6), pp.1034-43.

Schalk G. (2008). Brain-computer symbiosis. J Neural Eng. 5(1), Epub 2008 Jan 17. Review.

Sellers, E.W., and Donchin, E. (2006). A P300-based brain-computer interface: initial tests by ALS patients. Clin. Neurophysiol., 117(3), pp.538-548.

Sellers, E. W., Vaughan, T. M. & Wolpaw, J. R (submitted).A brain-computer interface for long-term independent home use. *Amyotrophic Lateral Scleroses.*

Taylor DM, Tillery SI, Schwartz AB. (2002). Direct cortical control of 3D neuroprosthetic devices. Science, 296(5574), pp.1829-32.

Townsend, G. T. et al.(submitted). A novel P300-based brain-computer interface stimulus presentation paradigm: moving beyond rows and columns. Clin Neurophysiol.

Velliste, M., Perel, S., Spalding, M.C., Whitford, A.S., Schwartz, A.B. (2008). Cortical control of a prosthetic arm for self-feeding. Nature 453(7198), pp. 1098-101.

Vidal, J.J. (1973). Toward direct brain-computer communication, Annu. Rev. Biophys. Bioeng., pp. 157-180.

Wessberg J, Stambaugh CR, Kralik JD, Beck PD, Laubach M, Chapin JK, Kim J, Biggs SJ, Srinivasan MA, Nicolelis MA. (2000). Real-time prediction of hand trajectory by ensembles of cortical neurons in primates. Nature, 408(6810), 361-5.

Wolpaw, J.R., Birbaumer, N., McFarland, D.J., Pfurtscheller, G., and Vaughan, T.M. (2002). Brain-computer interfaces for communication and control, Clin. Neurophysiol., 113, 6, pp. 767-791.

Wolpaw, J.R., McFarland, D.J., Vaughan, T.M., Schalk, G. (2003). The Wadsworth Center brain-computer interface (BCI) research and development program. IEEE Trans Neural Syst Rehabil Eng, 11(2), pp.204-7.

Zhang, H. (2009). A clinical study of motor imagery-based brain-computer interface for upper limb robotic rehabilitation, in Proc. EMBC, pp. 5981-5984.